Library of
Davidson College

The Political Mobilization of Peasants

A Study of an Egyptian Community

International Development Research Center

William J. Siffin, *Director*

Studies in Development: No. 8

The Political Mobilization of Peasants

A Study of an Egyptian Community

ILIYA HARIK

INDIANA UNIVERSITY PRESS

Bloomington and London

301.35
H281p

Copyright © 1974 by Indiana University Press

All rights reserved

No part of this book may be reproduced or utilized in any form or by any means, electronic or mechanical, including photocopying and recording, or by any information storage and retrieval system, without permission in writing from the publisher. The Association of American University Presses Resolution on Permissions constitutes the only exception to this prohibition.

Published in Canada by Fitzhenry & Whiteside Limited, Don Mills, Ontario

Manufactured in the United States of America

Library of Congress Cataloging in Publication Data
Harik, Iliya F
  The political mobilization of peasants.

  (Studies in development, no. 8)
  Bibliography: p. 293
  1. Villages—Egypt—Case studies. 2. Political participation—Egypt—Case studies. I. Title.
II. Series: Studies in development (Bloomington) no. 8.
HN783.5.H37 301.35′2′0962 73-16535
ISBN 0-253-34535-9

75-6076

Contents

Foreword vii
Acknowledgments ix

1. Shubra el Gedida 3
2. The Broader Context 13
3. Peasants, Princes, and Reformers 32
4. From Headmanship to Representative Government 50
5. The Single Party System: Village Leaders 63
6. The Single Party System: Mobilization 1965–1968 81
7. Political Leadership and Political Power 101
8. The Mobilization Regime and Mass Communications 128
9. Opinion Leaders and the Mass Media 147
10. Formal Political Ideology and the Village Response 165
11. Attitudes toward Policy and Change: The Humanizing Role of Ideology 186
12. Political Attitudes, Kinship, and Social Mobility 206
13. Elections to the Arab Socialist Union, June 1968 222
14. Crisis in the Modern Sector 242
15. Conclusion: Reflections on Political Change 260

Appendices 285
Selective Bibliography 293
Index 301

Foreword

Professor Harik and I have a colleague who sometimes claims that Gibson County, Indiana, is a true microcosm of the American political system—that one can find within it, and within its transactions with the larger political scene, evidence and example of all that really matters to the student of politics.

It is a long way from Gibson County, Indiana, to Shubra el Gedida, Egypt. But Professor Harik's book reminds me, in a number of ways, of the deliberately provocative argument of our colleague. Shubra el Gedida may not be a true microcosm of Egypt, politically or otherwise. But this study, which focuses intensely and informedly on that particular village, does indeed illuminate a larger milieu of concern for those who would understand social change in the United Arab Republic and for those who would enlarge their understanding of center-village interaction in Egypt, in the Middle East, and elsewhere, as peasant village societies are incorporated into more complex and dynamic sociopolitical systems.

At its core, this work portrays the response of a particular village to the revolution. The work is "systematic"—that is, it is ordered by a deliberate and defensible mode of analysis—but the product is more than an abstract set of survey research findings. It is palpable knowledge.

True to his methodological commitment, the author makes no claims to generalization about the response to the revolutionary movement in Egypt's 4,000 other villages. Yet his study is suggestive. It inspires surmises about more general patterns of change and development than those portrayed, and it lays a foundation of method and perspective that could convert those surmises into determinate knowledge. And this is one effect of the integrity and the perceptiveness—the compelling authenticity—with which the study treats its sharply bounded universe. As one reader of this work has said, ". . . almost for the first time I recognize in a written work by a political scientist the Egyptian villagers I have known."

Professor Harik's combination of sound scholarship and a manageable empirical field challenges some of the dogmatic generalizations—about communications in complex social systems, for example—that tend to be accepted as elements of the working lore of the social sciences. As a result, this work offers valuable contributions to the methods and methodological perspectives of social science.

But method and methodology are always intendedly instrumental. Their value must be judged in terms of substantive results. The quality of those results, in this work, is clear, as are some of the larger substantive implications. The study offers useful insights into the large and ubiquitous problem of relations between central governments with modernizing ideologies and social-change strategies (and stratagems) and the peasant communities at which such ideologies and strategies are aimed. In this study, one is exposed not only to the village but to the village-in-context, which is a splendidly germane way of perceiving what happens—what can happen under certain conditions—to the ideas, aims, and efforts that emanate from the center as they reach their intended targets.

This work exemplifies a certain kind of social science at its best, a social science inspired by significant questions and enacted with sound methods to produce valid answers and to stimulate further inquiry.

William J. Siffin
Director

Acknowledgments

A book like this one rarely shows the various contributions of all the people who were involved in making it possible. Only a modest tribute is paid to some of them here. The American Research Center in Egypt bore the major burden of financial support for the period I stayed in Egypt, and its grant was supplemented by the International Affairs Center and the International Development Research Center of Indiana University. IDRC made it possible for me to have research assistants and free time for one semester and three summers, during which the major portions of the book were written. I owe a great deal to Dr. George Stolnitz, former director of IDRC, who patiently supported me during this long period and generously gave of his time and advice to improve the quality of this book. Dr. William Siffin, who is now director of the IDRC, has continued in the same spirit and has kindly seen this work through the last stages. I am also grateful to the IDRC staff for their help throughout the period, and to Mrs. Karen Craig, whose interest and competence in editing this manuscript enhanced its completion. I would like also to acknowledge the continuous support of Gus J. Liebenow, a colleague and Vice President of Indiana University.

My greatest debt is to the people of Shubra el Gedida, who kindly and selflessly accepted and cooperated with me despite the many demands put on their convenience and privacy. The Ministry of Agrarian Reform and Land Reclamation secured official permission for me to undertake the research and helped me get established in Beheira Province. Many friends in Egypt helped me in more ways than I know how to thank them; in particular, I would like to mention Ibrahim 'Amir and Muhammad Zaydan.

Ronald Bolin, Philip Vernon, and Samir Sarhan, all former graduate students at Indiana University and now faculty members at universities in the United States, Canada, and Egypt, have helped me with competence and dedication. I also thank my students in the graduate seminar on social stratification and political elite for perceptive criticisms of the ideas expressed in chapter 2; special mention is due Mary Sharon Shouery, Jim McDavid, Martin Sampson, Walid Moubarak, and Richard Axel Magnuson. Professors Malcolm Kerr, Alan Horton, and Janet Abu-Lughod read the manuscript and made valuable comments. Chapter 9 of this book was originally published as "Opinion Leaders and the Mass Media in Rural Egypt: A Reconsideration of the Two-Step Flow of Communications Hypothesis" in *The American Political Science Review* LXV, no. 3 (September 1971) and is reprinted here, with minor changes, by permission.

The Political Mobilization of Peasants

A Study of an Egyptian Community

chapter 1
Shubra el Gedida

"Revolution is the science of changing society."
Nasser

The First Visit

We left early in the morning for Shubra el Gedida,[1] a village just ten kilometers to the east of Damanhur, the capital of Beheira Province. Before we made our exit from Damanhur, we had to stop at the Mahmudiyya canal, which separates the town from the countryside, for the bridge was open to let through a fleet of sailboats bound south from Alexandria. "It will take just fifteen minutes for the bridge to close again," remarked Hasan Faris, the secretary of the Arab Socialist Union for Markaz Damanhur.[2] "And another fifteen minutes for the traffic to clear up," added the driver, who was made available to us by the governor of Beheira Province and by the Beheira Executive Bureau of the Arab Socialist Union.

Across the bridge it was market day; we could see men, women, and children peddling their chickens, pigeons, fish, pots and pans, and trays of various vegetables. On both sides of the bridge, long lines of decrepit old taxis, trucks, and draft animal carts added to the confusion.

The colorful garb worn by the men and women left exposed little of the body except a small part of the face, but I observed that the people were slightly fairer than other Egyptians I had seen thus far. Children playing

---

1. Shubra el Gedida is a pseudonym, as are the names of all villagers. The names of national and provincial leaders are real.
2. Each province in Egypt is divided into several geographic parts, each of which is called a *markaz*. Markaz Damanhur is a rural district adjacent to Damanhur town. The town itself is not a part of the markaz.

underfoot in the mud were not only light in color, but many had strikingly blond hair. "They are from Qaraqis, the next village on our way," remarked my journalist friend from Cairo, who later explained the common belief in the area that Qaraqis had been one of Napoleon's military posts in Beheira.

The tale of that great adventurer in the land of the pyramids came back to me as a fresh and vivid sensation. It was indeed in Beheira Province at al Rahmaniya, where we had had occasion to inspect land reform farms, that Napoleon fought his first of two major battles in Egypt against the Mamluks in 1798. The second battle took place at Shubrakhit, a small town ten kilometers to the east of Shubra el Gedida. The people of Beheira, and those of Damanhur in particular, were later to resist the French when a self-proclaimed Mahdi, or the Chosen One, rallied thousands of peasants and townsmen to harass the occupying forces. Both sides suffered numerous losses before the French put down the revolt and burned Damanhur to the ground.

Thus the quiet country of the friendly *fellahin* where we were now visiting, like the rest of the Delta region, had been the scene of momentous national events. When Nasser was still an unknown, low-ranking officer, he was briefly stationed in Damanhur, a fact the people there still remember with pride. Barely three miles east of Shubra el Gedida is the birthplace of Shaykh Muhammad Abduh (1849–1905), once the Mufti of Egypt, an associate of Jamal al Din al Afghani, an accomplice in the 'Urabi revolution, and the greatest Muslim reformer of modern Egypt.

The bridge across the Mahmudiyya canal was eventually closed; the cries of cart drivers and the honking of automobiles suddenly rose to a crescendo, and we made our way out of the traffic jam. The road to Shubra el Gedida was well paved and stood high over the green fields on both sides. Built in 1959, it connected Shubrakhit with Damanhur and thus cut short the circuitous dirt road that the people of Shubra el Gedida formerly used when they did not want to ride the slow Delta Railway. The railway had been built during the British period to connect villages with the Delta towns along the present macadam route. It had been dismantled before I went to the area, but I was to hear numerous references, made in jest, to its obsolescence and slow pace.

The ride through the country was beautiful, amid fields occasionally interrupted by mudbrick houses and with cattle, chickens, and ducks slowing down the traffic. In the distance, we could see villages popping out of green fields like mounds surrounded by palm trees, minarets, and pigeon towers, which reminded us that these "earthy masses" were the homes of men and women.³ What could it be like there? A primitive existence not deserving attention? Could it have any political life, which Aristotle had designated as the highest form of existence, one to be found in city life only? Everything I had read and heard about the Egyptian village—I had not yet been inside one—faded very quickly from my mind, and doubts about my going to Shubra kept pressing with disturbing force.

Occasionally I could see large, modern buildings standing like intruders on the monotony and grace of the countryside. I was told that these were government buildings, bringing to the villages the services of modern life. Some were cooperative buildings, erected with local resources, and, though esthetically discordant, they revived my earlier questions about political life in the village. Surely if villagers could build cooperative centers out of the revenue gained from the cooperative enterprise, then political life could not be lacking.

About a mile outside of Shubra el Gedida, we were greeted by the mayor and two other men, who came in the village ambulance to meet us. At the first opportunity I asked Hasan Faris, the ASU official in our party, about the legality of using the ambulance for social or political business. I knew that the Ministry of Health had such a strict control on the use of its motor vehicles that not even the physician from the village health center could use the ambulance to visit a patient. In an emergency, the driver would bring the sick person to the health center rather than permit the doctor to make a house call. Hasan Faris immediately responded, "Yes, but this is the difference. The nature of political activity in the ASU is to break convention when it stands in the way of the public interest."

Ahmad Amir, the mayor of Shubra el Gedida, was a well-dressed young man, clearly not a villager; he came from the fashionable city of Alexandria. An articulate and enthusiastic mayor, he led us without delay into the combined-services center (*al wahdah al mugamma'ah*), where a large sign posted on the main gate announced, "The Arab Socialist Union." This day was special, as it was the graduation day for the village fire squad, a volunteer group of young villagers. The fire commissioner from Damanhur was to supervise the performance and pronounce them qualified village firemen. The event was the first of its kind in Shubra and perhaps in all of rural Egypt. After the ceremony, we were escorted to the center of the village, passing through the marketplace to the main mosque, the cultural club, and finally to the craft shops and cooperative societies. Though it was difficult to concentrate during this procession, the mayor's

3. "Earthy masses" is the expression used by Henry Habib Ayrout, *The Egyptian Peasant* (Boston: Beacon Press, 1968), p. 87.

words remained in my mind all that day. "Shubra has passed in recent times through two periods of feudalism," he had said, "and is just now becoming free." The reference was to political struggle in the community since the Revolution, but only later would I fully understand the meaning and nuances of his statement.

When we bid farewell to our Shubra friends, we still had three more villages to visit that day. One, al-Barnugi, was of particular interest. Two men in our party, the journalist and the secretary of the *fellahin* in the ASU of Markaz Damanhur, had played important roles in the recent history of this village. Al-Barnugi is a small village of some nine hundred people who used to be the subjects of the Nawwar family, one of the largest groups of landowners in the region. In 1963, ten years after the land reform had been put into effect in Beheira, the Nawwars, by evading the reform measures, still owned over twenty thousand feddans.[4] The journalist, assisted by the district ASU secretary for *fellahin* affairs, had researched the extent and means of the Nawwars' evasion of the law; his findings were printed in *Rose el Yusuf*, a weekly political magazine published in Cairo. The exposure led the government to confiscate all the Nawwar land.

During King Faruq's reign (1937–1952), a member of the Nawwar family had built himself a palace in al-Barnugi modeled after the King's Muntazah Palace in Alexandria. Such a spectacle in al-Barnugi is all the more intriguing since the village to this day does not have a paved road. Clustered outside the palace garden walls are the abject mudbrick dens in which the Nawwar *fellahin* lived. In 1966, the palace was converted into the Socialist Institute of al-Barnugi. Displayed in the main hall is a religious verse that says in effect that God made available for the faithful the homes of tyrants who had wronged them.

The Socialist Institute of al-Barnugi was established in 1966 with the express purpose of indoctrinating peasants over thirty years of age who had become free from the grasp of landowners and who, it was hoped, would become political cadres for the Arab Socialist Union. The palace, which had once witnessed lavish parties, was now a boarding school for peasants, who came for two weeks in groups of one hundred to learn about socialism, historical materialism, imperialism, the "tyranny" of the royal family, the Egyptian national struggle, and the cooperative system. They were instructed in small classes by trained cadres wearing workers' clothes.

The experiences of the day stimulated far beyond my original expectations my desire to study a Beheira village. Beheira, one of the provinces

4. A feddan equals 1.038 acres, or 4201 square meters.

most affected by land reform, was obviously a place where interesting events were unfolding.

Choosing a Research Site

A month later I packed to return to Beheira. The Ministry of Agrarian Reform had just given me permission to start my research whenever and wherever I wished, and the Agrarian Reform Administration, an agency of the ministry, sent one of its public-relations officials to help me choose a site where I could begin my research.

I had had occasion to make several informal visits to other provinces such as Beni Suef in Upper Egypt and Minufiya in the Delta region, but for many reasons I decided to concentrate on Beheira. I had better personal relations there and believed that I could count on the support and cooperation of the Arab Socialist Union leadership as well as local government officials.

Beheira is a large province, however, and the task of choosing a particular village community was still ahead. The purpose of the study was to examine national penetration of a local community and to assess the impact of such penetration on local leadership, the local power structure, and the political ideas and habits of villagers. It therefore was necessary that the community chosen have most of the agencies introduced by the national government to the countryside since 1952. Other, more specific criteria, which further narrowed my choice, are discussed below.

Community Size

Villages in Egypt are generally larger than those in other Middle Eastern countries, and the population size varies greatly from one village to another. Some social anthropologists consider the average size of a Middle Eastern village to be about four to five hundred people,[5] but village population size in Egypt ranges from a low of three hundred to a high of over twenty thousand. The larger villages do not differ markedly from smaller ones; all are inhabited predominantly by small cultivators and agricultural wage laborers. I was interested in a medium-size village of five to eight thousand, one sufficiently small to be within my control as a participant observer but large enough to have most of the organizations that I wished to study.

Social Composition

In Egypt, some villages are strife-ridden, whereas others are fairly peaceful. Strife usually occurs between different clans and rarely, if ever,

---

5. Carleton S. Coon, *Caravan: The Story of the Middle East* (New York: Rinehart and Winston, 1964), pp. 175–76.

between religious groups. Since endemic kinship strife and blood feuds, often inherited over generations, detract from normal change processes, I sought a village with a reasonable degree of heterogeneity and social conflict, yet one without excessive differences. Perhaps in contrast to Upper Egypt, such villages are quite common in the Delta.

Agrarian Reform

Egyptian agrarian reform represented the most direct intervention by the national government in the local community and involved compulsory redistribution of land and reorganization of the mode of production, with far-reaching political consequences. In some areas, including Beheira Province, villages that had before the Revolution been owned in their entirety by a single landowner have come under the administration of the Ministry of Agrarian Reform. I visited such villages in Beheira during my exploratory trips and found them run almost completely by agrarian reform officials. This form of administration reduces to a minimum the possibility of social choices for the inhabitants and would certainly prove unsuitable for my purposes. I preferred a village with a mixed population, one where some inhabitants were beneficiaries of land distribution while others were not directly affected by it.

Formal Organizations

The Revolution had established new organizations in villages to implement its policies and to establish socioeconomic reforms in local communities. These new organizations included village councils, cooperative societies, official party branches, extension centers, sporting clubs, and schools. A study of national penetration in the local community would thus have to take place in a village where these organizational innovations existed. Since the process of local reform was not fully completed by 1966, it was necessary to find a village having at least the principal new organizations.

Accompanied by officials from the Ministry of Agrarian Reform, I visited about ten villages that we had earlier designated as good possibilities. I then narrowed the alternatives to three villages, including Shubra el Gedida. Any of the three sites could have served my research purposes, and I chose Shubra el Gedida. The agrarian reform officials as well as the ASU leaders in Markaz Damanhur were agreeable but not enthusiastic. The Agrarian Reform Administration understandably would have preferred my studying a village where agrarian reform operated at a maximum, but the indifference of the ASU leaders still puzzles me, for the ASU was quite active in Shubra. It was only through the good will of these

Egyptian officials and party leaders in Beheira Province that, once I had made up my mind, they generously extended their cooperation throughout the period that followed.

The Village

A visitor to Shubra first notices a traffic sign printed in big letters, "Slow Down: Children Crossing," and next to it a fountain where swarms of noisy village girls fill their water jars. Two large, modern buildings stand out: the veterinary unit and the combined-services center. The center, a large compound situated on about six acres of land, includes the school, the hospital, the village council offices, and the social and agricultural extension units.

The "Casino" stands across the road from the combined-services center. Despite its pretentious name, the Casino is no more than a concrete room with a small open area, a few straw chairs, and softdrink bottles. Located on the outskirts of the village, it is not a meeting place for the villagers, but it does serve as a roadside resting place and often as a waiting room for the bus; it is of more use to the officials who live and work in the adjacent combined-services center. The village council leases the Casino to a man from Shubra, who brings baked bread from Damanhur, offers the daily newspaper for sale, and who never appears to tire of running back and forth with softdrinks for the officials and their guests at the combined-services center. Social entertainment is compulsory in Shubra el Gedida, and guests are usually offered a choice between dark boiled tea or a softdrink. Failure to accept even this small hospitality is a social blunder that inhibits free and friendly relations.

From the Damanhur road near the Casino, Shubra looks like an island surrounded by green seas. As in most villages in the Delta, the demarcation line between the sown land and the clustered houses of the village is very clear; cultivated vegetation extends to the doorsteps of the houses on the village's outer limits. Before using the extremely scarce and expensive fertile land to build new houses for their rapidly increasing numbers, villagers always look first for space inside the village proper. Walking for the first time inside the village, one may find the narrow, winding dirt roads and the dust oppressive, but the friendliness of the villagers soon makes a visitor forget any discomfort.

Shubra el Gedida is a compact community, where most social interaction occurs within its perimeters. But it is also opening up to the outside world. I had only to wake with the peasants at dawn and look through the window of my room at the combined-services center to appreciate fully the movements to and from the village. Villagers start out early in the morning, men in their plain white *gallabiyas* (peasant tunics) and women in their colorful costumes, to drive docile water buffalos (*gamusas*) into the fields or to walk to the bus station for a ride to Damanhur.

The population of Shubra in 1966 was 6210. Most villagers derived their livings from agriculture. About 60 percent of the employed were cultivators, and 21 percent were agricultural laborers. The rest were vendors, shopkeepers, government employees, tinkermen, and resident or itinerant craftsmen. The two major crops are cotton and rice. Maize, alfalfa, and beans are also grown, but practically no vegetables are cultivated, and the cultivation of fruit trees has just started.

One's first impression of Shubra's people is their homogeneity rather than their differences. Peasant attire is universally worn, and practically all the houses are made of sun-dried mudbricks, which indicate their owners' low standard of living. The observer can notice more redbrick houses in some neighboring villages where a higher standard of living exists. Like the rest of Egypt, Shubra is predominantly Sunni Muslim; a Christian minority exists, but it constitutes no more than 1.6 percent of the village population and in appearance can hardly be distinguished from the Muslim population. The people of Shubra view themselves as Arabic-speaking Egyptians, and I could detect no cleavages along ethnic or religious lines.

Administrative Ties

No sooner does one really get to know Shubra than one finds complex administrative ties with the surrounding villages that belie the first impression of clear, physical boundaries. For instance, the community of Shubra proper is linked to five hamlets by a single municipal council. Shubra is situated in Markaz Damanhur, one of eleven districts in Beheira Province. Markaz Damanhur is composed of seven municipal communes such as Shubra's, but no civilian administration tops them or coordinates their activities. Municipal administration is linked directly to the provincial government; there is no intermediate unit. A district is a geographic rather than a civil administration unit, created originally as a police administration center, hence its name *markaz*. Each district has a police commissioner responsible for public security matters. However, as a unit of intermediate size between a village and the province, the markaz has in recent years acquired political functions, mainly as an electoral constituency and as an administrative unit in the official party organization.

Subnational administration in Egypt is still based on two units: the province and the municipal commune, the first headed by a governor and the second, by a mayor. In 1966, Wagih Abaza was the governor of Beheira Province, appointed by President Nasser for a second term under pressure from the people of the province. A former army officer and an efficient, public-minded person, Abaza accomplished in the early years of his term many public projects, including housing, schools, health centers, roads, and craft training centers. He no doubt enjoyed the advantages bestowed on governors by the local government law of 1960, which gave provincial governors even greater powers and autonomy and raised them to the rank of deputy minister. An astute administrator and influential political figure, Abaza brought together under his strong leadership the officials of the various ministries in the province and prevented the ill effects of weak administrative coordination, which had prevailed in the past. He was very active as the patron-in-the-wings for the Arab Socialist Union in Beheira and can be credited with the appointments made in 1966 to the top offices of the official party in Beheira Province.

Shubra el Gedida is linked to other villages and provincial affairs in still another way—through agrarian reform. The Ministry of Agrarian Reform has drawn its own administrative lines in the provinces, taking into account the original boundaries of the large estates reclaimed by the government. The organizational structure starts with the village at the base and rises to the *mintaqah* (region) and then to the province levels. In each village, peasants who are beneficiaries of land distribution are organized in a cooperative society run jointly by their elected representatives and agrarian reform officials. Like other provincial agents of national ministries, agrarian reform officials are formally under the authority of the governor. From the start, however, the Agrarian Reform Administration has developed, and still maintains, considerable autonomy from the governor.

Just as the *mintaqah* of the Agrarian Reform Administration varies in its boundaries from the markaz, so does the basic unit of a village cooperative differ from the cultivation area (*zimam*) of a village. Occasionally, reclaimed land in one village is too small an area to justify the creation of its own cooperative society and becomes attached to another village cooperative. In Shubra el Gedida, for instance, all the land consolidated under the reform cooperative until 1961 had been part of Shubra's cultivation area. Later, newly reclaimed land adjacent to Shubra was also brought under its cooperative society.

There seems to be no logic to the different administrative boundaries that I have just described except the operational exigencies of each of the ministries involved: Local Government, Interior, and Agriculture. Consistency in this case is not necessarily a virtue, and no problems have been caused by these different administrative boundaries. Although Shubra is not exactly a rural center, I have seen villagers from different places in the region come to Shubra, some for errands in the cooperative, others to see the mayor about a school, and still others to attend the Tuesday market or to see their representative to the National Assembly. Similarly, I have accompanied Shubra's leaders on their business visits to neighboring villages that are related in one way or another to Shubra's various administrative units. Political and economic interaction in the region has been enhanced by administrative and business ties.

My stay in Shubra was cut short after three months by the sudden Arab-Israeli conflict in the middle of May 1967. Without any knowledge of the impending crisis, I fortunately had administered an opinion survey during the first week of May and then had taken off for a week's rest, during which period the crisis started. I had to leave Egypt shortly thereafter. In June of the following summer, I returned to Shubra for an additional stay of ten weeks and had an opportunity then to continue to observe village events as freely as I had in 1967. I will always remember the serenity with which the people of Shubra el Gedida faced their fate under national defeat and continuing crisis. In 1969, the Egyptian government banned foreigners' travel outside the major cities; the ban is still in effect to this day.

chapter 2

The broader context

In his famous essay on peasant society, Eric Wolf underlines the sobering thought that "industrial society is built upon the ruins of peasant society." [1] What future does this grave historical experience suggest for developing countries where peasants still constitute about three-quarters of the population? Wolf feels that "their continued presence constitutes both a threat and a responsibility for those countries which have thrown off the shackles of backwardness. While the industrial revolution has advanced with giant strides across the globe, the events of every day suggest that its ultimate success is not yet secure." [2] Whereas Wolf has emphasized the insecurity for a world divided by wide gaps in the socioeconomic standards of its peoples, Barrington Moore has stressed the threat that a large peasant population in a society poses for the development of democratic institutions.[3]

The state of deprivation in which peasants live is not a special problem limited to one region but a problem of global dimensions. Despite the impressive expansion of modernization forces in developing countries after World War II, peasants still constitute the majority of their populations. This leaves the question of change among peasants, and the conditions under which it occurs, a matter of continuing importance.

One anthropological tradition considers peasant society as a subordinate order which can be viewed only in terms of "its relationship to the social and cultural superstructure above. . . ." [4] There is no widespread agree-

---

1. Eric R. Wolf, *Peasants* (Englewood Cliffs, N.J.: Prentice-Hall, 1966), p. vii.
2. Ibid.
3. Barrington Moore, Jr., *Social Origins of Dictatorship and Democracy: Lord and Peasant in the Making of the Modern World* (Boston: Beacon Press, 1966).
4. Lloyd Fallers, "Equality, Modernity, and Democracy in the New States," in Clifford Geertz (ed.), *Old Societies and New States* (London: The Free Press of Glencoe, 1963), p. 168.

ment among anthropologists, however, on the nature of the superstructure that defines peasant existence. It has been viewed by different scholars as the culture area, a national society, the city, a subnational region, and a market community.[5] Although this is not the proper context for an exposition of various approaches to the study of the peasantry, it is nevertheless appropriate here to acknowledge my debt to these scholarly endeavors in perceiving the problem of studying a peasant community, conceptualizing its dimensions, and becoming sensitized to the issues. Since the points I discuss in this study have been raised in one form or another by other writers, I find it convenient to start elaborating the approach to this study of Shubra el Gedida in the context of established wisdom. Because the issues discussed here are not particular to Shubra, I hope this introduction will serve to put them in the broader context of Middle Eastern societies.

Views of Peasant Society

To some political scientists, the peasant is one of the least free agents in societies that have been dominated by urban interests. Yet peasants, it is maintained, will not be able to rise from poverty and backwardness without the assistance of urban elites, specifically the middle class.[6] The communist party of Iraq shares this view when it maintains that only through their alliance with industrial labor and the petty bourgeoisie will peasants be able to overcome the burdens of an exploitive social system.[7] Peasant leadership has been stymied by illiteracy and poverty and by being physically dispersed in work sites.[8] Extreme deprivation circumscribes the

5. A. L. Kroeber, *Anthropology* (New York: Harcourt, Brace, 1948); Robert Redfield, *Peasant Society and Culture* (Chicago: University of Chicago Press, 1956); Raphael Patai, *Golden River to Golden Road: Society, Culture and Change in the Middle East* (Philadelphia: University of Pennsylvania Press, 1962); Eric R. Wolf, *Peasants, and Peasant Wars of the Twentieth Century* (New York: Harper and Row, 1969); Edward Banfield, *The Moral Basis of Backward Society* (New York: The Free Press, 1967); Julian Pitt-Rivers (ed.), *Mediterranean Countrymen: Essays in the Social Anthropology of the Mediterranean* (The Hague: Mouton, 1963); Karl A. Wittfogel, *Oriental Despotism: A Comparative Study of Total Power* (New Haven: Yale University Press, 1957); Clifford Geertz, "Peasants," in Bernard Siegel (ed.), *Biennial Review of Anthropology* (1961); and G. W. Skinner, "Marketing and Social Structure in Rural China," *Journal of Asian Studies* 24, nos. 1, 2 and 3 (1964–65); Henry Rosenfeld, "An Overview and Critique of the Literature on Rural Politics and Social Change," and Robert A. Fernea, "Gaps in the Ethnographic Literature on the Middle Eastern Village: A Classificatory Exploration," in Richard Antoun and Iliya Harik (eds.), *Rural Politics and Social Change in the Middle East* (Bloomington: Indiana University Press, 1972).

6. Manfred Halpern, *The Politics of Social Change in the Middle East and North Africa* (Princeton: Princeton University Press, 1963), p. 97.

7. Second National Congress of the Iraq Communist Party, *Barnamaj al Hizb al Shuyu'i al Iraqi* (Beirut: al Nida' Newspaper Publications, 1970), p. 82.

8. Ibid., pp. 82–88.

life chances of the peasant who is poor, exploited, conservative, and passive.⁹ Manfred Halpern argues that the peasant, isolated from the rest of the world, is bound to kinship and community ties.¹⁰ Lloyd Fallers agrees, pointing out that in most developing countries, rural people "remain semisubsistence peasant cultivators, often producing for a market but nevertheless carrying out their productive work within a village context in which occupation remains embedded in kinship and community structure—in which workmates are kith and kin." ¹¹ The question here is whether these generalizations apply to peasant conditions during the past or to a persistent phenomenon in a changing world.

Whereas some social scientists have defined peasant society in relation to urban society, others, particularly Fallers and C. A. O. van Nieuwenhuijze, have conspicuously avoided this interpretation. Fallers and van Nieuwenhuijze believe that in the Middle East it is still too early to speak of a middle class (a basically urban phenomenon) comparable to that of Europe. Van Nieuwenhuijze considers societies in the Middle East as composite, pluralistic, and discontinuous.¹² He notes a variety of cleavages —ethnic, tribal, rural, traditional urban, and sectarian. Within each group exists the internal divisions between elite¹³ and mass, parallel to elite-mass cleavages that exist in the whole society. Traditionally, subnational groups have maintained autonomy vis-à-vis one another and have related themselves directly to the culturally and politically dominant group. Van Nieuwenhuijze views this pluralistic pattern of social composition as convergent, rather than integrated, social order.¹⁴

According to some writers, Middle Eastern societies lack a middle class, which has been the backbone of nationally integrated societies in the West. For example, van Nieuwenhuijze regards the middle class in the Middle East as still in the inception stage, weak and internally divided. It is composed of *effendis*, a category that includes government officials, military officers, educators, skilled industrial workers, engineers, and mechanics, among others. These occupational groups have not yet become large in number or integrated with traditional urban groups such as artisans and merchants; rather, *effendis* remain a weak congery of distinct groups in the social system, each rated by itself somewhere in the middle.¹⁵

9. Halpern, p. 87–97.
10. Ibid., p. 95.
11. Fallers, p. 185.
12. C. A. O. van Nieuwenhuijze, *Social Stratification in the Middle East: An Interpretation* (Leiden: Brill, 1965), p. 9.
13. Van Nieuwenhuijze uses the terms "top" and "mass," ibid., p. 21.
14. Ibid., p. 66.
15. Ibid., pp. 24–25.

Fallers also feels that the middle class in the Middle East has not yet come to its own. "In most of the new states," he writes, "the great majority of the population are not yet involved in modern differentiated occupational structures, and the occupational system remains little differentiated within itself. . . . The stratification systems of the new states remain much more sharply 'peaked' and more 'broad-based' than those of Western societies." [16] The massive reservoir of rural people in the new states is "the least influenced by modern occupational structures." [17] Contemporary society in the Middle East, and in the new states in general, is thus composed of elite and mass; at the top are bureaucrats and entrepreneurs and at the base, peasants and workers. Bureaucrats, however, are more numerous and more powerful than entrepreneurs, according to Fallers, and this is what distinguishes the contemporary Middle Eastern elites from earlier European counterparts.[18]

Unlike Fallers and van Nieuwenhuijze, Halpern is convinced that a "new social class" has emerged in the Middle East "as the principal revolutionary—and potentially stabilizing—force." [19] The "new middle class," as he calls it, is a salaried bourgeoisie composed of managers, officials, teachers, engineers, journalists, lawyers, and army officers.[20] The intelligentsia form the largest and politically most active component of the new middle class.[21] He distinguishes between the new middle class and the "older bourgeoisie," which was comprised of provincial and urban landowners as well as merchants and entrepreneurs.[22] In political orientation, members of the new middle class are ideological, whereas in background they are educated, of humble origin, and politically powerful.[23] Theirs is the responsibility to lift the peasantry from misery and backwardness.

Both Halpern and Fallers view the state as the dominant economic institution and note that it is staffed with the products of modern education—individuals who have acquired occupational skills and who by virtue of these skills have become the elite. There is no doubt that Halpern is justified in attributing a central role to the new middle class despite its statistically small size, because what it lacks in numbers, it makes up for in power. It may be observed that the sons of the "older bourgeoisie" are also

16. Fallers, p. 185.
17. Ibid., p. 190.
18. Ibid., pp. 185–90.
19. Halpern, p. 51.
20. Ibid., p. 52.
21. Ibid., p. 56.
22. Ibid.
23. Ibid., pp. 51–73.

the beneficiaries of the most modern education available in their societies, and they, too, hold occupations for which they receive salaries. Moreover, they are civic and national in orientation. Currently, many members of this class occupy important positions in most socialist regimes, as well as in nonsocialist regimes such as those of Iran, Turkey, and Lebanon.

Groups within the middle class can be broken down for descriptive purposes according to the wishes of the writer, but, when such social categories are used to explain other phenomena such as political behavior, the connection between variables should be established, not assumed. It is difficult to see, for instance, why the privileged among the middle class should be considered the leaders of the past but the political outcasts of the present. The literature on contemporary political elites in Middle Eastern countries shows them to come from both the upper and lower segments of the middle class.[24] This is true of both kinds of political systems, democratic and socialistic, whereas in Iran the upper and the upper-middle classes are predominant.

The entrepreneurial groups in the Middle East are easily misunderstood, perhaps because the most privileged among them in socialist states such as Egypt, Syria, and Iraq have recently suffered economic setbacks in addition to having had their privileges decried in official ideologies. Business entrepreneurs and landlords are relegated to a traditional status by van Nieuwenhuijze [25] and by Halpern, who feels that when the "older bourgeoisie" were in power they failed to integrate rural and urban societies into a single nation and have not identified with the goals of modernization.[26] Landowners usually suffer from the same criticism.

Such broad disparities in viewing social divisions in societies of the Middle East do not enhance the study of peasant politics. The issue, however, cannot be ignored. For if we accept the social science tradition of viewing peasant society within the context of a larger order, it becomes necessary to identify the superstructures that are most relevant.

Social Stratification Reconsidered

In almost all Middle Eastern nations, subgroups can be identified in a variety of ways.[27] Ethnic differentiation is the oldest and, to a large extent,

24. See note 30 below.
25. Van Nieuwenhuijze, pp. 24–25.
26. Halpern, p. 69.
27. For a detailed discussion of social cleavages and problems in the third world and in the Middle East, see Clifford Geertz, "Primordial Sentiments and Civil Politics in the New States," in *Old Societies and New States*; and Iliya F. Harik, "The Ethnic Revolution and Political Integration in the Middle East," *International Journal of Middle Eastern Studies* 3, no. 3 (July 1972).

the most persistent problem. Progress has been made in integrating sectarian or ethnic groups. In Lebanon, progress toward integration has been achieved by means of reconciliation, whereas, in Turkey and Iran, it has resulted from a balance between coercion and pacification. In Egypt, where tribal and ethnic divisions are marginal, the urban-rural differences, which are taken into account in this study, are more visible.

Urban-rural differences in the Middle East have been known since antiquity but never on such an extensive scale as in modern times. Before the nineteenth century, the urban population was very small and had weak ties with rural areas. Urban growth started in the middle of the nineteenth century as the domestic market flourished to meet the European demand for cash crops.[28] With the development of the domestic market, provincial and port towns grew rapidly and assumed important economic and political roles in the process of national integration.

Occurring simultaneously with the urban development, and related to it, was the imbalance in the new relations between urban and rural areas whereby regional differences began to correspond with class cleavages. During this time, two major occupational groups—landowners and merchants of agricultural products—appeared and, though mainly rural in origin, became associated with urban centers.[29] The majority of people in rural areas became sharecroppers, tenants, daily wage laborers, and small owners. Thus rural communities, which under the subsistence economy had been relatively egalitarian, changed into a stratified system with landlords at the top and agricultural laborers at the bottom. (Sharecroppers were in fact laborers who were remunerated in kind instead of in cash.) In the emerging class structure, most rural people worked for subsistence, whereas urban-based landlords and merchants extracted the surplus. Governments, in turn, contributed to this process in two ways: expanded government employment increased the numbers of urban groups, and government taxation and conscription further burdened the peasantry.

Urban domination of rural people and the economy has been severely criticized by modern reform-oriented regimes and by many scholars. Concentration on the injustices suffered by peasants has, however, resulted in biased assessment and failure to appreciate the role played by

28. For a more fully developed discussion on this point, see Iliya F. Harik, "The Impact of the Domestic Market on Rural-Urban Relations in the Middle East," in Antoun and Harik (eds.), *Rural Politics*, pp. 337–363.

29. I know of no study which determines the ratio of absentee to resident landlords, but evidence drawn from the literature, although not gathered systematically, suggests that absenteeism was predominant.

landowners, merchants, and state bureaucrats in national integration. As a result of their enterprise, urban and rural economies became interdependent, and the economic basis of nationhood was laid down; it was they who first became fundamentally concerned with national politics and central authority. Their concern for the protection of their recently acquired private property rights and the security of trade routes drove them to advocate the presence of a constitutional and centralized system of government. Having a vested interest in a centralized nation state, and being the forerunners of today's educated class, these groups played a major role in the genesis of modern nationalism in Middle Eastern countries.

Even as elites, these new occupational groups were hardly the custodians of traditional outlooks and culture or stalwarts of established power positions. Armed by their nationalist outlook, skills, and economic influence, they had to fight their way up against monarchies and imperialism. No sooner had they succeeded in attaining independence than they had to search for a politically regulating formula by which an orderly political community could be forged. Originally not very numerous or strong, their struggle against both royal autocracy and foreign domination left them weary and divided, a condition that did not contribute to the establishment of orderly and constitutional political communities. A premium, therefore, was placed on force, and the custodians of military power gained the upper hand.

By the end of World War II, the middle class had already expanded as a result of growth in central governments, business enterprises, and educational opportunities. The war had also stimulated local manufacturers and encouraged entrepreneurial activities. Though internally differentiated, members of the middle class had certain things in common: a moderate amount of education, modest income, and involvement in politics.

The gap separating the base from the peak within the bourgeoisie has been narrowed by the socialist orientation of the single party regimes and by the socioeconomic progress of other systems. In free enterprise societies, members of the lower bourgeoisie have advanced socially and economically, whereas, in socialist regimes, the privileged groups such as landlords, merchants, and entrepreneurs have been politically downgraded and economically contained. However, they still play a prominent role in the economy and the government of most countries, including Egypt, and one should not underestimate the ability of members of the more privileged sectors of the bourgeoisie to find a place for their skills in the new "socialist" state or to establish ideological ties with its leaders. Studies of elites in Turkey, Iran, Egypt, and Lebanon show clearly that those who occupy high positions in government come from both the privileged and the modest sectors of the bourgeoisie.[30] Rather than stress barriers between the old and the new bourgeoisie, it may be suggested that there has been a trend of upward political mobility among the modest groups of the middle class and a downward political mobility among the more privileged, especially in the single party states.[31] In brief, the bourgeoisie in many Middle Eastern countries, including Egypt, is growing and becoming more homogeneous.

It would be incorrect, however, to attribute to elites in competitive political systems, such as those of Turkey and Lebanon, the same trend of growing ascendancy of bureaucrats over entrepreneurs and professionals. In Turkey, when the single party system established by Ataturk was replaced by a multiparty system in 1945, entrepreneurs and professionals started to take precedence in elite positions at the expense of bureaucrats and military elements.[32] Downward mobility among the disestablished bureaucratic and military elite has led some observers to suggest that the coup d'etat of 1960 reflected the resentment of state officials toward political leaders.[33] In Lebanon, where a free parliamentary system dates back to the beginning of the modern state in 1926, bureaucrats have always been subordinate and have had limited political impact. Furthermore, landlords and lawyers, who had in the past enjoyed a predominant

---

30. Frederick Frey, *The Turkish Political Elite* (Cambridge, Mass.: M.I.T. Press, 1965); Leslie L. Roos and Noralou P. Roos, *Managers of Modernization: Organizations and Elites in Turkey* (Cambridge, Mass.: Harvard University Press, 1971); Leonard Binder, *Iran: Political Development in a Changing Society* (Berkeley: University of California Press, 1962); Marvin Zonis, *The Political Elite of Iran* (Princeton: Princeton University Press, 1971); Morroe Berger, *Bureaucracy and Society in Modern Egypt* (Princeton: Princeton University Press, 1957); Leonard Binder, "Political Recruitment and Participation in Egypt," in Joseph LaPalombara and Myron Weiner (eds.), *Political Parties and Political Development* (Princeton: Princeton University Press, 1966); R. Hrair Dekmejian, *Egypt Under Nasir: A Study of Political Dynamics* (Albany: State University of New York Press, 1971); P. J. Vatikiotis, *The Egyptian Army in Politics: Pattern for New Nations?* (Bloomington: Indiana University Press, 1961); Iliya Harik, *Mann Yahkum Lubnan* (Beirut: Dar al Nahar, 1972), pp. 24–44, and "The Lebanese Political Elite," in George Lenczowski (ed.), *Formation of Middle East Political Elite* (Washington, D.C.: American Enterprise Institute (forthcoming); Michael C. Hudson, *The Precarious Republic: Political Modernization in Lebanon* (New York: Random House, 1968). For subnational elite, see case studies of Turkey, Lebanon, Egypt, Morocco, and Tunisia in Antoun and Harik (eds.), *Rural Politics*; Yusif A. Sayigh, *Entrepreneurs of Lebanon: The Role of the Business Leader in a Developing Economy* (Cambridge, Mass.: Harvard University Press, 1962). Although no systematic analysis of the political elites of Syria and Iraq is available, an informal examination shows that members of the privileged middle class do occupy prominent political positions.

31. See, for example, Frey, pp. 156, 137; Roos and Roos, *passim*; and *Rural Politics*, pp. 301–10.

32. Frey, p. 195; Roos and Roos, pp. 48–51.

33. Roos and Roos, pp. 7, 82–84, 161, 164; and Frey, p. 390.

position among parliamentary elite, have been rapidly giving way to business entrepreneurs and professionals, who currently comprise the dominant group.[34]

A major development of the last two decades has been the growing importance of the central government and its changing relations to the countryside. Nationally inspired local reform may be narrowing the social and political gaps between the bourgeoisie and the rural people. In Egypt, the Revolution has intervened to modify the urban-rural relations prevalent before 1952. An expanded bureaucracy has spearheaded this drive, while measures have been taken to place a ceiling on landholding and private enterprise.[35] As a consequence, the imbalance between bureaucrats and entrepreneurs observed by Fallers has become more accentuated, and the central government has become considerably more powerful than it has ever been before. It also has become the major source and supervisor of developmental change in rural society, replacing urban business groups. As in other socialist systems, professionals and businessmen in Egypt have increasingly been transformed into salaried officials and managers of state-owned enterprises. As the central government assumes a more dominant posture, it becomes clear that the national political system is the context in which the peasantry may be better understood and studied.

In brief, we can *descriptively* identify a variety of social discontinuities —ethnic, religious, class, urban-rural, and elite-mass—in Middle Eastern societies. *Analytically,* very little work has been done to determine the relevance of these social differences to political behavior and the social order at large. Generalizations on these matters, therefore, have been informal observations and impressions that serve as hypotheses rather than confirmed empirical regularities. This is obviously not the context in which to undertake a comprehensive study of this kind. Only one aspect of it—the impact of national elite on a rural community—is examined here.

One of the basic observations in this study is that modernization under mobilizational and welfare-oriented regimes has had positive rather than disruptive effects on rural communities. Contrary to the social mobilization concept advanced by Karl Deutsch,[36] there is no sign that rural communities in Egypt will dissolve into cities or that rural occupations will

---

34. Harik, *Mann Yahkum Lubnan.*
35. See Harik, "Mobilization Policy . . . ," in *Rural Politics.* For a broader reference discussion on this same theme, see Harumi Befu, "The Political Relation of the Village to the State," *World Politics* 19, no. 4 (July 1967).
36. For the view that considers change to result in peasant dislocation, see Karl W. Deutsch, "Social Mobilization and Poltical Development," *American Political Science Review* LV, no. 3 (September 1961).

disappear as a result of modernization. Indications are that rural communities are being transformed without unnecessary dislocation. It is hoped that this study will shed light on the effects of social policy in undermining the conservatism of the peasantry, which Moore finds to be the major obstacle to modernization and democracy. Rather than being a birthmark, peasant conservatism is a defense mechanism against prevalent uncertainty and insecurity, and, despite their illiteracy and backwardness, peasants have been quite responsive to mobilization policies in their interest.

The farm cooperative system is a major feature of modernization in rural Egypt. By using and managing the cooperative, a peasant is not acquiring new cultivation skills so much as new organizational skills. He is adapting to new social relations that bind him to other cultivators in the community while retaining his independence, benefits, and property rights. As a social form of farm management, the cooperative has led the peasant to social and political involvement in the community and channeled his participation within an institutional frame. It has made it possible for low-income peasants to benefit from modern cultivation methods such as the use of mechanized farming and has freed them from moneylenders. Cooperative farming has already relieved peasants from part of the burden of field work and given them some leisure time. This tendency may increase in the future, but under the system of private land ownership and small holdings, owners will continue to farm their own land. In short, the cultivator is modernizing as cultivator, not as a worker in a new occupation.

It may be objected here that Egyptian peasants have responded to political and economic change because they have been favored by the Revolution and because they have been less isolated than peasants in some other Middle Eastern countries. Nevertheless, in other countries where social and economic reforms are taking place—for instance, in Iran, which stands in sharp contrast to Egypt in every other respect—peasants have responded just as favorably.

The Elite-Mass Outlook

The elite-mass gap thesis stressed in the literature is not altogether consistent with the underlying assumption of this book that the political elite in Nasser's Egypt have committed themselves to dealing with local and grassroots problems. As often expounded, the elite-mass gap theory points to class and cultural dimensions that deepen the cleavage between the elite and the mass. According to Halpern, the "new middle class" elite is self-centered and oriented toward its own needs.[37] Not only do these middle class elite exclude the majority of the population from decision making, but their political orientation, too, is distinct.[38] The gap between the "new middle class" and the rest of society is accentuated by several barriers. Contrast between those largely urban elements and the rural majority[39] is now wider than ever before,[40] moral and intellectual contact is broken between the generations,[41] and clerks and lawyers abound while there are too few organizers and managers to mobilize the masses.[42] The high illiteracy rates in rural areas and the reluctance of the intelligentsia to leave the cities compound the problem.[43] In short, Halpern feels that in "most countries, the new urban middle class has not yet broken through the great cultural barriers that have traditionally separated city from countryside." [44]

Van Nieuwenhuijze maintains that the "Middle Eastern intellectual is not likely to stand for a universe of thought and for a conception of society that are significantly at variance with those that characterized the Middle East and have done so for millennia." [45] He thus sees little change in the intellectual outlook of contemporary political and intellectual elites. When an intellectual communicates with the masses, he "tends to care for their compliance with his wishes . . . rather than for their understanding of his ideas." [46] Morroe Berger, who acknowledges that the political elite and intelligentsia in the Arab world have genuinely adopted modern ideas of nationalism and socialism, feels that the major impediments frustrating their efforts are the illiteracy and backwardness of the masses. The elite are forced to resort to ideological hyperbole and harangue "to arouse the masses whose national consciousness is still inchoate." [47] The masses in turn have become "a gullible prey to propaganda and extremism, easily swayed to violence. This is the social background, rural and urban, conducive to mob action; it provides the spontaneous mass base for the organized and paid mobs which so often set the larger movements in train." [48] Such observations on the general political unrest in the Middle

37. Halpern, p. 232.
38. Ibid., pp. 74, 232.
39. Ibid., p. 30.
40. Ibid., p. 88.
41. Ibid., p. 29.
42. Ibid., p. 273.
43. Ibid., p. 88.
44. Ibid., p. 95.
45. Van Nieuwenhuijze, p. 66.
46. Ibid.
47. Morroe Berger, *The Arab World Today* (Garden City, N.Y.: Doubleday, 1962), p. 308.
48. Ibid., p. 309.

East overlook the basic and far-reaching changes affecting the lives of the poor and their relation to the economically and politically powerful.

Ideology

In the opinion of both Halpern and van Nieuwenhuijze, the elite's ideology reflects the social origin and position of its members in the stratification system, the consequence of which is a failure in communications between the elite and the mass. Douglas Ashford, who has addressed himself to this problem as it exists in the Middle East and in other developing countries, feels that, by seeking to create social solidarity at the expense of individual liberty, the elite have been ideologically manipulative.[49] Moreover, the ruling elites' emphasis on ideology, he feels, is often intended to divert public attention from the regime's failures to satisfy the basic needs of various sectors in society.[50] Ashford does not indicate, however, whether this diversionary tactic is successful; what is clear is that Ashford shares the feeling common among Western intellectuals that ideology usually distorts reality and misleads the public. Such views are at variance with the hypothesis proposed in this study that the ideological orientation of the contemporary elite in Egypt and in some other Middle Eastern countries links them with the masses regardless of the elite's social background.

Drawing a distinction between the functions of ideology and scientific inquiry, Clifford Geertz warns that ideology should not be dismissed on the grounds that its pronouncements are not objective. In a seminal article on the interest and strain theories of ideology, he stresses its social functions in shaping public opinion and in serving as a guideline for action.[51] He views ideology as the effective use of symbols in "casting personal attitudes into public form."[52] In order to be an effective form of communication, ideological expression tends not to be descriptively accurate. The function of ideology is not to describe reality but to galvanize opinion groups and provide guidelines for effective action. Insofar as it is meant to affect the instructed and the illiterate alike, public ideology informs in a manner all its own.

---

49. Douglas E. Ashford, "Contradictions of Nationalism and Nation-building in the Muslim World," *Middle East Journal* 18 (Autumn, 1964), pp. 423–24. This theme is repeated in his *National Development and Local Reform: Political Participation in Morocco, Tunisia, and Pakistan* (Princeton: Princeton University Press, 1967).

50. Ashford, *M.E.J.*, p. 427–28.

51. Clifford Geertz, "Ideology as a Cultural System," in David Apter (ed.), *Ideology and Discontent* (London: The Free Press of Glencoe, 1964).

52. Ibid., p. 57.

Many able students of the Middle East have offered nearly exhaustive accounts and analyses of past and current political ideas expounded by Middle Eastern intellectuals.[53] Expansion of mass communications, however, and the emergence of mobilization regimes have given a popular dimension to ideas that can no longer be ignored. Moreover, increasing numbers of intellectuals in Middle Eastern countries are publicists, and they use the press to influence readers more often and more blatantly than do their counterparts in the West.

One direct way to assess the impact of ideology on the public is through empirical inquiry. This study, therefore, examines the political ideas of ordinary villagers and the means through which they have formed them. The mass media and the single party system, which have been used in Egypt as vehicles to convey the elite's views to the public, will be duly considered here. Nasser's political ideas are presented briefly to highlight his political strategy more than to analyze his art of expressive symbolism, although the latter task deserves the attention of anyone interested in Nasser's success with the masses as a wielder of ideological symbols. In Geertz's perspective, the test of ideology is in the effects—all the more reason to examine systematically ideological effects in Shubra.

Political Power and Elites

The emphasis on marked background differences between the political elite and the common man has reinforced the belief in a wide gap that separates the two. The elite-mass thesis assumes weak links between the rulers and the ruled and, in some cases, between elite and mass cultures. However, the elite-mass dichotomy thesis overlooks the distribution of power at different levels, and, in the context of the community under study here, leaves unanswered questions regarding lower- and middle-level elites—that is, those who have political or administrative positions in provinces and local communities, including those influentials who hold no formal positions.

Writers on political elites tend primarily to study personal qualities of

53. Albert Hourani, *Arabic Thought in the Liberal Age, 1798–1939* (London: Oxford University Press, 1962); Leonard Binder, *The Ideological Revolution in the Middle East* (New York: Wiley, 1964); Malcolm Kerr, *Islamic Reform* (Berkeley: University of California Press, 1966); Nadav Safran, *Egypt in Search of Political Community* (Cambridge, Mass.: Harvard University Press, 1961); Ibrahim Abu-Lughod, *Arab Rediscovery of Europe: A Study of Cultural Encounters* (Princeton: Princeton University Press, 1963); J. M. Ahmed, *The Intellectual Origins of Egyptian Nationalism* (London: Oxford University Press, 1960); P. J. Vatikiotis, *The Modern History of Egypt* (New York: Praeger, 1969), and *The Egyptian Army in Politics* (Bloomington: Indiana University Press, 1961); Serif Mardin, *The Geneses of Young Ottoman Thought* (Princeton: Princeton University Press, 1962).

leaders, their background characteristics and ideologies. They draw on the interpersonal theory of political power advocated most strongly by Harold Lasswell [54] and widely shared by others. Less significance has been attributed to leaders' relations to one another or to their power base, strategies, and interrelations at various levels in society. When the concept of power is conceived as a dyadic relationship whereby one actor induces or forces compliance from another, the power network of which their relationship is a part is overlooked. The compliance theory also simplifies the phenomenon of power and does not take into account the gradation of the power network; either there is compliance or there is not. In effect, society, too, is viewed in terms of the dyadic relationship of an elite-mass dichotomy: the elite have power and command while the masses are compliant and powerless. This theoretical tradition emphasizes elites as a "class" and as a "culture," concepts that in turn are used to explain elite political behavior. Perhaps the difficulty lies in considering personal relations as defining characteristics of power rather than as a power resource. A personal relationship that induces compliance is a resource that is brought to bear on others; it must not, however, be confused with power itself, which is the force necessary to achieve an objective.

Political elites, above all, are action-oriented individuals whose importance lies in what they do more than in who they are. Focusing on behavior rather than on personal characteristics would bring to light the connections that political leaders maintain with the rest of society and the importance of the power base in understanding their activities. There can be no doubt that background characteristics are useful indicators of power resources and of social groups who occupy strategic positions in the power network. The value of background characteristics as indicators of elite behavior, however, is less in evidence and has been shown to be variable.[55] To understand elite political behavior, the whole power network—its structure and its constraints—should be taken into account. A power distribution pattern is a gradation network; national leaders, regardless of how overbearing their power is, have to relate to other dealers in power at every level of society.

54. Harold Lasswell, *Power and Personality* (New York: W. W. Norton, 1948), and *Politics: Who Gets What, When, How* (New York: McGraw-Hill, 1936).
55. See Lewis J. Edinger and Donald D. Searing, "Social Background in Elite Analysis: A Methodological Inquiry," *The American Political Science Review* 61, no. 2 (June 1967). Also, recent studies on Middle East political elites have shown the modest and variable effect of background factors on elite political behavior; see William B. Quandt, *Revolution and Political Leadership: Algeria, 1954–1968* (Cambridge, Mass.: M.I.T. Press, 1969); Marvin Zonis, *The Political Elite of Iran* (Princeton: Princeton University Press, 1971); and Harik, *Mann Yahkum Lubnan*.

Emphasis on the study of elite behavior in a social context is based on the view that power is a system; interpersonal relations are only some of the forms in which it is manifested. A power system is an order of force units that coalesce and disperse according to regular principles. Leaders' behavior is subject to the organization of these forces, the objectives to be attained, and the principles governing their generation. Political elites are therefore highly disposed to attaining objectives under feasible conditions.

An analysis of the power network of a whole society is far too ambitious a task to undertake in one study, especially in the case of Egypt, where politics as social behavior has rarely been examined. When this study was begun, the concepts of power and leadership were only part of the design; political attitudes and structural change were the central concerns. Moreover, at that point, my views of leadership and power corresponded to the conventional concept. Only during the course of the study and after completion of data analysis has the new perspective taken shape; systematic analysis of the theory of power advanced in this chapter is not, therefore, to be expected. This book focuses on the structure of power in the community and the relations of the leaders with their base and with each other. In short, the study of Shubra has been more helpful in forming ideas on political power than in providing corroborating evidence, a task that goes beyond the findings of a single research project. The study's objectives are considered met if the intricate network of power relations within one community and its relations with a larger system are revealed. Moreover, the small social system of the community under study may illustrate the point that even at one of the lowest levels of the political order, interrelations of power dealers form a complex gradation network.

The Study Design

As an inquiry into political phenomena in one system, this is not a comparative study. Nonetheless, hypotheses developed and examined here should prove feasible to test in a number of other settings. The study has been designed to make possible the gathering and analysis of data and the testing of evidence.

The purpose of examining Shubra el Gedida as a single community is to attain precision in substantiating conclusions. Although one cannot generalize from Shubra to the rest of Egypt, a full grasp of the processes of change in one community should contribute to the study of development regardless of the relevance of those processes to the country as a whole. It should also be borne in mind that Egyptian national policies regarding the countryside have been fairly uniform and universally administered. These policies include land reform, cooperative farming, health centers, municipal administration, political party branches, mass communications, and schools. Their impact will no doubt differ from one community to another; for example, in one community, the cooperative may be slowed down by factional conflicts while in another it may be flourishing. However, whereas marked differences in particulars are bound to occur, basic trends should be comparable. For instance, if a community has been affected by mass communication despite widespread illiteracy, then comparable effects may be expected in other villages of similar size and conditions. Again, should national ideology fail to make a marked impact on agricultural laborers in this community, one may expect its effects on agricultural laborers elsewhere in the country to be limited. I wish to stress, however, that, whereas the community under examination is not exceptional in its social and organizational characteristics, the results of the study are not generalized to other parts of Egypt.

Despite its subordinate status within a dominant national regime, the community of Shubra el Gedida is in its own right a political field of action with ground rules and organizing principles of conflict and cooperation. The national regime has introduced general solutions to Shubra's problems in the form of institutional innovations, but the management and control of the resources of these new organizations have been the shared responsibility of the people of Shubra and the national government represented by officials. Therefore, while Shubra is still affected by external forces in the allocation of resources that it obtains from the national government, a major responsibility in these matters falls upon members of the community. Their political and economic behavior are considerably affected by their own attitudes and norms. Thus the focus of this study is on the villager and how he seeks to influence his fellow villagers and government officials.

The "field of action" concept entails the existence of both conflict and cooperation, whereas a mobilization regime emphasizes unity and seeks to impose uniformity. This study must therefore address itself to the issue of the political autonomy of the local community and to the significance and form of local political participation. Should Shubra's public affairs be run by the national government only, then the community would not qualify as a political field of action.

One major assumption of systems analysis is the presentation of the particular in relation to the whole, not descriptively but in the sense that a particular political activity should be viewed in terms of its relation to other political activities, the actors, and norms of the whole community. In other words, politics as an activity may be understood as a process affecting the overall picture of community life and exhibiting a discernible pattern. The political process in the community as I observed it during my stay in Shubra el Gedida is discussed here. Patterns that emerge from the study of political process—the initiation of issues, the course they take, and their resolution—are no less important theoretically than regularities discovered by other means such as quantitative analysis of survey data. Therefore, certain concrete political events and developments in village life are examined in detail, and the interactions of political leaders and citizens within the institutional arrangement of village life are stressed. Organizations such as cooperatives, the party branch, and municipal councils are arenas where issues are contested and resolved by ordinary citizens, officials, and local leaders. Process also implies time sequence; thus this book deals with the economic and political organization of Shubra before and after the 1952 Revolution. A number of political cases also are described and analyzed with a view to discerning and illuminating patterns of collective action.

I used three methods for gathering data on Shubra: documentary sources, participant observation, and an opinion survey.

Documentary Sources

Documentary materials were collected on the national government and society, the province, and the village community.[56] Statistical data on the national system were obtained mainly from the publications of the census bureau and the Central Bureau for Statistics (*al Jihaz al Markazi lil-Ihsa'*). Other government sources include statistical reports and accounts of various ministries, publications of the Arab Socialist Union, and books written by high-ranking officials. At the provincial level, various statistics and published material on Beheira Province were made available to me by the governor's aides and the Arab Socialist Union secretary. In Shubra, written record is limited to the unpublished files of local organizations. Various scholarly works, journals, and newspapers also were used and are identified in the text.

Participant Observation

I gathered most of my information on the political process in Shubra by attending meetings of the various organizations in the village and by talking to their leaders and members. In the course of about six months'

56. Two particularly useful sources on local affairs are the peasants' newspaper, *al Ta'awun*, which has nationwide circulation and is very informative on agricultural and other rural problems; and Damanhur's biweekly newspaper, *al Shabab al Hurr*, which covers local news of the province.

residence in the village, I accompanied officials and leaders on their daily business and conversed often with various groups and individuals in Shubra and in the province.

The Opinion Survey

The study of political attitudes and behavioral patterns is indispensable if we are to know the effects of national ideology, the mass media, and mobilization policies on individual citizens. For instance, it may well be that ideas transmitted by the national regime are modified to a significant extent in the course of their transmission to villagers, and the purposes of the regime may thus fail to be fulfilled in the manner intended. Similarly, the effects of ideological information may be partially subjected to a selective process determined by backgrounds and interests of the villagers. The most systematic effort to gather data on political attitudes and behavioral patterns was the administration of a questionnaire to a sample of adult males between ages 18 and 60 and to a separate group of 44 individuals who enjoyed leadership roles of varying degrees of importance. The sample respondents totalled 135 and represented 10 percent of adult males.[57] Because I observed no involvement on the part of women in the public affairs of the community, and because of practical research limitations, women were not included in the survey.

The questionnaire was designed to elicit information on four major areas of the respondents' lives: (1) mass media exposure and understanding of messages conveyed; (2) awareness of and attitudes toward selected local and national matters; (3) identification of and attitudes toward local leaders; and (4) respondents' backgrounds.

In presenting the research findings, I have also pointed out aspects of the national system that are relevant to the specific issues under consideration in Shubra. For example, before discussing land reform in Shubra or the use of the mass media, an account is presented on these topics as they are manifested nationally. This approach has been called for by the basic assumption in this study that the village of Shubra is directly connected with a higher political order to the extent that any statement made on the political process in Shubra becomes a commentary on the national system. Since the national aspect is prior to the local, I have preserved this order in the presentation.

Discussion of the national scene, presented in conjunction with the account of Shubra, is not to be viewed as a descriptive treatment of two systems—national and local—for the sake of drawing parallels between

57. Regarding comparison of the sample with the actual universe, see Appendix B.

them. Rather, the presentation is analytical and seeks to determine the relationship between the national and the local systems. Analysis of data from Shubra reflects primarily the manner in which national influences are received—accepted, rejected, modified, distorted, or overlooked—and the outcome of such encounters. At certain points in the book, the description of the national system proved more extensive than I had desired, primarily as a result of the need to develop the broader perspective adequately. Nowhere, however, does it overshadow discussion of Shubra itself. In only a few instances were the effects of local communities on the national system taken into consideration; neither the time nor the means were available to undertake such an important study. It may be hoped that other researchers will some day take on that task.

chapter 3

Peasants, princes, and reformers

For more than a century, the economic and political history of Shubra el Gedida was bound to nationwide forces, the most important of which were trade and state centralization. European demand for agricultural products during the nineteenth century and the ensuing breakdown of barriers to foreign trade had stimulated the domestic market and the cultivation of cash crops in Egypt,[1] which in turn led to the introduction of private ownership of agricultural land. As a result of both the emerging free market economy and the monarch's awarding of large land grants,[2] inequitable land distribution became a prominent feature of Egypt's agricultural economy.

The commercialization of agriculture gave rise to a variety of occupational groups involved in the agricultural economy of villages: landlords, merchants, sharecroppers, tenants, and agricultural laborers. These groups, all of which were present in Shubra in 1952, may be classified according to economic standards and status into a top layer of landlords and merchants and a lower stratum of sharecroppers, tenants, and agricultural laborers. This chapter outlines the system of rural capitalism and the fate of the various groups in Shubra under the Revolution. Because the restructuring of economic relations under the Revolution was a major cause of political realignments in the village, it is of primary importance in the context of this study.

The agricultural economy of Egypt during the last century and well into World War II can be characterized as a system of rural capitalism.[3] Rural

1. For a concise and authoritative statement on foreign trade in Egypt and the pressures on Muhammad Ali to lift barriers to it, see Abdel-Rahim Mustafa, "The Breakdown of the Monopoly System in Egypt after 1840," in P. M. Holt (ed.), *Political and Social Change in Modern Egypt* (London: Oxford University Press, 1968), pp. 291–307.

2. For the impact of the market and state centralization on peasant society in the Middle East, see Harik, "The Impact of the Market on Rural-Urban Relations," in *Rural Politics*.

3. Egyptian writers and Nasser use the term "feudalism" to refer to conditions of extreme

capitalism is a form of preindustrial, nonprofessional use of land by private owners for large-scale production of cash crops under a primitive mode of production based on sharecropping. Profits from agriculture were sought by both absentee and resident landlords through labor-intensive methods of production and preservation of the peasantry under subsistence conditions practically outside the market economy.

The Egyptian term "landlord" does not indicate whether an owner holds 10 feddans or 1000 feddans. Rural Egyptians refer to both *al mullak* (landowners) and *al mullak al qubar* (large landowners). Lately, they have started to use the politically pejorative term *al iqta'iyun* (feudalists) in reference to objectionable landlords who owned considerably more than 200 feddans before 1952. Since the appearance of land reform in 1952, the problem of terminology has become simpler, as the upper limit of landholding is now defined by law. Because of the social and political implications of the term landlord, however, the usage established by the Arab Socialist Union is more practical for the purposes of this study: a person who owns or cultivates less than 10 feddans of land is a peasant; if he owns more, he is a landlord.[4] The villagers' term "large landowners" is used here to designate only those who before the Revolution owned more than 200 feddans.

The main features of rural capitalism in Egypt were (1) extreme inequality in landownership; (2) commercial production of cash crops by means of tenancy; and (3) the preponderance of the national power of large landlords. After a brief account of rural capitalism on the national level, its form in Shubra el Gedida is examined.

The wide discrepancy between the estates of the large landlords and the holdings of the peasants indicates extreme inequality in landownership[5] before 1952. Figures show that 2000 large landlords, or about .08 percent of all proprietors, owned about 20 percent of the total cultivation area of Egypt—that is, more than 1 million feddans. In contrast, nearly 2 million peasants, or 84 percent of all proprietors owned only 21 percent of the total cultivation area in small plots of less than 2 feddans each. This

---

inequality. The inaccuracy of this usage has been pointed out by Ibrahim 'Amir in his books, *Al Ard wa al Fallah* (Cairo: Metba'at al Dar al Misriyyah, 1958), and *Thawrat Misr al Qawmiyyah* (Cairo: Dar al Nadim, 1957).

4. These two groups are included in the Egyptian social segment defined as "native capitalists" (see chapter 10).

5. For a detailed and scholarly account of landownership in Egypt, see Gabriel Baer, *A History of Landownership in Egypt, 1800–1950* (New York: Oxford University Press, 1962). A drawback to this otherwise excellent book is the author's limitation of his discussion to landownership; he ignores other, equally important kinds of tenure like tenancy and sharecropping.

means that the largest landlords, who comprised only .08 percent of the total number, held almost as much land as did another 84 percent of all proprietors. Thus a member of the privileged minority owned on the average 1377 times more land than a member of the poor majority. This may not seem excessive in a land-rich country, but Egypt is extremely poor in land resources and in 1952 had a cultivation area of less than 6 million feddans.

The second feature of Egypt's rural capitalism was its primitive production system. Professional farming, introduced in the last decade of the nineteenth century, was before World War II undertaken only by foreign firms. Then, in the 1930s a very small number of enterprising Egyptian industrialists started to run farms in order to produce raw material for their firms. However, since the large majority of landlords were not professional farmers, most of the land was sharecropped under an arrangement by which peasant families cultivated the land in return for pay in kind. The owner generally kept all the valuable cash crops such as cotton for himself, shared wheat with the peasant cultivators, and left maize and fodder for the peasant and his beasts of burden. As a result, a dual agricultural system emerged: on one side was the market economy and, on the other, the subsistence conditions of the peasantry.

The third feature of rural capitalism was the dominant role in the central government of landlords who enjoyed unlimited state support of private-property rights. Among the largest landlords in the country were the royal family, courtiers, cabinet ministers, and members of Parliament.[6] Because the system of unequal land distribution was in the best interests of the holders of national power, nothing short of a sharp decline in the value of agricultural land or a political revolution could ever have changed the socioeconomic structure in rural Egypt.

Shortly before World War II, a number of minor changes did occur in agriculture, all of which fell short of having a major impact on the dual agricultural economy. First, there was a widespread conversion from sharecropping to money rents, which tied the peasant cultivator to the market economy but did not improve his material conditions sufficiently to raise his standard of living from the subsistence level. Whereas only 17 percent of the land was under money rent in 1939, the figure jumped to 75 percent in 1952.[7] Other changes included the appearance of farm

---

6. For the role of large landlords in national politics, see Baer, *A History of Landownership in Egypt*; Henry Habib Ayrout, *The Egyptian Peasant* (Boston: Beacon Press, 1968), pp. 14–34; and P. J. Vatikiotis, *The Modern History of Egypt* (New York: Praeger, 1969). The prominent position of landlords in the national government is also shown in a dissertation on the social background of Egyptian elite in 1923 by Kathleen Merriam, *The Role of Leadership in Nation Building: Egypt, 1922* (Ph.D. diss., Indiana University, 1970).

7. Doreen Warriner, *Land Reform and Development in the Middle East* (New York: Oxford University Press, 1962), pp. 25–26; 'Amir, p. 106; Sayid Mar'i, *Al Islah al Zira'i wa*

operators on a small scale among landlords and the emergence of an extremely limited cooperative movement.⁸

Agrarian Reform

The Revolution of 1952 undermined the old system's main pillars of unquestioned property rights and a free market economy. When inconsistent with the new leaders' views of social justice, the right of private property was denied. The major steps taken by the new regime to change rural conditions were land reform and modification of market conditions.

The first land reform law was enacted less than two months after Nasser and the Free Officers took over the government in 1952.⁹ The law limited landholdings to 200 feddans per proprietor and allowed the same amount for his wife and adult offspring. Landholdings beyond this limit were to be sold by the owner within about one year, after which time land held in excess of the law was to be requisitioned and the owner compensated at the rate of ten times the rental value per feddan.¹⁰ Sale of land was made difficult in a number of ways. Government rules stipulated that land could not be sold to relatives or to owners already possessing more than 10 feddans, and sales were limited to 5 feddans or less per single buyer.¹¹ By 1966, nearly 1 million feddans, or about one-sixth of the cultivated area, had been requisitioned by the government. This figure includes additional lands requisitioned as a result of lowering the ceiling again in 1961 to 100 feddans per proprietor.¹² Land reform measures had the effect of reducing the size of large estates below the official ceiling as a result of the fear that further reductions would be made by the government in the future.

Land requisitioned by the government was distributed mostly to landless tenants, typically in the amount of 2 or 3 feddans per family.

Mushkilat al Sukkan fi al Qitr al Misri (Cairo: [al Dar al Qawmiyyah lil-Taba'ah wa al Nashr 1963]), p. 35. For an economist's point of view, see the excellent account on Egyptian agriculture by Bent Hansen and Girgis A. Marzouk, *Development and Economic Policy in the U.A.R. (Egypt)* (Amsterdam: North-Holland, 1965), chapter 3.

8. On the development of cooperatives in Egypt, see Zaki Muhammad Shabanah, *al Iqtisad al Ta'awuni al Zira'i* (Alexandria: Dar al Ma'arif, 1965).

9. For an authoritative and first hand report on the application of the law and other details by one of the engineers of reforms in Egypt, see Mar'i, *Al Islah al Zira'i*; and Warriner, *Land Reform*.

10. Proprietors were compensated in nontransferable bonds payable in 40 years and carrying an annual interest of 1.5 percent. For details, see Gabriel S. Saab, *Egyptian Agrarian Reform 1952–1962* (New York: Oxford University Press, 1967), pp. 24, 26, 41–47.

11. See Mar'i, p. 65.

12. In 1969, the ceiling was lowered again to 50 feddans, and for the first time the idea of converting the requisitioned land into state farms was adopted. This is a serious departure from established policy and one to be watched for comparative purposes.

Landless tenants were favored over agricultural wage laborers since the government preferred to have experienced cultivators operate the new farms in order to avoid declines in output. Beneficiaries paid installments equivalent to compensations extended to expropriated landlords.[13] In effect, the peasants reimbursed the former landowner through the offices of the government.

The number of feddans distributed by 1965 totaled 690,740 spread over 292,600 families, or 1.5 million individuals.[14] By the end of 1967, 754,487 feddans had been distributed to 317,376 families.[15] Land reclamation projects by 1965 contributed an additional 111,000 feddans, which were distributed among 20,000 families. Orchards became state property run by the Agrarian Reform Administration.

The extent to which land reform policy affected the existing economic stratification system between 1952 and 1964 may be observed in tables 1 and 2. The most striking difference, as may be expected, has been the disappearance of the 2000 topmost landowners who held 20 percent of the cultivated area before 1952. The largest single owner in this category was the King, followed by other members of the royal family.[16] The second category of large landlords, who owned more than 100 feddans but less than 200, were the next group to suffer a serious setback. Not only were they forced to give up all land over 100 feddans, but figures show that by 1964 their numbers had increased by 1,000, whereas the total area of land that they held had decreased by 16,000 feddans. All the categories of landowners whose individual holdings were 50 to 200 feddans lost acreage. In 1969, the ceiling was lowered again to 50 feddans and the upper categories of landlords were done away with altogether.

Beneficiaries of successive reduction in landholding ceilings were the small and middle-size owners who owned less than 50 feddans. They increased their numbers by 343,000 and their total landholdings by 1,369,000 feddans, the most striking turnover in landholding in the history of private property in Egypt. Not all in this group were direct beneficiaries of land distribution; it may be said, however, that almost all of the changes in landholding had been induced by land reform measures that made large landlords sell land on easy terms in anticipation of the further lowering of the official ceiling. The greatest beneficiaries have been owners of less than

13. For a detailed account, see Saab, pp. 24–26, 46–47; Mar'i, pp. 68–70, 104–5.
14. Nearly one million feddans passed to state ownership, of which these figures constitute a part.
15. Saad Hagras, *Agrarian Reform in the United Arab Republic* (Cairo: Agrarian Reform Organization, 1969), p. 20.
16. In 1952, King Faruq owned 48,000 feddans and managed another 45,000 feddans as waqfs; see 'Amir, p. 108.

Table 1
Social Stratification Measured in Landownership before 1952

Class	Farm Size (feddans)	Owners (1,000)	Area (1,000 feddans)	Percentage of Total Owners	Percentage of Total Area
I	Above 200	2	1,117	.08	19.70
II	100–199	3	437	.12	7.30
III	50–99	6	430	.20	7.20
IV	5–49	148	1,818	5.30	30.40
V	Under 5	2,642	2,122	94.30	35.40
Total		2,801	5,984	100.00	100.00

Based on data given in U.A.R., Ministry of Agrarian Reform and Land Reclamation, *Al Islah al Zira'i wa Istislah al Aradi, 1952–1966*, Cairo, 1966.

Table 2
Social Stratification Measured in Landownership, 1964

Class	Farm Size (feddans)	Owners (1,000)	Area (1,000 feddans)	Percentage of Total Owners	Percentage of Total Area
I	100	4	421	.30	6.90
II	50–99	6	392	.20	6.40
III	5–49	168	1,956	5.40	31.90
IV	Under 5	2,965	3,353	94.30	54.80
Total		3,143	6,122	100.00	100.00

Based on data given in U.A.R., Ministry of Agrarian Reform and Land Reclamation, *Al Islah al Zira'i wa Istislah al Aradi, 1952–1966*, Cairo, 1966.

5 feddans, who increased their holdings from 35.4 percent of the total area in 1952 to 54.8 percent in 1964. During the same period, cultivators who owned less than 50 but more than 5 feddans gained land 1.5 percent over what they held in 1952. At present, after a lowering of the ceiling to 50 feddans, there are basically three classes left in rural areas: those who own less than 50 feddans, those who own less than 5 feddans, and the landless.[17]

17. The landless who rent land for cultivation should be included among the category of owners of less than 5 feddans.

In short, the landlord class in Egypt has become less differentiated and smaller, and has experienced downward mobility, while most poor cultivators have moved upward by a small margin.

Agrarian reform in Egypt goes beyond land distribution to include land consolidation, reform in the tenancy laws, fixed rental rates, limits on the amount of land a single tenant can rent, water control for irrigation, partial mechanization of agricultural production, and establishment of cooperative societies.[18] The establishment of cooperatives had far-reaching effects on peasants not only because it freed them from dependence on moneylenders and merchants but also because it rationalized the system of agricultural production.

Although agrarian reform has provided solutions to the problems of production and marketing, it has fallen short of providing land for all landless peasants; concealed rural unemployment continues to be widespread. Scarcity of land and overpopulation are two very serious problems of the Egyptian economy and cannot be solved by agrarian reform programs alone. Land reclamation continues to expand the cultivation area, but it cannot provide land for the entire rural population of Egypt.

Rural Capitalism in Shubra el Gedida

Rural capitalism in extreme form was present in Shubra. Within its humble environment, Shubra witnessed the interplay of forces that loomed large on the national scene; royalty, resident and absentee landlords, and political bosses—all were powerful agents of national politics. Shubra's large landlords, including a prince of the royal family, were mostly absentees of Turko-Egyptian stock. The largest landlord was Prince Muhammad 'Ali Ibrahim, whose estate in Shubra was 1278 feddans, or 33 percent of the total cultivation area (*zimam*) of the village. Most of the rest was owned by five absentee families, two resident families, and a *waqf* (mortmain land) in the name of the Mihtab family. Ordinary villagers owned less than 100 feddans in very small plots. As notables and professionals who lived in Damanhur, Alexandria, and Cairo, the absentee landlords, with the exception of the Prince, who was represented in the village by a steward (*ma'mur*), did not participate in the social or political life of the community and leased their lands to middlemen. Two resident landowning families, who figure largely in this study, were the Kuras and the Samads, both native Egyptian families. The Kuras, 'Abd al Rahman

18. For details, see Saab. See also the excellent monograph by U.S. Department of Agriculture, *Agricultural Development and Expansion in the Nile Basin*, Foreign Agricultural Economic Report No. 48 (Washington, D.C., 1968); and Hansen and Marzouk, chapter 4.

and his sons, owned 800 feddans of land; the Samads, Mustafa and his brother Kamil, owned 400 feddans, and two cousins of theirs owned 100.

The term "landowning family," as applied to landlords like the Samads and the Kuras, is often used without precision in Egypt to refer to a group varying in size from the nuclear family to a larger group, including paternal uncles and second cousins but not including all the members of a patrilineal kinship group. The Samads, for instance, are known in Shubra and in the district as a landowning family, but only five individuals of more than one hundred who carry the surname Samad were landlords. It should also be noted that titles of land were held individually, not collectively, by members of an extended family. The term thus has no relevance other than to indicate the extent of land resources of various members of a patrilineal kinship group; a family member's landownership becomes politically significant for the whole family only when kinship solidarity exists.

Before 1952, inequality of landownership was much more pronounced in Shubra than at the national level. Proprietors with less than 5 feddans each held among them only 58 feddans, or 2 percent of the total cultivation area of the village, whereas nationally this category of proprietors held 35 percent. Middle-size landlords owning 10 to 100 feddans have played an important part in the politics of rural Egypt[19] but were practically nonexistent in Shubra.

Commercial agricultural production was carried out by labor-intensive means, with the produce of the village being tied to the cotton market of Alexandria and the ginning firms of Damanhur. Other cash crops in addition to cotton were rice, wheat, and maize. Vegetables were not grown, and the only fruit trees were the palms cultivated by the Prince's steward. The peasants of Shubra to this day buy their vegetables in the market, and only large farmers have started to cultivate fruit trees, mainly citrus.

Though cultivation of cash crops was a profitable capitalist enterprise, the production system was primitive. Renting land and sharecropping were the main forms of production with the exception of the Kura estate, which was operated by the owner. In accordance with the national trend, money rent became widespread during and after World War II and replaced sharecropping to a considerable extent.[20]

Money rents gave rise to a class of entrepreneurs who served as middlemen between landlords and cultivators.[21] In Shubra, Mustafa and

---

19. Middle-size landlords made up 3 percent of total landowners in Egypt but owned 29 percent of the land.

20. In 1966, it was estimated that half the cultivation area was still under tenancy and that 27 percent of that area was still sharecropped. The large area of land under tenancy clearly indicates that some small owners were absentees.

21. Egyptians refer to this practice in land rent as *ijar min al batin*.

Kamil Samad were landlords who, besides placing their own estates under tenancy, rented large areas of land at low rates from absentee landlords and leased them to cultivators at a large profit. From the Prince's estate alone, Kamil Samad rented about 300 feddans, and his brother Mustafa rented a comparable amount. They also rented from the *waqf* administrators and from other absentee landlords. The position of the Samad brothers as village headmen (*'umdah* and deputy *'umdah*) and their status as landlords gave them an advantage over competing middlemen.

The Prince, who is reported by villagers never to have set foot on his estate, managed it by means of an administrative staff (*al taftish*) under a steward (*ma'mur*). A complex of buildings constituted the steward's headquarters, warehouses, and offices, all of which were located not more than 200 yards from the village. Most of this estate by 1952 was under money rent, and only a small portion, including the palm grove, was cultivated directly by the Prince's staff. In the absence of written records, the extent to which the Prince, like other farm operators, had shifted to rent during the 1940s is not very clear.

Like landownership, agricultural trade was concentrated in only a few hands. The merchant who bought most of Shubra's produce was Kamil Samad, who was also a landlord and middleman. His brother Mustafa, himself a landlord and middleman, did not engage in trade beyond the sale of his own produce.

The story of how Kamil operated as a merchant illustrates the economic enterprise of this landlord-merchant group in Egyptian economic history. In May of every year, Kamil acquired a loan of about 20,000 Egyptian pounds [22] from the Agricultural Credit Bank (ACB), a government institution created in 1931 to assist peasants and landlords in obtaining credit at a lower interest rate than that offered by commercial banks. In order to expand his business, Kamil turned also to commercial banks such as the Barclay's (now the Alexandria Bank) for additional loans; he used the same estate of 200 feddans as security for each of the loans. (No formal evidence was requested by the ACB or other banks, he said, as his word was sufficient.) Sometimes he also acquired loans from private financiers. Kamil amassed from all these deals a yearly sum of about 70,000 Egyptian pounds.

Fortified with cash, Kamil approached the cultivators in June, before the cotton crop was harvested and while rice was being planted, and offered them a price for their crops. The price he offered was one pound

22. The official rate of exchange in the 1960s was commonly $2.87, and the free market rate was $1.60. In 1950, however, the free market rate was $2.40. See Charles Issawi, *Egypt in Revolution: An Economic Analysis* (New York: Oxford University Press, 1963), pp. 112–14.

per cantar (a cantar is equal to 99 lbs.) under the market rate, according to him, and at an outrageously low rate according to cultivators. Kamil's advantage in this transaction was that he approached the peasants at a time when they were most in need of cash and could ill afford to sell on their own terms. Peasants were victims of high interest rates whether they obtained credit from financiers or from crop merchants.[23]

Kamil Samad's extensive business depended not only on his ingenuity as an entrepreneur but, more importantly, on the economic and political conditions then prevalent in Egypt. As a landlord himself, he enjoyed the advantages of access to credit from national sources of finance, and of personal contacts with officials and absentee landlords. He benefited from being the brother and deputy of the village headman, and, as such, enjoyed extensive political connections throughout the province and in Alexandria. Thus the Samad brothers belonged to that class of privileged rural notables who were a link between the local community and the larger environment and who could exploit their advantages most favorably.

By 1952, Shubra had only two landlords who were farm operators. The first was Majid Rayyan, a literate peasant who managed to rent approximately 10 feddans and own about 3 until after 1952, when he became an owner of 10 feddans. The other was 'Abd al Rahman Kura, the largest landlord in the village besides the Prince. Originally a merchant, Kura had settled in Shubra in about 1913 on an estate of approximately 800 feddans that he personally managed by using hired labor. He trained his sons, three of whom had university degrees, to follow suit as professional farmers. Except for Muhammad, who as a young man frequented the cotton market of Alexandria with Kamil Samad, none of them became involved in trade. In the 1950s, another member of the family took up trading in fertilizers, but this enterprise was terminated by the socialist measures of the regime.

The role of the national government in the economic life of Shubra before 1952 was limited for the most part to regulation of water for irrigation; not until 1931 did it have anything to offer to cultivators and landowners. The Agricultural Credit Bank was then founded by the government to offer credit at low interest rates to landowners who possessed about 50 or fewer feddans (raised in 1949 to 200 feddans) and to cooperative societies.[24] Mustafa Samad and 'Abd al Rahman Kura, the largest resident landlords of Shubra, immediately organized a local

23. Baer, pp. 89–90; 'Amir, pp. 128–32.
24. The ACB was originally proposed by the *Wafd* government in 1930 without success. However, the worldwide depression forced the conservative Prime Minister Isma'il Sidqi to aid farmers. The ACB was a government institution in which private banks owned part of the stocks.

cooperative society to avail themselves of low-interest credit from the ACB and also of low-cost seeds and fertilizers. Each of these two men subscribed to the cooperative for 1000 shares; the rest of the shares were distributed among a score of individuals, all kinsmen, friends, and associates of the Samad brothers. In the 1950s, for political as well as economic reasons, membership in the cooperative increased to over forty individuals. Mustafa Samad presided over the cooperative for twenty-eight years from the time it was founded in 1931 until it was dissolved by the government in 1959, and the Kuras always had a seat on the four-member board. Mustafa, who directed the cooperative from his home, left the society in debt, as he too was indebted to the ACB for 12,000 pounds. The small membership of the cooperative clearly shows that most cultivators in Shubra did not benefit from the services of the society or from the ACB. Land rents were not regulated by the government, and rental rates were subject to the law of supply and demand. No accurate figure on the rental rates could be obtained from the oral testimony of the villagers themselves, but figures computed for the national average indicate a steady increase in rates, especially between 1945 and 1952.[25] The record of Shubra's first cooperative society confirms the view often taken by Egyptian writers[26] on agrarian problems: the free cooperative system was controlled by landlords[27] and worked to their advantage more than to the benefit of the bulk of the peasantry.

Land Reforms in Shubra

The agrarian reform program in Egypt has in all its aspects been manifest in Shubra. Since land had been concentrated in so few hands, redistribution of land was more extensive in this locality than it was on the national average. Three hundred feddans were sold by the Prince to small cultivators; the rest of his estate was requisitioned and distributed to tenants. In distributing land, the government followed a policy of granting

25. United Arab Republic, National Institute of Planning, Memo. No. 576. Figures in this report show that from 1945 to 1952 the average rent rate per feddan rose about 11 pounds. The author, Dr. 'Izz al Din Hammam Ahmad of the National Institute of Planning, maintains that average rental rate reached its optimum point by 1952. He compared the standard deviations of average rental rates for the years 1953 to 1960. The difficulty with his conclusion is that rental rates for these years had been fixed by the government, and black market rates could not be ascertained.

26. Mar'i, p. 187; also 'Izz al Din Hammam Ahmad, *Dirasat fi al Iqtisad* al Zira'i (Cairo, 1961), pp. 95–96. See socialist writers' views also in *al Tali'ah*; and Saad M. Gadalla, *Land Reform in Relation to Social Development: Egypt* (Columbia: University of Missouri Press, 1962), p. 17.

27. Nationally, membership in a cooperative in 1935 averaged about 100 members only, a figure derived from statistics offered by Shabanah, p. 165.

Table 3
Land Distribution in Shubra el Gedida, 1966

Size of Farm (in feddans)	Number of Proprietors	Amount of Land (in feddans)	Percentage of Cultivation Area (in feddans)
Large proprietors (5–60)	About 60	1124	31.5
Small proprietors (under 5)	About 400	1009	28.6
Beneficiaries of land distribution (under 5)	436	1058	29.6
Land held by Agrarian Reform Administration		368	10.3
Total		3559	100.0

the land to the same tenants who used to cultivate it. It is quite likely that political consideration played a role in the distribution process, but I could discover no sign of it in Shubra.

Land distribution in Shubra in 1966 (see table 3) reflects the combined consequences of free sales by landlords and of government requisition and reallocation. Though in 1952 one landlord owned more than 1000 feddans, in 1966 no proprieter was left with more than 60 feddans. Large proprietors in 1966 were those who owned 5 to 60 feddans; this group included former large proprietors such as members of the Kura and Samad families, approximately four absentee landlords, and peasants who had purchased land after 1952. Small proprietors have shown the greatest increase in numbers, from a handful in 1952 to about 850 in 1966, about half of whom were direct beneficiaries of land reform. They were also in possession of nearly 60 percent of the village cultivation area and were divided almost equally between beneficiaries of land distribution and peasants who bought land independently.

The middleman's role in tenancy has been abolished, and tenants are now protected by the law in two ways: rents are fixed by law, and tenants are entitled to all the cooperative services offered to landowners.

Cooperative Societies

One of the most important agrarian reform measures affecting peasants was the introduction of cooperative societies. By extending credit and seeds, cooperatives solved the most urgent problem of small cultivators who had no cash to use for cultivation expenses. In 1967, Shubra had three cooperative societies, two for beneficiaries of land reform and one regular cooperative for other cultivators. Reform cooperatives were established by the government to serve the cultivation needs of beneficiaries of state-distributed land. They distributed seed, fertilizers, and pesticides, marketed rice and cotton, extended credit at no interest, and retrieved loans at harvest time. The main reform cooperative in Shubra, founded in 1954, was later extended to serve other neighboring areas when more land was requisitioned in 1961. As a result, the original membership of 400 has tripled. After 1961, another reform cooperative was established to serve Shubra's Mihtab *waqf* lands of 390 feddans, which had been requisitioned and distributed to cultivators. It is still a small cooperative and is less involved in village politics.

The regular cooperative, introduced in 1961, was modeled after the reform cooperative society to meet the needs of peasants not served by the reform cooperative.[28] In 1967, it served 613 members, all natives of Shubra. The ACB provides interest-free credit[29] plus seeds, fertilizers, and pesticides, which the cooperative distributes to cultivators according to their needs. The ACB is repaid through the cooperative society after the harvest and sale of the produce.[30]

In addition to these resources provided by the ACB, each of the three cooperatives of Shubra receives revenues generated by members' shares, service fees, and charges on the use of agricultural machinery. Income from these sources has enabled Shubra's cooperatives to distribute dividends to members, increase their reserves, and enhance their capacity for service by buying more machinery, building offices and storage rooms, and the like. The two main cooperative societies have increased their stock of machinery by six to seven times.

Cooperatives in Shubra, as in the rest of Egypt, are controlled jointly by state officials and local cultivators. The state appoints a staff usually composed of an agronomist (*mushrif zira'i*), an assistant agronomist, a

28. Regular cooperatives are known as *ta'awuniyat al 'itiman*, literally "credit cooperatives," but since extending credit is only one of their many functions, the use of the literal name is misleading.
29. Interest on credit was introduced at the rate of 4 percent after the 1967 War.
30. For details on the finances and staffs of cooperatives before 1962, see Saab, pp. 70–81.

number of clerks, and, in the case of the regular cooperative, a manager (*mushrif ta'awuni*) to oversee ACB accounts in the cooperative. The agronomist is usually the head of the society and has greater power than the board's president or secretary. Cultivators are represented by board members elected every four years. According to government rules, all but one of the board members must be small owners or tenants holding 5 or fewer feddans. Each board elects a president and a secretary, but the latter office holds the real power.

In Shubra, the staffs for the two main cooperative societies were complete in 1967 and led by experienced and capable agronomists. The small Mihtab cooperative, however, had only one agronomist and two clerks, and most of the management fell to the elected board of three members. The main functions of the staffs are to manage the resources extended to cultivators by the central government, handle members' accounts, implement national agricultural policy at the local level, and deal with such land-management problems as crop rotation, irrigation, and drainage. The agronomist, as titular head of the cooperative, supervises all these functions.

Cooperative boards control the cooperative funds and advise the agronomist on local affairs. Many extension problems are discussed and solved jointly by the staff and the board. In Shubra, cooperative board secretaries put in almost daily appearances at the office and regularly attend to the cooperatives' business during the busy season; other members of the board vary in their participation on an individual basis.

An important function of board members is to control cooperative revenue obtained from services over which the agronomist has no power. Because the building and maintenance of the physical plant, acquisition of necessary machinery, and similar projects are paid for from these revenues, the board, in effect, is responsible for the growth and development of the cooperative society. Agronomists generally participate in discussions of these matters and offer expert advice, but the final decision on spending belongs to the board. If, in the opinion of the agronomist, the board's decision is detrimental to national policy, he can object and delay implementation until a ruling is obtained from the Ministry of Agriculture or, in the case of reform cooperatives, from the Agrarian Reform Administration.

Reform cooperatives were under stricter control by the official staff than were regular cooperatives, but since 1962 more authority has been vested in the elected boards of reform cooperatives.

Thus whether actual power rests with the staff or with the board depends on the quality of leadership. In Shubra's reform cooperative, for instance, the board secretary, 'Ali al Shawi, and the agronomist, Nasr Damardash, worked in close cooperation administratively and politically. 'Ali al Shawi was as influential as the agronomist, if not more so. Members generally took their problems to him, and even the agronomist had to depend on the secretary in matters requiring expert knowledge of the rules of the cooperative system. In contrast, the agronomist of the regular cooperative dominated the staff and the board by virtue of his strength of character, energy, dedication, and expertise, and also because the board in 1966–67 was losing strength for political reasons (see chapter 14). However, when Muhammad Kura was the board secretary between 1961 and 1964, he, not the agronomist, overshadowed and dominated the official staff.

Agrarian reform has preserved privately owned land under a cooperative system of production and marketing. Cooperative production made it possible for Egyptian agriculture to adapt large-scale farming methods to small, private plots and improved cultivators' economic conditions and agricultural productivity.[31] Crop rotation, cotton spraying, fighting the cotton pest,[32] and marketing rice and cotton have all become the responsibility of cooperatives. Implementation of the laws of tenancy and contracts are also under cooperative management. Though land is privately owned, the individual farmer is not allowed to neglect his land, and, should he fail to attend to the management of his field, the cooperative would take over and charge the owner for the services rendered him. The cooperative and the official political party are obligated to preserve national agricultural production at a high level in order to earn for the country the hard currency so essential for national development. Cooperatives in Shubra have also provided their memberships with recreational services, housing renewal, financial assistance, and other village-wide projects.

The free market in the agricultural sector became extremely limited as a result of the introduction of the cooperative system. Cooperative credit and marketing put an end to moneylending by private entrepreneurs and reduced the business of merchants to retail trade in vegetables, fruits, some cereals, and livestock. By 1966, the dominant features of Shubra's agricultural system, especially moneylending and free trade, had vanished.

31. See Gadalla, *Land Reform*, pp. 60–61; Issawi, *Egypt in Revolution*, pp. 162–163; also Hansen and Marzouk, pp. 91–92. For figures on increase in productivity, see U.S., Department of Agriculture, pp. 50–51.
32. Infested leaves are first picked by hand, then the plants are sprayed later as a supplementary measure.

Occupations and Standards of Living

In view of the extensive economic changes in the village, it may be useful to consider briefly occupational distribution and relative incomes in Shubra at the time the survey was conducted. In 1967, half the adult males were cultivators, 21 percent were agricultural wage laborers, 15 percent were employees, and the remainder were shopkeepers, vendors, and artisans.[33]

A cultivator in Shubra owned or rented, on the average, 2 feddans. After discounting expenses and taxes, 1 feddan yields an annual net income of about 80 pounds,[34] an estimate based on oral testimony and cooperative reports but supported by survey results. Thus the average peasant in Shubra has an income equal to or better than most local employees, with the exception of the top village officials.

Agricultural laborers are landless villagers employed locally by the cooperative societies, especially the reform co-op, and by large proprietors. Many of them also work as seasonal migrant workers, mainly at Liberation Province, the land reclamation site west of Beheira Province. Agricultural laborers receive a daily wage of about 11 to 20 piasters, depending on seasonal variation in demand for workers, but they are often unemployed during rainy days. According to survey results, the average monthly income of laborers was 3 pounds in 1967. It should be added that, although the minimum daily wage has been fixed by the government at 18 piasters, this rate has been impossible to enforce and has been violated even by the Ministry of Agriculture, which sometimes paid as little as 11 piasters. The national government thus far has failed to raise appreciably this low-income group's standard of living.

Employees, who comprise the third largest occupational category, include the top-level government officials such as the mayor, agronomists, and social workers and the lower-level employees of the village council and cooperative societies. In the latter category are teachers, clerks, master craftsmen, foremen, guards, janitors, and others. Agronomists and social workers receive a monthly salary of 10 to 17 pounds, depending on their academic degrees and work experience; the pay of lower-level employees ranges from about 3 pounds for a janitor to 8 pounds for a clerk.

Vendors and itinerant artisans make about 3 pounds a month, as do laborers and other unskilled workers, whereas village shopkeepers may make up to 30 pounds a month, depending on the size of the store.

33. According to survey results, 2 percent of the adult male population were handicapped dependents. Women were not included in the survey and those among them who owned land are not included in these figures.
34. For the rate of the Egyptian pound see footnote 24.

Conclusion

During the monarchical period, ordinary villagers lived under conditions in which avenues for economic and ipso facto political choices were practically closed. With land as the exclusive source of income for the majority of the villagers, ownership, tenancy, or labor on the land provided the only livelihood of most inhabitants of Shubra. The ordinary cultivator was dependent on landlords for land to till, on moneylenders for credit, and on merchants for the sale of crops. Since these agencies in Shubra were concentrated in a few hands, an extremely disproportionate amount of economic and political power lined up against the ordinary villager.[35]

In economic terms, cultivators were a factor of production, as was the land they tilled, and they lived under subsistence conditions. However, though the tiller of the land was at the mercy of the economically powerful, he shared with them social norms that precluded the powerful from taking full advantage of their economic position. For example, the Samad brothers were related to many villagers by extensive kinship ties and patronage relationships, and the Kuras' ties with most villagers in their service were based on patronage in lieu of kinship relations. Furthermore, Islamic religion was the common code of ethics for both villagers and their masters; it required of the wealthy a modicum of humane treatment and charity toward the poor. The Kuras showed more religious responsibility than the Samads; to this day the Kuras spend conspicuously on alms-giving (*zakat*) and religious festivities.

Under a political system in which economic and political powers coalesce for the preservation of a status quo of extreme inequality, the individual's opportunity for economic and political choices is severely restricted. Peasant inactivism in Shubra was the manifestation of such a condition. Emphasis on inequality, the market mechanism, and national sanctions of private property is not another way of presenting a deterministic explanation of the political behavior of rural people. It is, rather, an attempt to highlight another dimension to the exclusively cultural explanation in many studies of peasant societies.[36]

---

35. On the lack of economic freedom as witnessed especially in Upper Egypt during the 1930s, see Ayrout, pp. 16 and 58.

36. Cultural explanations of peasant behavior are not only common in anthropological tradition but also among political scientists like Edward Banfield, *The Moral Basis of Backward Society* (New York: The Free Press, 1958) and sociologists like Arthur J. Vidich and Joseph Bensman in their excellent book, *Small Town in Mass Society*, 1st ed. (Princeton: Princeton University Press, 1958). For literature on Egypt with strongly cultural orientation, see James Mayfield, *The Politics of Rural Egypt: Nasser's Quest for Legitimacy* (Austin: University of Texas Press, 1971); and Hamed Ammar, *Growing Up in an Egyptian Village* (New York: Octagon Books, 1966). Mayfield, for instance, completely overlooks agricultural cooperatives and their impact on peasant life and economy.

Peasants, princes, and reformers

Change in the national political system and the revolutionary outlook of the new regime undermined the main source of autocracy in Shubra. Private property in agricultural land continued under the new regime, but it was qualified by a new principle of social justice to which the new regime subscribed. In the political philosophy of the new regime, land should be held relatively equally among cultivators; any land held in excess of the criterion of relative equality should be requisitioned and distributed to landless cultivators. Not only did land reform conform to the ideals of the new national leaders but it also served their political objective of undermining leaders of the old regime by divesting them from the economic source of their political power. By making it possible for cultivators to become owners and by extending to them necessary means of cultivation at negligible cost, agrarian reform freed Shubra's cultivators from the crippling forces of a relatively closed economic system. It gave the ordinary cultivator not only independence but also control over the means of his livelihood and thus opened up for him opportunities for self-improvement. Though economic progress remains limited by scarcity of resources and by overpopulation, agrarian reform has improved peasant conditions.

The dispersion of economic resources among larger numbers and the rights acquired by villagers to manage their cooperatives and local affairs resulted in the villagers' greater political participation and thus the enlargement of the source of local leadership. Relative equality in economic resources in Shubra, as this study indicates, resulted in relative equality in political influence between the lower-income people and the wealthy. Stripped of their disproportionate economic advantage over ordinary villagers, Shubra's established political leaders were weakened and eventually removed from the political scene. The following two chapters describe the power shift as it occurred in Shubra el Gedida.

chapter 4

From headmanship to representative government

Just as the local economy was bound to the nation's, Shubra's political institutions were part of the relatively integrated political system of the constitutional monarchy. The King exercised executive authority in collaboration with national political parties,[1] but the strength of the political parties, theoretically measured by the number of representatives they raised to Parliament, had been largely undermined by the arbitrary actions of the monarch. Despite the tactics of the King, the marshaling of popular support remained a major goal of most political parties whose claim to executive leadership and influence was based primarily on their strength at the mass level.

Party competition for votes in villages was determined by the actual distribution of political influence in each community, which was almost invariably in the hands of the custodians of economic wealth. This chapter deals with the structure of local political authority under the old regime and the forging of new institutions of local government after the Revolution.

Hereditary Authority in Shubra

At the time of the Revolution in 1952, political power in Shubra was held by Mustafa Samad and his brother Kamil, who maintained close relations with the central government and with other landlords of the village. The authority of the Samads in Shubra had been hereditary, and no one in the

1. For a description of this system, see P. J. Vatikiotis, *The Modern History of Egypt*; Zaheer Quraishi, *Liberal Nationalism in Egypt* (Alahabad: Kitab Mahal, 1967); and Jacques Berque, *Egypt: Imperialism and Revolution* (London: Faber and Faber, 1972).

village could remember that there had even been any other. 'Abd al Rahman al Rafi'i, an Egyptian chronicler, mentions a certain Muhammad Samad from Beheira Province as being active in national politics in 1882.[2] In the village, Muhammad was remembered by the Samads as a courtier of Khedive Tawfiq (1879–1892).

The Samads in Shubra were vague about their origin, but the oral legend I obtained from Samad elders was that they had come from Upper Egypt. Of their ancestors, they could remember only Muhammad and his brother Khalifah. (See figure 1 for the Samad family tree as I have constructed it from oral legend.) Khalifah, whose offspring inherited the office of *'umdah* (village headman), was not remembered for specific attributes, whereas his brother Muhammad was clearly recalled as an illustrious personage and the owner of a very large estate, black slaves, and movable property. Muhammad Samad, however, squandered his wealth and left little to his offspring, who, like most other Samads in 1966, were poor peasants. Khalifah, on the other hand, maintained his wealth and passed on a considerable fortune.

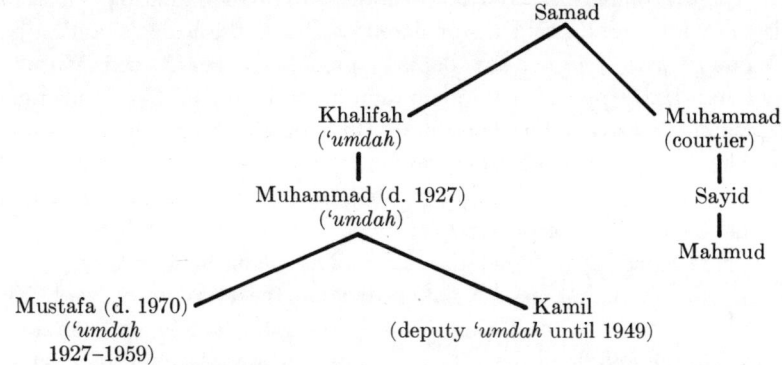

FIGURE 1. The Samad family

On his father's death in 1927, Mustafa, then only fifteen years old, immediately became the new *'umdah*,[3] circumventing the legal minimum age of twenty-five years by a false birth certificate. He told me that he had been elected by village landlords to become *'umdah*, but, since almost all Shubra's landlords were absentees,[4] it is doubtful that any such election

2. Since all local names have been changed in this study, I do not specify this source. 'Ali Mubarak's encyclopedia of nineteenth-century Egypt, *al Khitat al Tawfiqiyah*, unfortunately does not mention Shubra el Gedida.

3. For a discussion of the hereditary traditions of the office, see Gabriel Baer, "The Village Shaykh in Modern Egypt (1800–1950)," in Uriel Heyd (ed.), *Studies in Islamic History* (Jerusalem: Magnes Press, 1961), p. 128.

4. The only resident landlord besides Mustafa was 'Abd al Rahman Kura, who was not a native of Shubra.

took place. During the thirty-two years he served as *'umdah*,[5] his authority was challenged only once, and that was in 1953 when the sons of 'Abd al Rahman Kura took advantage of the change in national regimes and competed for influence with the Samads.

Mustafa's younger brother Kamil served as his deputy between 1939 and 1949. The conduct of the two brothers in governing the village was harsh but not ruthless; only two cases of major violence perpetrated by the Samads were reported to me. The first involved a peasant cultivator who had urgent business with Mustafa Samad and pursued him persistently, causing Mustafa to lose his temper and beat him. This incident accidentally led to the man's death, but the issue was settled privately by Mustafa and was never discussed by the villagers with outsiders, a practice quite common in Egyptian villages. A second case involved the accidental shooting of a woman by a member of the Samad family. Again, no official investigation followed the incident, and Mustafa settled the matter with the woman's family. The only other use of violence attributed to the Samads' government involved the beating, intimidation, and blackmail of villagers who caused problems or dared challenge the Samads' authority.

Kamil Samad resigned as deputy *'umdah* in 1947,[6] and Mustafa appointed Haj Hilmi, a compliant cousin and one of two remaining landowning Samads, to fill the position. Hilmi claimed that, when his ailing father lost his mortgaged land to foreign creditors in 1939, Mustafa shared in the spoils instead of extending a helping hand. Nevertheless, Hilmi responded to the call of duty.

Mustafa Samad was one of the first individuals in Shubra to receive a secular education, but he did not go beyond the elementary level. His power and prestige accrued from his social position, wealth, and contacts. Located in the middle of the village, his house was a tall redbrick building towering over the humble mudbrick huts of villagers. Because his house served both as the seat of authority and as *dawwar* (guest house), he posted two guards with rifles at the gate. Inside the house were two things of great symbolic importance to the villagers: the telephone and the guards' rifles. During the old regime, a telephone, because it could only be found in the *'umdah*'s house, became the main symbol of authority.

The extravagance of the Samad brothers contrasted sharply with the humble means of the villagers. Kamil vacationed in Europe and Lebanon while Mustafa built, in addition to his imposing *dawwar*, another mansion on the outskirts of Shubra, where he entertained his distinguished urban

5. In 1960, the national government changed the system of local government.
6. His resignation was not officially accepted until 1949.

friends. In 1935, he purchased an electric motor and was the only one in the village until recently to enjoy electric light in his home.

Except for a few prominent villagers, Mustafa's friends were outsiders such as the police officer of a neighboring town and officials of Beheira Province. He married the daughter of 'Abd al Rahman Kura, but, when she failed to give him a male heir, he took another wife. He kept the latter away from Shubra in order not to offend the Kuras; second marriages were generally frowned upon by the upper classes and the family of the first wife.

During the parliamentary elections, Mustafa delivered Shubra's vote to the political party of his choice. Before 1950, he favored the Sa'dist party, a nationalist group who split with the Wafd and, though they did not have the same strength as the Wafd in Parliament, were often favored by the King when he formed his cabinets. Keenly interested in maintaining national support for his position in Shubra, and being of nationalist sympathies, Mustafa found in the Sa'dists a powerful group to his liking. In 1950, however, he changed party affiliations and joined the Wafd, partly because his new wife was a relative of the wife of Mustafa al Nahhas Pasha, the strong leader of the Wafd. Through this personal contact, he saw an opportunity to rise in national politics as a deputy in Parliament. Knowledgeable villagers tell how he entered into a league with the Wafd, paid a lot of money to run on the strong Wafd slate, and was elected in 1950. His membership in Parliament, the height of his political career, was cut short by the King's dismissal of Parliament in March 1952. Four months later, a group of army officers under Gamal 'Abd al Nasser staged the coup that ended the monarchy, the political careers of its supporters, and all pre-coup political parties.

In addition to his office of *'umdah* and his wealth, Mustafa Samad's power was enhanced by strong support from the provincial government. He was a member of four important provincial committees: a Committee of Jurisdiction over the *'umdahs* in the province (*Lajnat al Shiyakhat*), the Irrigation Committee, the *Waqf* Land Committee and the Orphans Property Committee (*Lajnat al Hasibiyah*). On the Committee of Jurisdiction, he served with the provincial prefect, the *mudir* (now governor), the attorney general, representatives of the Ministry of the Interior, and three other notables, or *'umdahs*. These contacts were extremely valuable, strengthening his position against potential local challenge to his authority and enabling him to obtain personal economic advantages. For instance, through his membership in the *Waqf* Land Committee, he was able to rent the *waqf* land in Shubra, from which he made a large profit.

The Village Government

The 'umdah traditionally personified village government, and the nature of the office in 1952 had changed very little from what it was in the nineteenth century. In 1905, Lord Cromer wrote of the 'umdah, "It is not too much to say that the whole life of the village turns upon the Omdeh ('umdah)." Gabriel Baer makes much the same observation for the period between 1800 and 1950.[7] It would be a mistake, however, to think of all 'umdahs as powerful; many in small villages were poor, weak, and scorned—if not ignored—by provincial officials.

In the administration of the village, Mustafa was assisted by a deputy, the head of the village guardsmen (ghafir), and three shaykhs who served as heads of village quarters. The village had about fifteen guards, all of whom were villagers selected by the 'umdah from among his loyal followers. Each carried a rifle and wore an official uniform.

As stated by Mustafa Samad himself, the duties of an 'umdah were the maintenance of order in the village, collection of taxes, settlement of disputes, and dealing with agricultural problems of the village.[8] Mustafa saw himself as a mediator among the villagers, the landlords, and the government. Since Shubra had no police department until 1951, he was in charge of all local police functions. He could summon villagers to his office, or bring them by force if they resisted, and impose various punishments (from insults to short-term imprisonment). He was not permitted to inflict bodily injuries, impose pecuniary fines, or judge criminal cases. In the latter situations, his duty as 'umdah was to report the incident to higher provincial officials, a function that gave him considerable power, as he could attribute wrong deeds to anyone. Villagers had recourse to state courts if they could afford it; but courts in general gave great weight to the judgment of the local arbitration committee, which was headed by the 'umdah and whose other members were the village shaykhs and the ma'dhun (the official in charge of marriage contracts).

As 'umdah, Mustafa owed his power primarily to social position and ascriptive right of birth rather than to any outside force. It would be a mistake to describe the 'umdah as a representative of the national government to the villagers, as Baer maintains.[9] Though the 'umdah attended to such business of the national government in the village as assisting in the collection of taxes, reporting births, deaths, crimes, and

---

7. See Baer, "The Village Shaykh," p. 121.
8. For a detailed account on the functions of the 'umdah and changes in his functions, see Baer, ibid., p. 129.
9. Ibid., p. 123.

young men of conscriptive age, these duties by no means made him a government functionary; the government was as much in need of his services and power as he was of its recognition and support. Unlike government functionaries, he owed his authority mainly to his family and social position; the confirmation of that authority by the government was a matter of recognizing a *de facto* situation.[10] Thus Mustafa Samad had succeeded his father as '*umdah* of Shubra, and the government had dutifully confirmed his position even though he was below the legal age limit.[11]

Notwithstanding their privileged position in the village, the Samad brothers were not free from important constraints. In small Egyptian communities, established personal relations and accepted rules of conduct must be respected by everyone. The Samad brothers were not indifferent to local social norms, in particular those between patrons and clients or among kinsmen and friends.

One possible source of conflict in Shubra existed between the custodians of political power and the major holders of economic wealth in the community. As it may be recalled, the Samads belonged to a group of landowning families, but the Prince and the Kuras between them controlled about 60 percent of the land and were therefore the largest employers in the village. The major landlords, if they wished, could extend their economic power to political matters and by so doing overstep the boundaries of the Samads' influence on villagers. Only if each side had a serious interest in respecting the jurisdiction of the other could the Samads and the village landlords avoid conflict.

The Samad brothers were cautious in their relations with the Kuras and with the Prince's steward, since the Samads, too, rented a large portion of the Prince's estate. On the other hand, Mustafa was aware of the political limitations of the steward and of 'Abd al Rahman Kura; the former was a functionary without tenure and an outsider, and the latter was a recent resident of the community who had never been involved in village politics.

Mustafa's policy toward the powerful economic agents in the community was one of accommodation. Besides simply trying to stay on friendly terms with the Prince and his steward, he looked after their interests and provided them protection, making it unnecessary for them to seek political power themselves. He followed these same principles with other absentee

---

10. Ibid., p. 124. Baer confirms that in practice the office of '*umdah* remained hereditary. The national government during the monarchy removed very few '*umdahs*. Only in 1935 was a large number of '*umdahs* dismissed from office for partisan reasons. Six hundred '*umdahs*, or nearly 15 percent of all '*umdahs* in office, were then removed.

11. Mustafa told me that he had obtained a false birth certificate from a physician.

landlords. As for the Kuras, he gave 'Abd al Rahman Kura a privileged position in the cooperative and married his daughter. Between the two men, they owned 90 percent of the shares in the village cooperative, which they founded in 1933.

Despite his best intentions, Mustafa Samad had failed on two occasions to shield the steward from attacks by local citizens. The offenders were Mustafa's cousin and his brother, over whom he had no strong authority, and both incidents involved the rental and use of the Prince's machinery. Mustafa's cousin, Mahmud al Sayid Samad, quarreled with the steward; the Prince took the case to court, and Mahmud al Sayid was sentenced to jail. In the case of Mustafa's brother, who quarreled with the steward in 1949, the Prince decided to resolve the matter by requesting the national government to install a police station in Shubra, thereby robbing Mustafa and his brother of the responsibility to maintain order. The national government was already in the process of extending the provincial constabulary into villages, however, and Shubra easily qualified for a police unit. Mustafa had tried in both instances to calm the dispute and remain as neutral as possible, but when the Prince moved to introduce a police station to Shubra, Mustafa appealed to the leaders of the Wafd to prevent, or at least delay, the action. Two years passed before a unit was installed.

Though the functions of Mustafa Samad as 'umdah were obviously diminished in a formal sense, his powers were hardly affected. The police officer, as a stranger in a village with a strong leader, deferred to Mustafa on cases of local disputes, realizing that he had no chance of enforcing the law without the cooperation of the 'umdah. Mustafa continued to employ his armed guards as in the past, and the villagers detected no visible change in authority.

Despite limited effectiveness, however, the police station was a symbol of the growing power of the national government. As the only major change in Shubra's power structure before 1952, its appearance reflects two basic aspects of political reality in the community: (1) discrepancy in the authority between the custodians of economic wealth and local political leaders, as evidenced by the need of the large landlords for protection from the "boss's relatives," and (2) the expansion of the functions of national government to the countryside.

The Downfall of the Samads

Under the Revolution, Mustafa Samad was able to maintain his position for seven more years. Although the Nasser regime in its first eight years did not intervene directly in local rule, it created conditions that gradually undermined the *'umdah*'s predominance. The first blow to the Samad brothers was agrarian reform, which greatly reduced the land available for rent and thus terminated their roles as middlemen between landlords and tenants. (They themselves did not fall under the land reform law of 1952.) Mustafa Samad's hold over villagers not only diminished but vanished by 1960, giving way to political competitors, including peasant leaders.

The second measure taken by the Revolution that affected the Samads adversely was the creation in January 1953 of the Liberation Rally, a political movement with local branches in villages and towns. Mustafa's efforts to assume leadership of the local Liberation Rally were defeated by Muhammad Kura, son of 'Abd al Rahman.

From the start, the role of the Kura brothers in the official party had important political implications. It indicated that many villagers had become free from the Samads' control and were available for political recruitment. Moreover, the party served as a source of leadership for the municipal council, formed in 1961 according to a new law of local government which stipulated that councillors be drawn from the National Union local committee. Finally, it brought many new local leaders into contact with provincial and national leaders.

Power struggle continued when, in 1959, the Kuras and their allies challenged the Samads in the elections to the cooperative board. The Kuras' chances of success were poor, since Mustafa Samad ran the cooperative as a private business and restricted membership to his friends and kinsmen. However, the Kuras and one of their close allies, Haj Hammal, rallied villagers against the Samads' monopoly over such a vital resource in the village. On election day, a fracas resulted in the physical beating of Haj Hammal by the Samads. By taking his case to court, Hammal succeeded in bringing the cooperative society's problems to the attention of the provincial and national governments. It then was disclosed that for years Mustafa had been using money from the Agricultural Credit Bank for personal rather than cooperative purposes. Shubra's cooperative was found by the court to be in serious debt, and this discovery, together with his use of violence against voters, led to Mustafa's dismissal from his duties as *'umdah* and as head of the cooperative. The cooperative board that had been elected under him was dissolved, and new elections were postponed until 1961, when the national government's promised reorganization plan for cooperatives was enacted.

In 1960, the government abolished the old system of voluntary cooperatives and instituted new ones modeled after the reform cooperative. Election to the board of the new cooperative society took place in December 1961. For the Samads, this election proved to be their last effort to maintain some leadership in the village; they were soundly defeated at the polls. That they had been discredited in court and censured by the national government were the major reasons for the Samads' loss. However, other factors also were important. The new system of cooperatives—open to all peasants, both owners and tenants—broadened the base of support for the Kuras, who achieved a sweeping victory. All twelve members of their slate, including Muhammad Kura himself, were elected to the cooperative board.

The Creation of a Municipal Council

The transition of Shubra's local government from headmanship to a representative municipal council followed other developments in the community, primarily economic reforms in land distribution and the introduction of agricultural cooperatives. An official party branch had also been introduced. In addition to establishing the new organizations in the village, the regime tried to promote pluralism among leaders of local communities. To this effect, a cabinet decree stipulated that no individual was allowed to hold an elected office on more than one cooperative board;[12] and in 1968 rules were issued prohibiting close relatives from serving together in the Arab Socialist Union (ASU) basic unit. Similarly, councillors were forbidden from sitting on a cooperative board and on the village council at the same time. However, the law stipulated that councillors should be selected among elected officers of the local branch of the official party.

In 1961, Wagih Abaza, the governor of Beheira Province, appointed Sayid Kura as mayor of Shubra.[13] In addition to being on friendly terms with the governor, the Kura brothers had a majority in the local committee of the official party, the National Union.[14] Two other members of Shubra's National Union local committee, Haj Hammal and Majid Rayyan, were selected by the new mayor as councillors. (The other eight councillors came from the local party committees of Shubra's five neighboring hamlets, which formed the municipal commune of Shubra el Gedida.) Village officials such as the agronomists, the physician, and the school's superintendent were made ex-officio members of the council. In addition, the governor appointed two professional farmers to the council. The total

12. Cabinet decree number 165 in the year 1961.
13. In principle, the appointment of a mayor is made jointly by the governor, the director of municipal councils in the province, and provincial officers of the ASU. The choice in this case, however, was the governor's.
14. The ASU local committees were elected in 1963. Thus most municipal councillors were selected from local committees of the National Union.

number of councillors thus reached seventeen, and the formation of the council was in accordance with the new law.

The mayor and councillors made municipal policies, but officials who represented the service ministries of Public Health, Social Affairs, Education, and Agriculture managed the day-to-day business. Thus Shubra's council had a physician, a veterinarian, a social-services specialist, an agricultural specialist, school teachers, and clerks. In administrative matters, all these officials were under the authority of the mayor; however, in financial and technical matters, they were under the jurisdiction of their respective ministries, whose departmental officers were located in Damanhur. The mayor often complained about the ambiguity of the law and the division of authority over his staff. Other village councils suffered from friction between the mayor and ministry officials, but this sort of friction was not a serious problem in Shubra during my stay there.

Shubra's village council receives the bulk of its revenue from land taxes. These are shared with the provincial government, which retains 10 percent; the rest goes to the local council, giving Shubra's municipal commune a revenue of 25,000 pounds annually. The expenditures of the various ministries represented in Shubra are not part of this budget but supplied and controlled separately by each ministry. In 1967, Shubra's revenue from other sources was as follows:

£E 200, combined-services center
£E 200, provincial services council
£E 200, revenue of the crafts center and the marketplace
£E 400, wage-laborers project
___

£E 1000 total

The accomplishments of Shubra's village council during its first seven years were remarkable and deserve special attention. Sayid Kura was responsible for most of the achievements during his term as mayor (1961–1965), but his successor, Ahmad Amir, consolidated and added to them.

The first two projects of the council, the combined-services center and the marketplace, illustrate the programs that were achieved by local initiative. The combined-services center (*wahdah mugamma'ah*), which consolidates all the units of governmental services in the village within one compound, contains a hospital, a veterinary unit, the offices for the village council, a crafts center, a school, a children's nursery, and apartments for officials.

The combined-services center at Shubra was scheduled to be built in

1965. Not wanting to wait that long, the mayor and his council approached the governor in 1961 and offered two plots of land for the center as a gift from the community if the governor would authorize an earlier date of construction. The governor agreed to their terms, and the Kuras donated seven feddans for the center and three more feddans for the veterinary unit. By 1963, the completed center was in operation.

The second project was the marketplace. Shubra's traditional Tuesday market had survived the modern era but was crammed into the center of the village. Anticipating that a new marketplace would bring revenue to the village council and revive the market, the council drew up a plan to build a new marketplace and sought a loan of 1500 pounds from the provincial government.

Construction of the marketplace was completed in 1963. When the village council started to receive revenue from fees paid by merchants and customers, the Markets Department of the provincial government imposed a tax on the returns. The village council opposed the tax on the grounds that the Markets Department had not contributed to the building of the market. By pressing its case with the governor, Shubra was exempted from paying a tax; furthermore, the governor declared that the construction loan was a gift to Shubra from the provincial government for the improvement of the community.

Another project realized under Sayid Kura was the construction of a one-half mile road that connected the village directly with the combined-services center and the new marketplace, and also with the Damanhur road. Still another accomplishment, made possible by Sayid's personal contacts, was the acquisition from the government of a refrigeration unit, which enabled villagers for the first time to store milk for later delivery and sale in Damanhur. The village council during Sayid Kura's tenure undertook many other projects, including the establishment of a crafts center for the production of bamboo furniture and rugs (*kilim*), and for the teaching of sewing and carpentry skills.

The crafts center, intended primarily to train village youth to become artisans, sold the products in a special shop and accepted commissions for work. The apprentices were paid a small compensation by the council. A wage-laborers project was started in Shubra in 1965–66 when the national government sought to end the middleman role of labor contractors who recruited and transported laborers to Liberation Province, the land reclamation site near Beheira. Village councils were induced to provide labor from their own villages and received a compensation of six percent of the total revenue earned by laborers.

In 1966, Shubra's village council, under Ahmad Amir as mayor, introduced electrical power and service to part of the town. By 1968, the council had started to collect usage fees from village customers, but the service was not running at a profit because the council charged only a nominal fee as an inducement for villagers to use the service. Another project, introduced to the village in 1967–68 through the initiative and assistance of the village council, was a housing-renewal project on a plot of land contributed by the Agrarian Reform Cooperative. The village council was in charge of providing building material and making loans at low rates to prospective builders, who paid back the council in installments. The new houses were built according to specifications decided on by the government and the village council.

During their terms as mayor, both Sayid Kura and Ahmad Amir dominated the meetings and actions of the village council. As is generally the case in small committees, decisions were made by consensus, although a formal vote was legally required. During the council meetings that I attended in 1967 and in 1968, the councillors brought issues of community importance to the attention of the council and the mayor and contributed ideas on how best to solve problems. Within the council there was no opposition group, but differing views were expressed, and even Haj Hammal, the main ally of the Kuras, often openly disagreed with the Kuras' position on various issues. Most disputes concerned the wisdom of accepting or rejecting a resolution. On the whole, decision making was mainly the mayor's responsibility, since he conceived and initiated most of the issues, prepared the presentations, and swayed the opinions of the council members by being better prepared and more persuasive than anyone else. The mayor's primary duty of keeping the financial accounts of the council in good order was difficult because his clerk and accountants lacked expertise. Only the mayor's close supervision prevented financial mismanagement.

The mayor bore his enormous work load with the assistance of both his staff and special committees. Six permanent committees, which dealt with such areas of concern as agriculture, education, social services, complaints and grievances, and welfare management, consisted of council members in addition to others called upon by the mayor to serve on the basis of their leadership in the ASU or expertise in a certain field. *Ad hoc* committees were often formed to study a project for report to the council or to resolve a certain matter. In addition, two permanent councils were formed to administer the weekly market and the crafts center.

Conclusion

The political history of Shubra shows how strongly this village community had been tied to the national system. The status quo in Shubra had been largely maintained by institutions of the constitutional monarchy, and not until the old regime fell did Shubra undergo serious political changes. The Nasser regime created new political and economic conditions that were relatively free from the authoritarianism of national politics. Aside from compulsory reduction of ceilings on landownership and cooptation of local party leaders in 1966, the regime did not interfere directly in the management of Shubra's affairs. Instead, institutional means were created through which villagers could receive redress from injustice and manage their own economic affairs; such was the function of cooperative societies, which represented the greatest achievement of the agrarian reform policy. The second institutional innovation created to help villagers conduct local affairs by themselves was the municipal council.

Both cooperative and municipal institutions had administrative links to the provincial and national governments, but these were of a regulatory rather than managerial nature. Municipal councils, however, were more strongly linked to the provincial government and consequently were less autonomous than cooperative societies. The governor, the party's provincial secretary, and the director of provincial councils were instrumental in the selection of Shubra's mayor and its councillors. Municipal councillors were elected indirectly; candidates first had to be elected by party members in the community, and then the provincial authorities selected village councillors from the elected group. Shubra's first mayor, under whom the first municipal council was formed, played a central role in nominating councillors from Shubra and the rest of the municipal commune. The same councillors continued to serve succeeding mayors, and, by the summer of 1968, they had served for seven uninterrupted years, not because of distinction or power but because the national government had failed to call for new elections. Failure to hold new elections of local officers in cooperatives and municipal councils had detrimental effects on these organizations, which are discussed fully in chapters 13 and 14 of this book.

In addition to cooperatives and municipal councils, the new regime introduced a local party branch as early as 1953. With this measure, the national government had created the third major organization through which the people could manage their own economic, administrative, and political affairs at the local level.

chapter 5

The single party system: village leaders

The single party, common in many Middle Eastern nations, has served to disseminate ideology and to organize political participation. Many scholars feel that the single party system is more an instrument of ideological indoctrination than a channel for political participation. Both Douglas Ashford and Leonard Binder maintain that the single party regimes have not been able to solve the participation crisis. According to Binder, the single party regime is prompted, by both ideological and pragmatic considerations, to mobilize the entire population behind the goals of development, but at the same time it is responsible for preventing "premature diversion of resources from development to satisfaction of immediate popular needs."[1] In Egypt, Binder argues, "not all social segments have been admitted to political participation in any meaningful sense, although all citizens were considered to be members of the National Union, and the Socialist Union is only slightly more selective."[2] Furthermore, it is not certain that the purpose of the "revolutionary regime has been to resolve a participation crisis."[3] Ashford finds the drawback of such regimes to be the preoccupation of national leaders to forge a new society with "a high degree of homogeneity" at the expense of individual articulation.[4] Not only is such a system dominated by a single overbearing

1. Binder, "Political Recruitment . . . ," p. 219.
2. Ibid., p. 220.
3. Ibid.
4. Douglas E. Ashford, *The Elusiveness of Power: African Single Party State* (Ithaca: Cornell University, Center for International Studies, 1965), p. 31. The same theme is expressed again in his *National Development and Local Reform*.

leader, but its emphasis on ideological legitimacy tends to relegate the principle of representation to a secondary role. Representation of the masses on the basis of ideological affinity takes the place of free, competitive elections. Top national leaders in dominant regimes are not in power because they have been elected, nor do they intend to subject their privileged position to public discretion.

But if mobilization of the masses is a form of political participation, what exactly is the role of mobilization in single party regimes? Both Binder and Ashford feel that it is primarily to harness political resources for supporting the regime and neutralizing its enemies.[5] Lars Rudebeck, writing on Tunisia's single party, sees a developmental objective. He states that a single party may be an elite party, as in Liberia, "without effective mass organization" or, as in Guinea, a genuine mass party that seeks to dominate society completely.[6] His thesis is that "systematic and conscious efforts to overcome underdevelopment are causally connected with existence or growth of 'mass parties' as more or less effective instruments of mass mobilization."[7]

The prevalence of single parties in developing countries, especially in the Arab World, is undoubtedly related to the political importance in these countries of both populism and the dominance of a single leader. Here, the single party system combines populism with the authoritarianism of the elite in power, and national welfare is considered to be a function of strong leadership rather than of the representation of diverse social interests.

As seen by Ashford and Binder, the single party conforms to the revolutionary-centralized model developed by Coleman and Resberg,[8] which emphasizes mobilization of political resources for attainment of national goals and imposes ideological indoctrination as a basis of political solidarity. Nasser's single party is highly centralized; delegated authority is concentrated in the hands of appointed leaders who advocate the transformation of society by revolutionary means. However, this model breaks down at subnational levels of Egyptian party organization, where leaders are representative, power is diffuse among various groups, concern with ideology is limited, and political mobilization is carried out with

---

5. Binder, "Political Recruitment . . . ," p. 218–19; Ashford, *The Elusiveness of Power*, p. 31.

6. Lars Rudebeck, *Party and People: A Study of Political Change in Tunisia* (Stockholm: Alqvist and Wiksell, 1967), pp. 18–19.

7. Ibid., p. 23. It is noteworthy that Rudebeck's book provides evidence in support of the second part of his thesis concerning the growth of the party but not of the two main variables of his proposition.

8. James S. Coleman and Carl G. Resberg, Jr. (eds.), *Political Parties and National Integration in Tropical Africa* (Berkeley: University of California Press), 1966, p. 5.

moderation. In effect, Egypt's single party regime reflects the characteristics of the revolutionary-centralized pattern at the top level and those of the pragmatic-pluralistic pattern at subnational levels.[9]

It may be suggested that such a development has resulted from the inseparability of the party from the regime,[10] which is not unusual in Africa and in the Middle East. When Nasser's Free Officers seized power, they replaced the political institutions of the old regime with radically different economic and political relations. Nasser justified his actions in ideological terms and developed a system of ideas that became the official doctrine of the state. As an expression of Nasser's regime, the party was characterized by centralization and by ideological preoccupation, and its command structure was staffed by members of the national government. At subnational levels, however, these characteristics were greatly attenuated. Many factors contributed to the variance between the national and subnational levels. First, local power in developing countries is residual and has marginal outcomes on the power positions of national leaders. Second, the historical legacy of illiteracy and limited political participation leads to a slow response to and assimilation of formal ideology. Third, the highly developed mass media system in Egypt makes it possible for national leaders to reach the majority of citizens through means independent of the party organization. Such regimes as Egypt's need the collaboration of local leaders only as an auxiliary base for political support and for the implementation of policy, an objective that is attainable without heavy expenditure of political resources. In Egypt, the regime's real power rested on Nasser's popularity, the armed forces, the security police, and the civil bureaucracy. Thus, whereas the party's national leaders were Nasser's aides, Free Officers, and cabinet members, local party leaders emerged from nonofficial groups on a representative basis.

Discontinuity between the national party organization and those party officers whose jurisdictions are regions, districts, or localities has had serious implications for political behavior and leadership in Egyptian villages. For Shubra, it meant that local party leaders tended to represent a variety of social groups of diverse interests and political inclinations. Regardless of the highly centralized national government and the growth in the size and importance of the civil bureaucracy, government officials did not occupy a dominant position in Shubra's politics. One consequence of local pluralism and representative politics has been the development of five types of leaders, all of whom belonged to the official party without

9. For the pragmatic-pluralist model, see Coleman and Resberg, *Political Parties*.
10. See Harik, "The Single Party as a Subordinate Movement: The Case of Egypt," *World Politics* 26, no. 1 (October 1973).

being constrained by their membership to serve a single, monolithic interest. The five leadership types were representative leaders, organization leaders, government officials, activists, and "wise" men. This classification is made on the basis of dominant rather than exclusive characteristics. For example, one may find representative qualities among organization leaders and official status among some representative leaders. These overlapping characteristics are examined more closely in the discussion below and in the following three chapters, but worthy of mention here is that the patron-client relationship, which had its place in Shubra during the headmanship period, has considerably weakened, and no patron leaders as such were identified during the field-work period of this study.

The single party under Nasser changed its name and organizational structure three times.[11] The regime first launched the Liberation Rally in January 1953, about six months after the coup. By 1954, the Liberation Rally was allowed to die, and a more elaborate organization, the National Union, was designated by the Constitution of 1956 as the new party. Because of the Suez Crisis of 1956, however, the National Union was not launched until 1957, and its local branches were not elected until 1959, perhaps because of the regime's preoccupation with Egypt's union with Syria in 1958. Syria's secession from the United Arab Republic in 1961 undermined the National Union. Nasser then convened a National Congress of Popular Forces, a body of elected representatives that met in May 1962 to deliberate the future of the country subsequent to Syria's secession. The Arab Socialist Union (ASU), launched in 1963, was a product of that convention. Unlike its predecessors, the ASU was born with an elaborate ideology, which was proposed by Nasser to the National Congress of Popular Forces and distributed nationally, in book form, as the *National Charter*. In its first two years, however, the ASU was not more disciplined than the National Union; a reorganization plan, initiated in 1966 under the leadership of 'Ali Sabri, imposed more discipline on the party (see chapter 6).

The national party organization was run by a small directory headed by Nasser, the Higher Executive Committee, and the General Secretariat—in all, not more than forty individuals. The final decision in making appointments of officers to this command structure was Nasser's. Thus national party leaders did not rise from a popular base, and the channels through which local leaders could rise to national leadership positions were

11. Details regarding these changes may be found in Vatikiotis, *The Egyptian Army in Politics*, and *The Modern History of Egypt*; Binder, "Political Recruitment . . ."; and Dekmejian, *Egypt under Nasir*.

limited to two: (1) cooptation, usually of a very few to the General Secretariat, or the bureaucracy of the ASU; and (2) election to the National Assembly. The Higher Executive Committee was staffed by selected aides, cabinet ministers, and other top government leaders. As for the Secretariat, Nasser appointed a Secretary General who, in consultation with the President, recruited a group of less than thirty individuals, each designated to perform specialized party functions. As the organ that attended to the daily management of party business, the General Secretariat established a party bureaucracy to assist the various Secretaries in carrying out their regular business.

The ASU constitution had provided for the creation of a National Congress and a Central Committee as the two national representative bodies in the party hierarchy. However, these were not constituted until September 1968, when, after his military defeat, Nasser found it wise to make political concessions. In the past, he had felt no special need for these representative bodies and was reluctant to encourage the emergence of national party leaders from popular bases independent of him. Consequently, elections were not called for these party organs until a major crisis enveloped the country.

Since the party command structure was staffed by government leaders, distinctions between party and government are of a formal rather than substantive political nature. The official character of top party leaders has led observers of the single party phenomenon to assume that no real participation and freedom were allowed in single party organizations, an assumption that overlooks the dual structure of the single party system.

Viewed from the narrow angle of Shubra and Beheira Province, the party was active and relevant, and it drew more people into politics than did any other local institution. Many reasons contributed to the party's predominance in the political life of the village. Aspiring leaders had a better chance to capture positions in other community organizations such as cooperatives and municipal councils if they enjoyed a strong position in the local party branch. Similarly, those who aspired to higher leadership roles in the district or province found the official party to be one of their major channels. The party's role in recruitment to local institutions gave it weight in the allocation of local resources. Thus, regardless of its national impact, local party activity directly affected the ordinary villager.

An examination of the development and organization of the single party in Shubra reveals the party's relevance at the local level. Thus, the discussion in the following sections of this chapter emphasizes the emergence of new leaders, leadership struggle, local functions, and the party's contributions to community development.

Leadership Struggle and the Party

When the Liberation Rally was launched in January 1953, Shubra's *'umdah* interpreted the move as an invitation to represent the new government in his community. He promptly went to Damanhur and registered himself as the head of the local chapter, and his brother and another relative as members of the committee. This step was really no different from the traditional ways in which local influentials had always paid tribute to new governments, and the national leaders of the Revolution had then neither the time nor the organization to screen all those offering their services. As far as the national government was concerned, Mustafa Samad was its man in Shubra, and it took a handful of politically ambitious villagers to prevent this course from continuing.

Muhammad Kura understood that the change of regimes in Cairo was the beginning of a new era, and he saw his opportunity to challenge Mustafa's authority. He fought the decision that installed Mustafa Samad as the head of the Liberation Rally and exposed Mustafa's connections with the old regime. His efforts were successful, and a new committee was formed with Muhammad Kura as chairman and two young protégés, including Bashir Shubrawi, as members. Mustafa Samad's first political defeat gave Muhammad Kura the opportunity to establish ties with the new regime and to work toward ousting the Samads from positions of authority in Shubra.

Thus the Liberation Rally in Shubra was the arena for a power struggle between the new forces of Muhammad Kura and the old leadership of the Samads. Although the Samads saw in the new regime a threat to their position, they had wished to avert its immediate effects by assuming local responsibility for the official party. They had hoped to neutralize the party branch and, at the same time, make it clear to villagers that they still enjoyed official favor despite the changes in national regimes. The Kuras' challenge frustrated their designs, but the Samads continued to act as though they were on friendly terms with the regime, making sure not to allow the Kuras to appear as the only group favored by the government.

His position in the Liberation Rally gave Muhammad Kura no specific functions; it only bestowed on him the prestige of officialdom. He remained without jurisdiction or authority over the headman, but the party chairmanship served him as a legitimate channel for building up political support and for maintaining contact with the regime's representatives in Damanhur. Using this opportunity to the utmost, the Kuras brought private political resources and zeal into the local branch of the Rally and gave it more importance in the community than the regime had originally expected it to have. The Liberation Rally passed practically unnoticed on the national scene, giving way to a new political organization, but in Shubra el Gedida, its occurrence marked the rise of a competing elite and the beginning of a turbulent political course that resulted in the removal of the Samads and the rapid succession of new leaders.

In 1956, the National Union formally replaced the Rally, and Muhammad Kura was prepared to assume leadership of the new movement, especially since he had become known to the men of the new regime as a progressive local influential in their service. The contest for party leadership this time, however, was to be determined by local elections. The local, or basic, committee of the National Union was to be an elected Committee of Ten, who would then choose a representative to the district who, in turn, could be elected to the provincial committee.

Election to the Committee of Ten was of vital importance to those contending for power in Shubra. By the time the election for the Committee of Ten was called in 1959, it had become clear that members of municipal councils were to be selected among the officers of the National Union Committee of Ten and that election to the National Assembly depended on a person's standing in the National Union. The central party organization did not name or endorse candidates to local offices; only national candidates were screened for official approval. However, since both municipal councils and the National Assembly were projected in government plans to be formed within a year or two, the Kuras and the Samads realized that their political future depended to a large extent on capturing the local party unit. When elections were held in July 1959, amid a heated campaign charged with tension between the two groups, the outcome was six to four in favor of the Kuras. Both Muhammad and Sayid Kura were elected in addition to two prominent allies, Haj Hammal and Majid Rayyan; among the Samads, Mustafa and his distant cousin Mahmud al Sayid Samad were elected. All those elected except one were over forty years of age and enjoyed some standing in the community, a point that indicates that both sides had found it necessary to enlist support among nonpartisans.

The Kuras' majority in the Committee of Ten made it possible for four of their allies to become municipal councillors; Muhammad himself was elected by the Committee as a district delegate and eventually became a provincial delegate as well. As he was primarily concerned with gaining a seat in the National Assembly, Muhammad used his position in the National Union Committee of Ten to promote himself at the province level and to build support among province leaders. Shubra's politics and the municipal council were left in the hands of his brother Sayid, who was assisted by allies in the Committee. In the 1960 National Assembly elections, Muhammad Kura was elected as representative of Beheira Province. Then Sayid Kura was appointed mayor of Shubra by the governor. The Samads were not able to capture any office in the party or in the municipal council.

In 1961, when Syria seceded from the United Arab Republic, Nasser called for a national congress to be elected by the people to discuss the future political organization of the country. Two leaders from Shubra, Muhammad Kura and 'Ali al Shawi, were elected to represent the district of Damanhur in the National Congress of Popular Forces. 'Ali, a peasant, was the secretary of the reform cooperative of Shubra. The Kuras resented his rise to political prominence in Beheira Province; no sooner had they defeated the Samads and removed them from the political arena of Shubra than had 'Ali and other agrarian reform peasants emerged as major contenders in village politics. The competition for leadership between 1961 and 1965 revolved primarily around these two groups, although independent aspirants for leadership became visible contenders as well.

The Arab Socialist Union was born in the National Congress of Popular Forces in which Muhammad Kura and 'Ali al Shawi participated. It was created with much fanfare to give the impression that the official party had been transformed into a dynamic socialist movement with definite ideological commitment and the ambitious goal of combatting the subversive activities of antisocialist elements in the country. During its first two years in Shubra, the new party meant little more than the enlargement of the basic committee from ten to twenty officers and the allocation of half the committee seats to representatives from the lower village strata. However, the number of competitors for seats on the basic committee increased. In 1959, only two slates had competed for election to the National Union Committee of Ten, but, in 1963, three slates and a number of independents competed for leadership of the ASU. Among them, only the Kuras were landlords; the rest were small farmers, shopkeepers, agricultural workers, and professionals. There were, in all, eighty-three candidates for twenty seats. The Kuras won eight seats, agrarian reform peasants won seven, and independents won five. The Samads won no seats.[12]

Although the Kuras had only a slim majority over the agrarian reform peasants in the Committee of Twenty, they were able to maintain control; Muhammad Kura was elected secretary, and his brother Sayid, assistant

12. As a runner-up, Mahmud al Sayid Samad later became a member of the Committee of Twenty by filling a seat vacated by the death of a member.

secretary. Muhammad also succeeded in rising to the district and provincial committees of the ASU.

Despite his precedence over 'Ali al Shawi within the party organization, Muhammad could not prevent 'Ali from running for the National Assembly in 1964 as a candidate for the peasants' representative from the district of Damanhur. Since each district was entitled to one peasant representative and one representative of other segments of the population (in election terminology the *fi'at*, or "miscellaneous groups"), 'Ali and Muhammad Kura could have run on a single ticket instead of on competing slates. However, such was the rivalry between the two men that the election of one to the National Assembly was regarded as a threat to the other's position in the village. Thus Muhammad Kura opposed collaboration with 'Ali, whom he considered an arrogant parvenue. Both men lost. A lawyer, 'Abd al Mun'im Makram, who was a member of the ASU provincial committee and claimed to be favored by the governor, won the seat for the miscellaneous groups; a peasant leader of one of the large religious fraternities (*al Rifa'iyah*) won the other seat.

Thwarted in his bid for national office, Muhammad temporarily withdrew from politics, leaving his brother Sayid to look after their political assets in Shubra. Sayid continued to head the Committee of Twenty as its acting secretary and the village council as mayor. 'Ali al Shawi, meanwhile, continued to be active in Shubra and in the district through the ASU and the cooperative organization.

The New Leaders

One of the most outstanding developments in Shubra in the first decade of the Revolution had been the rapid succession and proliferation of leaders. Most prominent among them were those who formed political groups to become the main blocs within the ASU branch. It is appropriate here to take stock of these two groups and identify their leading members before turning to further developments in the ASU.

Representative Leaders

The Kuras. The Kuras acquired their leadership positions by means of elections. They had no clients but relied primarily on activists attracted by the Kuras' ideas and their challenge to the headman's family. Although it may seem that the early struggle between the Kuras and the Samads was a rivalry between two landlord factions, such an interpretation would be too simplistic. The Kuras were resident landlords who made farming a way of life and a profession. A handful of individuals without extended lineage in the village, they were educated young men who had acquired nationalistic and progressive ideas as they grew up in an era of great political agitation and turmoil in Egypt. Their rally behind the new regime in 1952 represented an authentic response to a national movement that conformed to their political views. The regime's land reform measures had not yet directly affected the Kuras, whose estate did not exceed the ceiling on landholding as stipulated by the decree of 1952. (In the division of the estate among the descendants of 'Abd al Rahman Kura, each had received less than 200 feddans.) Although their reactions to later reforms were to be different, in the first decade after the Revolution their political sympathies were with the new regime. Among the Kuras, three were politically active: two brothers, Muhammad and Sayid, and a nephew, 'Abd.

Muhammad Kura was an executive in a government-owned cotton firm in the town of Tanta. His farm work provided him with after-hours and weekend pleasure, but his brothers and nephews daily looked after his farm along with their own. Muhammad was born and reared in Shubra, as were his brothers and sisters. He and his brothers went to school in Damanhur, where they were considered "villagers" by their school mates, a social definition that made Muhammad aware for the first time of his identity as a rural person. While in school, the Kuras dressed in rural costumes and played with other villagers. When students struck or demonstrated, Muhammad and other rural students refused to join. Not until his late teens did Muhammad become aware of the differences between himself and the rest of the village students who rode with him daily to school on the Delta Railway. As he put it, "I gradually became aware that I was different from the other boys with whom I went to school. I was rich and the son of a landlord, or what in today's parlance is called 'feudalist.'" Muhammad's awareness of his social station may well have appeared at this time as a reaction to a similar self-awareness of village schoolmates who belonged to a deprived peasantry. One of these students, now a school teacher in Shubra, said that during their daily trips to school in Damanhur he and the other poor boys used to tell the Kura and Samad boys, "One day we shall inherit these large, well-built houses of yours, and you will become just like us."

Muhammad's political orientation as it may be reconstructed from discussions with him and from other reports I had from villagers is briefly described here. As he grew up, Muhammad, like most young men of his generation, became critical of the royal regime and identified with Egypt's nationalist struggle against the British. He was sympathetic toward peasants, with whom he grew up, and disapproved of his own class's indifference to the plight of the peasantry. He supported land reform in its early stages, the new cooperative system, and collective marketing. Muhammad's identification with the Nasser regime and his active support of its social policies attracted a large number of followers among the villagers, especially the educated and the young. It is not surprising, therefore, that one of his strongest supporters in Shubra has been none other than Bashir Shubrawi, his companion on the train who wanted to inherit the estates of the Kuras and the Samads.

Muhammad's political style in Shubra was to act whenever possible through second-order leaders; he preferred to devote his time to political activities in the province and at the national level. "I don't go into the village," he said.[13] "I work with a few chosen people." The Kura political following, however, was not built by Muhammad alone but through joint efforts with his brother Sayid and his nephew 'Abd.

Sayid Kura is the second member of the family to become a leading political figure in Shubra. Unlike Muhammad, his senior by two years, Sayid took a law degree from Alexandria University but chose to become a farmer rather than a lawyer. Although he had more education than Muhammad, Sayid did not have as many outside connections nor as much political skill. He did not aspire to political office beyond Shubra or Beheira Province, perhaps in deference to his brother. Instead, he concentrated on the political affairs of Shubra, became its mayor, and looked after his brother's political base in the village. Known to be credulous and egocentric, he also was generous and progressive. His career as mayor of Shubra attests to his desire and ability to improve life in his village.

'Abd is the third and last member of the Kura family who occupied a position of leadership in the village. Though about the same age, he was Muhammad's and Sayid's nephew. Like Sayid, he was a professional farmer, and both had received honorable certificates from the province for excellence in farming. In 1962, 'Abd was appointed by the governor to Shubra's municipal council as one of two agricultural experts. After Muhammad detached himself from the affairs of the cooperative in 1964, 'Abd acted as the family liaison to the cooperative board. His prospects for leadership were handicapped, however, by serious personal limitations. He was a compulsive talker and given to violent expressions of his feelings, qualities that were offensive to the villagers, some of whom described 'Abd as crude and objectionable.

Although the Kuras had their differences, they also shared a spirit of

13. The Kuras' compound is separated from the rest of the village houses by the main Damanhur road.

individualism and cooperated closely with one another. They lived in separate domiciles in one compound, looked after each others' farms, and acted politically as if they had one and the same goal. Their individualism, however, had created political conflict within the family in at least one instance. An intense rivalry is reported to have developed in the late 1950s between Muhammad and an older brother, Qadi, who, in the mid-1950s, had resigned from his position as a judge in Cairo and returned to Shubra to run for election to the National Assembly. His resignation, I was told, was a result of his disagreement with the government over the regime's attitude toward the administration of justice in the law courts. A man of learning and prestige, Qadi expected to have no difficulty in running for office; to his disappointment he found his brother Muhammad ahead of him in the political race, well established in the district of Damanhur and also determined to try for the National Assembly. A serious dispute between the two brothers developed, eventually breaking into the open. Muhammad carried his fight into the Secretariat of the National Union, which had the authority to eliminate undesirable candidates. After Qadi's candidacy was rejected by the committee, the political precedence of Muhammad was never questioned by his other brothers. Qadi died soon after his defeat, and the three Kura leaders have continued to advance the family's political standing.

The Kuras' Supporters. The Kuras' political base is different from the Samads'. The Kuras made no overtures to absentee landlords or to associates of the Samads but sought the support of villagers. At first, they followed a strategy of selective cooperation with potential leaders who, like them, stood for the reforms introduced by the Revolution. They have since broadened their circle to include a considerable number of cultivators who are respected in the community.

The first two political lieutenants the Kuras chose were Bashir Shubrawi, a school teacher, and Haj Hammal, a petty official of the Ministry of Awqaf and Religious Affairs. Bashir held a teaching certificate and taught elementary school in his own native village of Shubra. Not finding any other avenues for social and political action against the Samads before 1952, he became active in the village youth club. The Kura brothers' support of Bashir aroused Mustafa Samad's hostility toward him. Mustafa tried to intimidate Bashir by threatening to take action against Bashir's father,[14] against whom Mustafa had written false loans, but these measures were not successful.

14. Mustafa made Bashir's father secretary of the cooperative, and, as he usually did against those in his service, Mustafa wrote false loans against him as a means of controlling him.

Haj Hammal, the second main Kura lieutenant, was an official in charge of inspecting village mosques, work for which he drew a modest salary. Like Bashir, he was not a cultivator or landowner and thus was free from the direct economic control of the Samads. A man of personal integrity and shrewdness, Hammal shared Bashir's indignant attitude toward the Samad brothers. Both Bashir and Hammal were also known for their short tempers, which the Kuras considered a major handicap; Muhammad Kura viewed them as second-order leaders, on whom he relied for contact with villagers.

Other leading villagers who supported the Kuras were small but self-sufficient cultivators and a few competent individuals employed on the Kuras' estates. Another group of supporters were board members of the regular cooperative, which was comprised of persons who appreciated the opportunity to bypass the Samads' unquestioned authority over the community. Whereas most of the votes for the Kuras in electoral contests came through the efforts of second-order leaders, votes also came from employees on their estate, estimated in 1967 to be about 160 persons during the peak season. These, however, were not clients; they were wage laborers in a free labor market and had no personal relations with their employers that would entail responsibility and dependency. It is believed by informants that, although not all Kura employees voted for the Kuras, many of them did.

In addition to loyal leaders whom they recruited in the village, the Kuras established alliances in the late 1950s with three other village leaders: 'Ali al Shawi, of the agrarian reform cooperative; Majid Rayyan, a well-to-do resident landowner; and Shaykh Jalil al Shubrawi, the oldest *imam* in the village. All three supported the Kuras against the Samads and, in return, were supported by the Kuras for leading positions in the village organizations such as the agrarian reform cooperative, the village council, and the ASU basic committee. However, the alliance with Shawi broke off by 1960, and the other two turned against the Kuras by 1965, specifically because they felt that the latter were seeking to establish a hegemony over the village as a whole.

Organization Leaders: The Agrarian Reform Cooperative

Although isolated cases of peasant unrest had occurred before the Revolution, land distribution to peasants in Egypt was an official favor, not the result of previous peasant struggles. The peasants' first opportunity to assume leadership positions came in the cooperative, where they elected a board. From the start, the Agrarian Reform Administration took a paternalistic view toward the beneficiaries of land reform, helped them learn about cooperative systems, trained a select group in cooperative management, and taught them the election procedures for the cooperative board. In the late 1950s, the Agrarian Reform Administration further urged peasant leaders to participate in the politics of their communities, especially in the National Union. Those who ran for higher office were encouraged by campaign contributions to cover part of the campaign expenses. Thus members of the agrarian reform cooperative used the cooperative as the base from which to expand their influence in other village arenas.

In Shubra, the first board of the reform cooperative was elected in 1954, immediately after the cooperative was founded. Muhsin Tukhi, a literate peasant who had previously worked as a foreman and tenant on the Prince's estate, was elected board secretary, the only elected executive position. Tukhi was inclined to support the Samads, though he could be of little help to them in their struggle to maintain their leadership in the community. In the 1958 board elections, a slate of nine candidates led by 'Ali al Shawi, an intelligent, 26-year-old peasant and son of a former tenant in the Prince's estate, defeated Tukhi's team. In this campaign, 'Ali's slate included two others, Yasin and Hamada, who, like 'Ali, had acquired their management and political skills through the cooperative organization. During the campaign, the Shawi group challenged the incumbent's management of the cooperative but did not raise broader political issues. When the Shawi slate won, the Tukhi group accused their opponents of election frauds, and the Agrarian Reform Commissioner in Damanhur called another election, which took place in 1959 and ended with exactly the same results. 'Ali al Shawi was then elected board secretary by his colleagues; he and Yasin and Hamada remained throughout their tenure as the top leaders of the cooperative group.

'Ali did not have more than a few years of formal education, but he could read and handle simple accounts properly. One of the founders of Shubra's cooperative, he had been trained by the Agrarian Reform Administration. His father had received under agrarian reform in 1953 approximately three feddans of land, the management of which was passed on later to 'Ali and his three brothers. Before assuming responsibility in the cooperative, 'Ali engaged in part-time livestock trading. He was calculating, obstinate, and very ambitious.

'Ali's main political support came from fellow members of the reform cooperative in Shubra, although in 1961, when peasants from neighboring hamlets were brought into Shubra's reform cooperative, his political following included them. As cooperative board secretary and delegate for the *mintaqah*, he could facilitate each member's business both in Shubra and in Damanhur. He also benefited from the support extended to cooperative officers by the Agrarian Reform Administration. In addition, 'Ali built a constituency among friends and relatives in Shubra, and, in his early bid for leadership of the cooperative, he was backed by the Kuras. Finally, as a prominent cooperative leader, he attracted the attention of the Arab Socialist Union and enjoyed the support of party leaders both in Shubra and in the district.

Although the Kuras originally supported him, 'Ali al Shawi's rapid emergence as a leader alerted the Kuras to his potential as a political rival. The Kuras' concerns arose immediately after 'Ali's election in 1958, when they noticed him broadening his base of support among reform peasants in both the district and in the province. His election as delegate to the Associated Cooperative Society of the district[15] further aroused the Kuras' suspicions, and his election in 1962 as representative to the National Congress of Popular Forces confirmed their fears.

The rivalry between 'Ali al Shawi and Muhammad Kura accelerated as both men started to look forward to the 1964 elections to the National Assembly. True to form, 'Ali al Shawi ran in the elections to the National Assembly in 1964, as did four others, one of whom was Muhammad Kura himself. 'Ali also led the agrarian reform group in the Committee of Twenty against the Kuras, who had a majority in the Committee. 'Ali's political career has been one of the most enduring in Shubra, and he had always had his political bloc within the ASU local committee. He continues to constitute the main opposition to the Kuras in Shubra to this day.

The members of the agrarian reform group were not government employees. They were elected officers who represented cultivators and looked after their interests in the cooperative society and in the village at large. Like the Kuras, they were representative leaders who were elected in competition with others. However, their political base and point of reference was the cooperative organization for whose interests and development they worked.

The "Wise" Leaders

The "wise" leaders were a carry-over from the old regime but, nonetheless, possessed qualities that made them valuable also to the new systems. A wise leader in Shubra is generally an older person who, in addition to his public spirit, has some degree of wealth and education. Typical among the wise leaders in Shubra were Majid Rayyan and Jalil

15. For the administrative order of cooperatives in each province, see Saab, *The Egyptian Agrarian Reform*, pp. 51–70.

Shubrawi. Politically and materially independent, they were sought as running mates by other electoral candidates. In the past, the Samads had deferred to Rayyan and Shubrawi but had also expected cooperation in return. Once, when Shubrawi had refused the Samads an important request, they had used force against him—to no avail. The wise leaders tended to avoid partisan loyalties and maintained their independence from the various competing blocs. Both Shubrawi and Rayyan were elected to positions in the party branch and in the municipal council. Three others in Shubra could be classified in this group of local wise leaders.

Conclusion

Local leaders found in the official party the means to influence village-wide policy and to establish political contacts outside the community. Some leaders represented their community at the district or provincial levels, while others reached national office in the country's representative body. These outside contacts were valuable in keeping local leaders aware of the political situation in the broader arena and in providing a channel of communication between higher authorities and local communities. Above the village level, however, the party organization did not serve as a cohesive system of policy implementation. District and provincial officers had little authority over local leaders, since the latter owed their positions to local constituents. Thus, until 1965, the local branch of the ASU enjoyed considerable autonomy and represented the local power distribution in the community rather than the authority of a national movement.

It would be incorrect to view the single party in Egypt as primarily a centralized movement; there was too great a diversity between local and national party experiences. The party in Shubra has been more lively and more consequential to the lives of villagers than the national party organization has been to Egyptians in general. While forming an indirect link with the national leadership of the regime, the local party branch was basically a community concern with relatively strong provincial ties. Between 1953 and 1965, the government's reluctance to impose organizational and ideological discipline left communities free to develop local interests. Thus in Shubra the Arab Socialist Union, as well as its predecessors, consisted of various political groups with different backgrounds and political interests. Moreover, party experience in Egypt shows that the single party system serves multi-purpose functions rather than a single, all-important one. Neither political development nor political support for the ruling elite exhausts the various roles a party performs at various levels in the polity.

Members of the local party branch in Shubra enjoyed the freedom to select their own officers, form competing political groups within the organization, and maintain limited contact with higher party officials. Such political autonomy, which allowed villagers to feel that they had a stake in the outcomes of party activities, increased political competition, group coalescence on the basis of special interests, and leadership mobility. Moreover, the party provided a base for capturing other leadership positions both within and outside the community and for controlling local resources. In the absence of strict organizational and ideological discipline, the party served to generate and coordinate political diversity within the framework of the regime's legitimacy and reform orientation. However, local autonomy had also the effect of encouraging hostile forces as well as political opportunism, and such tendencies aroused the suspicion and distrust of the more doctrinaire elements in government—that is, the activists in the party and leftist intellectuals. Those national figures and intellectuals who failed to see the value of political freedom for local development had the opportunity in 1965 to offer an alternative policy for local development based on the principle of mobilization. Local mobilization and party discipline contributed to the rise in importance of official leaders and activists, whose role is the subject of the following chapter.

The identification of two levels of party politics in Egypt indicates that unitary political organizations do not necessarily prohibit the local development of diverse political groups or leaders. It thus may be important to revise prevalent views on change and politics in single party regimes of developing countries. In Shubra, villagers responded to external stimuli not only by accepting programs that bring about economic profits but also by being willing to organize, learn organizational skills, and actively participate in politics. They were neither submissive nor apathetic to modernization policies. Moreover, the expansion of the bureaucracy and the official party into the countryside did not result in a regimented village life or in domination by government administrators. On the contrary, villagers learned with remarkable speed how to gain strength and advantage by using local organizations both as a shield against encroachments and as a channel to relate to the national political system. In dealing with administrators within and outside their community, they dealt from a position of strength as members or officers of representative organizations who stood for legitimate rights, not as seekers of favors or charity. Official recognition of such organizations as the cooperative and the political party lent a certain respect for the interests that local leaders represented. Moreover, as there were several organizations in the village, the party branch became a significant vehicle for linking local leaders and smoothing business transactions among the different organizations. Government administrators in turn understood that villagers, as members of the party, could go through organizational channels to higher authorities to air grievances, obtain redress, or solve problems. Action outside the organizational structure was not prohibited, but it was less effective, and protagonists often enlisted the support of one organization or group against another to achieve their ends.

The emergence of officially recognized local leaders who were with government administrators jointly responsible for village organizations resulted in interdependence and increased exchanges between the two groups. Many administrators thus found it necessary to become, politically, "members of the community" in order to assume some of the representative qualities of native village leaders. Similarly, many village leaders were coopted to act in semi-administrative capacities to facilitate the implementation of official policy. (This symbiosis in leadership roles, which was carried out mainly through the party channels, is described further in chapter 6.)

In short, modernization forces have not led to geographic dislocation of rural people or to sociopolitical disorientation; rather, they have stimulated interest in politics and in the community itself and have encouraged the emergence of diverse political groups and leaders.

chapter 6

The single party system: mobilization 1965-1968

In 1965, a policy to transform the Arab Socialist Union into a mobilization movement introduced yet another unsettling element into the rapidly changing political scene in Shubra. This phase was marked by three novel steps: (1) leadership cooptation was extended to all subnational levels; (2) firm hierarchical relations among party cadres were established; and (3) a program for local action was adopted. In ways similar to the experiences of other African official parties, none of the aims was fully accomplished; in 1968 there was a return to the old system, that is, to the election of party leaders (see chapter 12) and to ambiguity in the community functions of party organs. Because of its direct effect on Shubra's politics and because of its significance in the single party experience in Egypt under the Revolution, the mobilization drive is given special attention here.

Reorganization of the ASU

Under the new drive, the central authority of the ASU went through changes in personnel rather than in structure. President Nasser called on 'Ali Sabri, former prime minister and vice president, to lead the mobilization drive. Sabri acted through a Secretariat of sixteen members who were selected to meet the challenge of mobilization and who therefore tended to lean toward the left and to be more active than previous Secretariat members. The leftward shift in the ASU was doubtless enhanced by the decision of the Egyptian Communist Party in April 1965 to dissolve itself and let its members join the ASU.

Despite these changes, the Central Committee and the National Congress remained unconstituted during the mobilization period, and the practice of running the party by a small national directory remained unchanged. The ASU, as a national movement, continued to serve Nasser's political purposes.

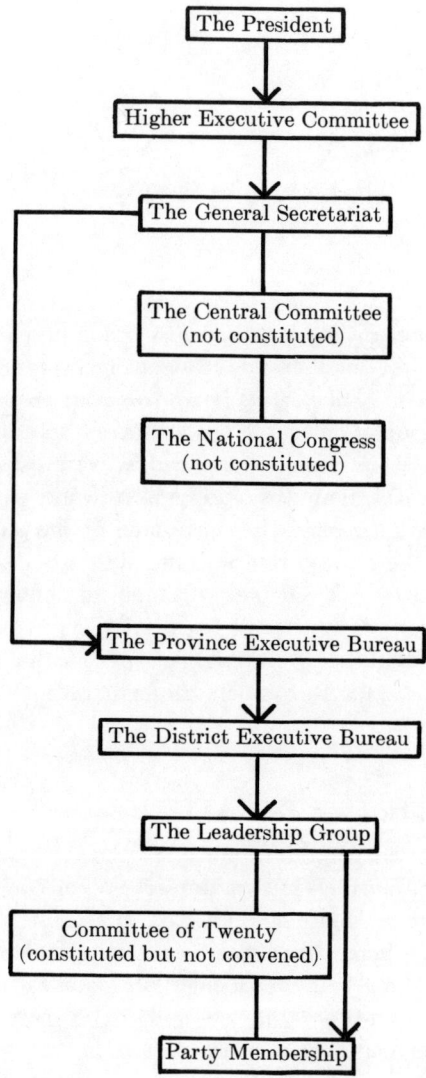

FIGURE 2. Formal structure of the Arab Socialist Union, 1965–1968

Major changes were instituted on the subnational levels, however, with the creation of a completely new party organization composed of executive bureaus at the provincial and district levels and Leadership Groups (*Jama'ah qiyadiyah*) at the basic level in villages, city wards, or places of work (see figure 2).[1] Each executive bureau was headed by a first secretary, who exercised authority over the other bureau members and lower organs of the party. Appointments to the provincial executive bureau were made by the Secretariat in cooperation with the provincial governor. The provincial first secretary appointed district secretaries, who in turn appointed the secretaries to the Leadership Groups.

Officers of the province and district bureaus were full-time, salaried party officials who were paid mostly from state funds and trained at party institutes. They were selected from the civil bureaucracy, the school system, universities, the business management sector, and private occupations such as law, farming, and other lines of work. Material incentive, in the form of a bonus added to the salary a person had received before joining the party leadership, was used to attract qualified cadres away from established careers. Party leaders were considered to be on temporary loan and were guaranteed the right to return to their former jobs after completion of their terms in the ASU. Incentives and assurances were necessary because political careers were considered less secure than other employment and more demanding in time, energy, and responsibility.

Another important feature of the ASU reorganization under Sabri was the well-disciplined, militant Youth Organization,[2] created in 1965 as an auxiliary body of the ASU. Youth was rather liberally defined to include individuals between the ages of sixteen and thirty-three. The Youth Organization was designed to move at a faster tempo than the mother organization and to give its members objectives and activities that suited their temperaments.

Training in the Youth Organization took two forms: ideological indoctrination and instruction in the practical skills of organization and endurance under hardship conditions. Through lectures and discussion groups, trainees were instructed in the principles of socialism, the national struggle of Egypt and other Arab countries, the achievements of the Revolution, and the developmental needs of Egypt. The *National Charter* was the main text on these subjects.

1. The following discussion on the national party structure is, for the most part, adapted from Iliya Harik, "The Single Party as a Subordinate Movement: The Case of Egypt," *World Politics* 26, no. 1 (October 1973).

2. For a concise account of the history of the Youth Organization, see *al Shabab al 'Arabi*, May 1967.

The Sabri reforms strengthened party leadership at all subnational levels and established firm lines of authority. Provincial party secretaries were invested with power over lower-level officers and given a privileged position on the governor's council. Particularly important in the new organization was the district first secretary, who linked basic unit leaders with provincial party leaders and who was the prime mover behind party activities at the mass level. Under his supervision, local leaders were selected, trained, and assigned official duties. He also led political education drives, helped the local cadres overcome political opposition, and assisted in solving local community problems. His instrument in these varied activities was the Leadership Groups, at the core of which were the most active and prominent ASU members at the local, basic level. Headed by a secretary, membership in a Leadership Group was fairly large and included key local officials.

The mobilization program in Shubra was closely bound to the district and provincial executive bureaus of the party, headed by Hasan Faris and Ibrahim Adam, respectively. Before assuming party leadership, Faris had been a school teacher. Adam, a lawyer who had already established himself in business and politics in Damanhur, was an executive in a government-owned firm and a provincial leader in the ASU. During the mobilization drive, he became the ASU secretary for Beheira Province at the suggestion of governor Wagih Abaza, who had close personal relations with 'Ali Sabri and who was unofficially the leader of the mobilization drive in Beheira. Both Adam and Faris were energetic individuals wholly committed to the new ASU policy.

Official Leaders and Local Resistance

From the start, the mobilization drive undermined the political power of representative leaders such as the Kuras in Shubra. It was part of the new system's design to disengage former local influentials, especially wealthy landowners. Although this policy was burdened with ideological jargon that stressed party discipline, its application at the local level remained flexible.

In dispensing with local influentials in Beheira, two steps were taken: (1) the prohibition of a native of a community from becoming mayor of his hometown, and (2) the recruitment of cadres for the Leadership Group. In Shubra, the services of Sayid Kura as mayor were terminated, and Ahmad Amir, an official of the local government, was appointed to take his place in the summer of 1965. Amir was slated to become not only the mayor of Shubra but also the leader of the ASU mobilization drive in the community. His was a prodigious task, and he faced strong local opposition. The political struggle between Amir and the Kuras illustrates the broader issues of representative leaders' resistance to national interference that encroaches on their prerogatives and the relevance of local political power to local reform. National efforts to impose some political uniformity on Shubra affected other local leaders such as the agrarian reform peasants, 'Ali al Shawi in particular.

Ahmad Amir had been a young official of the Ministry of Local Government in a village in Beheira Province. Born and raised in Alexandria, where he had earned a bachelor of arts degree in history from the city's university, Amir was twenty-eight when he became mayor of Shubra. His father, a successful engineer, belonged to a segment of the population which, as he put it, had suffered indirectly under the socialist policies of President Nasser. Nevertheless, Amir had come of age during the Nasser era and had been affected by its nationalist and socialist philosophies. A person of strong character and determination, intelligence and initiative, he had quickly abandoned his first job as a school teacher, finding its rules and routines too restrictive of his need for self-expression and action. He then joined the Ministry of Local Government as a municipal council secretary. His new assignment as mayor of Shubra was to tax his strength and abilities.

Not surprisingly, the Kuras made it very difficult for Amir to establish his authority in the community. His first confrontation with local opposition was Sayid's refusal to turn over to him the municipal offices and documents. Other high-ranking village officials were initially cautious and disinclined to give the new mayor any advice. The dilemma was interrupted by a political training program started in the late summer of 1965 by the Youth Organization, of which Amir was a representative at the provincial level. He and Shubra's physician were selected to attend the Halwan Socialist Institute. As successful graduates, they continued their training at the Socialist Institute of the Pyramids at Giza, where they received very high marks. In the course of their studies, the two men became close friends and acquired additional political skills and determination.

By virtue of his training and high position in the Youth Organization, Amir became the undisputed leader of the ASU mobilization drive in Shubra. He and the physician started a local chapter of the Youth Organization. A socialist institute also was created to offer a political education course about socialism, the Revolution, and Egypt's national struggle. Ninety villagers went through the training program, most of them literate young men who were given leading positions in the Youth Organization and the Leadership Group. At this early stage in the reorganization of the ASU, Amir became Shubra's main political liaison with the district executive bureau; Sayid Kura, though acting secretary of the Committee of Twenty, had been bypassed by higher party leaders. In forming the Leadership Group in February 1967, the district secretary depended almost entirely on Amir for nomination of the secretary, assistant secretary, and other members of the Group. Party reform measures and the creation of the Leadership Group to head the ASU locally was not accompanied by measures to abolish the Committee of Twenty.

Skillfully, Amir gradually overcame the Kuras' resistance. He first established friendly relations with village officials and formed a personal group among those who had been trained in socialist institutes. He also cultivated social and political contacts with the land reform peasants, who were political rivals of the Kuras. As for the Samads, Mustafa had already been officially banned from taking part in politics, the only person in Shubra to be so restricted. Mustafa's brother Kamil had become politically inactive and powerless by the time Amir started his work in Shubra, but other members of the Samad family and friends in the village were still active and were willing to cooperate with the new mayor.

Amir's ability to overcome the Kuras' resistance in Shubra was the result of both skill and local factors that acted against the Kuras. When Amir arrived in the village, the seeds of political pluralism had already been sown; he found politically independent individuals and groups in the village willing to stand with him against the Kuras. First there were the large number of officials in the village, whose local contacts were extensive, and the agrarian reform peasants, who had already emerged as a political force in their own right. In addition to these groups, Amir welcomed the remaining forces of the Samads and their friends, despite their suspect position vis-à-vis the regime. However, because the remaining Samads were peasants of modest and poor means, Amir viewed them in a different light. Amir was able to win the confidence of all these forces in the community by demonstrating strong leadership qualities and by facing up to the Kuras. On two occasions he struck directly and effectively where the Kuras were the most vulnerable.

When Sayid Kura was mayor, the council operated under a financial deficit, but apparently neither Sayid nor the councillors realized it. The deficit was the result of mismanagement and, according to some, the dishonesty of the municipal secretary, who enjoyed Sayid's confidence. Amir discovered the deficit, and, aware of the politically explosive nature of his discovery, made the facts public and took legal measures against Sayid. In addition to being publicly embarrassed, Sayid had to sell one-tenth of his land to pay for the deficit.

The second instance involved a television set that had been donated to the village council by the Ministry of Information to be operated for the public. Instead, Sayid kept the set at his home, perhaps to avoid the responsibility of running it. Amir recognized a suitable issue for a showdown. First, he ordered Sayid to return the television set to the village council; Sayid defiantly refused. Amir then threatened to send the village police to retrieve the set, leaving Sayid no choice but to comply. In a politically adroit maneuver, Amir had made his plans known in the village, and villagers waited to see who would emerge as the victor. The outcome firmly established Amir's authority. After these two encounters, the Kuras allegedly made only one other futile attempt to undermine Amir's authority, after which they apparently resigned themselves to accepting the new village leader and gradually cooperated with him.

Amir's victory in the face of strong local opposition reflected the success of the regime in disestablishing its former allies. Amir could not have succeeded without the support of the politically trained village officials, the ASU local supporters, and the party executive bureaus. Establishing a Youth Organization chapter and a Leadership Group also enabled him to create a broad base of support in the village. However, the role of the ASU in this instance should not overshadow the importance of political and economic changes that had taken place in Shubra and that had already created sources of support for the mobilization movement.

Recruitment of the Leadership Group

The Leadership Group was the basic party unit at the local level. Its members were selected among party activists in the Committee of Twenty, members of the Youth Organization, community officials, and independent villagers. (The Committee of Twenty was in effect immobilized but not abolished.) Membership in this basic party organ was divided into two categories: reliable cadres as a core group and a broader membership of promising prospects. The names of all Group members, approximately forty-five individuals, were given to the public; the twenty-eight core-group members among them, however, were not publicly identified as such.

The recruitment of the Leadership Group members differed from established practice in two ways: designation replaced elections, and party leaders at the district and province levels played a direct part in the selection. Despite the direct role of the party organization in naming local leaders, the outcome showed that flexibility and the accommodation of different forces in the community were the guiding principles in the selection.

After consultation with provincial party leaders, Hasan Faris, the district party secretary, appointed two peasants, Ahmad Suhdi and Fikri Haris, as secretary and assistant secretary of the Leadership Group. Both had been nominated by Ahmad Amir. The first was groomed for the job because of his cooperation, strong interest in politics, and independence from the Kuras. Suhdi's nomination had also won the approval of 'Abd al Mun'im Makram, a member of the province's executive bureau and also the district's deputy in the National Assembly, who particularly wanted to prevent Muhammad Kura and 'Ali al Shawi from being selected because both were contenders for Makram's National Assembly seat. As an independent who opposed the Kuras, Suhdi thus suited the electoral purposes of Makram. Furthermore, Makram's main supporter in Shubra was Mahmud al Sayid Samad.

Fikri Haris, the Leadership Group assistant secretary, was a friend of both Amir and the Kuras. He was also an active party member whose initiative and loyalty to Amir were demonstrated early when he became one of the first individuals to cooperate with the new mayor despite the Kuras' opposition. His position as a friend of the two antagonists made him valuable as go-between. His connections with the Kuras, however, strained his relations with Suhdi. The latter had originally objected to his appointment but was overruled by Amir.

As it finally emerged, the Leadership Group was run by three individuals who were supervised by Amir: Suhdi, Haris, and Mahmud al Sayid, although the last was a member, not an officer, of the Leadership Group. In view of their central political roles, a brief account of their backgrounds is in order.

Ahmad Suhdi was a peasant who owned three feddans of land and came from a very small patrilineal kinship group. Although his education was limited to a few years of elementary instruction, he improved himself by regularly reading newspapers and listening to the radio. In 1966, he was the only man from Shubra to attend the Socialist Institute of al Barnugi. Although he was politically ambitious and very articulate, he lacked the essential personal skills of politicians. He ran unsuccessfully for office in the local branches of the National Union (1959) and the Arab Socialist Union (1963). He was related to the Samads by marriage and was a friend and associate of Mahmud al Sayid. In the 1959 cooperative elections, when Mustafa Samad was under intense pressure from the Kuras, Mustafa selected Suhdi to run on his slate. As the Samad brothers were no longer of political importance in the community, however, Suhdi's earlier connections with the Samads did not seem to bother Amir.

Mahmud al Sayid was a distant cousin of the Samad brothers and a descendant of the illustrious Muhammad Samad. He was one of the first few individuals from Shubra to receive a secular education and earn a certificate from Damanhur's vocational institute. After a checkered and unsuccessful career that had taken him to all parts of the country, he returned to Shubra to become a tenant farmer on the Prince's estate, during which time he became subservient to his more successful cousins Mustafa and Kamil. As a landless tenant, he became a beneficiary of the land reform in 1953 and gained a degree of independence from his cousins, although he continued to associate with them until 1959. With Mustafa and Kamil completely removed from the political scene, Amir did not hesitate to give Mahmud al Sayid a chance to prove loyalty and commitment to the ASU. Mahmud worked closely with Suhdi and accepted some of the hardest, most time-consuming, and least politically rewarding assignments from Amir. As one of the most politically talented and forceful persons in the village, Mahmud was a great asset to Amir.

Fikri Haris was also a literate and honest peasant, who owned only four feddans. Like Suhdi, he came from a small Shubra family of modest means. His cousin Sayid Haris was a wealthy local merchant and partner in business with 'Abd Kura, but Fikri had cooperated with Amir from the beginning despite his friendly relations with the Kuras.

The most striking omission from the Leadership Group nucleus was 'Ali al Shawi. His absence implied that the ASU was steering away from prominent, independent local leaders, even when, like 'Ali, they were of humble peasant origins. In Shubra, at least, the ASU drive sought to create a new leadership, independent of existing political blocs. Had there been time, the drive might have succeeded in this task, but, as will be seen later, national events moved too fast and undermined the Leadership Group in Shubra before it consolidated its powers.

There were sound political reasons for Amir's exclusion of 'Ali from the Leadership Group, but none seemed advisable when viewed in the light of subsequent effects on the viability of the Leadership Group. 'Ali was known to be an independent, stubborn person who was difficult to sway; furthermore, he derived part of his political strength from the Agrarian Reform Administration, which had enjoyed administrative autonomy from both the provincial government and the ASU. Although Amir initially drew support from agrarian reform peasants, he was aware of their proclivity for political independence and wanted to contain their influence.

'Ali's exclusion from the Leadership Group was an exercise in the subtlety of village politics. Amir, who was indebted to 'Ali for his early support against the Kuras, was not ready to repudiate him directly and without provocation. Therefore, he appointed 'Ali as a member of the

Youth Organization, knowing that 'Ali would not be interested in associating with youth, including students, none of whom had 'Ali's prominent political standing. At the same time, he appointed 'Ali's younger brother, who was amicable but weak, to the core group of the Leadership Group. Outwardly, Amir was generous to the Shawis, placing two of them in the ASU organizations in the village; but actually he had tied their hands, since 'Ali would not take part in the Youth Organization meetings, and his brother was ineffective in the Leadership Group.

Outmaneuvered by Amir, 'Ali still could not openly oppose an official of Amir's standing without weakening his own position. As his name was in the expanded membership list handed out to the public, he participated actively in the meetings of the Leadership Group. For 'Ali, it was important to appear in public as someone favored in the official party circles, and he played that part to the best of his ability.

When the ASU national leaders planned the Leadership Group, they envisioned a membership drawn from various elements in the community, especially officials and board members of cooperatives, village councils, the Youth Organization, and even the Committee of Twenty. The purpose of broadening the leadership base was to enable the ASU to become the unifying agent amidst the proliferation of political and economic groups in the community.

In Shubra, however, the Leadership Group forged for itself an independent existence, paying only lip service to the idea of cooptation of representative elements in the various organizations and interest groups in the community. The two cooperative societies and the Committee of Twenty were represented by their weakest members, a deliberate move to exclude the Kuras and agrarian reform peasants. The representative from the regular cooperative was the agronomist, who was a member of the Youth Organization, closely allied with Amir, and indifferent to the Kuras. The same pattern of selection was followed in choosing a representative from the Committee of Twenty.

The Role of the Arab Socialist Union in the Community

Cooptation of local leaders was one of two major characteristics of the mobilization drive; the other was the party's new program and functions within the community. After 1965, the ASU played a prominent role in several local activities: (1) political education, (2) supervision of local organizations, (3) self-help projects for community development, and (4) the creation of auxiliary forces available to officials who needed assistance in special projects.

Political Education

As mentioned earlier, the first act in the mobilization drive of 1965 was to educate top community leaders in national institutes created for this purpose. When the newly trained leaders returned to Shubra, they opened a socialist institute to instruct selected villagers in the ideology and policies of the regime. Ninety villagers, including officials, went through the Shubra Socialist Institute, and from their ranks, Leadership Group members were drawn.

The Youth Organization, too, actively participated in political indoctrination. Members met regularly once every two weeks and discussed readings, specially designed for this purpose, from the Youth Organization biweekly organ, *al Shabab al 'Arabi*. New recruits were admitted to these discussions in preparation for membership.

A third aspect of the political education program was the training in socialist institutes of almost all village officials, including those who were politically indifferent. Many key officials used their ideological training to increase their political participation in community life, but those who were originally nonpolitical or who disliked such programs tolerated them only to oblige the mayor and provincial leaders. Politically indifferent officials who refused to participate were not punished or discriminated against.

The results of the survey conducted in Shubra suggest that political education and the subsequent increase of involvement improved the officials' public image and relations with villagers. Two survey questions dealt with this point. The first asked villagers to identify individuals regarded as most knowledgeable in the affairs of the cooperative society; the second asked them to indicate the most helpful. Most frequently mentioned were those officials and board members who were politically involved; in contrast, those who limited their activities to official duties, many of whom were hardworking and conscientious, were hardly mentioned at all. Responses to other questions designed to identify leaders in the community confirm these results.

The political education program did not, however, visibly affect the average villager. For instance, the survey revealed that village leaders in general were the source of political ideas and information only for a minority of villagers (see chapter 9); the majority, who had access to the mass media, received their political information and ideas first from national sources. What the survey does not measure, however, is the role of the ASU in sensitizing villagers to political ideas and messages transmitted through the mass media and in sustaining those ideas' relevance to village life.

Political Supervision

ASU watchdog activities covered local organizations as well as politically unreliable elements in the community. The Leadership Group secretary, Ahmad Suhdi, reported regularly to the district party secretary regarding the political situation in the community and the political opponents of the mobilization drive. He personally conveyed such information to the district secretary without involving other Leadership Group officers such as his assistant Fikri Haris or the Leadership Group liaison officer. When he returned from Damanhur, Suhdi would confer directly and only with Mahmud al Sayid and Ahmad Amir. Thus information transmission within the ASU was both personal and confidential.

The ASU also supervised the two cooperative societies in the village and examined members' complaints. The Leadership Group named a committee of three for this purpose. (See chapter 14 for a detailed discussion of this activity.)

Perhaps the most effective action taken by the Leadership Group was to silence subversive rumors aimed at undermining ASU policy. For example, a rumor spread rapidly in the village and elsewhere in the district that the purpose of medical examinations of students in village schools was to collect blood. The immediate reaction of parents was not to send their children to school. The Leadership Group quickly stepped in to combat the rumor, using a loud speaker to address the villagers. The Group also organized visits to parents to dispel their fears. These efforts had prompt effect; parents sent their children back to school that same day, and the medical examinations took place on schedule.

Another rumor arose in the spring of 1967 when the Leadership Group was conducting a survey of the village population and livestock for the ASU Secretariat of Peasant Affairs. News from unknown sources spread in Shubra that the purpose of counting livestock was to collect a tax of two pounds on each animal. Again, the Leadership Group acted immediately to dispel citizens' fears and completed the census satisfactorily.

Community Development through Self-Help Projects

Self-help projects (*hulul dhatiyah*, literally "self-induced solutions") were the main undertakings initiated and executed by the ASU basic units. Launched by 'Ali Sabri in 1965, the idea of self-help had first appeared as an ASU slogan to stimulate local initiative in community development. Projects such as draining local swamps, improving village roads, clearing irrigation canals, and building schools and mosques were considered by the

ASU national leadership to be within reach of local party members, who could thus improve the community without incurring expenditures from the national government.

The Leadership Group undertook such projects in Shubra and also participated in district-wide projects. In the district, the ASU constructed a road with the voluntary labor of party members and the free tractor service provided by cooperative societies. The road, twenty-three kilometers long, connected several villages with each other and with the main rural network, improving marketing facilities and introducing agricultural machinery to the cooperative societies.

ASU projects in Shubra included constructing and improving village roads, organizing a local fire squad, building a bus station along the road to Damanhur, lowering meat prices, lighting village streets, inspecting agricultural methods with a view to increasing production, and offering literacy classes. Three of those projects are discussed in detail here.

Lowering Meat Prices. Shubra had three meat stores, which sold meat at a standard rate of sixty piasters (a piaster equals approximately 1.5 cents) per kilogram. After young villagers returned from a training period in the Socialist Institute of the Youth Organization in Damanhur, they launched two projects: one to reduce the high price of meat and the other to medically examine school children for the early detection of tuberculosis and bilharsia. After making a study of the cost of meat, they found that shopkeepers were charging very high prices and tried to persuade them to lower their rates. When merchants refused to yield, the Youth Organization members decided to offer some competition; they took up a collection primarily among ASU cadres and opened an improvised meat store.[3]

The Youth Organization members sold meat at the rate of forty-five piasters per kilogram. To their surprise, their efforts brought them profits, and they decided to continue until the shopkeepers came to terms. During the second week of competition, the shopkeepers, believing that the whole thing was "children's play" and not likely to last, tried to put a stop to their young competitors with a perfunctory promise to sell meat on acceptable terms. When they failed to honor their promise, the youth group resumed the sale of meat, whereupon the shopkeepers came to terms and lowered meat prices to the rate suggested by the Youth Organization.

This dramatic and unprecedented incident brought the Youth Organization to the villagers' attention. During the price war, villagers supported the Youth Organization and increased their appreciation of the ASU. The

3. In Shubra, shopkeepers slaughter animals in front of their stores after clearance by the veterinary.

popularity of the Youth Organization's action compelled Fikri Haris and 'Ali al Shawi to side with the group despite their being related by kinship ties to the largest meat store owner in the village. Word of Shubra's activities reached other villages, where many meat stores were forced to lower their prices.

Agricultural Inspection. The purpose of this experimental project, started in February 1967 by the ASU Secretariat, was to change agricultural practices detrimental to productivity. Shubra was one of three communities selected in Beheira Province to test the possibility of using political means to educate peasants about better cultivation methods. Two officers of the Secretariat were sent to Beheira to launch the project and supervise the local cadres who carried out the plan.

The Leadership Group in Shubra held several special meetings, during which the national officers explained the project and organized inspection teams. At these meetings, local agricultural problems such as land fertility, drainage, irrigation canals, and waterwheels were discussed. Task forces were assembled to do the field work, while the national officers handled problems requiring action by the provincial bureaucracy. The village was divided into sectors (*hawd*), each to be supervised by a team of three party cadres whose main function was to advise cultivators and see that their work conformed to official regulations.

Required conformity with official dates for planting crops is one example of problem solving by political means. Before the cotton planting season, peasants in Shubra planted a broad bean known as *ful,* which is one of the mainstays of the Egyptian diet. Delays in harvesting the bean crop often resulted in delays in planting cotton. Failure to plant cotton on schedule makes it more susceptible to the worm pest, and a poor cotton crop means a great loss in revenue. In the Leadership Group meetings, local party cadres tried to explain to the national officers the peasants' reason for the late bean harvest. However, once the national officers had convinced everyone that the issue was urgent, inspection teams complied and ordered peasants to harvest the mature bean crop immediately and to pull out premature stocks.

The results were generally favorable, and cotton was planted on time. During this undertaking, however, the local cadres behaved less strictly than they were expected to by national officers. Marginal cases were ignored, and peasants who would have suffered a major loss of their bean crop by uprooting the stocks were allowed additional time. Justifying their tolerant attitude, local party cadres explained that it would be "inhuman" to force a poor cultivator to destroy a crop just at the time it was ripening for harvest and that special cases had not affected the overall picture.

When the national officers proved impatient, they were criticized by local cadres, who considered their peremptory manner to be prohibitive of useful dialogue. The local cadres had avoided bossism and were sympathetic to peasant difficulties, whereas the national officers were demanding and severe.

Repairing Village Streets. A third self-help project that may be of special interest was undertaken in the fall of 1967 by the Leadership Group secretary, his assistant, and Mahmud al Sayid to repair the main street in the village. The street was too low where it met the main road to Damanhur but a little higher than the thresholds of most houses in the middle of the village. Fikri Haris's idea was to lower the level of the street within the village and raise it where it intersected with the main road.

Tasks were assigned: Fikri took over the responsibility of raising money, and both Suhdi and Mahmud al Sayid were in charge of recruiting volunteer workers and supervising work in progress. Fikri managed to obtain only a few pounds from ordinary villagers, but his connections with the Kura group proved useful. Even though his cousin was a meat merchant who had suffered from another self-help activity when the meat prices were lowered, Fikri collected donations totaling twenty-four pounds from his cousin, the Kuras, and other well-to-do cultivators. With part of the required sum in hand, the project was started, tractors were hired, and volunteers were organized. (Not participating were the Youth Organization members who had become demoralized by the national policy aimed at immobilizing their organization throughout Egypt after the June 1967 war with Israel. See chapter 13.) In order to complete the project, Fikri requested that the mayor use public funds to match the amount collected from private contributions, hinting that the Kuras, the mayor's main opponents, had given generously. Amir donated twenty-five pounds from the village council's public works fund, and the project was completed.

Fikri's role as liaison between the Leadership Group and the Kura bloc was successful in this instance; both sides cooperated. The case further shows that party cadres were still active in community self-help projects despite the generally demoralizing atmosphere in 1967 after the nation had suffered a military defeat (see chapter 12).

The Arab Socialist Union as an Auxiliary Force

Another activity of the ASU was to assist local officials in implementing national policy and improving community conditions. The government's need for a mass organization to link officials with the public and to generate mass response to public policy was one of the main reasons for establishing a political movement. The need for local party cadres was expressed in a comment attributed to the governor of Beheira when he decided to send a committee to study housing renewal in Shubra: "We need a mass organization in the village that is able to respond to and cooperate with the executive branches of government." The ASU served in this capacity; its cadres received the governor's housing committee and gave them a tour of the village, pointing out urgent housing needs and discussing what the provincial government could offer.

The ASU in Shubra has assisted in programs concerned with family planning, savings, agriculture, combating the cotton pest, procurement of provisions, and recruitment of agricultural laborers. Many of the ASU's contributions toward these projects have been discussed elsewhere and only a few cases need be examined in detail here.

The Medical Examination Project. As mentioned earlier, the Youth Organization chapter in Shubra had proposed a general health examination for school children. The physician, who was also chairman of the Youth Organization chapter, offered to extend the program to include a chest X-ray for the entire village population. On a previous occasion, after arranging with the Department of Health in Damanhur for X-ray machines and specialists, he had been embarrassed when the medical mission arrived to find that only twenty-five villagers appeared for examination.

In order to prevent a recurrence of such an incident, he sought ASU assistance by raising the issue in the Leadership Group meeting and asking cadres to inform and urge villagers to appear for the examination. During the meeting, it became clear that it was more than a lack of information that had stopped people from going for examination. First, villagers had no incentive to take examinations because the results of similar tests made by the health department in the past had never been revealed. The physician promised to correct this.

A second deterrent had been the choice of the village club as the examination site. Although the club was conveniently located in the center of the village, men considered it shameful for their women to appear there. The doctor then explained that he needed a spacious place like the club where electricity was available. A lively discussion followed. The suggestion that won the approval of all the cadres was for members of the Leadership Group to take the initiative: they would tell villagers that they were taking their own women with them to the club for examination. By leading the procession in the company of their wives, ASU leaders broke the taboo, and other villagers followed their example.

Medical Examination of Livestock. The national government's plan to insure livestock for all peasants at negligible rates stipulated that animals first be examined by the village veterinarian. Although there was a standing Ministry of Agriculture requirement for every village veterinarian to examine all livestock, the veterinarian in Shubra had always objected, claiming that peasants would not bring their animals to him unless they were very sick and that the village council had never offered to help in such an undertaking. The Leadership Group decided to force the issue with the veterinarian and requested the insurance plan for Shubra. At the discussion in the Leadership Group meeting, the veterinarian stated that he needed the support and assistance of villagers if he was to examine such a large number of animals. The Leadership Group decided to organize teams of peasants to urge people to bring their animals to the veterinary unit and to help in keeping order.

The response of the villagers was beyond expectations. Shubra's veterinarian and another from a neighboring village who came to assist were overwhelmed. Twice, the Shubra veterinarian left his work to complain to the mayor about the pressure and the chaos, accusing the Leadership Group of not keeping order. The veterinarian's accusations prompted the mayor to conduct an investigation, which revealed that the Leadership Group had succeeded in getting villagers to respond to the plan and had tried to keep order but were unable to maintain complete control over the unprecedented crowds. Furthermore, it appeared that both veterinary doctors had acted rudely toward the peasants.

As this case illustrates, the Leadership Group's initiative made it impractical for an official to ignore its deliberations, even when he was openly hostile either to the Group or to the issue at hand. Henceforth, whenever the veterinarian learned that the Leadership Group meeting was to discuss an issue related to his work, he attended. He obviously wanted to defend himself against attacks and oppose any decision that would eventually affect him adversely. Those other top officials in the village who, like the veterinarian, had been uninterested in politics took similar attitudes. Thus one of the main advantages of the Leadership Group in stimulating public participation in village affairs was its open meetings. Elected party branches, with their closed-door meetings, had been inferior in this respect.

While the role of the ASU in community development was impressive in certain respects, it also had serious shortcomings. For instance, the ASU in Shubra failed to give effective support or guidance to the agricultural laborers' "trade union," which had been organized by the district secretary (see chapter 14). The union, in desperate need, had received local support only from the mayor, who had extended some financial aid and appointed the social worker of the village council to help them in accounting. Similarly, the Leadership Group effort to combat illiteracy in the village lacked deep commitment and the drive to sustain it; the number of villagers who received an education under the program was so small that it did not appreciably affect the total picture. There is still plenty of room for more initiative and work to improve village life, particularly in combatting diseases such as bilharsia.

Also on the debit side is the fact that self-help ideas were initiated by external sources and were being guided, to a large extent, by the district before taking root locally. The readiness of cadres and their heightened understanding of the importance of these activities did not lead to an impressive degree of voluntarism; the heads of the ASU often had to assign individuals to tasks when a lack of volunteers threatened the success of a project.

Motives, though hard to fathom, certainly were not all characterized by pure devotion to public interest. Many cadres were attracted to service in the hope of winning political prizes later or gaining useful employment. This attitude may be understandable; politics is an activity in which valuable resources are controlled and allocated, and those who remain indifferent to such inducements are not allowed to stay in politics for long.

Conclusion

The single party in Egypt has been reorganized several times, but in Shubra it is necessary to stress only two periods: collaboration,[4] 1953–1965, and mobilization, 1965–1968. During the mobilization drive, a new political group of peasants under the ASU banner emerged in Shubra, and political activity accelerated. The ASU imposed party discipline, undertook ideological indoctrination, and at the same time abandoned elections in favor of leadership cooptation. However, the new policy expanded, rather than eliminated, the pluralist political structure of the community; instead of imposing a strict, uniform formula on the community, it gave rise to a new partisan group under the leadership of local officials and peasants.

At the district and province levels, professionals, in addition to peasants and government officials, constituted a strong component of party cadres. Some formerly leading villagers were not invited to join the new ASU groups, but many nonetheless continued to be as politically active as possible, and many retained their bases of support without holding a political office. Those leaders regained their initiative and positions in 1968, when the regime stopped the mobilization drive and reverted the

4. For a definition of the collaboration model, see Harik, "The Single Party. . . ."

ASU to its pre-1965 role (see chapter 14). Indeed, the continuously changing policies of the regime have contributed to local leadership proliferation and instability, and have precluded the possibility of a new autocracy replacing the Samads. Successive changes in leadership positions in Shubra show that politics has become a precarious career. All prominent leaders in Shubra were successively weakened by a combination of national and local developments.

Under the mobilization drive, party activities were expanded to include community development projects and supervision of officials, in addition to keeping watch over former influentials. Political indoctrination was widespread; for members of the local branch of the Youth Organization, it was systematic and demanding. At no point, however, did ideological discipline become too strict, and villagers were not compelled to demonstrate their ideological conformity. The party's active role in village problem solving induced local and provincial officials to rely more often on party cadres in implementing official policy and administering daily tasks. Because of the cadres' regular contact with the people and their responsiveness to national policies, officials found in local party leaders an important liaison with ordinary citizens.

One of the most important features of the local mobilization was the open meetings of the Leadership Group and the officers' encouragement of villagers to attend. The open meetings gave villagers a chance for greater participation in party activities and provided a forum to discuss and settle village problems and policies. There, the villagers, especially members of the Youth Organization, questioned the officials' activities and called them to account. No less important was the generation of ideas that such meetings made possible by bringing many different points of view together. Neither the previous party branch nor the new Committee of Ten, which replaced the Leadership Group (see chapter 13), has offered such opportunities. By closing the meetings to the public, the Committee of Ten draws a curtain between party leaders and the party following in the village.

Political involvement of party members has been limited to subnational levels without significantly penetrating national institutions. The party organization suffers a separation between its subnational and national organs that circumscribes the party's influence in national affairs. There can be little doubt that national leaders prevail over lower-level leaders, but their relationship is one of remote, rather than direct, control. However, local affairs are not conducted in a sphere independent from national consideration; local institutions have been the creation of the national government and have performed functions consistent with national designs. Local autonomy has provided villagers with considerable freedom in making decisions regarding recruitment of local leaders and management of their local affairs, but it is not a substitute for participation in the recruitment of national leaders or for free ideological intercourse. Local autonomy has, however, given relevant and valuable experience to villagers in matters that mean a great deal to them.

So far, this book has described the processes through which local organizations have been forged and how those processes have affected various groups and leaders in the community. The evidence indicates that a revolution in the structure of political and economic relations has occurred in Shubra and that many new leaders have emerged. What structural analysis does not show, however, is how new local organizations and thus *ipso facto* how national leaders have been able to affect the attitudes and ideas of ordinary villagers and local leaders, what network of relations exists among local community leaders, and what has been the most effective means of communications between national leaders and villagers. The following six chapters of this book are therefore concerned with survey analysis of data on local leadership relations, communications, ideology, and attitudes.

chapter 7

Political leadership and political power

Proliferation of leadership and political struggle have been conspicuous features of Shubra's politics since 1952. The complexity of political relations and the instability of leadership roles have been underlined in the previous chapters on the political history and process in the community. The study of leadership, however, is rooted in the phenomenon of political power, which manifests itself in a pervasive way within a field of action.

Power is defined here as one's capacity to attain political objectives. It thus follows that the power of one leader or a bloc of leaders should be viewed in relation to the distribution of power in the field of action. As power relations often are manifested in personal terms, we may be able to obtain information on leadership alignments and divisions by finding out how leaders relate to one another. To identify the community leadership structure in Shubra, ordinary villagers as well as reputed leaders were interviewed. Two conventional methods were used: the reputational method and the observation of decision making in councils.[1] These methods do not exhaust the possible range of discovery, nor have they been equally applied in as rigorous a manner as I had wished; despite their shortcomings, however, they have proved useful in this inquiry.

Attributed Leadership

The reputational method is an information-gathering technique by which a researcher obtains data on leaders through informants, social registers, or panelists. In this study, it was decided to elicit information on attributed leadership by means of an opinion survey of a representative sample of

1. For an account of these methods, see Arnold M. Rose, *The Power Structure: Political Process in American Society* (New York: Oxford University Press, 1967); and Terry N. Clark (ed.), *Community Structure and Decision-Making: A Comparative Analysis* (San Francisco: Chandler, 1968).

adult males. It was hoped that through this method the villagers' perceptions of community leaders would emerge. In yet another step, I selected a second group of 44 native villagers who, by virtue of their positions, my personal observations, and informants' reports, seemed to be the leading political actors in the community. Results from the random-sample survey served as a check on this selection and produced very few leaders' names that had not been included in the selected group of 44. This group of 44 individuals (henceforth called the Select) were subjected to the same interviews as were the ordinary villagers in the sample.[2]

Sample respondents and the Select were asked three questions intended to elicit their opinions as to who were influential people in the community. The first question asked: "Who in the village, would you say, is liked by most people here?" Persons mentioned in response to this question will henceforth be called the Popular. The second question asked: "Who would you say are the most influential individuals in the village?"[3] Persons identified in response to this question will henceforth be called the Influentials. Unlike the first two, which tended to elicit information on the political standing of individuals, the third question asked respondents for the names of those having the actual power to solve village problems. A comparison between those reputed to be Influentials and those who actually attended to solving villagers' problems is presented later in this chapter.

The instrument to obtain information on attributed leadership was specifically designed to elicit the respondent's perception of community members who, to his knowledge, were considered popular or influential. The question did not, for instance, ask a respondent to identify people he personally liked best or to whom he personally deferred, but rather to state who in his opinion was influential in the community. Respondents also were asked to state why they considered the people they had chosen to be leaders. Responses to this question are discussed separately in chapter 11.

Relying on a representative sample of opinion in the community may have precluded the charge of partial selection of informants and the effects of bias often leveled against the use of social registers and informants' reports.[4] Furthermore, by interviewing 44 leaders specially selected,

2. For details on the randomness of the sample, see Appendix B.
3. This question was phrased in colloquial terms, which, in the village context, convey the idea of influence. Translated literally: "Who would you say are the individuals in the village whose word is generally obeyed and who are able to see people's business through?" Both questions on popularity and influence were adopted from Malikah's questionnaire, Lewis Kamil Malikah, *al Jama'at wa al Qiyadat fi Qaryatin 'Arabiyah* (Sirs-al-Layyan, Egypt: Markaz Tanmiyat al Mujtama', 1963).
4. For criticism of the reputational method, see, for example, Raymond E. Wolfinger, "Reputation and Reality in the Study of Community Power," *American Sociological Review*

additional evidence was provided and compared with that of the sample responses. Moreover, the reputational status of an individual will not be used here as an indicator of his special area or weight of influence, but only of his general leadership status. Greater frequencies or smaller ones will simply refer to the extent of recognition or consensus regarding a leader's political status, not necessarily to the weight of his influence. However, it would be unrealistic to ignore completely the size of the vote and its implications for other measures of degrees of influence.

Community Leaders

The survey responses show remarkable agreement between the Select and ordinary villagers in regard to the identity of top leaders in the community. Complete accordance exists between the two sets of respondents regarding the top 5, and a strong agreement on the top 9[5] Influentials. (Spearman's rho equals .91 for the top 9 Influentials and .77 for the top 8[6] Popular.) Agreement between the Select and sample respondents regarding local leaders continues to be relatively strong down to the person ranking 20 in order of the votes received. Of the top 20 names, 14 are mentioned by both groups of respondents. The disparity in the views of respondents on the standing of leaders in the village grows progressively wider further down the list.

The Select seem to agree more with one another on the names of top Influentials in the community than do ordinary villagers. The top Influential, for instance, received 89 percent of the Select's votes, compared with only 57 percent he received in the sample. A comparable difference can be seen in the case of the tenth-ranking leader on the two lists. This difference, doubtless, is due to the Select's greater homogeneity and knowledge of public affairs.

A group of 41 other leaders were identified by sample respondents and 31 by the Select, all of whom received less than 10 percent of the votes. Therefore, those will be considered as secondary leaders, in contrast to general leaders whose influence is village-wide, not particularistic.

Influence and popularity are highly associated in Shubra. Villagers view the most influential persons as also the best liked (Spearman's rho for the top 10 = .90).[7] The same is true of the Select's responses, where

---
25 (October 1960); and Nelson W. Polsby, *Community Power and Political Theory* (New Haven: Yale University Press, 1963).
   5. Significant at the .01 level.
   6. Significant at the .05 level.
   7. Significant at the .05 level.

association between attributed influence and popularity is clearly indicated by a rho of .81 [8] for the top 10 leaders. The Select, however, tended to discriminate more between influence and popularity than did the sample respondents, as clearly revealed by the smaller proportion of votes given to the Popular by the Select. The minimum-maximum percentage range of the Select's vote for the top 10 Popular individuals is 18 percent for the lowest on the list to 66 percent for the highest, whereas for the top 10 Influentials the minimum-maximum range is 27 to 87 percent. Presumably, the Select, who include in their ranks most Influentials, have stronger feelings of sympathy and antipathy toward one another as a result of rivalry and alliances. They also, more often than do ordinary villagers, find it necessary to deal with one another regardless of their personal feelings, which explains why some acknowledge others' influence without being sympathetic to them.

Leadership Role of Officials

An examination of the influence status of appointed village officials may reveal how the community views those appointed to serve it. For the purposes of this study, I have identified 60 nonelected leaders who occupied formal positions in Shubra and ranged in importance from the mayor down to a clerk in the village council or cooperative society (see table 4). The list is limited to official employees; villagers who were coopted or elected to formal positions such as municipal councillors, cooperative board members, or party branch cadres are not included in this special section but are included in the Select group. Each formal position discussed here can be considered sufficiently strategic in the life of the community as to affect the business of a fair number of the village population. For example, an agronomist in a cooperative society may affect the management of cultivation, while a teacher may affect the long-range attitudes and skills of youths. All 60 officials had been appointed by the village organizations or extra-community agencies such as the provincial or central governments; they may, therefore, be considered representative of outside forces of influence. The top officials such as the mayor, the head agronomists, and the physician were all appointed by the government, but some lower-level officials were natives appointed by top village officials, who had secured the formal approval of the provincial government.

Among the 60, only 18 were thought of as Influentials by sample respondents (see table 4). Officials who were considered influential were

8. Significant at the .05 level.

Table 4
Village Officials Designated as Community Leaders by the Reputational Method

Category	Co-op Officials	Village Council Officials	Teachers	Imams	Total
Occupants of Official Positions	13	21	21	5	60
Influential Officials by Reputation as Identified by Survey Respondents	6	6	3	3	18

Table 5
Villagers' Perception of Importance of Organizations

Rank Order	Order of Choices for Each Organization				
	First Choice	Second Choice	Third Choice	Fourth Choice	Fifth Choice
I Village Council	59	40	17	2	1
II Cooperative Society	41	25	22	11	10
III Youth Organization	14	28	26	22	7
IV Leadership Group	9	17	22	10	19
V Committee of Twenty	3	11	13	20	14
VI Village Club	2	1	9	16	27

involved in village political life beyond the call of official duty; officials who remained nonpolitical and limited their activities to their official tasks were not considered influential, nor even helpful. The least involved in village public affairs were school teachers, and only 3 out of 21 were acknowledged as influential and helpful.

Only one out of every two officials were involved in village politics. Those who were uninvolved politically failed to relate well to the villagers whom they served. This observation, however, should not apply to the performance of their official duties; many of the politically uninvolved were hardworking and competent in their jobs.

Political involvement in the village is greater among officials who are natives or residents in the community than among nonresidents. Non-native officials in Shubra outnumber native officials by more than three to one, yet the ratio of native Influentials to non-native Influentials is only one to one. Whether native or not, when we exclude the mayor, officials rank low in the order of attributed leadership in the community, with only three out of eighteen designated as among the top ten leaders. However, when elective positions are included, the list of Influentials who occupy formal roles rises sharply, yet it remains true that the majority of occupants of formal positions are not influential because many of them are middle- and lower-level officials.

Finally, it may be useful to indicate how the various organizations, whose officers have been under discussion here, rank in order of importance to the villagers. Respondents were asked to indicate the rank order of the most useful organizations in the village. The results (see table 5) clearly indicate the primacy of the village council and cooperative societies in the lives of the villagers. Fifty-nine respondents considered the village council to be first in rank of importance, whereas only one person ranked it last. Among the various branches of the ASU, the Youth Organization occupied the highest rank, no doubt because of its successful campaigns to lower meat prices (see chapter 6) and improve the physical conditions of the village. However, it is difficult to weigh the impact of ASU groups separately because their leaderships overlapped to a large extent.

Village Problems and Community Leaders

When leadership is defined by specifics such as solving problems, the names of individuals become fewer and the names of local organizations start to appear. To elicit information on leaders' capacities to solve problems, a question regarding general ability was asked first, followed by a number of other questions regarding specific matters. Villagers were first asked to identify village problems; then, those who were able to do so were asked to state who in their opinions could solve these problems. Problems that had been identified by respondents pertained to agriculture, housing, lighting, village streets, and the like. Only six leaders, all of whom were among the top ten Influentials, were identified as capable of solving these problems. Problem solving was viewed by some respondents as the responsibility of local organizations. (See table 6.)

Since most problems fell within the municipal council's jurisdiction, it should not be surprising that the mayor, Ahmad Amir, received the largest number of votes. Mahmud al Sayid, who came next in importance, was an associate of Suhdi, the ASU Leadership Group secretary; Mahmud al

Table 6
Attributed Leadership in Problem Solving in General

Type of Agent	Number	Percentage
Name of Individual		
1. Ahmad Amir	35	25
2. Mahmud al Sayid	16	12
3. Ahmad Suhdi	4	3
4. Fikri Haris	3	2
5. Sayid Haris	3	2
6. Haj Hammal	2	1
Corporate Body		
Government (national and provincial)	13	10
ASU	12	9
Cooperative	3	2
"Trade Union"	2	1
The Police	2	1
Informal Group		
Everyone in the village	25	18

N = 135

Sayid's receiving more votes than Suhdi is no doubt due to his forceful personality and skill in solving problems. Finally, it may be worth noting that 18 percent of the respondents felt that village problems were the common responsibility of the community as a whole, a reflection of civic consciousness.

For further comparison between reputed influence and actual ability to solve problems, each respondent was asked three questions about his own behavior when faced with a personal problem concerning finances, family matters, or disputes over property and livestock. A fourth question sought to find out how a villager reaches a decision on participation in community affairs, that is, whether he makes up his mind on his own or depends on others to advise him. It was assumed that those whose advice is most often sought influence those who seek it. A leadership pattern emerged from the responses to these questions.

Three types of political actors emerge from analysis of the survey results: specific individuals, corporate bodies, and informal groups (see table 7). The pattern of influence shows that some leaders in Shubra are "general" and others are "specialized." The names of the general leaders appear in regard to every issue raised in the survey—family problems, financial problems, personal disputes, and political participation. However, it may be noticed that the extent to which an individual person is considered a general leader by villagers varies, as the frequencies clearly indicate (see table 7). On political participation, more villagers follow the advice of Amir, Mahmud al Sayid, Suhdi, and Haj Hammal—all ASU leaders. Since these same names also emerged at the top in the reputational analysis, they may be considered the top leaders in Shubra.

Below the top leaders are so-called specialized leaders, who were mentioned in reference to some issues but not to others, such as Rayyan, Fikri Haris, Sayid Haris, 'Ali al Shawi, and a few others. It may be recalled that all these individuals were reputed to be leaders. It may also be noticed that specialized leaders consistently obtained lower votes in all responses than did the top leaders. The surprising appearance of 'Ali al Shawi among the specialized rather than among the top leaders points to his declining political fortunes by 1967 (see chapters 13 and 14).

Villagers also viewed organizations as effective and specialized agents in community life (see table 7). The ASU, for instance, was mentioned more often in regard to matters of public affairs than was the village council, but the two were mentioned with almost equal frequency in regard to solving personal differences. In communications, specialization of each of these organizations differs according to the issue; the ASU led in spreading information on socialism, while the village council led in spreading information on family planning.[9] It is difficult, on the whole, to draw hard and fast distinctions between the village council and the ASU since many of their officers overlapped.

As for informal groups, villagers resorted to kinsmen in family differences and financial problems more often than in property disputes or political matters. It is interesting to note that the police and courts were hardly ever sought out in personal differences in family or financial matters and very little in property disputes (see table 7).

The Kuras, who were only marginally active in public affairs when the survey was taken in May 1967, were not accredited with any influence in problem solving, although they were acknowledged as general leaders. Exclusion of the Kuras is understandable with respect to issues that require

---

9. The physician, who was the Youth Organization secretary and a leading figure in spreading information on family planning, was also an *ex officio* member of the village council.

Table 7
Village Leaders Identified by Problem-Solving Ability

Type of Agent	On Family Problems	On Financial Problems	On Property Disputes
Individuals	*Percentage*	*Percentage*	*Percentage*
Ahmad Amir	16	24	42
Mahmud al Sayid	15	15	10
Jalil Shubrawi	12	6	6
Ahmad Suhdi	4	5	2
Majid Rayyan	3	4	2
Haj Hammal	6	3	2
'Ali al Shawi	7	2	1
Corporate Bodies			
Village Council	4	4	8
Cooperative	—	4	7
ASU	4	3	7
The Courts	—	2	7
The Police	7	1	6
Informal Groups			
Nearest of Kin	21	20	4
Friends and Neighbors	7	11	7
"I solve it myself"	17	10	1

an official position, which the Kuras lacked in 1967, but it seems curious that in such areas as financial problems and personal disputes, the villagers did not resort to the Kuras. This could be due to the social distance and impersonality of the Kuras, whose interests had always been limited to handling major village policy rather than particular issues of importance to individuals.

In considering possession of power that can affect village-wide problems, respondents mentioned leaders in positions of authority in the municipal council and in the official party. Those who had leadership standing in the community but had been out of office were realistically assessed rather than neglected. While reputed to be leaders, the Kuras were also considered not in a position at that time to affect the resolution of village problems. Thus respondents clearly distinguished between the political standing of a person and his actual influence at a specific time.

The reputational method has in effect directed attention to the potential power contenders, whereas decision making reflected closely the actual power holders at the time. Influence reputation pointed to potential leaders such as the Kuras and kept them within sight, reminding us of their possible future resurgence, as indeed occurred in 1968 (see chapter 13). Another point that should be emphasized here is the ability of villagers to conceive of political relations in institutional, not just personal, terms, as their frequent mention of the leading role of local organizations clearly demonstrates. It is also worth noting here that villagers considered local leaders and organizations as the proper agents for solving community problems, not, as is usually the case in developing countries, the national government. The only problems whose solution some villagers felt was the responsibility of the national government were those of national significance such as unemployment. This attitude may be indicative of the villagers' growing confidence in their local institutions and leaders.

Survey results have not shown bias in favor of individuals with ascriptive qualities. The two leaders of the village religious fraternities (Sufi orders), who had succeeded their parents in their religious positions, were not once mentioned as leaders in public affairs and politics. My personal observation also confirms the absence of Sufi leaders from political life. Family elders or members of large patrilineal kinship groups rarely appeared among the top seventeen leaders; in fact, most of the top leaders came from small patrilineal kinship groups. Moreover, individuals such as the Kuras who enjoyed a high social status were not considered, probably for the reasons already discussed, leaders who could solve village problems. Religious leaders, or *imams*, some of whom were acknowledged as community leaders as well, were not traditional but modern leaders, as will be shown later.

Leadership in Shubra became quite diversified and was enjoyed by individuals who were generally powerful and also by others whose influence was limited to special spheres of action. However, influence structure in Shubra had a peak occupied by the mayor and members of the Leadership Group. And yet, there were many restraints on the powers of the top elite. Politically, they were watched carefully by their opponents; managerially, they could not assume the leadership role of other existing organizations in the village such as the cooperative societies that had autonomous spheres of action. As an obvious concession to other community leaders, the mayor and the ASU had to include most key officers of village organizations in the Leadership Group in order to secure their cooperation.

Under conditions of rapid change similar to those in Shubra, surveys such as this one are period bound. In 1967, there were political leaders in Shubra who had decided not to use their influence but rather to wait for a more propitious time. The outcome of the 1968 elections (see chapter 13) demonstrate that the political resources of those leaders could be activated successfully. To understand leadership more fully, political processes should also be closely examined, with particular emphasis on leadership changes and decision making.

Sociogramic Analysis

The results of the reputational method show a high degree of consensus concerning community leaders. Were one to accept this tendency without further analysis, one would no doubt conclude that a power elite exists in Shubra, producing yet another case in the list of community studies that confirms a distinct ruling class.[10] Although the same names occur in most cases, leadership lists do not in any way show the relations of leaders to one another.

The main question here is whether leaders in Shubra are cohesive or divided. No direct questions were asked, except of informants, regarding divisions and alliances of leaders, partly because such relations may be delicate as well as obscure. Instead, sociogramic analysis was applied to survey data in order to determine relationships among respondents by detecting their mutual or unilateral recognition according to their votes. When one of the Select, for instance, is asked to name influentials in the community, his choices are most likely to be other Select individuals. By charting such choices into sociograms, relations among leaders can be better gauged, and the results may further help detect objectivity of the survey responses, as will be shown later.

As sociogramic analysis reveals primarily interpersonal relations, its application is limited to relatively small groups whose members personally know each other. The Select constituted such a group, and analysis will be limited to them. Since the Select also included almost all individuals with leadership status in the community, their attitudes toward one another should be informative on the subjects of the leaders' cohesion and disunity.

The sociograms (see figures 3 and 4) were charted on the basis of data obtained from responses to the following two questions: "Who in the village, would you say, is liked by most people here?" and "Who would

10. This tendency has appeared in the original leadership study by Floyd Hunter and in several subsequent studies. See Floyd Hunter, *Community Power Structure* (Chapel Hill: University of North Carolina Press, 1953). For a discussion of the literature on the subject, see Polsby, *Community Power*.

you say are the most influential individuals in the village?" Each individual who was mentioned in response to either of these two questions was given a code number. Two sociograms were then charted, one for popularity and one for influence. Individuals who received less than five votes on popularity or influence were not included here in order to preserve the visual clarity of the sociograms in regard to the major leaders. The direction of arrows distinguishes the recipient of a vote from the voter. A circle drawn around a number indicates that an individual is a recipient of five or more votes and qualifies as a "star." Those who chose him comprise his "constellation." Double lines from one circle to another indicate reciprocal recognition.

Sociogram I (see figure 3) records the responses of the Select on the best liked individuals in the community. It shows that the Select split into three major clusters: the Leadership Group, the Kuras, and the agrarian reform peasants. The pattern also appears in Sociogram II on influence (see figure 4). When the stars in each sociogram and their constellations are identified, it becomes clear that the clusters represent three different political groups competing with one another for power in the community. The first political group, the ASU Leadership Group, is represented by Suhdi (40) and Mahmud al Sayid (60), both close associates of the mayor, who was also the senior ASU personality in the village. The second political group is led by the Kura family represented by Sayid Kura (42), Sayid Haris (43), Haj Hammal (44), and 'Abd Kura (46). The third group, the agrarian reform cooperative, is represented by 'Ali al Shawi (58). It is clear that this last group is very weakly linked to the other leaders in the community, with only one of its members acknowledged by other leaders.

The two sociograms show also that there are independent leaders such as Majid Rayyan (59) who do not belong to any of the three groups. A problematic case is Fikri Haris (57), who, according to the two sociograms, belongs to the Kura bloc but was actually the assistant secretary of the Leadership Group. His is both a complex and revealing case, and Fikri will be left temporarily unaligned until discussed fully later. The cases of two other leaders should also be clarified here. Ahmad Amir was omitted from the sociograms because as a non-native he was not formally interviewed,[11] and, though he received votes, his own choices remain unknown. Also, Jalil

11. As Amir's name does not appear in the two sociograms, the names of those who acknowledged him could not be observed. During the research period, I made a decision to interview formally only natives of the village. Though the decision may seem arbitrary, it caused no problem since the three ranking Influentials excluded were very well known to me. These included Amir, the physician, and the agronomist of the regular cooperative.

Political leadership and political power 113

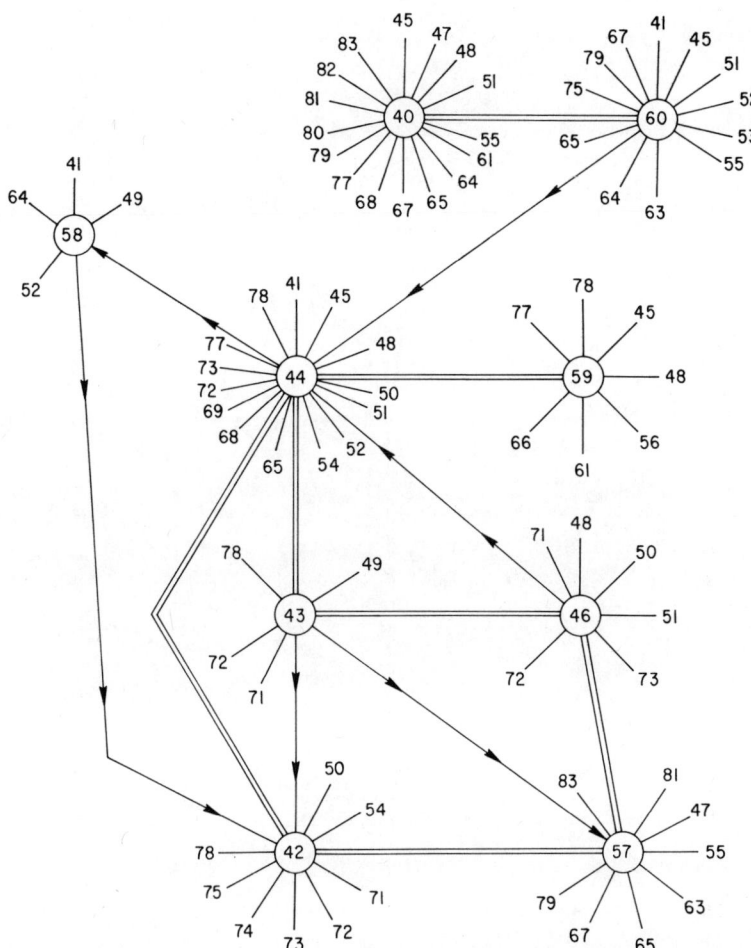

FIGURE 3. Popularity pattern (I). Choices made by the Select in Shubra's leadership poll. A star represents a leader who had been named by at least more than one other leader. Lines drawn to him indicate that he is the recipient of others' votes. Double lines indicate mutual recognition.

Shubrawi, who declined to be formally interviewed, had to be left out although he received many votes.

Before the sociograms are analyzed further, it may be useful to describe the political groups that have been identified thus far: the Kuras, the ASU Leadership Group, and the land reform peasants. These are, respectively,

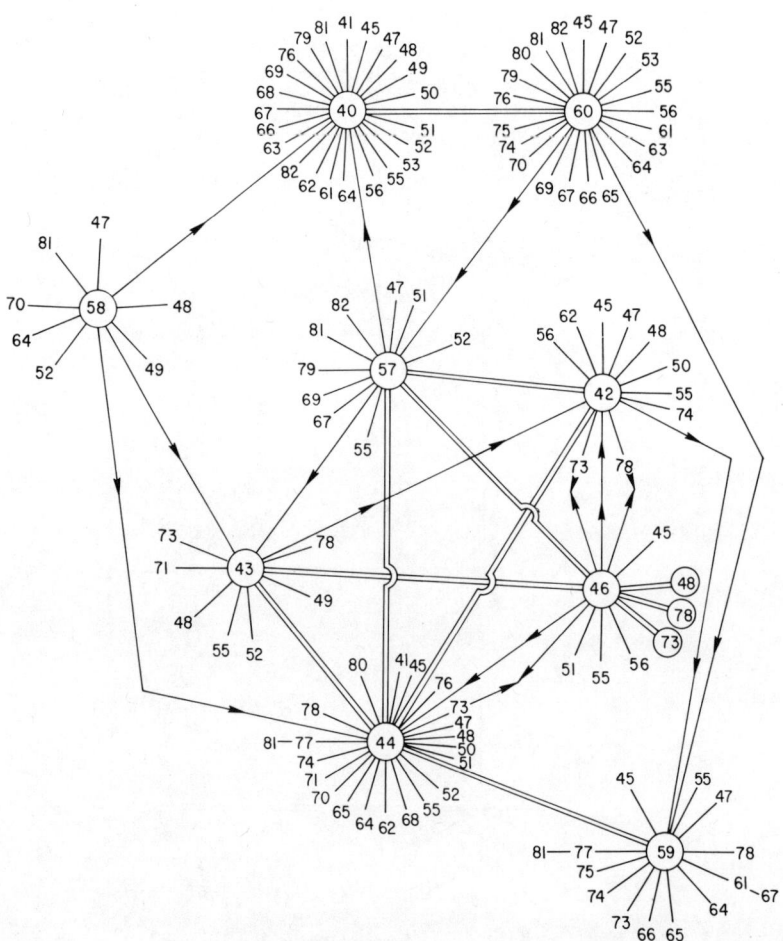

FIGURE 4. Attributed influence pattern (II). Choices made by the Select in Shubra's leadership poll. A star represents a leader who had been named by at least more than one other leader. Lines drawn to him indicate that he is the recipient of others' votes. Double lines indicate mutual recognition.

the representative, official, and organization leaders distinguished earlier.

The three political blocs in Shubra differed from one another both educationally and economically. The representative leaders—who include Sayid Kura, 'Abd Kura, Sayid Haris, Haj Hammal, and Bashir Shubrawi—

form a distinctly upper-income group in the community. They are, with the exception of the last two, the wealthiest individuals in the village. In 1967, three Kuras owned 136 feddans of land among them, and Sayid Haris was also a merchant who owned a meat store in the village and another in Damanhur, in addition to carrying on a lucrative trade in livestock. The only low-income persons belonging to this group were Haj Hammal, a retired petty official of the Ministry of Awqaf, and Bashir Shubrawi, a preparatory school teacher of modest salary. In educational background also, the Kuras were distinguished; one held a university degree, one had a high school diploma, and three had completed elementary education.

Among the three groups, the leaders of the land reform peasants had the most modest economic and educational means. They were all beneficiaries of land distribution and ranged from literate to barely literate. Having been landless tenants, none had been able to enjoy an extended period of formal instruction. However, the agronomist of the reform cooperative, who was politically on their side, had a technical institute degree in agriculture.

The third category is the ASU Leadership Group (LG), whose leaders include three cultivators and two government officials. Each cultivator in this group manages on the average about four feddans, and some of them engage in other part-time work; they have, thus, a little better than average income among the people of Shubra. The two officials, the mayor and the physician, are among the best paid officials in the village, yet their monthly income does not exceed thirty pounds, an income far below that of the Kura family and lower than the mean income of cultivators managing six feddans. On the whole, the LG cultivators are not better off economically than the agrarian reform peasants. In education, the LG have the edge over the land reform peasants, primarily because of the presence of educated officials in their ranks.

The leaders of the three blocs in the village had been exposed to educational influences beyond their formal school experiences. The Kuras, for instance, had been in touch, both socially and professionally, with the urban population. The leaders of reform peasants had received training at cooperative institutes and were in touch with provincial officials who advised them regularly on business aspects of cooperatives and agriculture. Members of the LG were exposed to indoctrination on socialism and politics in meetings with higher ASU officials and in socialist institutes.

The presence of appointed officials in the LG reflects its strong ties with elements outside the village community and underlines the fact that it was the instrument of the national government. The agrarian reform peasants also hold firm ties with higher officials outside the community, although only one local official belonged to their ranks. In contrast to these two groups, the Kuras in 1967 had very weak connections with the provincial and national governments but were strong in their local attachments and wealth.

As individuals, the leaders discussed here differed markedly from one another. In age, they ranged from 32 to 64 years and, in education, from barely literate to university educated. They included cultivators, merchants, officials, *imams,* and teachers. The most underrepresented occupational group was the agricultural laborers, who constituted 21 percent of the village adult male population, but only one of whom appeared among the leaders.

First, it is clear that each political bloc revealed in the sociograms had social characteristics relatively distinct from those of the other two. Second, Shubra's leaders were not politically cohesive but were divided into three groups plus a number of independents. Thus what seems to constitute a power elite vanishes under rigorous analysis. Relations among blocs were weak, as can be inferred from the fact that the sociogramic stars tended to acknowledge one another when in the same bloc but rarely when in other blocs. Third, leadership structure in the community tended to be stratified across the three blocs; the Select fell into top and second-order leaders (stars and constellations). In each bloc, stars were acknowledged by second-order leaders, but the latter were not acknowledged by the stars. Finally, it may be observed that the pattern of influence appears to be more complex than that of popularity (compare Sociograms I and II as shown in figures 3 and 4), as leaders were willing to acknowledge the influence, if not the popularity, of other leaders.

The Reputational Method and the Detection of Bias

By demonstrating that the leaders of Shubra were not cohesive but divided into three opposing blocs, it has been shown that the reputational method of studying community leaders does not necessarily result in affirming the existence of a power elite. Another charge usually leveled at the reputational method is the possibility of bias among respondents. Therefore, it is necessary to deal with the issue of bias before further conclusions are drawn.

An examination of the sociograms (see figures 3 and 4) reveals a considerable degree of personal bias in the responses of the Select. First, the leadership patterns revealed in both sociograms corresponded to the actual political blocs in the community known to exist from experience;

hence they reflect political alignment rather than objective assessment. Personal political sympathies appear to have affected the leaders' judgment. Apparently, partisanship on the part of respondents prevented them from acknowledging prominent leaders who belonged to other blocs.

Another indication of partisanship was the failure of some prominent leaders to acknowledge Ahmad Amir, the Mayor, as an influential and popular leader. Politically, the mayor belonged to the ASU Leadership Group, which was at odds with the Kuras; but since his leadership in the community was undisputable,[12] at least in terms of influence, Amir serves as an objectivity test, especially for the Kuras, who were opponents of the LG. Only one of the top Kura leaders acknowledged Amir's popularity; among the eight second-order Kura leaders, only four acknowledged his popularity. The same attitude, with minor changes, persisted with respect to responses on influence; only a few more of the Kura leaders acknowledged Amir's influence.

Another example of bias is the case of an independent leader, Majid Rayyan (59), who named four of his close friends, two of whom were in a low order of importance. He also named a weak leader (52) in the agrarian reform bloc, while he left out the truly strong man (58) whom he detested. Rayyan was a very knowledgeable older man in the village and could not have chosen simply out of ignorance.

Should bias in attributing leadership be sufficient reason for dropping the use of the reputational method? On the contrary, such bias can be useful in the study of the community power structure, provided, of course, that one allows for its presence. Political influence is an elusive phenomenon, often obscured by personal relations and emotions. It often is self-defeating for political actors to reveal their true feelings and positions, making it difficult for students of political influence to determine the facts. As an instrument that can elicit such personal bias of leaders, sociogramic analysis is of great value in the study of influence. It reveals concealed relations among leaders and draws attention to their alliances and divisions.

The most certain way to overcome distortions resulting from bias is for the researcher to assume it exists and then seek a representative sample of community members whose opinions and biases would reveal a wide range of perceived leaders. Those whose names are mentioned by respondents, supplemented if necessary by additional names obtained through informants, can be interviewed to determine the identity of, and alliances and

12. Amir received the highest number of votes given by both respondent groups, the Select and the Sample.

cleavages among, leaders. In the case of Shubra el Gedida, the leadership biases of all the population were included to yield a representative list of all community biases. In a small community of less than ten thousand, almost all individuals who play some leadership role can be included. The reputational method is, above all, a technique for identification of leaders in a small community.

By making use of personal feelings of political actors, the present sociogramic analysis has determined their relations and leadership stratification as well. When an individual showed bias against other leaders, he nevertheless reported objectively on the leaders of his own group. The sum of all reports is the total number of leaders of all the groups in the community plus their rank as top or second-order leaders. In the Shubra data, partisanship simply reduced the plurality of the vote each particular leader obtained, but it did not leave any leader out of the picture.

Demonstration of the existence of bias should serve as a warning to the user of the reputational method not to treat data on influence from informants and leaders at face value as political facts but as respondents' attitudes. On the other hand, the presence of bias should not discourage would-be users of the method; bias is part of political reality and should be elicited. When the source of information on leadership is the leaders themselves, their bias, if detected, proves to be very useful.

Revealing Covert Relations

Daily experience reveals that, in politics, the strategies and attitudes of leaders are often concealed. As part of the influence phenomenon itself, concealment of information is one of the challenges to political scientists engaged in empirical research. Information gained by a combination of the reputational method and sociogramic analysis may reveal concealed relations sometimes unknown to the outside observer or even to many community leaders themselves.

A sociogramic analysis of Fikri Haris (57), the assistant secretary of the Leadership Group, illustrates some of those concealed relations among leaders that generally elude the observer. The relatively obscure political position of other leaders, too, became clear in the sociograms, and the analysis of Fikri's case may be sufficient to make the point. Sociograms I and II align him with the Kuras, not the LG (40) and (60), an indication of the lack of sympathy toward them, and vice versa. In contrast, Fikri and two of the topmost leaders among the Kuras (42) and (46) mutually acknowledged each other's popularity, as the double lines drawn between them show. No other connections are revealed between Fikri (57) and any other group in the village.

Sociogram II (see figure 4) reconfirms Fikri's strong relations with the Kuras and weak relations with his LG colleagues. There is mutual acknowledgment between him and three Kura leaders and a unilateral acknowledgment of a fourth. In contrast, Fikri's senior colleague in the LG (40) again fails to acknowledge him as an Influential though (40) is acknowledged by Fikri as such. Lack of reciprocity between Fikri and the LG is manifested again in his relations with (60), who acknowledges Fikri, but is not acknowledged in return. Here again, Fikri shows no new connections with any other group.

The picture that emerges is that Fikri definitely belonged to the Kura group and that unexpected personal and political relations existed between him and his LG associates.

Fikri's actual position in the political network of the village was not entirely clear to me when I was there, and I took him at face value as an LG partisan. He was a regular LG worker, kept company with Suhdi (40), the LG secretary, and presided with Suhdi over every LG meeting. In personal and informal discussions with Fikri, I found his ideas closer to the LG's views on general political principles than to those of the Kuras. His connections with the Kuras remained concealed; he was neither seen with them nor did he frequent their residences. Finally, the fact that he was nominated to his LG position by Ahmad Amir, the major opponent of the Kuras, dispelled the possibility that he could be a Kura ally.

However, there were at that time also some reasons to be uncertain about his alliances. Fikri's cousin (43) and son-in-law (71) were both well-known allies of the Kuras. His relations with these relatives, especially with his cousin, were good, although politically they were somewhat restrained with his son-in-law.

Why was he nominated by Amir, a man who was too well informed about local politics to have been misled? The nomination, in fact, was made in full knowledge of Fikri's friendly relations with the Kuras. Politically aspiring, Fikri was favorably disposed toward Amir and the regime's reforms; thus Amir could view him as a friendly activist, one who could establish a rapport between the LG and the Kuras. The appointment of Fikri was a conciliatory move toward the Kuras by which Amir had hoped to abate their hostility toward him personally and toward the LG.

Politically, Amir's step turned out to be very well advised, since the Kuras were potentially the strongest political bloc in the village. Amir needed to find a way of dealing with them without surrendering leadership; moreover, this step was in line with the official policy of the LG, which aimed at creating cooperation among all groups, leaders, officials, and citizens. The struggle with the Kuras had not originally been

Amir's idea but had been forced on him by the Kuras after he was appointed mayor in place of Sayid Kura.

The political move met the needs of Ahmad Amir but not those of Suhdi, the secretary to the LG, who neutralized Amir's maneuver by isolating Fikri. Suhdi was an old opponent of the Kuras, and his new position as LG secretary put him in the forefront of the challenge to their position in the ASU. He was not quite willing to accept as an associate a friend of the Kuras and thus blocked Fikri's integration into the leadership. Instead, he coopted Mahmud al Sayid (60) as an associate without title and ignored Fikri whenever possible.

Suhdi, it seems, never quite approved of Fikri as his assistant secretary and intimated his feelings to Amir. When Amir made the nominations to the LG, he showed the list to Suhdi in my presence and asked for his opinion. Suhdi gleaned the list and returned it with an indifferent response, a gesture that aroused Amir to retort that the selection was the best possible under the circumstances. Suhdi politely concurred but without apparent conviction. He later told me that he did not approve of all the names listed in the LG, but did not specify anyone in particular. At that time, I could not make out what Suhdi's objections were; now, with the advantage of hindsight and data analysis, the picture seems to fit together.

The complexity of Fikri's position in 1967 eluded me as well as most of the Select. Analysis of the sociograms demonstrates clearly that even some of the Select did not know the real political position of Fikri. Sociogram II shows that the stars—(42), (44), and (46)—in the Kura bloc and Fikri reciprocally acknowledged one another, but that was not the case with the Kura constellation. Conversely, the LG constellations voted for Fikri, whereas the LG stars, (40) and (60), did not.

The full statistical evidence of this inverse projection of political images is unequivocal. In Sociogram I, of the eleven Select men who voted for Fikri, three were Kura stars, but none were Kura constellations. The remaining eight votes came from the LG constellations but none from the LG stars.[13] In Sociogram II, Fikri received thirteen votes, three of which again came from the same Kura stars and only one from LG stars. The remaining nine votes, as in Sociogram I, came from the LG constellations rather than the Kura constellations.

It may be, therefore, that Fikri so successfully concealed his real position that his public image was completely reversed. By publicly posing as closely allied to the LG while privately keeping strong ties with the

13. Only one voter among the 8 voted for the Kuras and the LG at the same time; the others did not vote for any Kura leader.

Political leadership and political power

Kuras, he may have misled many village leaders as well as the public, not necessarily to his political advantage. Analysis of the sociograms reveals that neither bloc was clear on how its core leadership related to him.

Ordinary villagers were just as uncertain about Fikri's political position as were second-order leaders. A check on the voting support that Fikri had received from sample respondents showed that his support indeed came from LG followers rather than from the Kuras. In the sample total of fourteen votes for him, thirteen were from individuals who had also voted for LG stars (40) and (60), but only three of the thirteen had also voted for the Kura leadership. Although the LG received more votes than the Kuras in general, the difference appears large enough to be significant. The results, in short, show that, politically, the public image of Fikri was identified with the LG.

Events that I witnessed in the summer of 1968 confirmed these findings. By the summer of 1968, Leadership Groups of the ASU had been abolished by Nasser, whose regime had reorganized the ASU to open the organization once again to free elections. A Committee of Ten was to be elected as the basic village unit of the ASU. During the elections for the Committee of Ten in June 1968, the former heads of the LG in Shubra did not run on the same slate.[14]

During the 1968 election campaign, Fikri behaved with much the same political duplicity as previously discussed. He ran as an independent on his record as a former LG leader. Privately, however, he made an agreement with the Kuras for mutual support. When the election returns were announced, Fikri had been elected by a very small margin. Disappointed, one of Fikri's cousins, who had helped Fikri in the campaign, complained in my presence to a Kura family member that Fikri had honored his pledge but that the Kuras had failed to reciprocate. This was the first explicit indication I observed of confidential relations between Fikri and the Kuras. After the elections, Fikri's relations with the Kuras ranged from cool to openly unfriendly.

It is possible that the Kuras had acted in bad faith, as Fikri's cousin charged. However, another hypothesis based on sociogramic analysis suggests that his poor showing was the result of the inverse projection of his position in the public eye. Being associated with the LG, which was already defunct formally and whose leaders were divided openly, his actual public support weakened.

Since his arrangement with top Kura leaders was confidential, there is

---

14. This was contrary to the trend in Beheira Province, where most former LG officers ran in the elections together and captured most of the seats in the new basic units.

reason to believe that it never became known to the Kura supporters. Moreover, the Kuras themselves did not campaign directly, but acted through representatives, who had appeared as constellations in the sociograms and who had not, as it may be recalled, recognized Fikri as an ally; and, inadvertently, one may assume, they had failed to recommend him to their followers. Why the Kura heads did not instruct them to support Fikri remains unclear, but one reason may have been indifference, since his link with the LG and Amir was no longer useful.[15]

It is hoped that what has been revealed through the use of the reputational method in this study will contribute toward a better understanding of its possibilities and limitations as well as reduce the intensity of the debate over its adequacy for scientific research.[16] In the present case, the reputational method and sociogramic analysis were used effectively (a) to identify the most widely recognized leaders in Shubra, (b) to reveal the pattern of leadership stratification, (c) to determine the extent of division and cohesiveness among leaders, (d) to point to areas of specialized influence, (e) to uncover concealed relations among leaders, and, finally, (f) to determine the extent of bias in the responses of leaders.

Decision Making and Leadership

Decision-making bodies in Shubra during the period under study here were the village council, two separate boards of the cooperative societies, and the Leadership Group. Only the ASU Leadership Group was a relatively large body of about twenty-eight members. The other groups had memberships ranging between ten and fifteen, but only about nine members of any of these groups attended meetings regularly. In all the groups, decisions were almost always made by consensus rather than by majority vote. Two other studies of relatively small communities with vastly different cultures have reached similar conclusions regarding decision making. F. G. Bailey, studying Indian village communities,[17] and Arthur Vidich and Joseph Bensman, studying Springdale, a small town in New York,[18] observed this phenomenon and tried to explain it. Vidich and

15. In addition to the LG's being dissolved, the mayor himself was in the process of being transferred from Shubra to a higher office in a neighboring province (see chapter 13).
16. See, for example, Raymond E. Wolfinger, "A Plea for a Decent Burial," *American Sociological Review* 27 (December 1962).
17. See F. G. Bailey, "Decisions by Consensus in Council and Committees," in Max Gluckman and Fred Eggan (eds.), *Political Systems and the Distribution of Power* (New York: Praeger, 1965), pp. 1–20.
18. Arthur J. Vidich and Joseph Bensman, *Small Town in Mass Society: Class, Power and Religion in a Rural Community* (Princeton: Princeton University Press, 1958).

Bensman remarked that consensus in councils was associated with minimization of decision making and the surrender of jurisdiction. In contrast to Bailey, who explains consensus in structural terms, Vidich and Bensman attribute this phenomenon to cultural factors.

Unlike Springdale, Shubra's recent history has been characterized by intense political activity, social reform, and leadership struggle. It therefore may appear curious that decision making by consensus prevails here, too. However, there was no reluctance in Shubra to bring issues to council or to make decisions, perhaps because of the action-oriented ethos of the community. As the struggle over the revenue of the village market (see chapter 4) demonstrates, Shubra's leaders did not surrender their jurisdiction to outside agencies, despite the strong role played by the provincial government in the affairs of local community. Since decision by consensus in combination with reluctance to act has not been the case in Shubra, as in Springdale, it may be instructive to turn to Bailey's explanation in trying to understand the behavior of Shubra's leaders.

Bailey contends that councils lean toward consensus when they are administrative in function and lack legal sanctions or when they are elite councils quite independent from their constituents. Despite the fact that all of Shubra's decision-making councils except the Leadership Group were elected, they qualify as elite councils. Each of the two cooperative boards, for instance, were internally very cohesive and relatively protected from external interference from other leaders in the community. No other village organization had the power to penetrate their ranks or interfere against their decisions. The unity among cooperative board members is demonstrated in sociogramic analysis,[19] which shows a high degree of mutual recognition among board members in both societies. It should be added that all the officers of the two cooperative boards had been elected on the same slate, and the opposition had failed to have any of its candidates elected.

The village council, in contrast, was composed of conflicting political groups, but it converted to an elite council as a result of the assertiveness of the mayor, who succeeded in isolating the opposition and winning the support of most council members. It is interesting to note that the only instance in which a formal vote was taken in the village council during the three years of Amir's tenure as mayor was the result of a challenge by the Kura opposition. When the mayor called for a vote, he won by ten votes against one. As a consequence, Sayid Kura, the main challenger, stopped

19. Sociogramic analysis of cooperative board members showed a high degree of reciprocal recognition.

attending village council meetings; his supporters then conceded to the mayor's leadership and cooperated with him. The mayor, in turn, tried not to provoke the other side but also not to surrender his prerogative to make political decisions. However, on another occasion when he and Sayid Kura locked horns, Amir proposed to the council that Sayid be dropped from membership since he had consistently failed to attend the council's meetings. Amir was unable to obtain action from the council members on the issue and no vote was ever taken, although council minutes mentioned the discussion and Amir's position. Thus, while the Kuras could not divide the council and set up one faction against the mayor, neither could the mayor lead the council into action, however legal, against his opponents.

Village political struggle failed to surface at the decision-making level in councils because Shubra's councils were internally cohesive. Resolution of issues was in effect predetermined at the leadership recruitment stage during bitterly contested elections. Shubra's major political conflicts thus occurred and were resolved in principle before they reached the decision-making councils. Moreover, political opposition occurred outside the councils and came from contenders who sought to replace the existing leadership. On the other hand, when it happens that councils are not cohesive, controversy rather than unanimity in decision making follows. In 1968, when two political opponents, 'Ali al Shawi and Muhammad Kura, were both elected to the ASU basic Committee of Ten, their political differences surfaced immediately during the first meeting, which ended without any political decision having been made. However, two decisions of a nonpolitical nature were made without opposition, one of which pertained to repairing a water fountain and thus affected no one's political standing.

Political influence and leadership cannot be viewed solely in terms of overcoming resistance; harnessing resources for effective action is just as important a part of the influence phenomenon. Leadership initiative or commitment was as important as decision making in Shubra. Individuals who were capable and willing to assume public responsibility were not numerous, and thus leadership qualities were generally valued. Overcoming resistance to proposed projects was not always the main problem that top leaders faced; enlisting active individuals in public affairs was just as important, if not more so. For those who aspired to leadership, many opportunities existed, especially in the 1960s, for them to prove themselves and rise in the ranks. Leaders with constructive ideas were well received in councils and encouraged to assume responsibility for implementing their ideas. Fikri Haris, for instance, found no political opposition for his street-repairs project; his only obstacles were obtaining funds and attracting volunteer workers. Many of Shubra's issues pertained to the need to coordinate human resources and expand the villagers' capacity for responsibility rather than to overcome resistance.

Bailey has argued cogently that decisions by consensus are characteristic of councils that lack legal sanctions to implement policy. Shubra's cooperative boards and village council enjoyed legal sanctions to implement their decisions and used those sanctions against offenders; however, for practical reasons, the emphasis instead was on persuasion and cooperation. If they were to invoke legal sanctions too often, not only would their policies be very costly in time, expense, and good will but also conflicts would no doubt arise within the community and eventually tax the limits of the unity that existed among council members. Shubra's councillors understood that they were often acting against a background of apathy and entrenched habits that had to be overcome by persuasive, not legal, means. As already mentioned, efforts made by the ASU to persuade peasants to grow cotton on official schedule proved necessary in order to gain the compliance of reluctant cultivators. When widespread cooperation is necessary for successful implementation of policy, possession of legal sanctions to enforce decisions is of no great value.

Conclusion

Analysis has revealed the subtlety of political relations in this small rural community of an underdeveloped country. Not only has there been leadership proliferation in the community, but leaders have also been drawn from different backgrounds to include laborers, tenants, small landowners, large landowners, petty as well as high-ranking officials. Government officials, who are generally reputed to be all-powerful in rural communities,[20] have been viewed by villagers as second to native community leaders in importance. Of particular interest has been the network of relations among leaders; rank ordering as revealed in sociogramic analysis demonstrates that top leaders are sustained by second-order leaders and by still less prominent leaders whose importance is limited to a specialized activity or particular group. The community's elite have, moreover, not manifested cohesive-power characteristics but have been shown to segregate into separate parties or blocs, each one having its place, characteristics, and political interests. But whereas leadership blocs in Shubra appeared distinct from each other, they were not incommunicable, nor did they split into hostile factions. As the sociograms have shown, the

20. See, for example, Harumi Befu, "The Political Relation of the Village to the State," *World Politics* XIX, 4 (July 1967).

relations among the blocs are weak but not severed, thus allowing for a degree of flexibility in their relations.

One important feature of Shubra's politics that has appeared in this analysis is that political blocs and influentials have formed around local organizations. The basic party unit was the center of one political bloc; the reform cooperative was the center of another. As for the third bloc, the Kuras, it too operated most successfully when it controlled the municipal council and the party branch. Elite behavior and attitudes have thus been affected by their organizational base in the community just as the leaders' ambitions and interests have to a certain extent modified the goals and policies of their organizational bases. The cluster of influence around village organizations has been further demonstrated by villagers' perceptions of their local organizations as the agencies through which problems are solved. Regardless of their social backgrounds, leaders conceived of political strategies in terms of loss and gain of influence in the context of countervailing powers in the community. With political bonds relaxed by socioeconomic change, each leader sought new ties as determined by his social or organizational base. In further illustration of this point, the 1968 ASU elections are discussed in chapter 13.

In Shubra, the power structure was pluralistic, that is, it consisted of several competing but internally cohesive groups. Decision making was relatively free of tension and concluded by consensus. This feature may not seem entirely consistent with Shubra's highly competitive political field of action, nor does it seem democratic, as pluralistic political structures tend to be. However, it must be pointed out again that competition has been very keen in Shubra but manifested on two levels: (a) at the leadership recruitment level, that is, during elections, and (b) in the interactions of the various blocs with one another in the community. Sharing and division of powers occurs by virtue of the fact that no single group, regardless of how internally cohesive it may be, has been able to control all the power bases or stand alone in making decisions in all spheres of community life. The absence of oligarchy in Shubra reflects the distribution of power over many political blocs and the vigilance of each one of these blocs to prevent any other from achieving exclusive control. This situation, of course, is not new or limited to Shubra. In his realistic assessment of Western democracy, Seymour Martin Lipset commented, "While most private governments, unions, professional societies, veterans' organizations, and political parties will remain one-party systems, since they do not possess the basis for sustained internal conflict, it is important to recognize that many internally oligarchic organizations help to sustain political democracy in the larger society and to protect the interests of their members from encroachments of other groups."[21]

---

21. Seymour Martin Lipset, "Introduction," in Robert Michels, *Political Parties: A Sociological Study of the Oligarchical Tendencies of Modern Democracy"* (New York: Collier Books, 1962), p. 36.

chapter 8

The mobilization regime and mass communications

On our way through the village we heard sounds of grief coming from the headman's house and women crying.

"Stop," I ordered the driver. "Could it be that the headman has died?"

A spectacle through the automobile windows struck my eyes, and I could not at first make it out. There was chief of the guards, his deputy, and some of his men with something in their hands marching through a cheering crowd of men, women, and children. Some in the crowd were beating tambourines while women trilled just as they do at weddings. I peered through all this and saw that what the guards were carrying was nothing but the official telephone apparatus! At my side, the doctor yelled, "The telephone! It is being given a bridal treat."

I called one of the guards, who told me that orders had just been received dismissing the present headman and appointing a new one from the rival clan.

"I see. It is then the customary transfer of the telephone to the house of the new headman."

With a smile on his face, the doctor said, "It seems that the telephone to the headman is like a scepter to a king."

From Tawfiq al Hakim, *Yawmiyat Na'ib fi al Aryaf*

This passage from Tawfiq al Hakim's perceptive short story tells of an incident that took place in a Beheira village more than forty years ago, when the telephone was the only means of modern communication in rural areas. In 1967, Shubra el Gedida had about nine telephones, four television sets, daily distribution of newspapers, and over eight hundred radios. Both the telephone and the village headman have been "uncrowned."

What impact has the spectacular spread of mass media had on Egyptian villages? Above all, what has become of the role of local leaders in communicating ideas now that the radio brings information directly into the mudbrick houses of villagers? As the medium through which the voice of the central government reached the village, the telephone in the past acquired the halo of authority; but now, with more than one medium speaking to villagers, what is the nature of the message and what effect does it have on political attitudes of villagers? This chapter and the next focus on the expansion of the mass media, its programs, and village reception of mass media output. The role of local leaders as mediators of information and ideas in a political order where a government-controlled mass media system is the source of almost all ideas and information is also discussed.

Mass Media on the National Level

We are witness currently to the unfolding of many human dramas of which the information explosion is not the least momentous. The entire world is the locus of the communications revolution, and though national disparities still exist in the use of the mass media, they are becoming less marked.

Egypt is not one of the world leaders in processing and transmitting news or mass media programs, but when compared to other developing countries, it becomes a force to reckon with in the communications field. According to UNESCO, *World Communications, 1966*, Egypt's official news agency MEN had 7 permanent news bureaus in 1966 and 18 foreign correspondents, almost all in the Middle East, Africa, and Asia. In the continent of Africa, Egypt has gone farthest in making use of the mass media, both for home consumption as well as for export, primarily to Arab and other African nations. In 1952, Egypt's broadcasting capacity was 2 programs and 15 hours of daily transmission; in 1965, it had increased to 10 programs and a total of 142 hours.[1] Three of these programs were transmitting a total of 55 hours to non-Egyptian audiences throughout the world.[2]

A look at the distribution of time per type of program is particularly useful for comparison later with local consumption of mass media programs. Table 8 gives figures for Egyptian radio programs in 1966. The same rank order of types of programs is maintained in television transmissions.

The Nasser regime very quickly took advantage of the political significance of mass publicity on a nationwide scale. Only four months after the Free Officers took over the government, the regime created the Ministry of National Guidance, and then the Ministry of Information. From the start, the Ministry of Information spread government messages

1. It reached 156 hours in 1967. See *Rose el Yusuf*, February 3, 1969.
2. Al Jumhuriyat al Arabiyat al Muttahidah, *Al Kitab al-Sanawy lil-Ihsa'at al 'Ama, 1952–1965*, p. 196.

Table 8
Egyptian Radio Programs

Type	Percentage of Weekly Broadcasting Time
Entertainment	59.9
Cultural Programs	19.2
News	16.1
Religion	04.8

SOURCE: UNESCO, *World Communications, 1966*.

to the public and sought to improve the means of transmission. By 1966, it was in charge of the three mass media systems: press, radio, and television. In 1958, a Ministry of Culture was created and has since promoted national culture programs in the provinces, particularly by sponsoring theater performances and movies.

Egypt is still a nation "led by its ears," with more people tuned to the radio than reading newspapers or other printed information. In order of importance, the radio comes first, followed by the press, television, movies, and finally theater. Aware of the people's habits of mass media consumption, the government has stressed audio-visual means for disseminating its word to the public. It is not possible to arrive at an exact figure for the number of radio receivers owned in Egypt because no license of ownership is required, but an estimate made by UNESCO in 1966 shows that Egypt had 6.6 receivers per 100 population, the highest rate in Africa.[3] An Egyptian government report on Cairo estimates that one-third of all families living in Cairo own a radio.[4]

For years, the Egyptian press has been the most developed in the Arab world, although 70 percent of the Egyptian population was still illiterate in 1966.[5] Newspaper readers are estimated by UNESCO at 2 percent; other sources confirm this estimate and put newspaper distribution throughout Egypt at 600,000 copies per day.[6] Newspaper reading in Egypt, however, is greater than the UNESCO figures indicate. Sales of daily papers is not an accurate measure of the number of readers because a paper is generally

3. UNESCO, *World Communications, 1966*.
4. See *Rose el Yusuf*, February 3, 1969.
5. We have no data on the possible loss of literacy since. Loss of literacy occurs because of lack of exposure to a literate world.
6. *Al Ahram*, February 6, 1967. Egypt's population then was 30 million.

read by more than one individual. There are no total figures for weekly magazine sales, but I have obtained figures for three of the most popular magazines, which, together with *al Ahram*'s figures, enable us to estimate distribution for 1966 as ranging from 20,000 for the relatively low-selling national magazines to 100,000 for the best selling.

Television made its debut in Egypt as recently as 1960 and has shown a phenomenal growth from about 57,000 sets in 1961 to 361,000 in 1966, the majority of which, of course, are found in Cairo and in Alexandria.[7] But the television audience can be considered much larger than the ownership figures indicate because the government has installed television sets in public places and distributed sets for public showing in villages. In 1964, the ministries of Agriculture and Information began to distribute television sets to cooperative societies and to village councils in rural Egypt to be operated for the public; by 1966, 1,050 sets had been distributed.

The movie industry and the theater, like the press, are more advanced in Egypt than in other Arab countries. The Egyptian movie audience, however, is still relatively small, reaching 28 million in 1967 and averaging approximately one show per person annually. The theater as a mass medium dates back to 1961, when the government stepped in to encourage the production of "guided" plays and to promote provincial performances. The peak of its success, measured by the number of performances, was reached in 1964; and though it has since shown a slight decline, today there are still twice as many performances as there were before 1961. Contemporary playwrights have shown considerable interest in peasant themes, which are popular in both the towns and the countryside.

The communications media in Egypt are all run and controlled by the government. The press, which was nationalized in all its forms in 1960, has passed theoretically from private hands to the public; the regime has claimed that this step has transferred the press to the people through the Arab Socialist Union. However, the ASU has no real control; press affairs have been in the hands of the President and the Minister of Information.

The press under the Revolution passed through two stages of control: the first was the time-honored practice of censorship; the second stage, after 1960, has been marked by managerial methods of control. The extent to which the press has been suppressed ebbs and flows in almost direct relation to the insecurity of the regime. The greater the insecurity, the more oppressive its measures tend to be. Nationalization of the press in 1960 was not, however, a real solution to the tendency among journalists to be critical of the government; what has really succeeded in achieving a

7. Al Jumhuriyat al Arabiyat al Muttahidah, *Al Mu'ashirat al Ihsa'iyah*, 1967.

relative peace between the regime and the intellectual corps of journalists has been the managerial control of the press and what was Nasser's progressive shift toward the left.

Managerial control is the method by which journalists, as managers of their own affairs, free from external interference of the censor,[8] exercise self-imposed constraints in the dissemination of news and ideas in the interest of preserving their own autonomy. In 1961, all newspapers and magazines were administratively consolidated under five publishing houses, with a director general for each house. Newspaper and magazine editors became directly responsible to the director general of the house, as the ordinary writers were responsible to their editors. Press control in effect passed to these top administrators who, by virtue of the confidence placed in them by the President and their own vested interest, have proved responsive to the general guidelines and wishes of the regime.

Managerial control has worked in Egypt for more than one reason. First, Nasser took a personal interest in the press and appointed to top positions journalists of high intellectual integrity who are respected by their colleagues. The fact that journalists were appointed as press administrators has been greatly appreciated by the press corps. Second, since 1956, the ideological gap between the regime and the strong socialist group in the press has narrowed in direct response to the regime's movement toward socialism. Finally, the press has been generously rewarded with high salaries paid by the regime. A director of a publishing house receives a salary comparable to that of a top industrial executive or minister of state; an ordinary writer is paid a salary equivalent to that earned by a university professor.

In effect, journalists themselves have been persuaded to exercise self-control and manage the news in a manner sensitive and responsive to the general goals of the regime, understanding its vital interests and the implications of its ideology and policy. To journalists, the censor stands for outside interference and suppression; self-management, though not free of controls, allows for some integrity for the writer and relative harmony between him and his political environment. These controls may be repugnant to individuals reared in a democratic system, where greater freedom of the press prevails, but it must be remembered that news, entertainment, and new ideas have been reaching mudbrick huts in the countryside. On the other hand, it may be argued that the mass media, nationalized or not, would have eventually reached the common man.

8. In 1967, after the war with Israel, the censor returned, much to the disappointment of journalists.

Since the days depicted in al Hakim's anecdote, the official character of the telephone has extended to all other media.

In short, the central government has been the major force behind the remarkable expansion of mass communication systems. The Egyptian government has no serious competitor in supplying information and propagating ideas. At any rate, a spirit of reconciliation has prevailed between the government and the intellectuals who have disseminated the news. Moreover, it is these intellectuals, as middlemen between the central government and the masses, who have provided some diversity in views under the new regime.

Travel Habits of the People of Shubra el Gedida

Before turning to the detailed discussion of mass communications in Shubra, it may be useful to examine first another form of communication in the village—travel. A look at this facet in the lives of the villagers may provide a better understanding of the context in which the mass media are received in rural Egypt.

Shubra at present is within easy reach of Damanhur, the provincial capital. A bus line, originating in a small town to the east of Shubra, carries passengers every half hour to and from Damanhur. A similar service is provided by a number of small, wayward limousines, which pick up passengers along the way. Shubra has enjoyed these transportation services only since the paved road was completed in 1959. Previously, one could reach the village only by a long, circuitous, unpaved road or by the slow rural railway, a minitrain used mainly for freight, which connected the agricultural centers in the Delta region. The Delta Railway was removed after completion of the macadam road.

Most people in Shubra el Gedida make use of these transportation facilities, traveling primarily to Damanhur for business and shopping. Almost all adult males, 93 percent, have traveled outside Shubra, and the majority have traveled rather frequently, as is revealed in the survey. Although peasants have a rather casual concept of time and the reported frequency of their travel is at best an indication rather than a precise account, from personal observation, I can, however, attest to the frequency of their movements to and from the village.

Fewer people have traveled to other cities: 24 percent of the adult males reported having visited Cairo and Alexandria, whereas only 8 percent reported visiting other villages. Whether or not these reports are very accurate is not easy to say for the simple reason that villagers may not consider visiting neighboring villages as travel. Mass transit to many small villages, however, is not readily available, and one often has to ride a donkey or walk. Furthermore, most of the villagers' travels, as they have indicated, are for purposes that for the most part can be fulfilled only in the city and not in other villages.

Of the trips made by the men of Shubra, 47 percent are for private business and 40 percent are for shopping, mainly in Damanhur. Other, less frequently cited reasons are to visit family, friends, and religious shrines or, simply, pleasure. Except for the students who go to Damanhur for preparatory and vocational education, very few visitors stay overnight. Most visits terminate within the same day and are restricted to business.[9]

The town of Damanhur is a small, conservative community of about 127,000 people. As the administrative center of Beheira Province, a large proportion of its inhabitants are employees of the government in the various bureaucracies and in the public-sector enterprises. Next to government employment comes trade and work in firms, mostly in cotton ginning, rice husking, and other rural occupations. The town is partly urban, partly rural: water buffalos (*gamusas*) and cows pass by morning and evening in front of its only modern hotel and in front of the governor's mansion; from the hotel windows, one can see brush and chickens on the roofs or balconies of apartment houses.

The Mass Media in Shubra el Gedida

While in Shubra, I once stopped to watch a man threshing. The power was supplied by a water buffalo and a cow, tied together to the harness. I was struck by the one discordant note in this pastoral scene: a transistor radio hanging on a twig of a tree near the threshing grounds. The man was quietly listening to the broadcast of a play. When it was over, I heard the radio announcer say that we had just heard *Bilad Barrah* (*Foreign Lands*) by Na'man 'Ashur. The play was about the taming of the aristocracy under the Revolution and the elevation of the common man to a prominent place in the socialist order of Egypt.[10]

It so happened that I had talked with the author of that play one week earlier in Cairo, and we had discussed intellectuals and peasants. 'Ashur had not been aware of the extent to which villagers were becoming

---

9. I did not come across any villager from Shubra who had seen a movie in one of its theaters.

10. 'Ashur sees a more subtle theme in his play, which I have chosen to ignore because it is the aspect of mass culture that concerns me in this discussion, that is, the direct meaning that the play conveys.

Table 9
Places of Exposure to the Radio

Location	Number	Percentage
At home	82	60.7
At the market place	30	22.2
At friends', neighbors', or relatives'	15	11.1
At Anwar's (village tailor)	6	4.4
Miscellaneous places	5	3.7
Do not listen	6	4.4
Total Responses	144	106.5

N = 135. Total responses exceed N because multiple responses are possible.

Table 10
Frequency of Television Watching

Frequency	Number	Percentage
Watches daily	25	18.5
Twice a week	33	24.4
Weekly	29	21.5
Once a month or less	14	10.4
Does not watch	34	25.2
Total Responses	135	100.0

N = 135

exposed to national influences and seemed quite interested to hear what I had to say about the subject. He is not an armchair intellectual but an activist writer of socialist beliefs, although not necessarily those of the regime; his first play, which brought him to the attention of the intellectual community, was about peasants. Whether 'Ashur was aware that he expressed the main themes of official ideology in that play and that, by using his words, the official radio transmitted official ideas to the villagers is another matter. The fact is that the mass media have been conveying voices like 'Ashur's to the countryside for over ten years.

In Shubra el Gedida, as throughout the rest of Egypt, the radio is the medium most used by the villagers. All but 4 percent of the respondents to the survey said they listen to the radio. Since almost all of them have been exposed to the radio, differentiation is made here not between listeners and nonlisteners but between owners of sets and nonowners. The respondents were asked whether they listen to the radio and, if so, where (see table 9). Assuming that those who listen at home are radio owners, we can estimate that there are 13 receivers per 100 persons. This figure equals the world average for 1961,[11] although it is below the level of most rural provinces in Lebanon, where there are radios in 91 percent of all households.[12]

The next most frequently used communications medium in Shubra is not the press, as it is in Egypt as a whole, but television. In May 1967, there were only two private television sets in Shubra, one owned by a landlord and one by a merchant. Two public sets were provided by the reform cooperative and the village council. In the summer of 1968, I found two more private sets owned by shopkeepers, who also played them at their stores for the public. In the survey, respondents were asked how often they watched television (see table 10).

Fewer people are exposed to the press in Shubra than to the radio and television (see tables 11 and 12). Of the 69 adult males in the sample who are exposed to the newspaper, only 19 reported reading the paper daily. Although Egyptian newspapers are inexpensive and accessible to villagers, the low frequency of newspaper reading can be explained by the high rate of illiteracy, which afflicts 51 percent of the adult male population of the village. Newspaper reading in Shubra also varies directly with differences in age. Individuals under age 40 read newspapers more often than do those age 40 and older. The ratio of these two age groups in the total sample is 2 to 1 in favor of the former, whereas for newspaper readers it is 3 to 1. Newspaper reading in Shubra should also vary with sex because the illiteracy rate among women in Egypt is higher than among men.

Comparable data on the exposure of villagers to the mass media is available in two studies, one conducted in 1956 and the other in 1960, in villages of Minufiya Province in the Delta.[13] The results are compared with

11. Wilbur Schramm, *Mass Media and National Development* (Stanford: Stanford University Press, 1964), p. 95.
12. See Michael Hudson, "Democracy and Social Mobilization in Lebanese Politics," *Comparative Politics* (January 1969), p. 256.
13. Gordon Hirabayashi and M. Fathalla el Khatib, "Communication and Awareness in the Villages of Egypt," *Public Opinion Quarterly* 22 (1958), pp. 357–363. The second study is by Lewis Kamil Malikah, *Al Jama'at wa al Qiyadat fi Qariyatin 'Arabiyah* (Sirs-el-Layyan [Egypt], 1963), pp. 62–63. Hirabayashi and Khatib took a five-percent sample and included females, whereas Malikah dealt with the natural number of a small village and excluded

Table 11
Exposure to Newspapers

	Number	Percentage
Neither reads nor hears paper read	69	51.1
Reads himself	42	31.1
Listens to someone else read	23	17.0
No answer	1	.7
Total	135	100.0

Table 12
Frequency of Exposure to Newspapers

	Number	Percentage
Daily	19	14.1
Twice a week	15	11.1
Once a week	20	14.8
Once a month or less	9	6.6
No answer	2	1.5
Total	65	48.1

the data from the Shubra sample (see table 13). Although the data from all three studies do not reflect conditions in the same village, they do represent one homogeneous region of the Delta and suggest an increase in the number of radio listeners between 1956 and 1967 commensurate with the national trend. No trend, however, is visible in the figures on newspaper reading in these villages.

Exposure of the Select to the Mass Media

All 44 selected leaders in Shubra are radio listeners; 96 percent of them own radios, compared with 61 percent for the whole sample. Similarly, 98 percent are exposed to the newspaper either once weekly or daily; only 4

females and young people below the age of eighteen. Gadalla, in a study of agrarian reform peasants in one Delta community, reports lower figures for 1956 than do Khatib and Hirabayashi. Only 33 percent of his sample were exposed to the radio; see Gadalla, *Land Reform*, p. 81.

of them read it less frequently. As for television watching, 93 percent are exposed to television, 86 percent once weekly or daily and 13 percent less often. The most striking fact is that 98 percent of the Select read newspapers, whereas only 33 percent of the ordinary villagers do.

As compared with the sample villagers, the Select are exposed more to the mass media. The mean score in media exposure[14] for the sample villagers is 54, whereas for the Select it is 78. The Select obtain their information directly from the media much more than ordinary villagers do (80 percent compared with 48 percent). Another interesting difference is that none of the Select gives as his source of information neighbors, friends, or relatives; the only personal sources they mention are state ministers, the governor, or high provincial officials.

Summary

The survey data on villagers' exposure to mass media showed that (1) the availability and use of mass media by the villagers of Shubra el Gedida is extensive (oral history of Shubra also shows that access to mass media is of recent origin); (2) both private and public access to mass media exist in the village; (3) gregarious habits of listening to the radio are declining as more households own their own receivers; (4) the output of mass media, whether it be in the form of messages directed to the nation, entertainment, or services such as Koran recitation, reaches the ordinary villager now through all three media; (5) the Select village leaders have shown a markedly greater use of the mass media than have the ordinary villagers; and, as will be shown later, (6) the Select are also better informed than ordinary villagers.

As pointed out in the first part of this book, there is very little social differentiation among the villagers of Shubra. The different responses to the mass media shown by the Select in comparison with the ordinary villagers suggest that a new social stratum is emerging in this community: the great consumers of mass media. Second, the responses show that even in a rural community in an underdeveloped society, leadership and information go together. If, in the course of this analysis, the leaders consistently distinguish themselves from the ordinary villagers, then evidence in support of these two points is provided.

Mass Media Output and Village Response

What has been the reaction of the villagers to the mass media? One can assume that, while the mass media output is very large, the consumption

14. For the index of mass media exposure, see chapter 9.

capacity of the ordinary man is quite limited, perhaps even more so for the villagers. Therefore, it may be hypothesized that an increase in transmission does not result in an equal increase in mass media consumption, and that consumption, as indicated by preference for programs, is just as selective.

This section explores the phenomena of marginal utility of mass media and selective exposure. How much are villagers exposed to the mass media, and what, in particular, attracts their attention? What ultimately determines a villager's choice is his personal interests, but the extent of exposure and the kind of messages selected depend on other variables as well. Most relevant variables turned out to be (a) the mode of exposure, that is, private or public reception; (b) the medium used, that is, radio, television, or newspaper; and (c) the personal and social attributes of the villager.

A comparison of the number of hours of national broadcasting (see table 8) and the preferences for radio programs in Shubra (see table 14) shows a striking disparity. For instance, very few hours of religious programs are broadcast, but such programs draw the attention of the second largest group of listeners, who, at the same time, give very little attention to cultural programs despite the larger number of hours these programs are broadcast (see table 8). This finding suggests a preference of the religious over the secular, yet such an interpretation should not be carried too far. The low educational levels of villagers give them little interest in intellectual matters per se, and their lack of attention to cultural programs is no evidence of an aversion to secular matters. Indeed, the tendency in the village is to prefer entertainment programs (see tables 14 and 15) over every other type of program, including the religious.[15] Although villagers seem to be attracted to the mass media mainly for the entertainment it offers them, it would be erroneous to assume that this particular interest lacks social and political implications; the organization of leisure time may have an integrative effect on the village community. Nationally broadcast entertainment programs give precedence to national songs over local songs, and to patriotic and nationalistic themes over folk themes.

Also, television coverage of sports events arouses the interest of villagers in national athletic heroes and teams, and makes it possible for villagers to identify with them. The top three national soccer teams in 1966 gained fans throughout the nation. I found people in Shubra, as in Cairo, passionately supporting one team against another, and I was often asked to take sides.

It may well be that entertainment offered by the mass media is a form

15. A similar result is reported by Gadalla, *Land Reform*, p. 81.

Table 13
Villagers' Exposure to Mass Media over Time (in Percentages)

	Source		
	Hirabayashi and Khatib, 1956	Malikah, 1960	Harik, 1967
Radio Listeners	55 (includes females)	77	97
Radio Owners	—	17	61
Newspaper readers	20 (includes females)	43	31
Listen to others read paper	—	18	17

Table 14
Villagers' Favorite Radio Programs

Type of Program	Number	Percentage
Songs	81	60.0
The Koran and religious talks	74	54.8
News and political programs	46	34.1
President's speeches	40	29.6
Plays and various entertainment shows	24	17.8
Everything	13	9.6
Rural broadcasts	7	5.2
Sports	0	0.0

N = 135. Maximum score per item cannot exceed 135.

of vicarious learning for the villager whereby overt messages of any program may convey many covert meanings. By organizing the villager's leisure time through the mass media, national leaders impart to him new values. Villagers assimilate new ideas, often unconsciously, as they watch the plays, movies, and variety shows on television. For instance, television has introduced rural people to scenes from city life that reflect, among other things, a liberal disposition toward man-woman relationships in single as well as in married life.

The organization of leisure time by means of the mass media is an aspect of cultural change that may contribute to (1) the realization of uniform cultural patterns throughout the nation; (2) the bridging of the gap between local and national communities; and (3) dissemination of political and ideological messages. Another consideration, however, is that, with the radio, it is possible for individual villagers to be entertained privately in their homes. Private listening may lead to the development of more individualism in village life. Television is almost always viewed in a public setting, but each person seems to watch as if he were alone. As I frequently observed them, villagers watched a public set in complete silence; no comments or chatting was tolerated, and thus each person was forced to rely primarily on his own faculties to interpret what he was seeing on the screen.

The news and the President's speeches are popular programs. Nasser's speeches ranked third on television and fourth on radio, with 21 percent of viewers and 30 percent of listeners choosing to give him attention.[16] Nasser was not a conventional head of state; he was a charismatic leader, according to some observers. But there is another aspect to the popularity of his speeches. Nasser's speeches contained no fiery rhetoric; they were monotonous, flowing slowly and incessantly like the great Nile. His words were pronounced with deliberation; his pauses and repetitions were frequent. His style was not ornate; rather, he spoke in a colloquial, conversational manner. The villagers sat listening as if at a seance. Nasser took them into his confidence, or seemed to do so, by explaining affairs of state in uncomplicated language. He discussed governmental business, how it would affect them, and why. He congratulated himself for what he had done for them, called on their patience for hardships that had to be endured, and lectured them on socialism. The villagers were entertained, moderately enlightened, and, above all, flattered by his special consideration of them.

Finally, it is interesting that programs designed especially for village audiences are not very popular. Rural programs on both radio and television rank next to last. This ranking suggests that the preferences of villagers differ little from those of urban dwellers.

As suggested earlier in this section, what mass media audiences choose to pay attention to can be partially explained by the kind of medium used. Programs that villagers watch on television differ to some extent from

16. Political news and events assume greater importance in the newspapers than on radio and television, as revealed by informal interviewing of Shubra's newspaper readers and by information available on national patterns. See *Rose el Yusuf*, February 3, 1969. The same is true of Malikah's *Jama'at*, p. 68; and Hirabayashi, *POQ*, p. 359.

Table 15
Villagers' Favorite Television Programs

Type of Program	Number	Percentage
Plays, films, and variety shows	60	44.4
Songs	35	25.0
President's speeches	28	20.7
Sports	20	14.8
News and political programs	14	10.4
Everything	10	7.4
Rural programs	7	5.2
The Koran and religious talks	5	3.0

N = 135. Maximum score per item cannot exceed 135.

those listened to on the radio (see tables 14 and 15). On the latter, for instance, news ranks third in popularity; television news ranks only fifth. Although a large number of villagers watch television, it has not yet become a very useful source of information, perhaps because sets are not yet privately owned. Very few respondents mention television in particular as their source of information on national policies (see below). Religious programs, which ranked second in order of radio listening, ranked last on television. A similar difference appears with regard to sports, news of which is obtained mostly by television.

In order to measure the extent of disagreement between preferences on the radio and on television, I computed Spearman's rho, which yielded a correlation coefficient of .41.[17] The extent of disagreement in preferences on the various media revealed by this correlation coefficient suggests that each medium has a relatively different value to the public. We may refer to this phenomenon as specialization of medium function, that is, as a medium of communication, television offers to its audience programs of interest markedly different from what the radio offers them, and vice versa.

The extent of exposure to the mass media is another factor that sheds some light on the marginal utility of the mass media. I offered the hypothesis earlier that the extent of an individual's exposure to the mass media is partially determined by the mode of reception and the individual's background characteristics. Survey data from Shubra are analyzed to provide the evidence for this hypothesis.

17. Significant at the .20 level.

"Mode of reception" refers to the conditions under which an individual becomes exposed to the mass media; reception may be either private or collective. "Private reception" is an individual's personal control over the medium used, that is, his ownership of a radio or television set and the purchase of his own newspaper. For the purposes of this study, the private mode of reception will be considered identical with ownership of a radio set and reading one's own newspaper. "Collective reception" is the individual's dependence on others for access to the mass media. In Shubra, collective reception usually occurs in public places such as the marketplace, the cooperative society, the village council hall, or in the homes of neighbors and friends.

To measure mass media exposure, a scale was constructed;[18] each respondent's score was computed on a scale of 100. The mean score was then computed for respondents who had private access to the mass media and for those who were dependent on others. Individuals with private access were found to be considerably more exposed to the mass media than those whose mode of reception was collective. The mean score for the first group is 65, whereas for the collective reception group it is 34. In short, consumption of media output is qualified by the mode of mass media reception.

It may further be observed that awareness of mass media messages varies according to the relevance of informational items. On the basis of the political awareness index,[19] a wide variation of awareness exists, indicating that villagers are best informed on national policies that affect them directly and least informed on matters that are remotely related to their daily lives. A 58-point difference between the highest awareness score and the lowest confirms beyond doubt that learning from the mass media is a selective process affected by personal interests and concerns. Villagers' responses to the Five Year Plan is an example of this highly selective understanding of national policy. In order to finance the Five Year Plan, the national government proposed that ordinary citizens save a certain amount of their income. In Shubra, 76 percent of respondents had not heard of the "Five Year Plan," whereas 77 percent had heard of the "savings policy"! This suggests that mass media communications tend to be modified by their functional relevance to local life and concerns.

Media Preference of the Select

Differences between the Select and ordinary villagers with respect to choices of mass media programs are fairly wide (see tables 14, 15, 16, and

18. For explanation of the scale, see chapter 9.
19. For the index, see chapter 9.

17). The primary interest shown by the leaders in the mass media is political; news and other political programs rank first in the leaders' preferences on both radio and television, whereas these programs rank third and fifth, respectively, for ordinary villagers. Another distinction between leaders and other villagers is that the former show greater interest in rural programs; perhaps they are more sensitive to national policy aimed at changing village life. A third difference is that village leaders show greater interest in cultural and social programs (see tables 16 and 17), in which the ordinary villagers show practically no interest at all.[20]

When all preferences of the two groups are considered, one learns that the listening habits of the Select and those of ordinary villagers are not extremely different (rho = .79),[21] whereas television preferences are very different (rho = .35).[22] It seems that the Select have resisted the strong appeal of television as an instrument of entertainment and continue to look primarily for news and political programs, as they do with other media, whereas the public are attracted mostly by the great entertainment value of the screen.

Survey data suggest that the Select exercise greater discrimination in making their media choices than the public at large. The Select's independence in choosing programs may be due to their private ownership of radios (96 percent), compared with a smaller number of ordinary villagers who own radios (61 percent). The free choice that the Select enjoy with respect to media programs is further evidenced by the fact that the specific medium affects a leader's preferences less than it does those of ordinary villagers. For instance, the similarity of programs preferred by the leaders on television and radio is higher (rho = .50)[23] than that of the ordinary villagers' choices (rho = .41).[24] Ten percent of the ordinary villagers (see tables 14 and 15) reported that they listen and watch everything indiscriminately, compared with only 2 percent of the Select (see tables 16 and 17). The lack of a choice is clearly expressed in the words of ordinary villagers. "I have no choice; I watch everything," said one of them. Another respondent declared, "I say anything on television is good." In short, the kind of medium affects leaders' choices less than it affects the ordinary villagers'.

20. Questions on media preferences were open-ended (see Appendix A), and the argument that leaders have public images to maintain is not likely to apply in this case.
21. Significant at the .05 level.
22. Not significant at the .10 level.
23. Significant at the .10 level.
24. Significant at the .20 level.

Table 16
Radio Program Preferences of the Select

Type of Program	Number	Percentage
News and political programs	37	84.1
Songs	31	70.5
President's speeches	21	47.7
The Koran and religious programs	20	45.5
Rural programs	14	31.8
Plays and variety shows	9	20.5
Cultural programs	7	15.9
Social programs	5	11.4
Everything	1	2.3
Sports	0	0.0

N = 44. Maximum score per item cannot exceed 44.

Table 17
Television Program Preferences of Leaders

Type of Program	Number	Percentage
News and political programs	21	47.7
Plays, films, and variety shows	20	45.5
Rural programs	12	27.3
President's speeches	11	25.0
Cultural programs	8	18.2
The Koran and religious programs	7	15.9
Sports	7	15.9
Songs	6	13.6
Social programs	1	2.3
Everything	1	2.3

N = 44. Maximum score per item cannot exceed 44.

Summary

The main points revealed by the survey data on media preferences can be summarized briefly: (1) preferences vary according to the medium used and the mode of reception; (2) considering both radio and television together, the three most preferred types of programs are entertainment, political news, and religious programs, in that order; (3) entertainment programs may perform a significant function in facilitating social and political integration of the village with the national system; (4) leaders are distinguished from other villagers by their greater interest in news and political programs, rural broadcasts, and cultural programs; and (5) leaders are more constant in their political interests and demonstrate greater independence of mind and freedom of choice in selecting their media programs.

Conclusion

The mass media experiences of villagers have been more rich and more complex than has been suggested by generalists. National elites have shown considerable interest in communicating with the people of the countryside, and the messages transmitted have been varied, some functional, others not. While the news is no doubt managed and ideas controlled, official mass media have not served to obtain simple compliance to national policy. Exhortations do not play as great a role as one might expect; functional programs such as entertainment, religion, culture, and practical advice have not been subordinate to political and ideological communications. Furthermore, villagers have proved to be as discriminating as other rational beings in selecting mass media programs. In addition, they have shown interest in a wide variety of subjects. This may suggest that villagers' attitudes toward the mass media are not greatly different from those of other social groups.

Although village leaders have appeared to be greater consumers of the mass media output and more politically attuned than ordinary villagers, they have not proved to be less selective. Furthermore, they have had no power over the dissemination of mass media information. In the next chapter, their role as mediators in conveying information to ordinary villagers is compared with the direct effects of the mass media.

chapter 9

Opinion leaders and the mass media

"The word of God can reach further if one hires a loudspeaker."
F. G. Bailey, *Stratagems and Spoils*

The spectacular increase in the accessibility of radio sets, especially in the third world, underlines once again the importance of determining the effects of the mass media on the public. In particular, the issue of direct versus indirect conveyance of mass media messages assumes special importance in the context of general illiteracy and poverty.

Interest in this question was aroused in the 1940s when Lazarsfeld and his colleagues drew attention in their pioneering study, *The People's Choice*, to the prominent role played by opinion leaders in conveying information obtained from radio and newspapers to the politically less active sections of the population.[1] For a short period after the book was published, a succession of studies supported the two-step flow of communications hypothesis.[2] As stated by Lazarsfeld et al., "Ideas often

---

1. Paul F. Lazarsfeld, Bernard Berelson, and Hazel Gaudet, *The People's Choice: How the Voter Makes up his Mind in a Presidential Campaign*, 2d ed. (New York: Columbia University Press, 1948).
2. See the three studies on which Elihu Katz reports in "The Two-Step Flow of Communication: An Up-to-Date Report on an Hypothesis," *Public Opinion Quarterly* 21 (Spring 1957), pp. 61–78; Robert K. Merton, "Patterns of Influence: A Study of Inter-Personal Influence and of Communications Behavior in a Local Community," in Paul Lazarsfeld and Frank N. Stanton (eds.), *Communications Research: 1948–1949* (New York: Harper and Brothers, 1949), pp. 180–219; Elihu Katz and Paul Lazarsfeld, *Personal Influence: The Part Played by People in the Flow of Mass Communications* (Glencoe: The Free Press, 1955). It is interesting to note that these last two studies focus on how individuals are influenced to act

flow *from* radio and print to the opinion leaders and *from* them to the less active sections of the population." ³ It was not stated *how often* ideas flow in this pattern, only that, "It is commonly assumed that individuals obtain their information directly from newspapers, radio, and other media. Our findings did not bear this out. The *majority* of people acquired much of their *information* and many of their ideas through personal contacts with the *opinion leaders* in their group." ⁴

In a study of the impact of national policies and ideas on ordinary citizens, such linkages as the mass media and opinion leaders deserve special attention. The dissemination of new ideas and information is directly related to the reform process and can broaden a villager's perspective and contribute to the development of attitudes consistent with the new economic and political institutions implemented in his community. Because reform ideas are nationally conceived, the question of whether rural people are receptive to or able to assimilate them must be explored. Claims are frequently made that the mass media language is not wholly intelligible to the common man in developing areas,⁵ yet the dearth of systematic inquiry⁶ limits our ability to assess such claims. This chapter, therefore, examines the effects of the mass media on the villagers of Shubra el Gedida and, in particular, on their politicization, first by determining how messages reach the population of the village, then by comparing the roles of the mass media and opinion leaders in contributing to the political awareness of villagers.

The survey conducted in this study was designed to elicit information on the exposure to mass media and political awareness of individual villagers with respect to three national policies: savings, family planning, and socialism. Exposure to mass media is defined as the use of at least one of the three formal media available in the community: newspaper, radio,

---

on certain matters by various forces, including the mass media, rather than on the flow of mass communications. Other studies influenced by the opinion leaders hypothesis are S. N. Eisenstadt, "Communication Processes among Immigrants to Israel," and J. Mayone Stycos, "Patterns of Communication in a Rural Greek Village," both in *Public Opinion Quarterly* 16 (Spring 1952), pp. 42–58 and 58–70, respectively. The first of these two articles does not deal with mass media but with personal communication, and the second deals with a community that had practically no access to the mass media; they can hardly, therefore, serve to confirm the two-step flow of communication hypothesis.

3. Lazarsfeld et al., *The People's Choice*, p. 151.
4. Ibid., p. xxii.
5. See Ithiel de Sola Pool, "The Mass Media and Politics in the Modernization Process," in Lucian W. Pye (ed.), *Communications and Political Development* (Princeton: Princeton University Press, 1963), p. 244; and Lucian W. Pye, *Politics, Personality and Nation-Building: Burma's Search for Identity* (New Haven: Yale University Press, 1968), pp. 20–21.
6. An exception is the recent work by Everett M. Rogers, *Modernization Among Peasants: The Impact of Communications* (New York: Holt, Rinehart and Winston, 1969).

and television. Extent of exposure is determined by a scale that is explained below.

Political awareness is defined here simply as knowledge of a particular policy. The general awareness index is explained below. "Aware" respondents were also asked to identify their sources of information for each policy item. When it was found that the source was one of the mass media, the respondent was asked further about the mode of his reception. For instance, if the source was a newspaper, the individual was asked whether he read it himself or had someone else read the paper to him. Persons citing the radio as a source of information were asked where they heard the radio. In this way, it was possible to determine the extent of personal ownership of radio sets in the village and to discover in what places villagers assembled to listen to radio programs.

Before analyzing the data, it may be helpful to describe briefly the three policy items used in this study to test respondents' knowledge and sources of information. The *savings policy* was a part of the first Five Year Plan, which at the time of its inception in 1959–60 was projected by the government's economic analysts as primarily dependent on national savings for its success. People were urged to establish savings accounts, and local organizations such as cooperatives, village councils, and official party branches informed and assisted the public toward this end. Although the campaign counted on voluntary compliance, government officials were subjected to monthly deductions from their pay checks in an amount equal to a quarter of a day's wage, refundable with interest after five years. Similarly, the agrarian reform cooperative deducted 3.5 Egyptian pounds annually on each feddan owned by a member.

As to *family planning*, the Nasser regime was rather indifferent, if not hostile, until 1962, when, in the *National Charter* delivered to the National Congress of Popular Forces, President Nasser stressed the ill effects of the high birthrate on the economy. Not until 1965, however, did the government attempt vigorous administration of the family planning program, implemented primarily by doctors and nurses in local health centers.

Socialism in Nasser's Egypt has emerged gradually over the years. A very large number of nationalization measures were adopted between 1958 and 1961; however, the definitive statement on socialist ideology appeared in 1962 in the *Charter*.

The Flow of Information

The Shubra data show that the largest number of people, 48 percent of the total sample, acquired their information on the three policy issues directly

Table 18
Direct and Indirect Flow of Communications from the Mass Media
(by Radio Ownership Status)

Radio Ownership Status	Direct Reception of News through the Media		Oral Reception of News		Had Not Heard of Policies		Total
	Number	Percentage	Number	Percentage	Number	Percentage	
Owners	51	62	23	28	8	10	82
Nonowners	14	26	27	51	12	23	53
Total	65		50		20		135

$X^2 = 16.72, p < .001$.

through the mass media, whereas 37 percent heard only oral reports from news mediators.[7] The "mass media group" consisted of respondents whose sources of information on at least two of three issues—savings, family planning, and socialism—were media sources. The "oral reception group" was determined in the same way, except that the main source of information was personal contact rather than the media.[8]

What determines the manner in which communications flow to the public? I hypothesize that the greater the exposure to the mass media, the more *direct* is the flow of communications. It follows that as the mass media become more accessible to and more widely used by the public, the role of mediators in disseminating information will decline. The Shubra data is analyzed to test this hypothesis.

Radio was the medium most commonly used in the village (96 percent of the respondents listened to it), but not all individuals were exposed to the same extent. About 40 percent of the respondents did not own a radio but listened to it. It seems reasonable to assume that ownership of a radio set at home gives comparatively free and frequent access to at least one of

7. The remaining 15 percent were not aware of these policies.
8. A negligible number of respondents mentioned both the mass media and news mediators as their sources of information on a particular policy item. These numbered 3, 9, and 5 for savings, family planning, and socialism, respectively. All these cases were included in the mass media group because we were testing for outreach of the mass media; anyone indicating the media as a source of information in effect became a member of the mass media audience regardless of other sources he mentioned.

the mass media, whereas nonownership is an indicator of limited access and less exposure. Table 18 shows that radio ownership is directly related to the flow of information.

Among radio owners, those who obtained their information directly through the mass media outnumbered those depending on oral reception by more than 2 to 1. Among nonowners, the reverse was true; those who acquired information through news mediators outnumbered the mass media reception group by about the same ratio. The percentage of owners who acquired policy news directly through the media was much higher than it was among the general public, 62 compared with 48 percent.

Variables other than exposure may account for this relationship. Background characteristics of the mass media group and of the oral reception group were therefore examined for possible variation. No significant difference was found except for literacy.[9] The media group was 62 percent literate, whereas the oral reception group was only 40 percent literate. Control for literacy (see table 19) has shown that direct reception of news continues to be significantly related to radio ownership, even in the absence of literacy. Coefficients of tetrachoric correlation[10] determine separately the variance in direct reception of information explained by radio ownership and that explained by literacy (see table 20). Radio ownership accounts for .623 of the variance in direct reception, whereas literacy accounts for .396; when variance in radio ownership was considered, literacy accounted for .441 of the variance.

The newspaper was a source of policy news in the village.[11] Again, not all those familiar with the newspaper in Shubra were equally exposed to it; some read the paper themselves and others depended on someone else to read it to them. Analysis shows that only a small number of newspaper readers[12] depend on opinion leaders for news of policy (see table 21).

The hypothesis that the greater the exposure to the mass media the more direct is the flow of communications tends to be confirmed again by the overall mass media exposure index (see table 22; for definition of index, see below). In further support of these results, radio owners tended to favor the news broadcast more often than did nonowners.

9. Chi-square test shows significance beyond the .05 level. See below for an account of other background factors.
10. Tetrachoric correlation coefficient was developed by Pearson as an estimate of the product-moment correlation for dichotomous variables.
11. Television did not turn out to be a major source of news comparable to the radio and newspaper, perhaps because it was not privately used in the village, and free access and choice of programs were limited.
12. Analysis of data on those who read the paper more often has not revealed a significant difference in the manner in which communications flowed. This is perhaps due to the fact that the time span between them was not markedly different.

Table 19
Direct and Indirect Flow of Communication from the Mass Media among Illiterates (by Radio Ownership Status)

Radio Ownership Status	Direct Reception of News through the Mass Media		Oral Reception of News		Total
	Number	Percentage	Number	Percentage	Number
Owners	18	62	11	38	29
Nonowners	7	26	20	74	27
Total	25		31		56

$X^2 = 7.52, p < .01.$

Table 20
Variance in Direct Reception of Information (by Radio Ownership and Literacy)

	Direct Reception	Radio Ownership	Literacy
Direct Reception	—	.623	.396
Radio Ownership		—	.441

$N = 135$

In short, the two-step flow of communications hypothesis is not supported by the facts. The greater the exposure to the mass media, the more directly political information is obtained. Moreover, the evidence suggests that the role of mediators in disseminating information may decline in relation to the increase in exposure to the mass media.

Are we faced here with the problem of choosing between the credibility of one case study and that of another? The answer is, simply, no. Lazarsfeld and his colleagues discovered that undecided voters are *influenced* more by personal contacts than by the mass media, but nowhere do they provide evidence that in the majority of cases the mass media reach the general public indirectly. As a matter of fact, data in *The People's Choice* show that mass media messages actually reached the majority of the people directly; 68 percent (n = 401) stated that the radio was a " 'helpful' source" in making their voting decision.[13]

Observing the gap between the evidence and the generalization, Elihu Katz wrote that it "may be . . . that influences stemming from the mass media first reach 'opinion leaders' who, in turn, pass on what they read and hear to those of their every-day associates for whom they are influential." [14] Stated in this way, the hypothesis suggests that opinion leaders inform *some* individuals, and it does not preclude the possibility that the majority of the public has direct reception of information. The question of influencing others in making a decision, the main subject of *The People's Choice*, should not be blurred with patterns of dissemination of information.

The Opinion Leaders

Communications studies in developing countries indicate that traditional figures such as headmen, priests, shopkeepers, and teachers are the main mediators of ideas and information in villages.[15] In Shubra, as indicated, 37 percent of the adult male population still depended on mediators for political information. The marketplace was an important center for the diffusion of mass communications: a sizable number of survey respondents who owned no radio sets were found to be exposed to the news in the marketplace, where someone read the newspaper to them, or where a shopkeeper let them listen to his radio. It may be assumed that those who served as radio hosts or public readers of newspapers were also likely to be mediators of information on public policy.

Before presenting the evidence in support or rejection of this hypothesis, it is necessary to make clear a change in terminology. So far, those who transmit information orally have been called "news mediators," but in this

13. Lazarsfeld et al., p. 127.
14. Katz, p. 61.
15. See, for example, Daniel Lerner, *The Passing of Traditional Society: Modernizing the Middle East* (Glencoe, Ill.: The Free Press, 1963), Chapter I; Stycos, "Patterns of Communication . . . ," pp. 59–60; Stycos, "The Potential Role of Turkish Village Opinion Leaders in a Program of Family Planning," *Public Opinion Quarterly* 29 (Spring 1965), p. 124; Ibrahim Abu-Lughod, "The Mass Media and Egyptian Village Life," *Social Forces* 142 (October 1963), pp. 97–104. In a systematic and very informative article, James N. Mosel finds that shopkeepers play an important role in disseminating information, but he also identifies officials of the government as playing a similar role in a most interesting discussion of personal mediation of news in Thailand; see James N. Mosel, "Communication Patterns and Political Socialization in Transitional Thailand," in Pye, pp. 200–206.

Table 21
Direct and Indirect Flow of Communications (by Newspaper Reading Status)

Newspaper Reading Status	Media Reception of Policy News		Oral Reception of Policy News		Had Not Heard of Policies		Total
	Number	Percentage	Number	Percentage	Number	Percentage	
Newspaper readers	30	71	12	29	—	—	42
Secondary readers	11	48	9	39	3	13	23
Don't read	24	35	29	42	16	33	69
Total	65		50		19		134

$X^2 = 6.52$, (df $= 2$), $p < .05$; computed for the first two columns only.

Table 22
General Mass Media Exposure and Directness of Information Flow

Media Exposure Score	Mass Media Group		Oral Reception Group	
	Number	Percentage	Number	Percentage
High Exposure Score	36	57	16	32
Low Exposure Score	28	43	34	68
Total	64	100	50	100

N $= 114$
$X^2 = 6.64$, $p < .02$.

section the term will be used alternately with "opinion leaders"; as will become evident, news mediators in Shubra are also by occupation opinion leaders.

Survey data do not confirm the hypothesis; no connection was found between the role of public newspaper reader and dissemination of news of national policy. Twenty-three respondents said they listened to the newspaper read, for example, by their own children, a well-known tailor in the village, or some of the shopkeepers. When the sources of information given by these 23 respondents were checked, it was found that a newspaper reader was in no case the source of information on any of the three policy issues.

Checked next were the sources of information for the 48 respondents[16] who owned no radio set but listened to the radio outside their homes, usually in the marketplace. Only 2 of the 48 respondents gave the names of shopkeepers as their source of information; the rest mentioned the medium itself or mediators other than the radio hosts. Casual contact with friends and neighbors also played a very small part in spreading information on public policy; only 6 percent of the respondents[17] received information on the three policies from friends and neighbors.

In short, evidence reveals that the public reader of the newspaper and the radio host had, as news mediators, no personal influence on those who got their news in the marketplace. Indeed, it was among this group of marketplace listeners that we found the largest number of individuals who were uninformed on public policy (see tables 23 and 24). There can be no doubt that shopkeepers were not playing the kind of educational role that their strategic position in the community qualified them to play. The public reader and the radio host were just a means to make mass media messages accessible to individuals who had no private access. The shopkeepers in Shubra viewed radio, and more recently television, as a business attraction to draw the public to their shops. (Indeed, these small village entrepreneurs even resorted to the use of microphones to announce their products during special weekday markets.)

As already observed, some adult males (37 percent) received their information on national policies through mediators (little less than half of them[18] had radio sets in their own homes). Who, then, are the news mediators who attended to this minority section of the population and passed on to them the news of national policies? We have already ruled out shopkeepers, public readers, and radio hosts. Mediators of policy news in Shubra turned out to be representatives of new village organizations such as the local political party branch, the village council, and cooperative societies.[19]

16. Remaining nonowners did not listen to radio.
17. This figure represents a mean score for the frequencies on the three policies.
18. 46 percent.
19. Respondents tended to mention an organization as such by name or refer to an officer by personal name or office held. References to an officer by personal name or office were coded under the name of his organization.

Each organization varied from the other in complexity and area of jurisdiction, but they all stood as agents attending to various aspects of village affairs and as the channels through which the national and provincial governments conveyed ideas, information, and policy to the local community. Their roles included simple dissemination of information, inculcation of ideas, and, in certain cases, demands for conformity to policy. It is thus appropriate to refer to the leaders of these organizations as opinion leaders as well as mediators of information.

The officers of the village organizations, who performed the main task in spreading information to the oral reception group, all occupied modern roles such as head of the party organization, mayor, physician, agronomist, or member of the cooperative board. They were locally elected officers and government officials, some native to the village and others outsiders. These people were, on the whole, young, they were the most educated in the community, and they had obtained their posts on the basis of merit or political competition in elections. Most of the elected officers were very small cultivators; a few were salaried individuals and agricultural laborers. Traditional roles as such had little relevance in disseminating political information in the community.

In view of the diversified functions of village organizations, the information and ideas they passed on to others also tended to be specialized.[20] On socialist ideology, for instance, party officers of the ASU were the major opinion leaders, on savings policy the cooperative societies assumed a more prominent information role, and on family planning the physician and nurses (officials of the village council) played the leading role. On no single policy item, however, was one organization or individual found to be playing an exclusive role.

The role of opinion leaders in Shubra was purposeful, not casual or informal. A physician who informed villagers about family planning was acting within the framework of his official duty, and the same may be said of the ASU officer who explained why it is important to comply with family planning or who lectured on socialist ideas. To pass on information and

20. In a survey conducted in rural Turkey on attitudes toward family planning, specialization of opinion leaders was also noted: "professional sources and authoritative mass media channels are rated as much more influential on family planning than are local religious or political leaders"; see Stycos, "The Potential Role . . . ," pp. 128–129. Lerner wrote in "Communication Systems and Social Systems: A Statistical Exploration in History and Policy," reprinted in Jason L. Finkel and Richard W. Gable (eds.), *Political Development and Social Change* (New York: John Wiley, 1966), p. 196, that in "the model type . . . messages usually emanate from sources authorized to speak by their place in the social hierarchy, i.e., by status rather than skill criteria." The emphasis on social status has not been supported by the facts in this study, and the separation between skill and position of news mediators does not seem to take into account modernizing rural communities where skill determines position.

influence others' opinions and attitudes was part of his formal or perceived role in the community. Spreading information orally on national policy in Shubra was thus a functional activity, organized rather than haphazard.

No data from Shubra are available that would allow a direct comparison between the dissemination of policy news and the diffusion of other kinds of information such as the death of a head of state, victory of a national soccer team, or a scandal involving a known public figure. Fortunately, however, there is a study of how news of such events spreads in six villages of the Delta,[21] which gives at least an indication of the difference according to item in the oral transmission of news. Thirty-six hours after Radio Cairo announced the death of the King of Morocco, a team of interviewers queried 272 heads of households to find out how they had learned the news. A little more than one-third of the respondents[22] in the six villages heard of the King's death through the oral reports of relatives and friends.[23] In contrast, news of policy was orally conveyed in Shubra by officers of village organizations, not relatives and friends. This may suggest that, in rural Egypt, oral transmission of nonfunctional information occurs casually and without purpose, while functional information is disseminated by specialized agents in charge of local organizations.

In the absence of comparative data it is difficult to assess the role of mediators of information in Shubra. It is true that they reach fewer people than do the mass media, yet the fact that they are first to transmit information to 37 percent of the adult males is by no means a modest performance. In their various roles as political, cooperative, and administrative leaders, these men are in direct contact with the majority of villagers; even if they are not first to inform villagers about family planning or savings, they are the ones who explain and administer these policies.

It is possible to maintain on the basis of observation that, despite the independence of most villagers in obtaining information, opinion leaders played an important role in sustaining and relating mass media messages. Because they were more informed than ordinary villagers and by virtue of their official duties in local organizations, opinion leaders have played the role of interpreting policies and ideas to villagers in an effort to mobilize them. Although a cultivator first may hear about collective marketing or a savings policy through the mass media, it is the cooperative leaders who administer these policies for him. Similarly, ideas about Arab socialism bear relevance to the activities of the ASU branch in the community. In other words, institutional bases founded in the village provide an anchor

21. Ibrahim Abu-Lughod, "The Mass Media and Egyptian Village Life," *Social Forces*.
22. Ibid., p. 99.
23. Ibid., p. 103.

for messages transmitted on the airwaves. Local organizations have given concrete meaning and relevance to many ideas and policies originating at the national center. Indeed, some national ideas have been understood locally in terms of how they have been manifested in the village, not in their intellectual form (see chapter 10).

Mass Media Exposure and Political Awareness

The fact that the mass media reach more of the public directly in Shubra raises the further question of their political effects on those who come in contact with their messages. Does exposure to the mass media make a villager more informed politically? There are some commonsense reasons to question the extent to which the mass media can affect the political knowledge of a villager. First, the language used in the media is mostly literary, whereas the majority of villagers are illiterate and use the vernacular. In the second place, not all villagers are sensitized to politics; only 33 percent mention the news as one of their favorite programs. Entertainment programs rank first in order of preference among the villagers in Shubra; news and political events rank third. It cannot be assumed that mere exposure to a mass medium is an adequate indicator either of exposure to political news or of an understanding of the program transmitted.

In order to determine whether or not exposure to the mass media is associated with political knowledge, indices for degrees of mass media exposure and political awareness were constructed. These indices also provide a means of comparison between the mass media and personal mediators as effective sources of information. Exposure to the mass media was conceived in terms of frequency of contact with any one or all three of the media available in the village. Thus if a respondent reported that he daily read the newspaper, watched television, and listened to the radio at home, he received a weighted score. The individual scores for each medium were then averaged, and a mean score was assigned to each respondent. Notice that the index of mass media exposure does not take into account the individual's choices of programs, and thus it should be considered an index of general media exposure, not of exposure to the news only.

The political awareness index is based on weighted scores assigned to each survey respondent on seven questions relating to national and international affairs.[24] It takes into account both the respondent's recogni-

---

24. The seven questions on which the index is based are knowledge of the Five Year Plan, savings policy, family planning, socialism, the name of the prime minister, the names of four

tion of an issue and, in certain cases, the correctness of his understanding of an issue.

The Shubra survey reveals a positive correlation between mass media exposure and political awareness ($r = .53$);[25] 28 percent (r^2) of the variation in information gained by villagers was associated with their exposure to the mass media. For a closer look at this point, data on mass media exposure and political awareness have been cross-tabulated. Frequencies shown in table 23 tend to cluster along the diagonal line, that is, the greater the mass media exposure the higher the awareness score and vice versa.[26]

Furthermore, those who possessed a radio at home, an indication of greater exposure, were found to be more sensitized to political information than those who did not. Conversely, 40 percent of all radio owners regard the news as a favorite program, compared with only 23 percent of nonowners. Among these who considered the news as one of their favorite programs, 75 percent had radio sets at home. Since private ownership of mass media receptors has also been found to correlate positively with political awareness (see table 24), we may conclude that the mass media in rural Egypt contribute to politicization of villagers.

Are the mass media more effective or less so than opinion leaders as channels for passing on political information and ideas? Analysis has shown that the mass media group was better informed politically than the oral reception group and also more literate. Table 24 compares mean awareness scores of all respondents whose source of information was the mass media with those who received their information through mediators. As can be clearly seen, political awareness scores of the mass media group were significantly higher than those of the oral reception group. Since no significant difference was found in the travel experience of the two groups,[27] exposure to the mass media rather than physical mobility explains the higher level of political awareness.

As to other background differences between the two groups of respondents, only literacy was found significant;[28] occupation accounted

---

socialist countries, and the names of four "reactionary" Arab states. The last category was clearly defined by the Nasser regime; awareness of it was indicative of the respondent's knowledge of his nation's attitude toward other nations.

25. Significant beyond the .001 level.

26. Scores for High, Medium, and Low are, respectively, 67–100, 34–66.9, and 0–33.9.

27. Almost everyone has traveled to Damanhur. It was found that 58 percent of the mass media group and 55 percent of the oral reception group have traveled to Cairo or Alexandria, or to both. Difference of percentage test is insignificant ($Z = .244$).

28. Chi-square test shows significance beyond the .05 level.

Table 23
Relation of Mass Media Exposure to Political Awareness

		High	Medium	Low	Total
Political Awareness	High	15	9	0	24
	Medium	22	29	11	62
	Low	4	16	29	49
	Total	41	54	40	135

Mass Media Exposure

$X^2 = 42.58$, $p < .001$ (critical value 18.47). The incidence of a zero cell (upper right) may raise questions regarding the computation of chi-square. However, with 2 or more degrees of freedom, this is admissible. See Helen M. Walker and Joseph Lev, *Statistical Inference* (N.Y.: Holt, Rinehart and Winston, 1953), p. 107.

Table 24
Level of Political Awareness for Mass Media and Oral Reception Groups

	Source of Information				
	Mass Media		Opinion Leaders		
	Mean	Standard Deviation	Mean	Standard Deviation	Difference of Means Test (t)
Mean Scores for Knowledge of Provincial Affairs	60	21	51	23	2.11*
Mean Scores for Knowledge of National and International Affairs	57	20	42	22	2.48*

* $p < .05$.

Table 25
Political Awareness of Illiterates (by Radio Ownership Status)

Radio Status of Illiterates	Mean Score for Mass Media Exposure	Mean Score for Provincial Awareness	Mean Score for National and International Awareness
Owner	55	48	45
Nonowner	36	42	34
Difference of Means			
Test (t)	3.56	.92	2.20
Significance Level (p)	.001	N.S.	.05

for some difference in awareness but not at a statistically significant level.[29] Control for literacy has revealed that mass media exposure accounted for a higher level of political awareness even in the absence of literacy (see table 25). Illiterate radio owners showed greater political awareness than did illiterate nonowners.[30]

In conclusion, the mass media again were found to be a more effective channel for disseminating political information than were opinion leaders in Shubra. Since both agents represented an authoritative source—the national government—the notion that the radio is an authoritative source of disseminating information does not by itself explain very much. In view of the higher level of literacy of the media group, it is reasonable to conclude that opinion leaders in Shubra transmitted information to the less-educated section of the population and to those who did not have much access to the mass media. Thus an unplanned division of labor between opinion leaders and the mass media seems to have developed in Shubra.

The effectiveness of the mass media as instruments of communication even in a rural setting weakens the claim that mass media messages are generally unintelligible to the majority of people in developing countries. These data also throw doubt on the notion that opinion leaders are more effective disseminators of information than the mass media.

---

29. The chi-square test did not show that occupation and reception of the news are significant.

30. In view of the demonstrably greater impact of the radio on villagers, Lerner's emphasis on literacy as a pivotal variable in the modernization of an individual's social orientation becomes insufficient. See Lerner, "Communication Systems and Social Systems," in Finkel and Gable, pp. 202–203. Levels of education, it may be suggested, should be taken into account in Lerner's theory of communications.

The positive relationship between mass media exposure and political awareness becomes clearer still when the data are broken down in terms of age, mode of reception, and occupation. Correlation between exposure and awareness is slightly higher among the younger set ($r = .54$) than among those respondents who were 41 years of age and over ($r = .50$). It is also higher among those who had private ownership of a radio or newspaper, .38, compared with .29 for those who were exposed to the media in public locations such as the marketplace.

For occupational differences, the mean may be a more reliable indicator of association than the product-moment correlation because of the small number of cases in three out of the four occupational categories. The more informed respondents were again found to be more exposed to the media among all occupational groups; the single exception was agricultural wage laborers, who showed a slightly lower exposure mean than cultivators but a relatively higher awareness mean. This last may be explained by the fact that a larger number in this group than among cultivators were young and read the newspaper, which is generally considered a more informative medium politically than radio or television.[31] The latter two media, especially television, are particularly noted for their entertainment programs.

The wage laborer group deserves further attention in this context. The group consisted of 28 respondents, or 21 percent of the sample, and ranked as the lowest-paid stratum of village society. However, the low social and economic status of this group seems to have had hardly any effect on their level of political information, a result that probably can be explained in terms of their relative youth and literacy. Since schools in Shubra have been a phenomenon of the last two decades, youth and literacy have a higher association among laborers than in the sample in general. Young agricultural laborers under 40 years of age in Shubra outnumber older ones by a ratio of 4 to 1, whereas in the total sample the age ratio is only 2 to 1. As for literacy, 46 percent of laborers were literate, and 36 percent of them read newspapers, compared with 24 percent readers among cultivators.

Comparative data on mass media exposure and political awareness are scarce. Two recent articles, however, offer measures comparable to that of the Shubra survey. In a study of five Colombian villages, Everett Rogers[32]

---

31. For complex reasons that need not be presented here, the exposure index assigns equal weight to each of the three media and thus does not reflect the educational difference in favor of the press.

32. Everett M. Rogers, "Mass Media Exposure and Modernization Among Colombian Peasants," *Public Opinion Quarterly* 29 (Winter 1965–66), p. 61. In "Socialization to National Identification Among Turkish Peasants," *The Journal of Politics* 30 (November 1968), p. 951, Frederick W. Frey confirms the positive association between exposure to the mass media and awareness but provides no specific value for the association.

noted a high correlation between exposure to the mass media and level of political awareness, ranging from a high of 0.74 in the most advanced community to a low of 0.37 for the least advanced. But in another such test in Quito, Ecuador, McLeod and his associates[33] found a low correlation, 0.24, between mass media exposure and political awareness. This finding has led the authors to conclude that there is "no clear and unequivocal confirmation of the hypothesis that mass media exposure leads to greater political knowledge." [34]

These comparative data are drawn from independent studies, and the problem of equivalent research instruments tends to complicate the picture. For instance, McCleod observed a high correlation between possession of media at home and political knowledge ($r = .58$), which is much higher than the correlation obtained from the total media exposure index ($r = .24$).[35] This difference obviously suggests that the greater the access to the mass media, the higher is the level of political awareness, a generalization confirmed in the Shubra study.[36]

Conclusion

The Shubra survey has shown that mass media messages reach the majority of the public directly and effectively. Opinion leaders serve as mediators of information and ideas to a smaller group of the public, mostly those who have less access to the mass media. The mediators of information and ideas in Shubra are also modern agents who represent local official and semi-official organizations. Information on public policy in Shubra is transmitted as a specialized and functional activity, not casually or without purpose. Finally, this study indicates a significant correlation between exposure to the mass media and political awareness.

These findings obviously do not confirm the role attributed to oral dissemination of information by the authors of the two-step flow of communications hypothesis; neither do they deny that mediators continue to play a role in passing information and ideas to some sections of the population. On the other hand, the Shubra, Quito, and Colombian village studies confirm a positive but not commanding relationship between the

33. Jack M. McLeod et al., "The Mass Media and Political Information in Quito, Ecuador," *Public Opinion Quarterly* 32 (Winter 1968–69), p. 583.
34. Ibid., p. 585.
35. Ibid., pp. 582, 583, 578.
36. It also suggests that the index of mass media exposure in the Quito study was too general (see McLeod et al., p. 578); otherwise the association identified for those who possessed media at home would not have been so different (difference is significant beyond the .01 level).

mass media and political knowledge, an observation that does not justify the ebullient faith in the effects of the mass media expressed in such works as Lerner's *The Passing of Traditional Society*.[37] Comparative data on the subject are still limited, however, and more needs to be done before broadly applicable generalizations about mass communications can be made.

Modernization involves more than communication of information and new ideas, and in Shubra the communications revolution was subsequent to an economic and political revolution. For a villager to be able to make decisions consistent with his welfare and development, conducive political and economic conditions should prevail. In Shubra, such change included the redistribution of economic resources, the creation of facilities that channeled the new economic possibilities for villagers, and change in political power distribution in a way that precluded the monopoly of economic resources by political means. Cultural change and its main vehicle, mass communications, so often stressed by some writers[38] as the dominant forces and features of modernization, have in Shubra been concomitants of other processes of change that facilitated transition and contributed to its consolidation. The cultural aspect of political change in Shubra is the topic of the following three chapters.

---

37. See particularly pages 52–54.
38. Lucian W. Pye, *Politics, Personality, and Nation-Building*, and *Aspects of Political Development* (Boston: Little, Brown, 1966); Everett M. Rogers, *Modernization Among Peasants: The Impact of Communication* (New York: Holt, Rinehart and Winston, 1969); Lerner, *The Passing of Traditional Society*.

chapter 10

Formal political ideology and the village response

"They have changed their masters,
their religion, their language and their crops,
but not their way of life."
Father Ayrout

"We used to tell ourselves, submit to this man
obey him . . . we no longer do this."
A peasant from Shubra

The mass media in Shubra el Gedida has not only provided entertainment for hardworking villagers but also has exposed them to ideological messages produced and disseminated by a national elite. The ideology of the present regime includes ideas that are new to village culture and its way of life, and their assimilation requires a special effort on the part of villagers. The preceding two chapters examined the ways in which ideological messages reach villagers and affect their political awareness. Here, the focus is on the contents of the messages and how villagers understand them.

National Ideology in Contemporary Egypt

National ideology incorporates ideas enunciated and articulated by the elite in government, primarily ideas advanced by Nasser himself, who first wrote *The Philosophy of the Revolution* in 1954 and then *The National Charter* in 1962. Nasser's speeches and the *Charter* constituted the main official ideology when the survey was conducted in 1967. The *Charter*, which he delivered to the National Congress of Popular Forces in response to the Syrian secession, provides a set of principles that justify the series of socialist and other reform measures taken by his regime, particularly since 1958. The *Charter* has also laid down the guidelines for the policy, doctrine, and intellectual position of the regime toward other ideologies and nations.

The principles of the *Charter* have been considered binding on all individuals in the ASU and others in the service of the regime, but in a manner that would never put anyone seriously to the test. Conformity to official ideology has been a mild demand easily satisfied by ritual performance; unbelieving bureaucrats, sipping coffee in government offices, use slogans from the *Charter* to impress bored superiors with their loyalty. The regime has, however, rigorously promoted the *Charter* through the mass media and widespread political education programs. Intellectuals whose vocation is the dissemination of ideas have been put under exacting demands to profess faith in the official doctrines. Any advocacy of a competing ideology would bring severe sanctions against the offender. A relative degree of ideological diversity can exist within the framework of the official ideology, but mild public dissent is tolerated only if presented in line with the spirit of the *Charter* and embellished with quotations. One of the Nasser regime's cultural "commissars" summed up the role of the *Charter* as the official ideological guideline:

> In my opinion, the *Charter* defines a number of issues and intellectual positions. If we cease to take it as the foundation of our ideology, then we would be taking a course leading us away from basic agreements to basic disagreements. Take for instance scientific socialism; it constitutes the principle that defines the minimum basis of agreement binding on everybody. Points that have not, on the other hand, been covered by the *Charter* are not similarly binding on everyone. I may hold a point of view on matters not taken up in the *Charter*, but it should not be inconsistent with its principles. In such a case, my ideas would not be harmful. Any differences in interpretation may be a subject for consideration and debate, but the *Charter* is the foundation. This point must be absolutely clear and decisive.

What are the principles of the *Charter* that have such a decisive power in setting ideological differences? In this introductory resume, only the salient principles of the *Charter* are discussed.

Arab nationalism and Arab socialism are the two main doctrines of the *Charter*. Arab nationalism had already been developed as a theme and practiced as a political arrangement in the union with Syria since 1958. Until the Syrian secession of 1961, Nasser's view of Arab nationalism was similar to the doctrine preached east of the Mediterranean, based on political unity among the Arab states in the form of a merger. Reluctant to admit defeat after the failure of this experiment, Nasser reasserted his faith in Arab nationalism and sought to retain his popularity in the Arab world. He embarked on a new Arab adventure in the Yemen that inflated the sagging posture of his Arab policy after the Syrian debacle. Unlike the eastern Arab countries, where nationalism has been an agonizing confirmation of cultural and political identity against "insidious" doubts from local nationalism, Arab nationalism as defined in the *Charter* was a confirmation of membership in the family of Arab states with no commitment to political unification. Nasser rationalized this position by stating that liberation comes before unification and that it is first the responsibility of each Arab state to free itself from reactionary forces.

Most of the *Charter* is devoted to the doctrine of "Arab socialism," that is, the version of socialist doctrine that the regime in Egypt has practiced over the last few years. It is a doctrine that regulates economic relations in such a way as to make it possible for society to enjoy a fair distribution of wealth and decent economic standards for everyone (*kifayah wa 'adl*). Socialism stands for the economic and social freedom of the individual, just as democracy stands for political freedom. Democracy, it is maintained, cannot prevail where economic security for the individual does not exist. Nationalization of the means of production is the major step in the realization of a socialist system; however, the *Charter* recognizes private ownership—on a small scale—of land and of businesses such as manufacturing, crafts, retail trade, and contracting. The economy, it is argued, consists of two sectors—public and private—but the latter is subordinate and should be responsive to the imperatives of the public sector.

The *Charter* also deals with class conflict as a major phenomenon of Egyptian social history. It argues that class conflict was inevitable in a society with a capitalist past such as Egypt's, but it favors a gradual resolution of class differences. In the pre-Revolutionary period, "feudalists" and capitalists extracted most of the wealth of the country while the masses toiled under exploitative conditions. The Revolution liquidated the economic and political roles of the "feudalists" and capitalists, allowing them to live on a relatively equal basis with others in society. Having abolished extreme inequality, Egypt has become a society of "working forces" (*qiwa 'amilah*), whereas during the past most people worked for the benefit of a few "nonproductive" elements in society. The working forces, however, are not an entirely homogeneous group but are composed of peasants, workers, soldiers, intellectuals, and native capitalists. ("Native capitalist" refers to all self-employed individuals who are not cultivators and to occupational categories ranging from shopkeepers to manufacturers and merchants. It may be added here that merchants were limited to domestic trade, and only small manufacturing industries were left in private hands.)

Social differences and struggle, it is maintained, will continue under socialism, but as a healthy phenomenon, without violence or political dissension. It is obvious, however, that, of all the working forces, the regime has considered peasants and workers, who are the most populous and most deprived, as the vanguard of the Revolution. Eventually, Nasser maintained in the *Charter*, differences among working forces would disappear in the socialist society of Egypt; however, he fell short of committing himself to the idea of a classless utopian society.

The Arab Socialist Union is considered the proper organizational channel through which working forces may compete politically. In socialist Egypt, the masses are united in one movement with one purpose; whatever differences exist among the masses can be resolved by constructive cooperation and legitimate competition within the framework of the national movement, the ASU. (It may be noted in passing here that the idea of the working forces' collaborating politically in one movement against imperialism and exploitation reflects the influence of the congress of eighty-one Communist parties who met in Moscow in 1960. At that time, the *Manifesto of 81* declared that a "national front" should be formed "of the working class, peasantry, intellectuals and the petty and middle urban bourgeoisie" to work for national independence and combat imperialism.)[1]

Many other topics are discussed in the *Charter*, but only those specific to this study are discussed here. First, a deep commitment is expressed toward revealed religion and toward freedom of religious belief and practice. Nasser leaves no doubt of his own faith in Islam, making it quite clear that the principles of the *Charter* are consistent with the Koran and adding that the principles of socialist justice constitute one of the main tenets of Islamic religion.

Science and technology are viewed as the *sine qua non* for establishing an industrialized and progressive society. As in most developing societies, faith in industrialization is unbound and is considered the main course toward national development.

The *Charter* inspires a spirit of political and social activism. It condemns objectionable aspects of the past and advocates socialist justice and belief in science and technology. It condemns inactivism, resignation, and isolationism. Political action should be rational, inspired by the ideology of Arab socialism and consistent with national planning and technological development. Work is considered a social value of the highest order, as illustrated by the slogan "work is honor." In contrast to the high value

1. George Lenczowski, *Soviet Advances in the Middle East* (Washington, D.C.: American Enterprise Institute, 1972), p. 16.

attached to social status in the old regime, work is ranked at the top of the hierarchy of values.

The *Charter* is an informative document on the guidelines for political action and organization in Egypt, but it is not an original contribution to socialist doctrine or Arab nationalist thought, as Nadav Safran pointed out when he examined the *Charter* in the light of a century of Egyptian intellectual development.[2] Any claim to distinction for the *Charter* as a political document should go not to its ideas per se but to the skill exhibited by Nasser in constructing a formula that cuts the middle ground and serves as an acceptable guideline consistent with the basic interests of the five different working-force groups designated in Egyptian society. The *Charter* offers something for each one of these groups without quite antagonizing the others. It succeeds in presenting a progressive outlook and serves as a common ideology for the various segments of Egyptian society. Its success is perhaps best exemplified by its appeal to intellectuals of right and left. It has also served as a basis of agreement among leftist intellectuals—the most vigorous, articulate, and divided group in Egyptian life—including Communists, who have found in the *Charter* the right step in the inevitable historical march toward the victory of socialism. On the opposite side of the political spectrum, native capitalists and cultivators have found the *Charter*'s recognition of private property rights reassuring.

The search for national unity within a framework of political radicalism inevitably leads to ideological eclecticism such as Nasser's philosophy. Nasser was not alone among leaders of developing nations to follow a course designed to reconcile different social groups in society. The following statement of Sukarno could have been made by Nasser himself:

> I am a follower of Karl Marx, but, on the other hand, I am also a religious man, so I can grasp the entire gamut between Marxism and theism . . . I know all the trends and understand them . . . I have made myself the meeting place of all trends and ideologies. I have blended, blended, and blended them until finally they became the present Sukarno.[3]

The Impact of National Ideology on the Local Community

The communication revolution that has overtaken Shubra el Gedida in the last decade served as one of the main nexuses between the nation and the

---

2. Paper delivered at a conference on Egypt, the School of Oriental and African Studies, University of London, 1965.

3. Quoted by Clifford Geertz, *Islam Observed: Religious Development in Morocco and Indonesia* (New Haven: Yale University Press, 1968), p. 85.

local community. Local leaders of the ASU have been responsible for organizing a political education program aimed primarily at training individuals who occupy positions of responsibility in the community and those who were considered prospects for occupying such positions in the future.

The number of people who went through the political education program in the so-called Socialist Institute of Shubra is not very large, 9 percent of the adult males, among whom only the top leaders had further training at socialist institutes in Damanhur or at other national centers. Those who had extra training were leaders of the ASU and the Youth Organization, and members of the cooperative boards. When political and ideological awareness in the village was surveyed in May 1967, the formal political education program was still in its infancy and had only reached the most politically active in the community. Thus a true test of the results of this program cannot be found in the sample survey, but rather in the interviews of the Select, most of whom had received political training courses. The sample survey constitutes a test of political awareness in the village at large and should be considered the cumulative effect of more than a decade of participation and exposure to the mass media.

Understanding of socialist ideas is a major indicator of local response to national ideology. In an open-ended question on the meaning of socialism, villagers were allowed to express for themselves what they understood socialism to be. Their responses indicate a complex array of ideas (see table 26) markedly different from those of the Select (see table 27).

The strong feeling that socialism fosters a community of people sharing similar interests and problems is reflected in the respondents' most frequent statements that socialism means unity of the people. An underlying sense of the phrase "unity of the people" is equality and the disappearance of social differences on the basis of status. In the words of one of them, socialism means that "we are one group, and [act together as if we have] one hand. We eat from the same loaf of bread, with no ones who are haughty and others humble. . . . It is like a peasant's lunch in the field, we all dip in the same pot." Another responded by saying, "I mean there are no [social] differences as in the past." The leveling effect of national policies since 1952, whereby villagers have been treated on a relatively equal basis, has come to mean socialism to them.

The regime's ideas on class struggle and exploitation also were understood in relation to particular experiences of the community itself. Exploitation was indeed keenly felt in Shubra; it was not, however, associated with social classes but rather with a type of individual, specifically the merchant middleman. Curiously enough, villagers' re-

Formal political ideology and the village response 171

Table 26
Villagers' Definitions of Arab Socialism

Category	Number	Percentage
Unity and cooperation with one another	38	28
Equality	24	18
Participation in public affairs	22	16
Sufficiency and justice	16	12
Abolishing class differences and exploitation	11	8
Reforms to improve general conditions of people	8	6
National independence or rule of the people	6	4
Cooperation among nations	6	4
Negative responses: additional financial impositions	2	2
Does not know	11	8
No answer	24	18

N = 135. Maximum number of responses per item should not exceed 135.

sponses did not indicate that the "feudalists," debased in official ideology, were the exploiters. No responses condemning landlords appeared in the survey. A very large majority of respondents stated strongly that the cooperative system freed them from exploitation by the merchant middleman (see table 28, chapter 11). The merchant belongs to an occupation that, to use a respondent's words, "is by nature exploitative."

Most striking is the absence of a sense of class solidarity among the large group of agricultural laborers; however, evidence of class consciousness exists among the smaller number of nonagricultural workers such as tractor drivers and mechanics in the two cooperative societies. Thus some class consciousness no doubt exists in Shubra, as can be inferred from such frequent references as "the big people," or "the poor folks."

Despite the sense of social differentiation from which each social group in the village views the other, I had the impression that class struggle and hostility were not part of the villagers' social behavior. This impression is borne out by the fact that only 8 percent of the sample respondents identified socialism with class differences. When the text of their statements were checked, they were found not to be charged with resentment, in contrast to statements regarding merchant middlemen. The villager, it seemed, wanted to have a fair deal and improve his lot, but he did not nurse a grudge against landlords or the urban rich; nor did he conceive of his welfare as relative to the deprivations of others. I do not remember a single reference made by an ordinary peasant regarding lowering the ceiling on landownership below 100 feddans. In 1967, no single landowner in Shubra possessed more than 50 feddans, yet 50 feddans is a large amount of land in a village where more than 21 percent of adult males are still landless agricultural laborers. The lack of agitation on this matter may be due to the fact that most of the large landowners in 1967 lived in the village and were considered part of the community rather than outsiders. Of these, only Kamil Samad had been a middleman, and, though villagers made disapproving statements about Kamil's past exploitative behavior, none expressed disapproval of the Kuras, who in 1967 were the largest landowners in the village. That the Revolution has spared the villagers from the *'umdah*, his brother Kamil, and the royal family may indeed have taken the bitterness out of local social relations. No one seemed to think that the wealthy in Shubra were responsible for his poor lot in life; rather, there was a clear idea in the village that one's condition continues to be poor because of the limited resources of the country and the population pressure on the land (see chapter 11).

In short, the villagers' perception of "class" is different from the common usage of the term. In their eyes, the world consists of rural people and undifferentiated "others." They did not entertain the idea of a group of people who have a conscious feeling of solidarity on the basis of their similar occupation or economic condition and whose interest is basically in conflict with other classes in society.

The dissemination of socialist ideas in Shubra has resulted in a version of socialism that can be characterized as rural socialism—a view that emphasizes equality and community rather than nationalization or class struggle. The concepts of equality and community are not, of course, unrelated to the idea of class differences, for only those who share similar life conditions, that is, equals, could really be part of one and the same community.

Nationalization of industry is not only a concept difficult for the villager to understand, but it is also remote from his economic and social situation. As already observed, mass media messages that were not immediate to life conditions of the peasant were not often noticed. As for making agricultural land public property, the idea was neither preached as part of the regime's philosophy nor did peasants seem sympathetic to it. The peasant in Shubra is interested above all in becoming a landowner, a feeling shared with peasants elsewhere in the world. Because of the scarcity of land, however, should the idea of communal property appear in Shubra, I would doubt that a strong resistance to it would emerge, except perhaps from those whose property exceeds two feddans.

Rural socialism is egalitarian in orientation; collective ownership or state capitalism are not part of its dimensions. The state, it is true, advocated an egalitarian ideal and implemented policies that narrowed the gap between the rich and the poor, but absolute equality in income has been neither officially advocated nor locally demanded. Shubra seems quite content with relative equality, and shows more concern over the ability of the state to continue to find better opportunities for the coming generations.

The most important dimension of rural socialism, the principle of community, is also distinguished by its local rather than national definition. Social or economic barriers no longer divide the village population into exclusive groups based on special privileges. Expressed most often as "unity and cooperation," the term "community" is not a vague expression used to ward off the probing of a stranger, nor is it alien to the doctrine of Arab socialism. Unity of all the people of Egypt as an expression of national solidarity is, of course, a highly sought objective of the regime. There is, however, an overriding local dimension to this term as it has been used by respondents that is not quite the same as that connoted in the *Charter*.

As it is understood in Shubra, "community" means active membership in the village, not formally or ecologically but through political participation and responsibility for public affairs. For example, a cultivator, explaining what he understood by socialism, said, "Everyone is now involved in the affairs of everyone else. . . . This is socialism." Another respondent said, "People now deal with one another. I mean we are free." It is not easy to understand these statements without appreciating their implied reference to the former stringent control of the headman and the Prince's steward, to a past when recourse to the national government for protection from local authoritarianism was absent. Without free political participation and public responsibility, no community existed and the individual stood alone to face the headman or the steward. Now, under socialism, every man has had a chance to vote or compete for public office and by such participation affect other villagers; he has come to think of himself as a free agent, free to be socially and politically involved. "Everyone is now involved in the affairs of everyone else" and "No one of us can afford any longer to ignore the other's lot" are perfect expressions of the community of fate and the sense of interdependence and unity.

These ideas are expressions of the villagers' own reading of the community history under the Revolution put in their own words, not in the formal language of the literati. In effect, the language of the rustic is not after all too different in substance from that of the national ideologues, for when Nasser wrote or spoke about political democracy as contingent on the existence of economic democracy, he expressed the idea of equality and community that the peasant has come to understand so well and so realistically. Much of the official language, however, remained intact among the Select. Their definitions of socialism (see table 27) were not only more national in orientation but also closer to the formal definition of socialism as expressed in the *Charter*. When asked to define socialism, the most common response (48 percent) was the official slogan "sufficiency and justice," that is, sufficient production and fair distribution of resources. In comparison, only 8 percent [4] of the sample respondents used the official slogan to define socialism.

Repeating long-standing socialist slogans like "To each according to his needs and ability" also distinguishes the Select from ordinary citizens, who were not familiar with such ideas. Similarly, the idea of exploitation as articulated by many of the Select reflects more accurately the national rather than local sense of the term. The leaders used it to impart the idea that capitalists take advantage of laborers. As one of them put it in words borrowed from the *Charter*, "Socialism means sufficiency in production and justice in allocations. Also, it means putting an end to exploitation by capitalists and giving every man an opportunity to work." Another respondent added that under socialism "man does not exploit man." Again, the Select are more sensitive to class differences because they take the national scene and ideas wholly within their purview. The Select come closest to ordinary villagers when they describe socialism in terms of equality.

Another contrast between the two groups is that the Select, unlike sample respondents, were all able to define socialism. It is noteworthy that in the much-celebrated socialist Egypt, 26 percent of ordinary villagers in Shubra were unable to identify or give meaning to the term. This uninformed group is mostly illiterate (74 percent) and rarely exposed to the mass media; the mean score for mass media exposure for this group is 38 on a scale of 100. What is surprising, however, is that the majority are young people whose average age is 35, a curious finding that speaks strongly to the point that the isolation of the past era has left its mark on the mobilization system. In the past, as I was told in Shubra, some villagers lived and died without ever having left their home village, and some others had not even been to another quarter of the village. At present, however,

4. Table 26 shows that 12 percent used the slogan; in fact only 8 percent used it in its original form, and 4 percent used the idea of justice in one form or another. In coding, these responses were included under one heading.

Table 27
The Select's Definitions of Arab Socialism

Response	Number	Percentage
"Sufficiency and justice"	21	48
Equality: fair and equal opportunity	20	46
Abolishing class differences and exploitation	15	34
To each according to his needs and ability	13	30
Nationalism and democracy	11	25
Social teachings such as those in Islam	7	16
Land distribution	7	16
The cooperative system	6	14
Raising standards of living	3	7
Political participation and awareness	3	7
Better deal for labor	3	7
Other	3	7

N = 44

many may not be able to identify the term socialism but almost everyone has been outside the community or exposed to the mass media.

The concept of socialism has obviously been localized in Shubra, yet without being divested from meanings conveyed through national ideology. The emphasis villagers placed on ideas was clearly of a different order of importance and indicative of their selective perception. Socialism has been understood mainly in terms of the villager's own perception of social reform in his community, and he expressed this personal view in his colloquial language.

Most striking is the regime's lack of concern about the villagers' particularistic understanding of socialism. Indeed, it may even be suggested that the regime itself has fostered such a tendency by stressing equality and freedom from exploitation as the main ideas of socialism in its ideological pronouncements directed at the countryside. This course, however, is quite consistent with the eclectic and pragmatic approach of the regime, in which philosophy has been adapted to particular situations. Use of effective symbols in addition to emphasis on relevant ideas for each group is testimony of the regime's ideological skills. The regime had a vested interest in establishing a basis of common understanding with rural people that goes far beyond its desire for their compliance to its policies.

Villagers' Attitudes Toward Socialism

Ideology as a cognitive system has been stressed so far, and only by intimation have villagers' attitudes toward socialism been clarified. No clear evidence from the survey or from my observation indicates that they were not in favor of socialism. Only two respondents made unfavorable remarks to the effect that socialism means additional pecuniary impositions in the form of dues to the party branch. Among the privileged few, the Samad brothers and, to a lesser extent, some Kura family members showed open dislike for socialism. The most positive expressions of approval were made in response to questions on the cooperative system (see chapter 11).

Assessing the intensity of a villager's feelings about a public issue is difficult because Egyptian villagers have the tendency to shy away from expressions of emotions, to appear publicly agreeable, and to resort to extreme brevity in their expressions. In order to avoid getting meaningless compliments as responses, the attitudes of villagers toward socialism was elicited indirectly by asking if the respondent wished to see socialism spread to other countries. Assuming that one would not wish to see something he dislikes spread, a positive answer is interpreted as favorable toward socialism and a negative answer as unfavorable or indifferent.

The majority in Shubra turned out to be in favor of socialism; 52 percent of all respondents and 70 percent of those who knew what socialism meant wished to see it spread to other countries of the world. When asked where they would like to see socialism take hold, practically all of them mentioned Arab countries toward which, one may suppose, the villagers were well disposed. African countries were also mentioned. Textual evidence, too, in many of these cases indicates a favorable response. Many respondents, for example, commented that they wished to see "the good" prevail everywhere and wished to see the whole world go socialist. One said that he wished to see socialism obtain in Saudi Arabia, commenting that "maybe God will inspire Ibn Saʻud to do what is good for his country and turn to socialism."

Textual evidence, however, does not support the second part of the assumption, that is, that those who do not wish to see socialism obtain in other countries are not in favor of it. Those in this group who were able to define socialism, with one exception, used words that could not in any way be interpreted as unfavorable toward socialism. Lack of knowledge of rather than hostility toward socialism seems to explain their responses. About 70 percent in this group are illiterate; their mean score on knowledge of international affairs is 13 points below the general average. Furthermore, 23 percent were not able to say what socialism meant.

However, despite the fact that they are more unaware than unfriendly, their attitudes indicate indifference toward socialism and perhaps toward the rest of the world.

Arab Nationalism

As a concept of remote relevance to the daily lives of villagers, nationalism is not generally assumed to be an aspect of peasant life. Father Ayrout, who spent a lifetime working with Egyptian peasants, wrote that the peasant "is still not conscious of belonging to a nation." [5] Yet, in Shubra, the prevalence of the idea of Arab nationalism clearly demonstrates that villagers can give thought to issues of wider national and regional import. What is worth noting though, in this respect, is that of the many themes in the *Charter* the idea of Arab nationalism has been least subjected to particularization and reflects a remarkable conformity to the official version. Observers of contemporary Egyptian life, including this writer, are of the opinion that Arab nationalism has, perhaps for the first time in recent years, reached the common man.[6] The people of Shubra el Gedida leave no doubt of their awareness and interest in Arab political affairs.

To find out if respondents knew the relations of their government to the various Arab countries, two survey questions asked them to identify Arab countries that are still dominated by "reactionary regimes" and to identify a number of socialist countries. It should be remembered here that Egyptian propaganda has portrayed the countries with which Egypt had unfriendly relations as reactionary, including the Republic of Tunisia, whose political system is most like Egypt's. When asked what he learned at the village socialist institute, one respondent replied, "They talked to us about the Revolution, the *Charter*, and the countries that are good and those that are bad." The "good" and the "bad" were classified by the regime into the "progressive" and the "reactionary" camps, the former including Syria, Iraq, and Algeria (sometimes including the Yemen) and the latter including Saudi Arabia, Jordan, Tunisia, and others.

The majority responded with a surprising conformity to the official view, a finding that confirms the observation made above about the effectiveness of the mass media. Saudi Arabia, true to the official view, topped the list of reactionaries, followed in order by Jordan, Tunisia, and a number of other Arab and non-Arab countries. On the question of socialist countries, a similar conformity to official view was demonstrated. Countries identified as socialist by the majority of respondents were Egypt,

---

5. Ayrout, p. 109.
6. Hourani, *Arabic Thought;* Anis Sayigh, *al Fikrah al 'Arabiyah fi Misr* (Beirut: n.p., 1959).

Syria, Iraq, and Algeria. The fact that the people of Shubra have become conscious of Arab nationalism is reflected in their wish to see a progressive and socialist Arab world. As observed earlier, 48 percent expressed their wish to see socialism prevail in Arab countries, but rarely did they extend the same feeling to non-Arab countries.[7]

It is also striking that Arab nationalism was expressed as a sentiment rather than as a program in much the same way as in the *Charter*. No view or desire for Arab political unity, for instance, was expressed. Some of the village leaders, when discussing the subject informally, repeated the official line adopted since the secession of Syria that Arab unity is an ideal that would not be realized until each Arab state individually establishes a firm and stable socialist system. Similarly, they accepted without question the official line that the Syrian secession in 1961 was the act of reactionaries, not the wish of the Syrian people.

It is interesting to compare these findings on the villagers' awareness of the Arab world in Shubra with observations made in Egypt during earlier periods. An Arab journalist, living in Cairo in 1920, was dismayed by the lack of interest in Arab affairs. The initial response of the Egyptian press to the fall of Damascus to French troops in 1920 was limited to a brief cable, "Damascus has fallen to the French."[8] Of course, almost fifty years separate that event from the period in which the survey was taken, and official Egyptian interest in Arab matters did not start until the late 1930s and early 1940s. At present, however, Arab nationalism is the concern of the ordinary Egyptian, even in remote villages. In 1966, I observed elementary school children in villages in the province of Beni Suef, as well as in the Delta, identify the names of Arab states and leaders, the Arab League, the friends of the Arabs as well as their enemies. Much of this acculturation in Arab nationalism should be credited to the Nasser regime.

Religion and National Ideology

Observers of the Egyptian contemporary scene cannot fail to ponder the regime's attitude toward religion. Revolutionary changes have affected the political system, the economy, and the country's orientation, but religion went through no changes that had not already been in progress. There is a boundary that marks off the revolutionary from the traditional as visible as the line that separates the desert from the sown in the Nile Valley. Nowhere can this frontier line be seen as clearly as in the regime's attitudes toward women and toward religion.

7. The next category was African states, which received only 5 percent of the vote.
8. As'ad Daghir, *Mudhakirati 'ala Hamish al Qadiyah al 'Arabiyah* (Cairo: Dar al Qahira Lil-Tiba'ah, 1959), p. 10.

Formal political ideology and the village response

Why has the regime not adopted a revolutionary stance toward religion and the status of women in society? Revolutionary change in Egypt stems from and is guided by pragmatic considerations. The regime's eclectic ideology promoted the adoption of functional solutions to fundamental and pressing problems; ideas by themselves had no spell or force of their own among the leaders of modern Egypt. An ideological campaign against religion in the name of an abstract idea would only whittle away mass political support, not offer solutions to a practical problem facing the regime. An attack on Bank Misr, for example, is not the same as an attack on a religious norm, such as the divorce law. Tampering with the divorce law is a direct assault on Islamic religion, the body of sacred and cultural symbols to the majority of Egyptians.

Changing the status and conditions of women in Egypt can hardly be considered irrelevant to that country's problems, however, and one would expect the regime to do something to fundamentally change the inferior status of women. The point is, however, that the position of women as it was viewed by the new regime was not one of the urgent problems of the country. When Nasser came to power, there were already more men than there were jobs, more cultivators than land to cultivate, and more school-age children than schools. It was not, therefore, practical to give priority to liberating women and giving them a status equal with men. At best, the regime encouraged educated women to participate in national life[9] and did not discourage whatever initiative Egyptian women had already shown. In short, the situation of women at the time of the Revolution was not a high-priority issue arising from either developmental needs or public pressure.

Keeping in mind the preceding discussion of the principles that govern the adoption of a radical policy in Egypt, let us look at religion and the challenges of a rapidly changing community as they were manifested in Shubra.

Men of religion, *imams*, in Shubra have supported most secular changes in the community and acted to advance them. In most Islamic societies, established religion is subordinate to the political system, but, in Shubra, the *imams'* attitudes reflected more than official compliance; they have been influenced positively by the regime and its political ideology. The *imams* in Shubra did not differ much from the secular supporters of the regime in Egypt, and their rural or poor backgrounds, youth, and education undoubtedly affected their response to the leadership and philosophy of the Revolution.

9. The first woman minister in Egypt was appointed under the Nasser regime.

In 1967, there were five *imams* in Shubra, four of whom were graduates of al Azhar University in Cairo; the fifth received his education in a provincial religious institution. *Imams* are paid officials of the state, and Nasser put them on a pay scale almost equal to that of other civil servants of the same grades.[10] All but one resided in Shubra, although only two of them were natives of the village. Four of the five *imams* were in their early thirties, and the fifth was in his sixties.

The oldest *imam* in the village, Jalil al Shubrawi, was an active and enlightened individual who was descended from a learned religious family going back centuries in history. A graduate of al Azhar, he has served Shubra all his life. A thoughtful and mild person, he kept in close touch with the young *imams* in the village despite the age difference. He was one of the village's best liked individuals[11] and headed the arbitration committee of the village council.

Serving with Jalil al Shubrawi on the arbitration committee is the other native *imam*, Hadi Hammal. Born in 1934 into a poor family, he nevertheless managed to receive an *'alim*'s degree from al Azhar University and spent two additional years of study in the field of education. Like al Shubrawi, he appeals to many people in the village, who consider him enlightened and honest. He is active in politics and has close, friendly relations with young people of his generation as well as with Jalil al Shubrawi. In 1967, he was a member of the Leadership Group and was elected in the summer of 1968 to the Committee of Ten, which replaced the Leadership Group.

The Azharite *imams* of Shubra share, to a great extent, a common attitude toward the regime and its rural policies. With some individual differences, they all subscribe to Arab socialism. The three *imams* who are not native to Shubra, however, are less active in the political life of the village.

Hadi Hammal, one of the most active *imams*, is typical of the generation of *imams* in Shubra who came of age under the Revolution. Shaykh Hammal learned his first lessons in socialism while studying under Dr. Hilmi Murad, a secular lecturer at al Azhar. Dr. Murad was a well-known nationalist and progressive educator, who rose to the prestigious position of rector of the University of Cairo and who, in 1968, became Minister of Education. Shaykh Hammal took note of Dr. Murad's references to Marxism and consulted books at the national library, Dar al

10. On the subject of *imams* and mosques in Egypt, see Morroe Berger, *Islam in Egypt Today: Social and Political Aspects of Popular Religion* (New York: Cambridge University Press, 1970).
11. Survey results show him to be the fourth most liked person in the village.

Kutub, because they were not available at al Azhar. He was impressed by what he learned about economics and did not find it irreconcilable with the teachings of Islam; both Marxism and Islam, according to him, called for social justice.

Back in the village, Shaykh Hammal became active in the ASU and was one of the first persons chosen to attend Shubra's socialist institute. After completing the course, he was chosen to teach at the institute, where socialist ideas, achievements of the Revolution, and the Revolution's version of the modern history of Egypt were the subjects of his course. He did not refrain from drawing on the teachings of the Revolution in the sermons that he gave in the mosque, pointing to the Islamic character of socialist ideas and the regime's policies.

Shaykh Hammal's approach to family planning and savings illustrates the position of the socialist *imams* on these issues. In supporting family planning, the *imams* were in part acting in response to their own sense of urgency about the population explosion in Egypt but were also encouraged by officials of the Ministry of Awqaf and Religious Affairs to discuss the subject. They were quick to find religious justification for the policy of family planning, following in that path the leaders of the religious establishment. Shaykh Hammal was able to unearth from religious books some traditions of the Prophet that suggested the Prophet's consent to limiting the number of children in a family. Not only did he preach on the subject himself, but he also opened the mosque to the physician and the mayor to lecture on the same topic, a step not quite in accordance with mosque regulations. However, much of the political activities of the ASU in Shubra waived administrative regulations when, in the leaders' judgments, national interest called for that.

Shaykh Hammal followed the same practice with regard to the savings policy, an issue that differed from family planning in two ways: first, he was not required to provide religious justification for this policy, but acted out of his own interest as a leader in the ASU; second, it was not as easy to find a religious justification for savings as it was for family planning. In principle, the interest on savings and loans is clearly prohibited in Islam, and, despite the writings of Shaykh Mahmud Shaltut, a former rector of al Azhar University, in support of interest and banking, there was no noticeable conversion among religious authorities in Egypt to accept his point of view. At any rate, Shaykh Hammal found in the writings of Shaykh Shaltut the authority that he needed to advocate savings in his Friday sermon.

Shaykh Hammal used religious argument also to promote the ASU self-help projects in the village. Instead of giving away your offerings to the

Sufi order, he told the congregation, you can put them in a special account to use for public projects in the village. Using the money for village projects, he argued, is like fulfillment of the religious commandment of alms-giving (*zakat*). At that time, the ASU leaders had proposed the installation of electric lights in the main streets of the village. Shaykh Hammal told his congregation that the implementation of such a project would prevent accidents and harm from happening to others, and to prevent harm is to fulfill God's commandment. Using the same argument, he explained that savings contribute to the betterment of national conditions of life and developmental goals.

The active role that the *imams* played in advocating national policies is more important as an example of the manner in which religious men in Shubra responded to modernization than as an indicator of the effectiveness of *imams* in converting the public to government policies. The *imams* were among those in the community who led the modernization drive, but they were by no means the most prominent ones. To judge from survey results, as opinion leaders they reached fewer people than did their secular counterparts. The point here is to show how the religious element in the community sided with social change and progress rather than, as it is sometimes the case, dissociated itself from social activity or clung to outdated practices and views.

The overriding political aspects in the interpretation of Islam by the village *imams* may be viewed as another illustration of the subordination of religion to politics in Egypt. Be that as it may, it should also be understood that the *imams* were not only concerned with politics; they also sought, independently from government policy, to modernize religion. Indeed, they resisted some religious practices that were either tacitly recognized or tolerated by the government. The difference between the government's and Hadi Hammal's attitudes toward religion can be illustrated by their respective positions vis-à-vis the Sufi orders, who are still active in rural as well as in urban Egypt.

The regime did not seriously concern itself with the Sufi orders in Egypt, except perhaps to prevent subversive or hostile forces against the regime from taking refuge under the guise of religious fraternities. Indeed, rather than disavow Sufi orders and practices, the ASU maintained a friendly relation with them. A visitor to Sufi festivals would often see posters welcoming visitors in the name of the ASU. In Shubra, however, the ASU was indifferent to the local Sufi orders, neither interfering with nor encouraging them.

The only opposition to the local Sufi orders in Shubra came from the *imams* rather than from secular forces. Shaykh Hammal's religious training led him to oppose Sufi orders in favor of orthodoxy and a rational attitude toward religion. In 1967, there were two fraternities in Shubra, both of which belonged to a local order, *al Ibrahimiyah*.[12] On their saint's day, they organize a procession and carry colorful flags. Their festivals consist of Sufi exercises accompanied by music and religious chanting, and the Sufis also hold celebrations on occasions such as a birth of a child or in memory of the dead. Those who request special celebrations make offerings to the head of the order and its members, often by slaughtering a lamb or giving a feast. The Sufis do not, however, teach religious doctrine but rather adhere simply to performing religious rituals.

Shaykh Hammal clashed with the Shubra Sufi fraternities when he urged the people not to take part in the festivals or in the ritual exercises. He told the people that these practices were against Islamic teachings and explained the theological basis for his argument. Shocked, the villagers hostilely wondered why no one else had ever taught such teachings before. The leaders of the orders, all members of a single family, interpreted the *imam*'s move as a personal affront to them. Anyone who knows the principles of Islamic religion, however, also knows that Sufi practices in some respects depart from orthodox Islam, a concept not easily explained to villagers who, from time immemorial, practiced Sufi exercises as part of their religion. However, aside from the worship of the saints, which went against orthodox doctrine, the Sufi practices had over time been reduced to a ritual dance that brings on a state of exhaustion, allegedly a spiritual trance or elation. Many enlightened villagers felt that the Sufi dances were healthy diversions that gave young men spiritual and physical satisfaction in an environment lacking recreational opportunities. By attempting to stop the Sufi orders, Shaykh Hammal was acting, in the name of the rational tradition of the learned, against accepted traditional practices of Islam. He was not heeded. There was no official endorsement of the *imam*'s activities against the Sufi orders. Shaykh Hammal was obviously continuing the fight of the modernists to reform Islam and raise it to the challenges of the day.

By calling for reformed religious practices and also by responding to modernization policies, the *imams* of Shubra stand among the modern agents of change in village life. They can be considered as agents of change on several grounds. First, they sought to broaden the religious perspective of the faithful by advocating and teaching a rational approach to religion in line with the Muhammad 'Abduh's [13] enlightened approach, and, in so

12. In the summer of 1968, I witnessed the rise of a third Sufi order in the village, apparently one among several manifestations of religious revival in Egypt after the 1967 War.

13. Shaykh Muhammad 'Abduh, the greatest nineteenth-century reformer of Islam, was born in a hamlet within walking distance from Shubra.

doing, they opposed the Sufi orders as symbols and agents of socially unprogressive traditions and religiously heterodox practices. Second, they have supported secular policies initiated by the regime by bringing religious legitimacy to secular policy and by urging the public to respond positively. Finally, they personally became involved in the social-political activities of the community by accepting responsibility for the arbitration committee and by participating in the ASU programs. As implied earlier, the *imams* of Shubra differ from their stereotype image in Egyptian literature.[14]

The modernizing effect of religion in Egypt may be compared with that of Lebanon, where religion offered a bridge between traditional and modern life. In a study of political change in Mount Lebanon during the nineteenth century,[15] I found the Christian religion and clergy to be effective agents of political change. They helped to break up particularistic political ties and advance nationalist ideas to replace them. A study of immigrants from mountain villages to two suburbs of Beirut has shown that, once in their new environment, the immigrants broaden their political orientation and identification from primarily kinship ties to the broader religious community.[16] If it is granted that a departure in social and intellectual orientation from the particular toward the universal is a modernizing trend, then religion in Egypt and Lebanon has played a modernizing role.

Conclusion

Formal ideology in Egypt is more of a program for action than a coherent system of ideas. Through its policies, the Nasser regime sought to generate political cooperation and to provide a political explanation of its views and goals. Arab socialism was not, however, a list of policy directives; on the contrary, its perspectives provided balance between the ideal and the practical by relating peremptory policy directives to a value system shared by the rulers and the ruled. Political ideology has taken both the forms of a guideline and an article of faith. In other words, it may be viewed as a set of selective ideas on politics that are the objects of emotive attachments. Ideological statements are neither true nor false; they are strategies for action about which people feel partisan or resentful.

Within the framework of radical social reform, the regime balanced the

14. See, for instance, 'Abd al Rahman al Sharqawi, *al Ard*; and Taha Husayn, *al Ayyam*.
15. See *Politics and Change in a Traditional Society*.
16. Fu'ad I. Khuri, "Sectarian Loyalty among Rural Migrants in Two Lebanese Suburbs," in Antoun and Harik (eds.), *Rural Politics*.

divisive effects of social reform with emphasis on national consensus. The *National Charter* was an eclectic body of ideas wherein practically every segment in society found recognition and legitimacy. The regime protected its own interests by portraying minimal social conflict as legitimate, while at the same time warning that class warfare would not be tolerated.

The cognitive aspects of Arab socialism have broadened the political perspectives of villagers and generated an action-oriented culture. Those aspects of ideology that were directly related to the conditions of rural life were best understood, whereas abstract and remote ideas reached only a minority—the best educated and most alert—of the citizens. As was pointed out in chapters 8 and 9, general and abstract principles were better understood when embodied in concrete policies or form. For instance, socialism was most commonly understood in terms of agricultural cooperation and political participation. Arab nationalism, which was understood by a very broad segment of the village population, had also taken a concrete form under Nasser and was expressed in dramatic terms not likely to be missed in a community highly exposed to the mass media.

A final word of caution: Formal ideas do not become universal just because there is widespread use of mass communications. That 21 percent of adult males in Shubra had not heard of socialism in Nasser's Egypt indicates the diffusion limits of formal ideas among an economically and culturally lagging population. That socialism was understood in terms of the actual reform measures rather than of principles and abstract ideas serves as a warning that political ideas divested from practical import will not have significant effect on the lower strata of the population. Nasser was keenly aware of this phenomenon, and, in effect, his ideology was made to order. In its prescriptive aspects, it followed the principle, "To each social group, the remedy it needs and the rewards it deserves." The following chapter examines the villagers' responses to concrete issues such as the cooperative system and policies of local reform, and, hopefully, adds to our knowledge of the regime's communication with the rural masses.

chapter 11

Attitudes toward policy and change: the humanizing role of ideology

A truck loaded with heavy sacks of various kinds of clothing was on its way to deliver its cargo to a large store in Cairo when one of the sacks fell into a canal. Later, when the water receded, the sack was found by some destitute villagers. A great rush followed and each took from the sack what he or she could lay hands on. Before long, security officers, who noticed the villagers wearing new attire, became suspicious and uncovered the secret.

The villagers were herded to jail and put before the prosecutor. [In the following, the prosecutor narrates the court proceedings.]

I asked for the next case. Two soldiers came forward, opened both sides of the door, and dragged more than thirty men, women, and children, tied with coarse ropes, into the courtroom.

"By God! Who are they? Animals from the Saturday market? Untie the ropes!"

My first thought was to question them collectively in the hope of obtaining a confession and finishing my job quickly. I screened them all in one quick look and said:

"You stole the clothes, didn't you?"

One of the peasants replied in a deep and weary voice: "I swear by God we did not steal, nor do we ever steal. The river threw the sack into our hands and each one of us got what fortune permitted."

I shouted back: "What fortune? Do you think the river owns the sack or is it owned by gentlemen [khawajat]?" [1]

1. *Khawajat* (pl.): "gentlemen" (used in Egypt in reference to foreigners who controlled most businesses during the monarchy).

186

Attitudes toward policy and change: the humanizing role of ideology 187

He replied in the same deep tone: "We did not think of it that way, sir. May God's blessing be on you; pity the poor peasant folks."

"It is a question of law and the law is clear: Anyone who finds an object that belongs to someone else and keeps it with the intention of appropriating it is treated as a thief. Do you understand?"

"Yes sir, but the clothes were right in front of our eyes, the gift of the river, and we are, if you will excuse the expression, practically naked."

"What? Do you think the world is without order? Or is there a law and a government?"

The poor man seemed to have lost his patience and said, as if to himself: "Would that the government just spare us its evil deeds. It did not clothe us nor does it let us clothe ourselves."

"I am obliged to put you in jail."

"But sir, why jail? You searched our homes and took away all the new clothes. Children who had been rejoicing are now crying and we are back to our original state: we have nothing and owe nothing."

"I can only let you out on bail."

"What bail? We are destitute, don't you see, sir?"

"Away with you! You give me a headache. It is impossible to talk with the likes of you. The law is the law and I am bound to the letter of the law by a force stronger than the ropes in which you were bound. The matter is for me a question of law above everything else."

Then out went the villagers, muttering: "They put us in jail because God covered our shame."

From 'Tawfiq al Hakim, *Yawmiyyat Na'ib fi al Ariyaf*

During the old regime, the language of the law did not cross the barrier between the ruling class and the peasantry, as the prosecutor admitted: it was impossible to talk to peasants. Nor did any other medium of communication exist to bridge the gap between the few elite and the rest of the overwhelmingly peasant population of Egypt.

Government is in principle impersonal and severe, but the regimes that are sensitive to this fact and develop a common language to communicate with the people, especially with the rustics, turn out to be the most popular with them. The authoritarianism of the current regime is perhaps neither greater nor less than that of the preceding constitutional monarchy; the difference lies in the present regime's awareness of its powers and the efforts it makes to mitigate their harsh effects on citizens.

Mobilization regimes often enjoy an advantage over other types of political systems by showing intellectual and political interest in drawing the public to the ideology of the regime. They tend to substitute doctrinal persuasion for popular participation in national policy making. Under a mobilization regime, ideological persuasion serves as a humanizing force that mitigates the severity of authoritarian decisions. In Egypt, the regime's understanding of the need to speak to the people is evidenced by its use of the mass media and other local means of persuasion to convince the public of the value of policies made in circles far removed from the ordinary citizen. National and local policies are explained and justified to villagers in practical and moral terms, often by invoking the principle of fair and equitable allocation of resources.

The Egyptian ideological concept of Arab socialism can be characterized as a functional system of ideas that bears a minimal degree of ontological assumptions. As already observed, Arab socialism has been formulated in such a way as to reconcile various segments of the population. On the village level, it appears as an ideology especially designed for rural communities; for example, the deep-seated religious feelings and traditions of the villager were not in any way disturbed by the regime, and, despite relatively progressive ideas in the *Charter* on the status of women, the ASU leaders in Shubra and Beheira Province have not been forced to include women in political life. In Shubra, seclusion of women continues despite the "progressive guidance of socialism." (A peasant who improves his social and economic conditions tends to seclude his women, while the very poor continue to send their unveiled women to work in the fields.)

Militant adherence to ideology offends villagers when it inhibits reasonable discourse. In one instance, during a political party meeting in Shubra, a villager who resorted to the customary "God willing" was rebuked by an ASU national delegate, who said that he was seeking their will to act, not God's. The national delegate's persistently authoritarian manner offended some villagers, who in turn gave him very little cooperation.

The fact that the Nasser regime favored the rural population and industrial workers was a major asset in its efforts to win the good will of villagers. However, the regime has had also to make difficult demands on the rural population, but ideological persuasion eased the impact and softened the harshness of national decisions. Such was the case in March 1967, when the peasants were advised to plant cotton by the officially set date, at the expense of the broadbean crop (see chapter 6). Other examples of the use of persuasion to offset immediate hardships caused by national policy are the savings and family planning policies.

In order to finance the Five Year Plan, the government sought to generate capital from savings made by citizens voluntarily or through compulsory deductions. Government employees were subject to a payroll deduction equal to a quarter of a day's pay per month, not redeemable until the end of a five-year period. Members of the agrarian reform cooperative [2] were also subject to deductions of 3.5 pounds per feddan annually, a considerable sum for cultivators earning about 100 pounds per year. Saving money in the post office or in the bank was a new idea not in line with the peasant's usual practice and longstanding fears. For very poor peasants, the accrued interest was hardly worth the hardships caused by saving part of their meager incomes. Ideological arguments advanced by the ASU and the mass media to explain the savings policy and its national importance made conformity to policy more tolerable.

Family planning met with similar initial resistance, which required persuasive ideological explanation to offset villagers' traditional attitudes. Policy makers have sought to assure the public through religious decisions (*fatwas*) and secular arguments that family planning is in the best interest of the nation and that it is not inconsistent with religious teachings. Survey results indicate (see below) that government efforts have proved quite effective.

Attitudes toward Cooperatives

Agricultural cooperation, as described in the *Charter*, is a system designed by the Revolution to free peasants from exploitation by large landlords and merchants. Since it has been an especially helpful innovation, it should not be surprising that Shubra peasants showed a clear understanding of the ideological language in which the regime extols the virtues of the cooperative system. Nationalization of marketing through the cooperatives is not, however, as obviously advantageous to peasants as cooperative production is. Villagers therefore were questioned on the issue of collective marketing. The majority indicated that it has saved them from exploitation and unfair middleman practices; only 9 percent viewed cooperative marketing as a means for the government to retrieve the credit it had advanced to cultivators (see table 28).

Villagers also objected more strongly to merchant middlemen than to landlords, a distinction not to be found in the regime's formal ideology. The majority, 59 percent, singled out merchants as "exploiters," compared with the 5 percent who mentioned exploitation by landlords. When describing the purpose of the cooperatives, protection from merchants rather than from landlords was stressed (see table 29). This response points to the fact that cultivators were often in debt to middlemen and thus

2. Members of the regular cooperative societies responded to the savings program at the request of the Peasant's Secretariat (*Amanat al Fallahin*) of the ASU, not at the request of the Ministry of Agriculture.

resented them more than landlords. In accusing the merchant, one cultivator declared that "the merchant is by nature an exploiter, and the [cooperative] society has rid us of him." Another explained that "people used not to find fertilizers and seeds because merchants were in agreement to exploit [the peasant] . . . but now, it [the cooperative society] gives us seeds and fertilizers."

There has been consensus in Shubra that "the cooperative society is good. It gives us what is rightfully ours and takes its own. This way no one takes advantage of anyone else's situation." Similar views were expressed by noncultivators who represent widely different social strata. A wage laborer who makes sun-dried mudbricks explained that, from his own observations and those of his cultivator friends, the cooperative society "helps the peasant in cultivation. The peasant now delivers his crops to the government, which sells his produce for him. This way he does not stand in need of any merchant exploiter." A livestock merchant, one of the richest nonlandowners in Shubra, agreed that the cooperative society "has served the peasant. In the past [before the Revolution], it used to serve a small monopoly group. The peasant did not [at that time] deal with it because he who borrowed a piaster [from the society] turned out to be in debt to the society for twelve piasters. It used to consist of moneylenders (*murabin*). We have had enough of that kind of humiliation and unfairness in this village."

Cooperative production and marketing have also contributed to the change in the villager's traditional image of the state. No longer viewed as a remote and unfathomable force in Cairo that functions primarily to tax and conscribe villagers, the government is now viewed in Shubra as a source of individual and social well-being. One cultivator, though viewing cooperative marketing as advantageous to the government, commented that "the government helps [the cultivator] all year round through the cooperative societies. Therefore we too should help the government [by selling it the crop]." The new confidence in the state is reflected in the identification made between government policies and village welfare. For example, one respondent said, "Is it not a government project? Then it is entirely in our interest. Do you think anyone would go along with what is harmful to himself?" Furthermore, the repetitive use, in describing the functions and purpose of the cooperative, of such terms as "to provide," "to serve," or "to protect" (see table 29) gives a clear indication of the positive attitude villagers have toward the cooperative system.

The beneficiaries of agrarian reform went even further than the ordinary villagers in their new concept of the government. The government was viewed as paternalistically favoring the peasant and shielding

Table 28
Views of the Purpose of Collective Marketing

Purpose	Percentage Citing Response
To prevent exploitation of peasants by merchants	59
To protect peasants' interests (by raising income)	19
To prevent unfair purchasing prices and black market	16
Inapplicable (noncultivators)*	14
To retrieve co-op's debts from peasants	9
To protect peasants from feudal exploiters (landlords)	5
Interest of the state and society	4
No answer	2

N = 135
* Some individuals who were not cultivators considered this question irrelevant to them, but those who did answer were coded.

Table 29
Views of the Purpose of the Cooperative Society

Purpose	Percentage Citing Response
To provide and distribute farming provisions (credit for seeds, fertilizers, etc.)	74
To serve cultivators and the village public	60
To provide services, technical advice, and guidance	17
Inapplicable	14
To protect peasants from exploitation by capitalist merchants	10
Do not know	4

N = 135

him from traditionally oppressive forces. As expressed by 'Ali al Shawi, secretary to the reform cooperative board, "The state is extending to us a protective arm (*'amilah lana hadanah*) until we become [economically and socially] independent." Testimonies of this kind make it clear that the favoritism that the Revolution had shown toward peasants was well understood by the villagers in Shubra. However, a certain sense of insecurity among these peasants still lingers. When seeking national unity in 1967–68, the government relaxed its grip on formerly discredited landlords; uncertainty and fear were felt among some politically active peasants in Shubra and Beheira Province. Again, as 'Ali al Shawi put it in a rhetorical question that he himself answered, "Do you think we [small cultivators] have become ready to stand on our own? I don't think so." Some peasant members of the ASU Executive Board of Beheira Province were apprehensive that "reactionaries" were going to make a comeback in the elections scheduled for the summer of 1968. They feared that these forces would blame the 1967 defeat on socialism and socialists.

New Habits of Thought

Changes in village culture were not limited to new ideas about socialism, cooperatives, and nationalism but also affected villagers' traditional attitudes toward personal matters and relations. Today, attitudes toward planning the size of one's family, toward kinship ties and loyalties, or toward the elder in the family are different from those held in the past.[3] To conjure up the image of a traditional villager, one is not entirely dependent on the literature. The survey results identify a residual personality typified by those scoring very low on awareness and other change-oriented indices. This group, of course, stands out as a minority in the village. In addition to survey results and the literature, I have resorted to informants to reconstruct the history and past culture of the village.

As an example of the traditional peasant, 'Abd al Mawla is a 55-year-old cultivator who has not often been out of the village. He lives in the same compound with twelve members of his family, including a married brother's family of three. Under the dim light of a kerosene lamp, I talked with 'Abd al Mawla in his house one evening. He was courteous, though ill at ease. I asked about the Leadership Group in the village:

"I don't know anything about them."
"You mean you have never heard of them?"
"I have, but I do not know anything about them. I just mind my own business."

3. See Ayrout, *The Egyptian Peasant*; Winifred S. Blackman, *The Fellahin of Upper Egypt* (London: Cass, 1968); and Ammar, *Growing Up in an Egyptian Village*. It should be observed here that these findings differ also with Mayfield's conclusions on peasant attitudes in *The Politics of Rural Egypt*. Mayfield's study was undertaken in 1966–67, but his report on peasants' attitudes and culture relies heavily on Ayrout and Ammar, whose studies predate the Revolution, the first written in the thirties, and second based on field work done in 1951.

"How did you hear about them?"

"From my children." He paused for a moment, then said, "I am told they go to meetings and talk politics. They want to appear like big people."

"You don't think this is right for them to do?"

"A peasant should not mix with such things, this is the big peoples' job. These men have left their fields unattended and are going around doing things that are none of their business."

We changed the subject and talked about village problems. "There are no problems," he said. "We just need a bakery," he added, "not much grain these days in the village and people baking at home are causing fires."

"You think you can do something about it?"

"No, I am a poor man, and nobody listens to a poor man."

"Who can do something about it?"

"The government should do it."

"Suppose a project like this was started in the village and you were asked to participate, would you ask somebody's advice before you decide or not?"

"We follow the big peoples' example in the village and it is up to them to decide."

"Have you heard about family planning?" He did not understand the term, so I used the local phrase, "prevention of births" (*mani' al khilfah*).

"Yes."

"What do you think of it?"

"This is really sinful (*haram*). Children are the gift of God and no one can stop God's work."

The subject changed again. I asked, "Suppose you have a family problem, where would you go to solve it?"

"We solve it among ourselves. We go to my older brother, he is the elder of the family and we act according to his advice."

"Do you think young men should have more say in running the village?"

"No."

In holding to these views, 'Abd al Mawla is not alone in the village, but he decidedly belongs to a minority. As the survey results show, the majority of adult men in Shubra disagree with 'Abd al Mawla on practically everything he said. Regarding the political and social prerogatives of the "big people" [*al nas al kubar*], the rich and traditionally influential, 67 percent of the respondents disagreed with 'Abd al Mawla.[4] "That was the source of our trouble," commented one respondent. "It was true in the by-gone days," added a second, but "today there is no such thing as big and small people." Others made similar statements: "I disagree," said one respondent, "it is a man's deeds not his family that matters. Leadership is not a question of family and status today." Repeatedly, the individual qualities of a person were said to be the basis for his leadership.[5]

4. Survey questions did not include a reference to 'Abd al Mawla; see Appendix A.
5. Although the questions were of the agree-disagree type, the interviewers were instructed to record any additional comments the respondents made.

In societies where experience is the only avenue for acquiring knowledge that culminates in wisdom at an advanced age, respect for elders is strong. In Shubra, the conditions under which age is highly respected are changing, as are attitudes toward the generations. Knowledge is acquired at the school now and through practical training in local organizations. Wisdom is no longer the custody solely of the elders; indeed, it is suffering from obsolescence in a rapidly changing social order, as more youth become equipped with the knowledge necessary for the times.

Villagers of all ages readily agreed that leadership in the village should be assumed by younger people; 84 percent agreed, leaving 'Abd al Mawla in an even smaller minority in regard to this issue. Villagers in Shubra have already seen younger people take charge of most of the village affairs and have not been disappointed. They have become well aware that young people are better informed than older ones; 91 percent, the highest percentage yet, agree that younger people are better informed on public issues. This result is not significantly affected by the 2 to 1 age ratio in favor of the young who are under 40 in the sample, since those who thought that young people are better informed constitute a ratio of 10 to 1. There can be no doubt that the older generation has conceded precedence in leadership to youth.

Villagers' views on leadership qualities show that kinship, class solidarity, and status do not, in the expressed opinions of villagers, constitute ideological qualifications for leadership. The most frequently mentioned attributes are the individual's moral qualities such as decency, trustworthiness, and being "a good man" or "a helpful man" (see table 30). Attributes that identify a person as influential differ in certain respects from those that make him popular. Moral qualities are more often cited as reasons for popularity than for influence (95 versus 77 times; see table 31). Despite some differences, however, strong similarity (rho = .89)[6] exists between the qualities that make up influence and those of popularity.

Studies of attitudes do not explain social behavior, but they unravel some of its underlying determinants. Villagers in Shubra, who almost unanimously agree that younger people are better informed and qualified for leadership, will not unquestioningly support every young man who runs for office against an older one, but neither will they refuse to consider a man for office on the basis of his youth. Elected village leaders in the 1960s were not, on the average, very old; officers of the ASU local committee at the time of their election in 1963 were 46 years old on the average, and this average dropped to 42 years in the 1968 committee.

6. Significant at the .05 level.

Table 30
Reasons for Considering a Person Influential in the Community

Leadership Attribute	Number	Percentage
Nominee's personal qualities (moral character)	77	57
Public orientation and ability to solve problems	72	53
Personal attributes such as education, age, and position	61	45
Active contributions to village affairs	42	31
ASU position and identification with the Revolution	36	19
Affinity with the public; responsiveness	19	14
Personal reasons	1	0.7
No answer	4	3

N = 135. Maximum number of responses per item cannot exceed 135.

Table 31
Reasons for Considering a Person Popular in the Community

Leadership Attribute	Number	Percentage
Nominee's personal qualities (moral character)	95	70
Public orientation and ability to solve problems	67	50
Personal attributes such as education, age, and position	38	28
Active contributions to village affairs	77	57
ASU position and identification with the Revolution	16	12
Affinity with the public; responsiveness	14	10
Personal reasons	3	2
No answer	7	5

N = 135. Maximum number of responses per item cannot exceed 135.

Young leadership, however, has not been won unconditionally or without a struggle. Tension arose among leaders of different generations and burst into the open in the councils of the ASU in Shubra. Members of the Youth Organization were consistently critical of the leaders of the Committee of Twenty and of its successor in 1966, the Leadership Group. During the ASU meetings, members of the Youth Organization insisted on formal order during the meetings and openly criticized the officers of the Leadership Group. Pressed by the impatient younger set, the older leaders adjusted to the youths' demands as best they could, though in private they admonished the behavior of the Youth Organization members. In the elections of 1968, the two groups openly opposed and criticized one another.

It is not surprising, therefore, that a critical attitude toward youth was reflected in the responses of the Select, who were not as ready to concede leadership to the young as were the ordinary villagers. While agreeing with the sample respondents that younger people were better informed, fewer (79 percent compared with 84 percent of the sample respondents) agreed that leadership in the village should be in the hands of the young.

Traditional societies have looked at age and kinship as the objects of respect and loyalty (except in aristocratic traditions, where title is stronger than age as an attribute of authority and respect). In Shubra, the change in attitudes toward age accompanies a change in attitude toward kinship as well. Respondents acknowledged that a weakening in kinship ties had occurred; 92 percent agreed that a person could not depend on his relatives as in the olden times, and 77 percent agreed that young people of today did not seek their parents' advice as they used to in the past. This awareness of the deterioration of kinship ties is quite consistent with the earlier conclusion that the clan no longer enjoys either its former solidarity or traditional social functions.

Other indicators also reveal a decline in the social functions of kinship. Respondents were asked to whom they went for help in solving family differences, financial problems, and property disputes. In none of these three areas did kinsmen play a prominent role. With respect to family problems within the immediate family circle, only 21 percent said they would resort to other relatives, usually starting with nearest of kin. A smaller group, 17 percent, depended on themselves alone in solving family problems and expressed a strong feeling against involving outsiders. A majority, 56 percent, sought help from nonrelatives, mainly the village council and its arbitration committee.[7] Thus not even private disputes were solved primarily inside the mudbrick walls of the family compound but, in the main, were taken to village leaders.

The role of kinsmen diminishes still further when the problem is financial; only 20 percent turned to relatives for assistance in financial matters. The rest of the responses fall into the same pattern as in the case of family problems, except that fewer depend on themselves.

The role of the family declined most noticeably with respect to property disputes, for which a third party was usually sought; only 4

---

7. The remaining 6 percent gave no answer or other responses.

percent resorted to an elder in the family. (One interesting response has come mostly from agricultural wage laborers, who refused to answer this question on the grounds that they were not propertied.) Only 6 percent sought out the police to solve property disputes; evidently the community resolved most of its problems by itself, avoiding the police and the courts. In all three problem areas, the majority of villagers seek the help of village leaders, particularly with regard to property disputes.

Resort to local organizations for resolutions of conflict constitutes a departure from the past and an adjustment to secondary relations not only in matters of self-government and production management, but also in resolving personal conflicts. Concomitant change in attitudes and socioeconomic structures is perhaps what accounts for the painless course of social development in the village community.

Religion and Attitude Change

Since religion has often been singled out by students of developing countries as one of the forces that inhibit social change, an attempt was made to elicit the respondents' attitudes on family planning, a national policy with religious implications. The question here is not the villagers' belief in Islam but rather the behavioral implications of their religious beliefs.

As observed earlier, the regime supported orthodox Islam and did not challenge the peoples' religious practices, not even those that were viewed uneasily by the learned *'ulema*, such as the worship of the saints. Furthermore, the regime made a special effort to imbue some of its policies with religious legitimacy. Family planning thus serves as an indicator of religious attitudes toward policy, for, although the *'ulema* have supported the religiosity of family planning, an individual may still feel an innate religious sentiment against tampering with the natural order.

Respondents who were aware of the family planning policy in the village constituted 90 percent; 82 percent supported it, and 8 percent opposed it.[8] Almost all of those who were opposed to family planning gave religious reasons for their opposition; of the 110 who were in favor, only 2

---

8. A similarly positive attitude is shown in another Muslim country; see Stycos, "The Potential Role. . . ." Our findings clearly disagree with such common views that the Egyptian peasant is turned off from family planning by his religious attitude; see Peter Mansfield, *Nasser's Egypt* (London: Penguin African Library, 1965), p. 130. For the practical problems of implementing the project in Egypt, see T. Paul Schultz, "Fertility Patterns and Their Determinants in the Arab Middle East," in Charles A. Cooper and Sidney S. Alexander (eds.), *Economic Development and Population Growth in the Middle East* (New York: American Elsevier, 1972).

gave religious reasons for their approval. Thus while it is clear that religion is more often the cause of opposing than supporting this policy, its effects on the whole are minimal. The proportion of adult men who found it offensive to their religious beliefs was negligible and constituted no obstacle to policies of social change.

No opposition to the policy of family planning was encountered among the Select, and almost all of them indicated their strong support of it. They also demonstrated a degree of sophistication in understanding its religious implications. A villager corrected me during an informal conversation when I used the term "birth control" and said he preferred the term "family planning" because Islam prohibits the prevention of life, which is implied by the first phrase. This may of course be rationalization on his part, but if rationalization occurs as a mechanism for religiously reconciling oneself to a policy of social change, then religion can hardly be considered an unbending force blocking the path of progress.

The Idea of Progress

The villagers' responses to family planning reflect their ideas of progress. Asked why they were in favor of family planning, almost all approving respondents gave secular reasons pertaining to their well-being. A rational attitude that accepts scientific means for changing one's social and economic conditions was clearly underlined in their responses. They wanted to limit the size of the family in order to improve their socioeconomic standing. A group of 58 respondents volunteered information on the ideal family size, the majority of whom wanted only one or two children. Those who wanted a family of three children constituted 87 percent of the total group.[9] In view of the common belief that peasants desire large families, it is interesting that views expressed in Shubra are rather similar to urban attitudes toward family size.[10]

Family planning "is the right thing," one small cultivator explained, "because when a person has two or three children only, he is able to send them to school, bring them up properly, and clothe them adequately. Then they grow up like good people instead of [spending their childhood] prowling around naked and sick." Some of the respondents were particularly struck by the urgency of the population problem and felt that the government was already very late in implementing the program. "I know what it means," said one respondent, who complained that the

9. These make 36 percent of the total sample.
10. T. Paul Schultz, "Fertility Patterns . . . ," pp. 413–14, found urban fertility rates in Egypt to exceed rural ones.

program came too late to benefit him, "I already have five children." One educated small cultivator and employee, who served on the village council, went further to say that only sterilization would now help. Nor did villagers fail to understand family planning in terms of traditional wisdom. One respondent said that a "peasant saying beckons us to keep our cattle few and spend generously on them, to keep our landholding small and service it well. The same applies to human beings," he added. Health, education, and economic security are uppermost in their consideration of family size.

The high expectations of ordinary villagers in Shubra are frustrated by their keen awareness of the vicious circle of Egypt's economy, which is based primarily on agriculture. The simple arithmetic of population pressure on the land is against the Egyptian; he already feels cramped on a small plot of land that resists expansion while the population increases by leaps and bounds. Villagers rejoiced at land reform, but they were also keenly aware that it was a temporary solution. The average cultivator in Shubra el Gedida today manages about two feddans; assuming that he has only three children (women are equally entitled to inheritance in Shubra), each one of them will end up with less land than is sufficient for his livelihood. The daring efforts of the national government to reclaim swamps and desert land and to irrigate them by the Nile water stored in the Aswan Dam has not yet noticeably affected the average cultivator in Lower Egypt, and the cost of reclaiming land has so far not been fully justified.[11] Already, the government is trying to prevent further fragmentation of cultivated land by stipulating that a beneficiary does not have unqualified rights to pass the land to his children in fragments; inheritance is now subject to the approval of the Supreme Committee of Agrarian Reform.

Those who were religiously opposed to family planning viewed the scarcity of economic resources in an entirely different manner than did those in favor of it. The religious argued that "God will provide for the livelihood of children. The scriptures say that God will give to each man the means of his livelihood." The same thing was repeated: "God gives and God will provide."

Those in favor of family planning viewed the matter rationally: "Our numbers are multiplying rapidly and our cultivation area is still the same. What will they [our children] do? Where will they go?" But will rational planning of social action solve the vicious circle of the Egyptian rural

11. Officials of land reclamation say now that the cost of reclaiming one feddan will be equal to or less than the market rate and that the high costs incurred earlier were caused by initial costs of machinery and expertise.

masses? Only time will tell; and on the outcome depends the stability of the political system, for the villager is no longer resigned to poverty and unhealthy social existence. His ideas of well-being and progress clearly indicate that his expectations of the future are high. His continued faith in the government is contingent on the regime's success in solving these problems.

Should the family planning program in Egypt prove a failure, it would not be for lack of support among villagers, if Shubra's results are at all typical. Even though women in the village were not interviewed, the answers in response to informal inquiry indicate that they were not less eager to limit the size of their families than were their husbands. Despite this general support, the family planning program in Egypt and in Shubra during the survey was not impressive. Some of the obstacles observed in Shubra may give an idea of the kind of difficulties encountered. In the first place, the intent of the national government was not as serious as the urgency of the issue would call for. Not until 1965 did the administration of the program enjoy reasonable government support, and even then, not enough. In the district of Damanhur, the ASU bureau showed much more interest than the government officials did, but then it could only affect attitudes rather than actually implement the program. There has also been very little experimentation in Egypt with methods of contraception, and advocation of "the pill" was not very successful. Uncertainty regarding the side effects of the pill and a poor sense of timing among peasant women dampened enthusiasm. Moreover, the administration of the program in the village was in the hands of the local physician and nurses, who were already overworked and had no time for additional duties. Instead of trying to establish confidence in the contraception methods used, the government resorted to poor methods of inducements that were to no avail.

Attitudes toward Political Change

The Samads, the Kuras, and the reform peasants have, at one time or another, played leading roles in the politics of Shubra during the last two decades. Each of these groups has been affected differently by the Revolution, and their reactions to rapid political change, as expressed by the leading members of each of the three contending groups, is the subject of discussion here.

Kamil Samad, once the deputy 'umdah of Shubra and a wealthy landlord, is currently a petty official in Alexandria, his power gone and his wealth dispersed. He has managed, however, to keep his imposing house in Shubra, where he spends long weekends during the summer. The future is not just bleak; he has no future, he feels. "I wish they would finish us once and for all, not in this piecemeal fashion," he said. "Our condition is similar to a cancerous body whose limbs are being amputated part by part, a slow and agonizing death." He is not fighting back any longer, nor is he trying to adjust to or infiltrate the regime's political organizations the way he and his brother tried in the 1950s. However, he readily criticizes the regime in private.

Kamil Samad does not give the regime any credit, not even grudgingly, as do some members of the Kura family. Because of the Revolution, his class of landlord-merchants is facing certain extinction, he feels, but the state of decline as he visualizes it is general. He views the situation in Egypt as suffering from moral decline, from a state of disintegration whereby everyone lives for himself with no sense of a collective good, as was the case in the past. "Look at the Suhdi brothers," he told me in July 1968, "the two are running in the elections against one another in a bitter fight." "Gone," he continued, "is the respect and deference by the young in the family to the elders." Citing another example of moral decline, he said, "Look at Maray, the vegetable vendor; he too has run for political office. Have you ever in your life known of such conceit?" The principal moral evil in the village as he sees it is selfishness: "Life in Shubra today is governed by selfish considerations, not general principles of respect for age and status." Under his family's government, he explained, the people willingly submitted because of the social position that gave the Samads the ability to bear responsibility and dispense resources for the interest of the common man. "We generously maintained," he said, "a *dawwar* (*'umdah's* guesthouse), where everyone in the village could find succor and help. This," he explained, "was very costly to us but we did it out of a sense of social responsibility that befitted our status in the community. People were united, unlike these days when everyone is set against everyone else." Respect for age, kinship relations, and status were, in his view, principles of social solidarity that have now disintegrated, to the detriment of the whole populace.

The Kura brothers represent a different case. Like the Samad brothers, they were landlords but wielded no political power under the old regime. The Revolution in 1952 opened up their option for political leadership, and they made the best of it. Yet, by 1965, it had become clear that their common political course with the Revolution had started to split into opposite directions. Radical changes in the economy and in the political party had already affected their fortunes; though they still enjoyed considerable wealth, their political position had declined to its nadir in 1966.

Sayid Kura, the lawyer and professional farmer who became both mayor of Shubra and acting secretary of the Committee of Twenty from 1961 to 1965, was confined to his home while a new mayor and a new party leadership took over the village. He felt that these changes had been directed against him and his family personally. But it was the loss of his political leadership and the frustrations of a man aware of his personal strength and ambitions that made him most unhappy. "I feel like someone in a straitjacket. I want to act but I cannot do anything. Previously I was the mayor of this village, and introduced many projects to it. . . . Now I just sit here watching. My projects are like children of mine living with foster parents while I sit watching them from a distance."

Sayid Kura has an action-oriented personality, a sense of concern for others, and a desire for public service. It is primarily because of these qualities that he felt terribly frustrated. He was not, of course, selfless, and, while he and his family viewed their public service as an extension of their status and power in the community, he also identified the interests of the community with his leadership qualities. He deplored not the prevailing social or moral order but rather the fact that it deprived him of presiding over the leadership and development of the village. He was not in agreement with the growing socialism of the regime as it was manifested in 1966 nor with the radicalization of the ASU, but he certainly felt that he could live with it, had he only been given a chance.

Like Kamil Samad, he feels that politics is the vocation of the wealthy and those of social status, not of the poor, who lack the necessary leadership qualities and the financial ability to afford politics. The village folks are dependent: "The countryside," he said, "needs strong leadership because it is still like a minor in need of someone who could bring to him social awareness and socialist justice." He thought that he could bring to these rural "minors" political leadership and guidance more valuable to them than the current version of socialism. Socialism, as it had been lately advocated from Cairo, he believed, had bypassed the interests of the country people. "What is socialism, and how should it be applied here?" he asked rhetorically. "In the countryside, it should be presented in a manner relevant to the peasants' level of understanding." He feels that he can bring socialism to the villagers, but the new leaders of the ASU cannot. It's obvious that his idea of socialism is no longer the same as that of the regime but corresponds more closely to the reform spirit of the mid-1950s.

The new elite of rural notables had a political outlook and a position in society to protect, just as the rural elite of the monarchy did. However, what distinguishes this professional and moderate rural elite from the country bosses of the old regime is their feeling that they deserve to lead by virtue of their abilities, education, wealth, and public-mindedness. They understand and accept the need to develop the countryside, and they hold to a moderate version of socialism, including the land reform program. They also feel that they have the prerogative to interpret socialism in a manner "relevant to the level of understanding of the villager." The Kuras have accepted all this except for socialism in its official 1966 version, which had crippled their economic enterprise by its restrictive measures against private business. For instance, after their realization that the ceiling on landholdings possibly would be lowered and thus continue to diminish their estates, they sold land and invested in trade, mainly in agricultural products such as fertilizers, pesticides, and cotton, until this trade was nationalized in the period 1961 to 1964. Still, they went along with collective marketing of agricultural products, and Muhammad Kura, an executive in a cotton firm, was one of the first to advocate and implement cooperative marketing of agricultural produce in Beheira. The loss of trade did not depress the Kuras because they were able businessmen and turned to livestock. However, the political pressures of 1966 and the radicalization of policy made them feel insecure about the future of this new economic venture. Consequently, they kept their operations in the livestock business at a low level, not exceeding a specific number of animals at any one time, in fear of new restrictive measures against this business as well. Kamil Samad claims that he forewarned the Kuras that their turn was coming next, and perhaps by 1966 they started to think that he was right.

Muhammad Kura, for instance, explained all the changes caused by the national government not in Kamil Samad's terms of moral decline but in terms of haste. He admits that progress has taken place under the Revolution: "The country has advanced economically and in morale under the Revolution," he said. "Indeed," he continued, "this is not just progress, it has now become a leap (*ila had al tafrah*)." His tone was plaintive, and his mixed feelings were expressed again when he referred to the fact that people have become aggressive and will no longer be fooled. "People [referring to his electoral district in Markaz Damanhur] are now like wasps, no one can impose anything on them."

Realistic and fair, the Kuras admit to and approve of the progress in the countryside that has taken place under the Revolution; they are, nevertheless, disappointed in the turn of events against them. This shift is no longer progress but "a leap" with no continuity or clear consequences. In 1968, changes on the national level gave Muhammad Kura another chance to run for office. He started at the village level and ended up in the newly elected National Assembly, but he was still disappointed because he soon realized that a member of the National Assembly enjoyed no real powers. He also could not forget that a small cultivator from Shubra whom he had once helped against the Samads rose to a political position strong enough to compete against him for national office. That man was 'Ali al Shawi, the secretary of the reform cooperative society, whose unsuccessful bid for membership in the National Assembly in 1964 also cost Muhammad Kura his seat. To Muhammad, 'Ali was a clear example of the aggressive attitude of the peasant under the Revolution, and he could never forgive 'Ali, whom he described as "conceited and ignorant of his station in life."

What does 'Ali think? 'Ali feels that "the Kuras are good people, but they have outlived their usefulness. The times have passed them by and their patronizing hegemony over the peasants is no longer feasible." He added that "if they had a chance to return to the village political arena, they would once more dominate the village by their usual tactics such as charity and similar methods." He believes that "agrarian reform has created a new situation [in the village]. Now, no person stands in need of any other person. Each one of us now is independent." 'Ali's vision is strikingly clear, and he has perceived that the social, political, and economic changes in the village have created conditions whereby the individual could be economically and politically independent from the charity and tutelage of others. In a sense, official ideology is to him real and true when it asserts that political democracy is contingent on economic freedom.

But 'Ali himself, the beneficiary of the Revolution, has by no means unlimited confidence in the future. He realizes that the situation is still one of struggle against possible return of the influential notables, who are still strong and who still appeal to a number of villagers who have not been seriously affected by the Revolution. In 1967–68, when the regime relaxed its measures against the notables and permitted free elections to the ASU, 'Ali and party activists felt politically insecure. 'Ali revealed his state of mind: "Do you think that we [peasants] are now strong enough to stand on our own? I think we are not," he said, in answer to his own question. He still feels the need for what he had once called government protection (*hadanah*).

In short, rapid change has been conceived in Shubra in three different ways according to each group's—the Samad's, the Kuras', or the reform peasants'—political position. The new thing in the village is selfishness and moral decline to Kamil Samad; peasant aggressiveness and a "leap" to Muhammad Kura; and a spirit of individualism and independence to 'Ali al Shawi.

Conclusion

It may be observed that diversity and change in village life had affected not only economic and political relations but also attitudes toward lifestyle and politics. Testimonies by villagers have confirmed the disparity between the literature's portrayal of them and their present condition and self-image.

To judge from villagers' attitudes toward family planning, religion, the good life, generational differences, and secular leadership, their ideological outlook is not so widely different from that of the national elite. Since there is no baseline against which to mark the beginning of change in villagers' attitudes, one can at least say that the gap between the world view of the elite and that of the peasantry has to a considerable extent been bridged in Shubra.

It is interesting, moreover, to note that, although national ideology has been conveyed to villagers in a uniform way, its effects on individual villagers have varied. It has again been found that local considerations affect the individual's selectivity of national ideas, and the individual shows a constant preoccupation with what is relevant to his own life conditions.

As a cognitive system, ideology serves as a guidebook to assist individuals in reading the signs by which they must live in society; as an affective system it seeks to rally support by means of symbolic appeals. The emphasis on persuasion has had the effect of creating a language intelligible on both the national and local levels. By virtue of its emphasis in Shubra, ideological persuasion has proved to be a humanizing force that tempers the authoritarian character of the regime. If there is a single point with which to credit the Nasser regime's improvement over the old system, it is that peasants now better understand why they have to suffer and the purpose of their suffering.

chapter 12

Political attitudes, kinship, and social mobility

As a mobilization system, Egypt can be considered a dominant regime of the kind that has become familiar in contemporary times, where populism and authoritarianism coexist. Populism takes the forms of plebiscites, mass organization, egalitarian ideology, and such formal institutions of popular representation as national assemblies, local government councils, trade union boards, rural cooperatives, worker management boards, and party organs. Competitive political activity is not so much lacking as it is restricted and guided. The rules of the game are laid down by the leadership of the regime, which limits the recruitment for and the functions of representative bodies.

The common belief that political participation under a dominant regime is a facade intended for gaining legitimacy in the eyes of the public and in world opinion is partially true but falls far short of reality. Since the task of implementing broad changes in economic-political structures, allocation of resources, and sociocultural beliefs cannot be accomplished by a minority elite acting alone, participation and responsibility may have to be spread widely throughout the political system in order to enlist the support and cooperation of a sizable number of the population. By actively seeking public support and cooperation, mobilization leadership neither submits its privileged position of power to public discretion nor puts it in question; rather, it attempts to use persuasion and secure voluntary cooperation on the widest scale possible. Political participation in a mobilization regime may therefore be viewed as a collaborative, or cooperative, effort between the rulers and the ruled to resolve problems and arrive at legislation without prejudice to the dominant position of the leadership.

Pragmatic considerations that may lead a dominant regime to encourage political participation include the desire to (a) reduce the harshness of its extraordinary powers over the people; (b) obtain active cooperation from the public in the implementation of its policies; (c) share the burden of management of public affairs in local communities and organizations; (d) obtain advice for legislation in which it needs guidance and assistance; and (e) divine the public mood. The major problem is arousing enthusiasm for participation when the public is aware of its secondary role in national policy. In a developing country like Egypt, other longstanding obstacles hinder such efforts: traditional beliefs and social ties, ignorance of the rules of the political game, and absence of a tradition of representative local government or collective management. On the other hand, citizens may voluntarily respond to political participation because of shared ideological commitment, vested interest in the regime, realistic or imagined belief in the possibility of affecting decisions, desire for a share in the spoils, or the need for self-protection.

By emphasizing ideology, mobilization regimes tend to assume that each individual is able to respond to new ideas and imperatives. The question, therefore, is whether the Shubra villagers had developed individual characteristics that enabled them to respond to national challenges and plans. The survey sought (1) to determine the extent of public response to the regime's campaign for mass participation and (2) to identify and explain attitudes of different respondents. The discussion here is limited to attitudes, in particular the self-perception of individuals in the context of local issues and policies. The aptitude for free political participation among men of Shubra should reflect not only on the regime's experiment in local government but also on its underlying principles of reform.

The Responsive and the Dependent

The terms "individualism" and "conventionalism" are given operational definitions here to denote two types of attitudes. Individualism refers to a respondent's self-perceived ability to decide for himself in matters related to the public affairs of his village community. Conventionalism, in contrast, is the self-perceived inability to decide on or affect local matters, that is, a nonparticipatory attitude. An obvious limitation of these operational definitions is their exclusively local application. Although it might be interesting to examine villagers' attitudes toward and perceptions of national issues and leaders, in a mobilization system attitude toward local policy is a more critical test of political participation and freedom. The villager is tangibly involved more in local than in national matters, and one may expect his responses to local issues to be more concrete in meaning and reference.

Each respondent was subjected to a battery of questions intended to elicit his attitude toward participation in community affairs. The first set sought to obtain personal testimonies as to whether a respondent independently decided to participate in village projects or relied on others to guide him. The second set of questions was designed to elicit a respondent's self-assessment of efficacy by asking him first to identify one or more village problems and then to state whether he thought he could contribute to their solution.

The results by question are first presented separately. When asked how they would respond to an invitation to participate in a village project, one of every two respondents said that he would decide independently; the rest relied on others for guidance (see table 32). Those classified as dependent fell into two subgroups: those seeking advice from others in the village and those who would "wait and see" before deciding.

It might be supposed that those who would "wait and see" wished to postpone judgment until the situation became clearer, or until their group took a stand on the matter. Neither assumptions turned out to be true. Respondents in this category neither expressed a desire to understand the situation better nor mentioned any specific group whose example they wished to follow. On the contrary, their hesitation was induced by a desire to see how the community at large would proceed. Only 3 of the 27 stated that they would follow the example of "elders"; the rest preferred to follow the consensus of the community. In most cases, respondents used the collective pronoun *we:* "We do what the rest will do"; only occasionally did one say, "I am like the rest and will do what they do." This suggests that most respondents found their security by becoming lost in the crowd and avoiding individual responsibility.

The compelling urge to submit to community norms and consensus was expressed in a telling way by one of the respondents. "There is a saying we use [that commands]: If you pass your enemy's place and see that people are building him a house, then you too should put in a brick." Or, as expressed more prosaically by another, "When we see the majority taking part in a project, we too should take part, even when it is against our own will."

Whereas a desire for anonymity and consensus seemed to overshadow any sense of individuality and partisanship among the "wait and see" group, those seeking the advice of others tended, in comparison, to be more free, reserving for themselves the choice of selecting an advisor.

Table 32
Attitude of Social Dependence or Independence

Question: "Suppose a project was started in the village by people here, such as opening a new school or draining a pool, and you were asked to participate as a member of this community. What would you do?"
(a) Ask someone's advice?
(b) Wait and see who will participate first?
(c) Decide on your own?

Response	Number	Percentage
Decide on my own	65	48
Ask someone's advice	41	30
Wait and see	27	20
No answer	2	2
Total	135	100

With respect to identification of village problems, 90 respondents (67 percent) were able to identify at least one; two-thirds of these felt that they could do something to solve these problems.

An attitude index was constructed on the basis of responses to the three questions just presented. Three attitude groups were thus identified: highly individualistic, moderately individualistic, and conventional. The first group includes those whose responses were positive on all three counts, that is, those who decided on their own whether to participate, could identify at least one village problem, and expressed an ability to affect its solution. The moderately individualistic were those whose answers were positive on two out of the three counts, whereas the conventionalist had negative answers on at least two of the three. Table 33 presents the distribution by the three-class attitude index.

The conventionalist group had a self-image of impotence in social matters and a belief that "no one reckons with the poor man." Most felt they had no weight in the community to affect matters; a few unwilling to accept public responsibility expressed the feeling that village problems were the business of leaders only (see table 34).

Individualists, on the other hand, felt they could assist in solving village problems. The majority expressed readiness to contribute work, money, and time to persuade others or to talk to village and provincial leaders about the matter.

These results may suggest the proportion of the population available for mobilization in Shubra el Gedida and perhaps in communities similar to it. The number, interestingly, corresponds closely to election results in the summer of 1968, when 59 percent of Shubra's eligible voters chose to go to the polls to elect the local committee of the ASU. With survey results showing that 62 percent of adult males possess a participatory attitude, and an overall village voting record of 59 percent,[1] it seems clear that the politically active population of Shubra constitutes a ratio of approximately 2 to 1. Whether a ratio like this is a credit to the regime depends largely on how one looks at it. A voting participation record of 59 percent of eligible voters is by no means a poor one, but as evidence of the regime's expressed intentions to activate all citizens, this record falls short.

The Correlates of Political Attitudes

Attitude groups have so far been identified. It remains now to show what may account for these differences among members of the same village community.

A possible explanation of participatory attitudes in Shubra seems generally consistent with a number of basic propositions in Lerner's *The Passing of Traditional Society*. A low level of individualism in Shubra seems clearly associated with lower degrees of exposure to the outside world and the mass media. For instance, more individualists than conventionalists (69 percent of the highly individualistic respondents, 50 percent of the moderately individualistic, and 32 percent of the conventionalists) had made visits to Cairo and Alexandria. (Travel to Damanhur was a common practice for all three groups.) Similarly, the greater a respondent's exposure to the mass media, which emanate almost entirely from Cairo, the greater the probability that he would manifest an individualistic attitude (see table 35).[2]

Table 33
Attitude Groups in Shubra El Gedida

	Individualist		Conventionalist	Total
	High	*Low*		
Number	37	47	51	135
Percentage	27	35	38	100

1. Only males voted in the ASU elections in Shubra.
2. For the mass media exposure and political awareness indices, see chapter 9.

Table 34
Respondents' Ability to Form Opinions about Village Conditions
(in Percentages)

Attitude Type	Able to Identify One or More Problems	Unable to Identify Problems
Individualist		
High	100	0
Low	68	32
Conventionalist	41	59

$X^2 = 27.22$, significant at .001 level.

NOTE: Total for column one is 90 and for column two, 45. For totals of rows see table 33.

In this connection too, positive correlation exists between awareness of national and international affairs, and individualistic attitude (see table 36). Political awareness, however, is primarily attributable to mass media exposure and, to a lesser extent, to literacy (see chapter 9). The media also turned out to be more extensive and effective in impact than were opinion leaders, contrary to the two-step flow of communications hypothesis.

Another factor found to be affecting attitude was membership in formal organizations introduced into the village since 1953 such as the cooperatives, the single party branch, and the village club. Conventionalists were

Table 35
Relation of Media Exposure to Attitude Type

Attitude Type	Exposure to Mass Media (Mean Score)	Difference of Means Test (t)		
		Individualist *High*	*Low*	Conformist
Individualist				
High	67	—	2.95 ($p < .01$)	2.77 ($p < .001$)
Low	52	—	—	0.87 (1/)*
Conventionalist	47	—	—	—

* 1/ not significant.

less in touch with organized political groups in the village than were individualists, and fewer belonged to village organizations. Individualists showed a membership ratio in village organizations of nearly three members to one nonmember; among conventionalists the ratio was less than half, 1.3 to 1. In short, those who make more use of the mass media, local organizations, and travel are more individualistic in attitude and show readiness to take part in village politics.

These specific observations on attitude toward political participation in Shubra and national influences on villagers suggest a minor modification in Deutsch's concept of social mobilization that involves, *inter alia,* a shift away from illiteracy and agricultural occupations in addition to a change from rural to urban residence.[3] The findings of the present study suggest that modernization, or rather the integration of an illiterate rural population into the national society, may occur within the local community itself, independently of migration to urban centers or change in occupation. Forces emanating from the center are now reaching rural communities and affecting every aspect of peasants' lives. It may be that the association between modernization and urbanization, so often encountered in the literature based on aggregrate data,[4] neither precludes modernization under rural conditions nor implies that modernization is inseparable from a change toward urban living. Due in part to effective national influences on local communities, the gap between the countryside and urban centers is becoming narrower in many countries, and, unless disaggregated into their component parts, the concepts "urban" and "rural" communities may prove less analytically useful.

Political Attitudes and Background Factors

Very little of the variation in attitudes of the Shubra population can be explained by background factors. Younger people, for instance, did not turn out to be more individualistic than older ones. The distribution of individualists and conventionalists by age groups is almost uniform.[5] Likewise, the attitudes among literates, illiterates, and various occupational groups were not distinctive.[6] Socioeconomic differences in the

3. Karl W. Deutsch, "Social Mobilization and Political Development," *The American Political Science Review* LV, no. 3 (September, 1961).
4. Notably, Daniel Lerner, *The Passing of Traditional Society.*
5. A slight tendency appears among those in their thirties and forties to be more individualistic than the rest, but it is not statistically significant.
6. Chi-square was computed for individualists-conventionalists among cultivators and noncultivators. It was found to be significant. Similar computations regarding attitudes in relation to other background factors showed a slight tendency for literates and cultivators to be more individualistic than others, but the difference did not prove statistically significant.

Table 36
Relation of Political Awareness to Attitude Type

Attitude Type	Awareness (Mean Score)	Difference of Means Test (t)		Conformist
		Individualist		
		High	Low	
Individualist				
High	61	—	33.4($p < .01$)	5.18 ($p < .001$)
Low	44	—	—	2.09 ($p < .05$)
Conventionalist	34	—	—	—

community were not sufficiently wide to lead to marked differences in attitudes, leaving exposure to external forces as the main factor contributing to attitude change.

Nothing has so far been said of primary associations of villagers, such as extended kinship groups. Much of the literature on rural societies in the Middle East stresses the influence of primary groups or corporate structure on behavior. Clans and sects are often emphasized as the basic units of societal action; the individual is expected to conform to the imperatives of the primary organization of which he is a member. Since the community of Shubra is fairly homogeneous religiously (there are too few Christians to make any difference), the following discussion examines the effects of kinship and residence only.

Kinship

Patrilocal residence has long been common in Egyptian villages.[7] Adult sons and daughters often live with their parents under one roof, abiding by the authority of an elder who determines shares of labor and crops. Common residence among kinsmen is still widespread in Shubra though not the dominant pattern (see table 37). About half the population live in nuclear family residences with no relatives. However, since half still live

7. For example, see Lucie Wood Saunders, "Aspects of Family Organization in an Egyptian Village," *Transactions of the New York Academy of Sciences* 30, no. 5 (March 1968); Winifred S. Blackman, *The Fellahin of Upper Egypt*; and Hani Fakhauri, *Kafr el-Elow: An Egyptian Village in Transition* (New York: Holt, Rinehart and Winston, 1972).

with relatives in the same compound, their attitudes were examined to find out if lack of individuality was related to kinship ties.

The most striking finding is the absence of association between residence based on kinship ties and conformist attitude. As the survey shows, 72 respondents in Shubra lived in the same compound with other relatives; these were compared with the nuclear family residents (couples who live alone or with their unmarried children) to see if living with kinsmen made a difference in a person's political attitudes. No connection between living with relatives and a participatory attitude was found. The two groups were distributed in practically the same proportion over the three attitude categories—highly individualistic, moderately individualistic, and conventionalist—with no significant difference (see table 38).

The possibility was explored whether individuals who lived in father-headed family compounds showed a more conventionalist attitude than others within the extended-family residence group. Among the 72 respondents living in family compounds, only 30 lived with their parents; the rest boarded with other relatives. It may now be hypothesized that patrilocal residence gives rise to an authority structure based on subordination to the fatherhead. Accordingly, attitudes in three groups—patrilocal, miscellaneous, and nuclear—were examined on this point. Once again, however, the expected association was not found (see table 39). Respondents in patrilocal residence did not manifest a conformist attitude any more or less than persons in other types of residence.

This finding is consistent with the observation made in this study that kinship relations in Shubra have little social or political consequence. Patrilocal residence fails to show correlates of authoritarianism. Two speculative comments may help put these results in a broader context. First, although patrilineal solidarity has been known to exist in the village until recently, Shubra never really had family clans with historical associations and memories binding them strongly together. Second, in fifteen years under the present regime, national forces have impinged on Shubra in such a way as to reduce the need for primary associations. Third, survey results discussed elsewhere (see chapter 10) show that young adults in Shubra are generally considered better equipped to meet the challenges of contemporary society. An elder in the house, therefore, does not necessarily enjoy greater respect from or authority over his offspring.

In short, the view that is commonly held of the Middle Eastern villager as inextricably bound to a corporate primary group is not borne out in this particular rural community. This finding of course does not disprove the kinship dominance proposition, but it should draw attention to the need for determining more specifically the weight of kinship ties vis-à-vis

Table 37
Mode of Living

Type of Residence		Number	Percentage
Nuclear Family Residence: No Relatives		63	47
Extended Family Compound		72	53
Number of Relatives	*(Frequency)*		
1–3	33		
4–9	14		
10–15	10		
unspecified	15		
	72		
Total		135	100

Table 38
Relation between Attitudes and Kinship (by Residence Status)

| Residence Status | Individualist | | Conventionalist | Total |
	High	Low		
No relatives living in the house	17	22	24	63
Relatives living in the house	20	25	27	72
Total	37	47	51	135

political behavior and attitudes. In Shubra, the political system has, by and large, replaced the kinship system.

Class Structure

Seen through urban binoculars, a village may seem an undifferentiated mass of peasantry. As Karl Marx once put it, villagers are as similar as potatoes in a sack. In Shubra, occupational divisions are clearly marked, and they seem to be associated with characteristics of social class, hazy as the class structure in the village still appears to be. Agricultural workers, vendors, and itinerant craftsmen constitute the lower stratum; cultivators, shopkeepers and officials enjoy higher economic and social standing. Except for a handful of individuals, however, most villagers have very modest incomes, about 50 Egyptian pounds a year for an economically active member of the lower stratum and about 150 pounds for his counterpart in the higher stratum. Residing in family compounds stretches incomes a little but does not seem to change significantly the economic picture.

Some politically articulate young villagers have referred to a presumed emergence of a local "bourgeoisie," by which they mean cultivators who had improved their lot as a result of land reform and cooperative farming. There is no doubt that most cultivators have improved their standard of living, an improvement clearly visible in their dress and housing. They have also become regular consumers of such relatively expensive items as meat, vegetables, and fruits, which in the past used to be limited to special and rare occasions. Local reform since 1952 no doubt has increased the economic differentiation between cultivators and the lower stratum of agricultural laborers and vendors.

It is true that a certain degree of socioeconomic differentiation is apparent in Shubra, though one can hardly call the emerging group of cultivators "bourgeois." Social differences take the form rather of an incipient sense of superiority, the origin of which is not often clear. While occupation, economic condition, and education are factors, social status seems to depend on the individual and the impression he makes. One cultivator, for instance, who had been practically landless but accumulated an estate of sixteen feddans in the last fifteen years has not been accorded any special prestige in the community despite his present wealth and success. On the other hand, another cultivator who had also emerged from conditions of poverty enjoyed respectable social standing and referred to other cultivators as "ignorant peasants."

Similarly, membership in a kinship group does not seem to bestow on an individual either special privileges or disadvantages. The Samad family, for instance, who monopolized the office of headman for generations and among whom one could find some of the wealthiest individuals in Shubra, included very poor persons such as agricultural laborers. In 1967, a politically active peasant who came from a very small patronymic group showed a condescending attitude toward an agricultural laborer who belonged to one of the largest and most respectable patronymic groups.

Defining social status has been further complicated by the fact that individuals of low standing such as agricultural laborers and vendors appeared as serious contestants in the 1968 local election of the ASU. When asked what makes them view an individual as a community leader,

Table 39
Relation between Patrilocal Family Residence and Attitude

Residence Status	Individualist	Conventionalist	Total
Patrilocal Family Residence	17	13	30
Miscellaneous Relatives in Residence	29	13	42
No Relatives	38	25	63
Total	84	51	135

$X^2 = 1.30$, not significant, (df $=$ 2). Critical value at the .05 level is 5.99.

many villagers mentioned individual characteristics rather than family background (see chapter 10).

These observations suggest that any effort to make sense of the current Shubra scene has to focus on individuals rather than on social classes or primary groups. The sense of social superiority recently acquired by some individuals has been the product of personal achievements such as skill, education, and political involvement or rank. The condescending cultivator, cited above, is one of the most literate, politically involved, and advanced inhabitants of the village. The peasant who was found to view his fellow peasants as ignorant was a very knowledgeable clerk and accountant in the cooperative who had quickly moved up in the ranks to become the factotum of the organization. The agricultural laborers who contested the ASU elections were products of the Youth Organization's political indoctrination program. As to the peasant who had become a wealthy landowner, neither is he distinguished for political leadership nor has he sought to use his wealth to gain social prestige.

These selective examples are presented here not only to highlight the flux in the community but to illustrate the point that neither the size of landownership nor family background account for differences found in the political attitudes of villagers toward social esteem and political participation. Moreover, no hostile attitude or accusation of conflict of interest has been directed toward those who are socially and economically privileged at present. The average villager tends to be indifferent to class categories designated in official ideology and harbors no hostility toward the wealthy few in the community.

Class conflict occurs when a contender relationship exists whereby one group's gains can be made only at the expense of another's and, second, when the contender can consciously generalize particular grievances or fears to the adversary's social group or class. In Shubra, peasants' articulation of their interests under the old regime was limited, and their grievances focused primarily on moneylenders and merchants. Under the Revolution, those who previously extracted the surplus from the peasants have disappeared from the village scene. The more recent social differentiation in the community still lacks both conditions of class conflict. Laborers, primarily agricultural, are a distinct social group who stand in a contender relationship vis-à-vis other groups in the village and may eventually develop class consciousness and form a protest movement. The practical reasons for the containment so far of such a development are discussed in the following account and in chapter 14.

Lateral Mobility

Villagers of Shubra have been drawn into activities extending beyond traditional routine or personal spheres. Politics have in recent years involved villagers in the affairs of others both in manner and degree unprecedented in village history. Yet marked upward social mobility among the inhabitants has not occurred; rather, political participation has created horizontal, or lateral, mobility, whereby individuals move within and between groups that in the past used to be beyond limits or simply did not exist. Whereas a person formerly belonged to a neighborhood or kinship group, he now belongs to political, occupational, and entertainment groups such as the political party, cooperative society, trade union, village club, self-help team, and the like.

Moreover, social and political organizations alike have no strong binding force on individuals; membership tends to be overlapping rather than exclusive and to be often just as undefined as that of informal groups. With increasing involvement in new activities, individuals cross group-membership lines frequently and easily. Upward social mobility may develop and become more pronounced, but there seem to be compelling reasons to believe this development would fall short of creating a sharply stratified social structure. Under conditions of scarce economic resources and unstable social groups of contiguous existence, change is more likely to result in lateral than upward mobility. Economic scarcity and socialistic controls on the allocation of resources will tend to press down on individuals trying to break away from the common economic conditions of the village. At the same time, the instability of social and political groups should prevent the factionalization of village politics, that is, it should contain the emergence of exclusive group memberships associated with antagonistic relations toward other groups.

Finally, social contiguity, like economic scarcity, should tend to check upward mobility. Such contiguity prevents the rise of social stratification when a person's self-image and his social definition are more strongly affected by qualities he shares with the community than by disparities. When a villager becomes distinguished in certain respects—for example, in education—he remains bound to the village folk by other ties such as neighborly and family relations, poverty, and cultural norms that prevent his escape to an exclusive social class. Spatial proximity can enforce social definitions that are generated by face-to-face conditions. "Who's who" in the village is recorded in the villagers' minds, not on the pages of a book.

For example, consider the case of Hadi Hammal, a young man of thirty-three and *imam* of the largest mosque in the village. An intelligent person, he had been able to take advantage of the free educational system in Egypt to obtain university degrees (in religion from the prestigious University of al Azhar and another degree equivalent to a master of arts in education at the University of Cairo). In this endeavor, he was guided and encouraged by an older *imam* in Shubra who had been impressed by the boy's character when Hadi was still a child. Hadi first served two years in another part of Egypt, then returned to his native village, where as *imam* he is a salaried official of the government. Despite his advanced education, he is of humble origin; his father owns less than one feddan. He has three brothers, one a janitor at the village council meetinghouse, another an agricultural laborer, and a third, a soldier. As an official, he receives a meager salary, which though sufficient for living in the village, is not enough to alleviate the poverty of his immediate relatives. He nevertheless bears part of the financial burden of supporting his parents, and, to make ends meet, he and his wife and two young children live with the rest of the family in the same mudbrick compound. Furthermore, Hadi's advanced education did not prevent his marrying an illiterate village girl, who remains secluded as do the rest of the village women who do not have to work in the fields. His children are no different—either in clothing or in hygiene—from the peasant youngsters in the village.

The most educated person in the village, Hadi is not wealthy and shares too many characteristics with his kin and the village population at large to permit an independent status for himself. He could, of course, leave Shubra, but the fact that he was away and then returned suggests either that he does not think of his chances as better elsewhere or that he has strong personal obligations to his family. I found many educated villagers in Shubra to be in a similar position.

These sharp social contrasts are too conspicuous not to be seen by other people in the village. Hadi is highly educated but lives with his illiterate parents and wife; he is politically and intellectually distinguished but economically poor. As an individual and a political leader, Hadi is widely respected; at the same time, he does not assert himself strongly in politics or socially, since he cannot afford the expenditures of political leadership nor the trappings of social status. He is daily reminded of his kin's humble status when, as he deliberates with other village leaders, his brother, as janitor, serves them tea and water. Keenly aware that he cannot elevate himself over others, Hadi makes a virtue out of modesty by deliberately assuming the humble posture of a villager and by wearing the *ghallabiya* (peasant tunic) rather than the drab Western dress of the urban Egyptians.

Living in a small community, as Hadi does, means also that he must conform to local norms of proper conduct if he is to maintain the respect of others. Accordingly, his wife must remain secluded, he must not indulge publicly in recreational activities or entertainment not generally accepted by others, and he must fulfill social obligations toward villagers regardless of their social standing or attitude toward him. In short, Hadi may well be able to help deal with village problems as one of its leaders, but he must follow the community's norms of social and moral conduct like everyone else. Such cultural considerations add to the tendency of maintenance of relative equality among the populace.

The concept of lateral mobility can now be clarified by the following observations: Acquired characteristics of an individual in Shubra are not transitive; if one is educated he does not tend to be also a member of an educated family, the wealthy class, or a status group. Similarly, if one is wealthy, he does not necessarily have a wealthy family or an education. Individuals do not move socially upward into an exclusive class but sideways into open and mutable groups. Upward political mobility has been more visible in Shubra, as a minority of less than one hundred individuals have ascended to political leadership roles above that of the average villager.

Conclusion

A political process that has been the product of national forces has given the people of Shubra a greater sense of identity and political involvement. Most of these external forces have been planned, suggesting that even a dominant regime tends to encourage a participatory attitude as an imperative of its development program. The Shubra data reveal that those who have tended to be more individualistic and participatory in attitude have been also those with greater exposure to the mass media. Villagers, regardless of their background differences, responded individually to new stimuli and to new ideas of political involvement. Background factors such as literacy, occupation, and kinship were not found to be associated in any significant way with attitudes either for or against political participation. Furthermore, patrilocal residence showed no effect on the attitudes of kinsmen; particularly, elders were not found to enjoy special influence in the compound.

One effect of the development of a participatory attitude in Shubra has been the expanding social ties and relations among individuals involved in new functional and political groups. In adding new social relations to primary ties, however, participants have not created new structures of social stratification. Social mobility has been lateral rather than upward; individuals belong to several groups while they remain in the same social stratum. Overlapping group membership has contributed to the spread of personal interests, ambition, chances, and calculations as prominent features of political behavior—in effect, a lively political atmosphere. The Shubra social system may not allow for much social climbing, but it is sufficiently mobile to encourage more participation in public affairs and to enhance personal aspirations.

chapter 13

Elections to the Arab Socialist Union, June 1968

This study has been concerned with the impact of the national policy on a local community. Developments of the economic and political structures in a historical perspective have been outlined. The emergence of cooperative societies, a municipal council and a political party branch have been discussed in detail. The emergence of leaders to fill positions in the newly created village organizations, leadership structure, and decision making, as well as the mass media, ideology, and attitudes, were analyzed. The following two chapters focus on the political process that highlights the concrete features of the structural and ideological systems outlined above. Presented here are a number of case studies relating to local party elections, crises in the cooperative societies, and conflict between agricultural laborers and the reform cooperative. Other cases and concrete events relative to the creation of new organizations have been briefly discussed in other chapters; here, assuming previous knowledge of the structural framework of community life, the focus is primarily on the process itself.

The impact of a mobilization policy on the local community has progressively promoted political participation and has created conducive conditions for political competition. At the national level, however, the trend has been to narrow the avenues of free political choice. The elections of ASU officers in the summer of 1968 illustrate this inverse relationship between the local and the national levels of politics in Egypt.

It may be recalled that, subsequent to Egypt's defeat in the 1967 war, the party mobilization drive was slowed down; by March 1968, the Sabri organization was abandoned and plans were made for returning to the election of party officers in the hope of maintaining a national consensus in the wake of a national crisis. Except for reducing the number of officers in the basic ASU committee to ten members, the 1963 formal party structure was restored unchanged.[1] The elections that followed in stages, starting in June and ending for all practical purposes in August, were perhaps one of the most freely conducted elections under the Nasser regime.[2] It was Nasser's wish to have free elections, and this wish was by and large fulfilled, as indicated by the relaxed atmosphere on election days, voters' conduct, and statements on how the elections were conducted. Electoral committees and the police conducted themselves in an exemplary manner in Shubra, thus contributing to the calm and conciliatory atmosphere that followed the elections.

Members of the regime were well aware from past experience that in some villages a single dominant family or some wealthy farmers made a mockery of free elections. There were instances in Egypt in which the Committee of Twenty elected in 1963 consisted exclusively of the members of one extended kinship group or of a local potentate and his clients. Measures were passed by the government preceding the elections of 1968 to give relatively equal weight to the vote of each participant and to free him from customary coercive practices. First, the election regulations specified that not more than one individual from a "family" (*usrat*) could be seated in the same ASU basic unit. A family was defined as consisting of parents, children, and grandchildren, aunts, uncles, nephews, and nieces. This definition falls short of including all the members of a patronymic group and was based on the most closely knit kinship ties. By preventing a kinship group from being represented by more than one person, the government hoped to curtail the influence of rural clans in many village communities. Exceptions to this rule were permitted,

---

1. See Harik, "The Single Party . . . ," *World Politics*.
2. Doubt has been cast on these elections since May 1971 by President Sadat, subsequent to the showdown between him and the 'Ali Sabri camp in the government. The only evidence to substantiate Sadat's charges of unfairness in these elections came from Ahmad Kamil, the chief of intelligence, in his court testimony. Evidence showed that Sha'rawi Guma'ah and Sami Sharaf used the Secret Apparatus, which they headed, to secure the election of some supporters in Alexandria and perhaps elsewhere. The chief of intelligence seemed to know only of the Alexandria situation.

It should be made clear that only at the higher levels of the Central Committee was free choice seriously constrained, and evidence has yet to be produced to confirm Sadat's controversial statements. Furthermore, it may be added that the 1968 elections were by far freer than those called by Sadat in the summer of 1971, despite all his pledges to conduct free elections.

In some small villages, several cases were noted where illiterate villagers would ask the electoral committee chairman to choose for them. While in the cases reported to me chairmen declined to assume the role of voters, some influenced the choice by suggesting names to unprepared voters.

especially when it was deemed necessary for two persons of the same family to be elected in order to give both peasants and laborers representation on the committee.

Another measure sought to preclude the concentration of local power in the hands of one person. Thus a decree was issued prohibiting *'umdahs* and village shaykhs from running for office in the ASU unless they resigned their positions. The office of *'umdah*, as mentioned earlier in this book, had been either abolished or reduced to minor functions, and a village shaykh was no more than a notary public. However, in small villages or hamlets, *'umdahs* continued to be strong local leaders, representing their hamlets in the village council of the commune. The measure, therefore, was aimed at preventing such *'umdahs* from consolidating all offices and power in their persons.

In 1963, the regime sought to limit the hegemony of local potentates by assigning fifty percent of all seats in the ASU and the National Assembly to peasants and workers. A "standstaat" system of representation was thus introduced, whereby occupational or other corporate groups would be guaranteed by law a specified number of representatives. Although the *Charter* mentioned five social segments that constituted the coalition of working forces in the ASU, only two categories were used in elections: (a) peasants and workers and (b) "miscellaneous groups" (*fi'at*), which included all those who were not peasants or workers.

Legal measures by themselves cannot fully produce a dispersion of political power within a short period of time, and had there not been more fundamental reform measures taken in years past, legal steps would have been easily circumvented. However, as shown in the case of Shubra, economic resources had been reallocated more equitably, and villagers had become more politically involved and independent. The following report on the elections in Shubra and at higher levels illustrates the extent to which these efforts have been successful or limited in their results.

Shubra, like other communities, was called upon to elect ten officers to serve as the basic party unit at the local level. The village as a whole formed a single constituency, and every voter was to vote for ten candidates. Once elected, the basic unit (the Committee of Ten) was to choose its own officers—a secretary and his assistant—and then elect among its members four delegates to represent Shubra in the ASU Markaz Committee. The district committee would do the same by electing its own officers in addition to eight deputies to represent the markaz at the Province Committee (*Lajnat al Muhafazah*), which also elected its own officers and representatives to the National Congress. In all these committees, from the basic unit to the Province Committee, the same rules applied regarding kinship relations, combinations of offices, and corporate representation.

In Cairo, representatives of all the provinces would form a National Congress that would elect a Central Committee of 150 members. The Central Committee would elect a Supreme Executive Committee to serve as the top executive body of the ASU under President Nasser.

The elections from the basic units to the National Congress lasted from June 25 to July 23, 1968, when the National Congress convened in Cairo. The election of the Central Committee, which had been scheduled to take place in August, was postponed by President Nasser, who went to the Soviet Union for medical treatment. Nasser called upon the National Congress to elect a Preparatory Committee of 100 to prepare, until his return, for the election of the Central Committee. Whatever purpose such a move was to serve, the manner in which the Preparatory Committee members were selected and President Nasser's unwillingness to hold the elections in his absence made it clear to members of the National Congress that freedom to select leaders at the national level suffered from serious official constraints. In selecting members of the Preparatory Committee, each provincial delegation elected a number of representatives from its own province, but the President exercised his prerogative of replacing those he did not wish to have by others of his own choosing. In addition to the 125 elected representatives of the Central Committee, the President appointed 23 ministers and 2 aides, making a total of 150. On October 19, 1968, the Supreme Executive Committee was elected by members of the Central Committee, but only 8 received more than the minimum votes necessary for election to the 10-member body. Both Anwar al Sadat and 'Ali Sabri were elected to the Supreme Executive Committee, but Sabri received the highest number of votes.

The composition of the Supreme Executive Committee clearly reflected President Nasser's wishes, since three of its members were original officers of the Revolutionary Command Council and the rest were ministers appointed to the Central Committee by the President himself. Of the eight-member executive body, only two were elected at the basic unit level: 'Ali Sabri and Anwar al Sadat. Little did President Nasser know then that these eight would select Sadat as his successor two years later.

The 1968 elections thus illustrate the political phenomenon of an inverse relation between conditions of free political choice at the local levels and limited freedom nationally. While political participation was encouraged and, by 1968, freed from official constraints, free political choice at the national level was limited by the wishes of the President.

The following section describes the manner in which the people of

Shubra responded to the elections from the beginning of the campaign to the time they sent their representatives to the markaz and province committees.

The Campaign

Campaigning for elections in Shubra was a novel experience for most candidates, many of whom found it distasteful, burdensome, and tricky. "We are not craftsmen," said one candidate from the defunct Leadership Group (LG), "we do not have the experience or the skill in electoral matters." Some found it embarrassing because it forced them to conspicuously draw public attention to themselves in a culture where the individual lowered his voice in respect of the group and the judgment of others. The norms of individual modesty were upset by an institution that required aggressiveness and unabashed personal publicity. Modesty, however, was a matter of social etiquette rather than an actual relinquishment of identity, and villagers felt obliged to bow to etiquette.

Many candidates who felt embarrassed to call attention to themselves did not campaign but simply let it be known, usually to those who were in leading positions in the village and to their immediate friends and relatives, that they were running for election. They were soon to discover from experience what the survey had already indicated: communication by word of mouth does not travel very fast or far enough. Many voters on election day did not know that these candidates were running for office.

Ahmad Suhdi, the proud secretary of the LG, was repelled by the idea of campaigning for himself: "You think I would go around begging people to vote for me? They know my record in the village and it is up to them to make up their minds." He lost the election. Another, Hadi Hammal, refused to become a candidate until several individuals, including some leading figures in the village, approached him. Once he became satisfied that his candidacy would be a response to public request, he obliged and commented, "The will of the people is like delegation." Nevertheless, he refused to campaign, feeling it below his dignity. Also, he felt constrained by his candidacy and could not freely discuss other candidates. "There were candidates of whom I did not approve," he said, "yet being a candidate myself, I could not speak up against them. Otherwise I would sound as if I was indirectly drawing attention to myself by showing the faults of others." Fortunately for him, he was not a politically controversial figure like Suhdi and was elected.

The desire for anonymity was not the only factor inhibiting individuals from campaigning. A feeling prevailed among some candidates that there was something basically immoral about politicking. One had to be crafty, make promises that he knew in advance he could not fulfill, and perhaps trick others while expecting similar behavior from them.

The feeling of propriety on the part of some candidates illustrates the normative constraints that prevented candidates from utilizing the most productive methods of obtaining votes. The cultural norm of dignity and self-respect required a certain pattern of behavior inconsistent with the requirements of electoral politics. Obviously, the cultural norm of self-respect did not greatly impede campaigning; skilled individuals could satisfy both, and the discussion here has dealt only with candidates inexperienced in the art of politics. In short, the cultural predicament of men like Suhdi and Hammal is presented not to illustrate cultural barriers to competitive politics but rather to draw attention to the manner in which villagers' lives are complicated by the advent of new institutions.

Skillful candidates in Shubra as well as members of the Youth Organization, however, were by no means distracted by conflicting normative demands. The youth group campaigned vigorously; in a clear departure from the prevalent campaigning styles, its members criticized other candidates publicly. Like gadflies, however, they provoked others more than they rallied support. They taunted villagers for being complacent and congenial, and pointed out the evil of voting to please friends instead of to serve a political principle. Elections, they argued, were a highly important opportunity for the people to choose leaders who would attend to the people's interests and serve the nation as a whole; they should not waste it by giving the elections away to opportunists who dominated the village for personal advantage. The youth group viewed campaigning as a duty and requirement of the democratic process. To speak out was not considered a means to draw attention to the self but to the principles for which one stood.

The shock-effect methods of the youth group did not lead to victory for any of them but was rewarding, they felt, in that they considered the campaign an educational experience for them and for the people. As some of them rationalized their defeat in the elections, "It was just expected. We are still young and running in elections for the first time. A sudden victory might make us conceited, but the struggle is on and we shall run again."

Politically experienced candidates such as Muhammad Kura, Mahmud al Sayid, and 'Ali al Shawi held professional attitudes toward elections and felt that campaigning was perfectly legitimate so long as it was conducted with decorum and unoffensively. Such was the spirit and the manner in which they conducted their campaigns and made contacts with as many voters as possible.

Finally, it should be remarked that all candidates campaigned, although in different styles. Those who were sensitive to proper conduct talked to their friends and acquaintances and encouraged them in their own way to help. The "professionals" focused on the most productive contacts and alliances, whereas former members of the defunct Youth Organization were publicly defiant.

Since posters were prohibited, campaigning was limited to personal contacts. Youth Organization candidates who had used posters at the beginning of the campaign tore them down upon learning of the prohibition. Pamphlets were permitted, but no one resorted to that method in Shubra. It may be recalled that shopkeepers in Shubra used loudspeakers on market day to attract attention to their commodities, but no candidate was foolhardy enough to copy them.

Candidacy

Aspirants to political office in the ASU nominated themselves; some did so independently, others by arrangement with the political group to which they belonged. In the summer of 1968, the three major political groups in Shubra—the Kuras, the agrarian reform peasants, and the ASU under Amir—were still in the center of the village political arena. A number of independents also nominated themselves and contested the elections. Two independents were of the higher social stratum: a school teacher who had not previously been involved in politics and a shopkeeper, Abdo Suhdi, younger brother of Ahmad Suhdi of the Leadership Group. It seems that Abdo Suhdi was also behind the nomination of the school teacher. Three other independents from the lower socioeconomic stratum nominated themselves: one was a very humble vegetable vendor, the second was a school janitor, and the third was a laborer. The candidacy of these last three aroused more curiosity than political problems, and although some village leaders considered such a venture presumptuous, the public viewed the nominations with respect. Indeed, thanks to the personal efforts of the vendor, he received enough votes to rank eleventh among the candidates. Only Kamil Samad, as was mentioned in an earlier chapter, saw in this political venture of the humble members in the community a sign of moral decline.

Old political veterans such as Haj Hammal and Majid Rayyan declined to run in this election, giving way to younger men. As they explained their decisions, young men in the village had distinguished themselves in the last three years and should be encouraged to take the lead. These two men, who had played a central role in the politics of the village, seemed overtaken by a sense of rapid movement and change with which they could no longer comfortably keep pace.

Among the political groups that had formed electoral slates, the Kuras played a very active role. Muhammad Kura, who had withdrawn from politics since 1965, sensed that the tide after the 1967 war was starting to turn in his favor after three lean years. Therefore, he decided to return to active politics in Shubra and renewed his visits and his contacts in the village. His brother Sayid, who had formerly acted as his deputy in Shubra, had withdrawn from active politics and left Shubra in the summer of 1967 to live and work in Alexandria.

Muhammad's political strategy during this election was to avoid open confrontation with his opponents and create an image of himself as a seeker of unity. Such a strategy was generally favored by ordinary villagers, but Muhammad Kura had additional reasons for adopting it. Many things had changed in the village during his absence, and he was aware that the ASU drive under Amir had made valuable contributions and won over many young men from whom he would like to receive cooperation in the elections. Indeed, many young Kura sympathizers were active members of the Leadership Group. Should he come back with a war cry against the men and the record of the ASU in the last three years, he would no doubt split his own following and consolidate the opposition against his slate. He could use more subtle means to weaken his opponents and win the elections.

Anticipating the electoral contest with him, former LG leaders were suggesting to villagers that Muhammad Kura was using Egypt's defeat in war to take revenge on his opponents in the village and on the regime. Rather than fall into this trap, Muhammad posed as an avant-garde candidate, a progressive supporter of the regime and socialism. He even had favorable comments to make about the ASU record in the village. This attitude baffled some of his opponents, one of whom remarked defensively to me, "We know this man is not a socialist." However, to the majority of villagers, Muhammad Kura was not casting a new image but was acting as they had known him before his political defeat.

Muhammad's electoral tactics, namely, his alliances with other candidates and nominations that may have proved valuable to him, were very crafty. His main opponents were Ahmad Suhdi, Mahmud al Sayid, 'Ali al Shawi, and members of the Youth Organization; had they united, they would have become a formidable opposition. Muhammad's strategy was to keep them divided and avoid launching a frontal attack on any of them, a step that could have led to their unity against him. First, he renewed contacts with promising young leaders who had become part of the LG drive during his absence such as Hadi Hammal, Bashir Shubrawi, 'Abd Ata, and Shatir. The last three were very favorably inclined toward the

Kuras even when they were fully cooperating with the LG and Amir, as illustrated by their refusal to take part in the political quarrel between Amir and the Kuras. Shatir was a landless laborer who worked as a foreman for the Kuras, but he was also a very bright young man who had worked hard for the LG. Evidently, the Kuras were not entirely opposed to maintaining links with the dominant group in the village then. Should they have asked Shatir to withdraw from LG activities, he probably would have had no alternative but to do so. However, his intelligence and skill made it possible for him to operate within both opposing groups without creating the impression that he was inconsistent in his alliances.

Three months before the elections, Muhammad Kura started to use his village house again and held meetings with these young men and other supporters. The only difficult case for Muhammad was Hadi Hammal, whose ties to Amir and the LG were stronger than those of the other three. Hadi Hammal hesitated to run, although he was urged to do so by both Muhammad Kura and Amir. When he did decide to become a candidate, he confided to this writer that the man who had really convinced him to run was his former village tutor, a modest religious man who was instrumental in Hadi's education. Both Muhammad Kura and Amir were pleased with his decision and maintained contact with him. Muhammad's successful efforts to attract moderate young leaders of the ASU ruined the chance for an opposing united slate made up of former leaders of the Leadership Group. Hadi Hammal ran as an independent, and the three other former LG members ran on the Kuras' slate.

Muhammad's design was still far from complete. His next step was to undermine the electoral base of Ahmad Suhdi, the secretary of the defunct LG and the protégé of Ahmad Amir. Suhdi was vulnerable on two counts: his younger brother Abdo had political ambitions of his own, and his LG assistant secretary, Fikri Haris, was not on good terms with him. Abdo Suhdi was inclined not to run on the Kura's slate in order not to alienate Amir more than necessary. Amir had urged him not to run at all but to support his brother Ahmad. Muhammad Kura understood Abdo's situation and encouraged him to run as an independent candidate. As it turned out, Abdo's candidacy was a severe blow to his brother Ahmad. In addition, Muhammad Kura concluded a confidential agreement with Fikri Haris for mutual support, should Fikri run as an independent. In effect, Ahmad Suhdi was isolated, and the only course left for him was to form a front with 'Ali al Shawi and Mahmud al Sayid.

The possibility of forming an election slate with 'Ali al Shawi was complicated by several factors. The dissolution of the LG, his brother's rivalry, the differences between Suhdi and the Youth Organization, and the success of Muhammad Kura in taking away the young and promising members of the LG did not make Ahmad Suhdi an attractive candidate to anyone. Moreover, Amir himself had strained relations with 'Ali al Shawi because he had tried to isolate 'Ali from the LG and because he had been involved in the efforts to unseat 'Ali from the cooperative board (see chapter 14). However, under the circumstances, Amir probably would have been able to reach an agreement with 'Ali had he not been preoccupied with his new but unconfirmed appointment as head of village councils for Gharbiyah Province.

For the former ASU leadership, everything seemed to fall apart. There were general factors not in its favor—for example, the defeat in the war—that opponents blamed on the socialist drive led by 'Ali Sabri. Also contributing to its decline in popularity were the banning of the Youth Organization in the fall of 1967, the eventual dissolution of the LG, and the reorganization of the ASU on a national scale. These last two steps amounted to an official rebuff to the former party leaders. In addition, Ahmad Amir, who was the mastermind behind the LG and the Youth Organization, was in the process of being transferred to another province as the chairman of the bureau of village councils. The news of Amir's impending move did not enhance the chances of a strong stand by former allies in the LG, as Amir's own bargaining power had been undermined by his becoming a "lame duck" mayor. Amir had not yet decided to accept the promotion not only for personal reasons but also in appreciation of the critical political state in Shubra, but few believed that he would turn down the offer.

In effect, the ASU leadership in June 1968 did not even run a slate; its members ran as independents or in alliance with the Kuras. Ahmad Suhdi, Mahmud al Sayid, and Hadi Hammal ran as independents, Fikri Haris was in league with the Kuras (see chapter 7), and three other LG members were actually on the Kuras' slate. With the situation generally unfavorable for the ASU former leaders, they evidently decided not to run a slate. To do so would have had the effect of polarizing the LG against the Kuras in the campaign, a move that would have been in the Kuras' favor since by then everything had gone against the LG record. Ahmad Suhdi and Mahmud al Sayid supported each other but without forming a slate. The Youth Organization, on the other hand, nominated two candidates, despite the fact that it had been suspended from political action as a national movement. Not only in Shubra but in other places as well, many individual leaders of the Youth Organization continued to act as if they still had a viable organization. Both candidates of the Youth Organization were workers; one was a driver of a tractor in the reform cooperative, and the other performed clerical duties at the village infirmary. Neither had any social status or family name to back him.

Unlike the former ASU leadership, the agrarian reform board united in the elections against all opposition from the Kuras or the Leadership Group itself. Under the strong leadership of 'Ali al Shawi, they formed a slate of four board members—'Ali and three others of the ablest among them—in the hope of attracting votes in the village at large, not only from cooperative members. Electoral alliances were also made with Mahmud al Sayid and a respected school teacher, who had been teaching away from his native Shubra. Although he was still able to find some allies, 'Ali's network of alliances was not really impressive, for he, too, had been suffering from setbacks (see chapter 14). The weakened position of the Leadership Group prevented him from forming an alliance with them. On the whole, it seemed that 'Ali and the former ASU leaders were paying the price of the power that they had enjoyed in the previous years, while the Kuras collected from all the disgruntled elements in the community.

The Election and Its Aftermath

The elections took place on June 25 in an atmosphere of calm. Written tickets were not permitted inside the election booth, and the voter had to name his candidates orally. Counting on his social position and connections in the province, Muhammad Kura tried early in the morning to enter the election room, as people of his social standing had been prone to do in the past. He was rebuffed sharply by the police officer at the entrance, who was not willing to tolerate any infraction of the election rules. Abdo Suhdi, who claimed to be a friend of the police officer, told me that the officer had given him an early warning not to count on their personal relations and to keep his distance from the election booth.

Election results, which were not announced until a couple of days later, showed a lead but not an overwhelming victory for the Kuras. Muhammad Kura was elected with only three of his allies: Shubrawi, Ata, and Shatir. The former two were popular in their own right. Also elected were Fikri Haris and Abdo Suhdi, two of the candidates with whom he had made alliances, and Hadi Hammal, a friendly independent. Ahmad Suhdi and the Youth Organization candidates were defeated, but Mahmud al Sayid was elected. The land reform group won two seats, 'Ali al Shawi and Sa'd Hamid, and lost two. The breakdown of the newly elected Committee of Ten was Kuras 4, Land Reform 2, Independents 4.

It was obvious that Muhammad Kura would lead in the Committee of Ten, but he had no clear majority that would permit him freedom of action. Instead, he had to rely on alliances with independents. It appears that the composition of the committee, as described above, may have been illusory because most of its members, with the exception of Muhammad Kura himself and Abdo Suhdi, were former members of the Leadership Group. The fact of the matter is that the membership of the Leadership Group was not clearly defined and consisted of coalition groups. Only its top leaders constituted politically a hardcore, ideological group. However, by the defeat of its secretary Ahmad Suhdi, the core force of the LG suffered a serious blow in Shubra, contrary to other places in the markaz, where most secretaries of the former Leadership Groups were re-elected to the new committees. In view of Suhdi's circumstances in Shubra, his defeat was quite understandable and, in many ways, inevitable. Nevertheless, Mahmud al Sayid and Hadi Hammal could be referred to as independents or former members of the Leadership Group.

The first decision expected to be made by the new ASU Committee of Ten was to elect its secretary and his assistant in addition to four delegates to the Markaz Committee. Ahmad Amir, who had practically kept a hands-off stance before the elections, was quite displeased with the results, especially with the defeat of Ahmad Suhdi, his trusted "deputy." Consequently, he snapped back quickly and conducted a strong campaign among the members of the new Committee in a last minute effort to contain Muhammad Kura. The possibilities seemed weak but not lacking, since there were six members who were not allies of the Kuras. He hoped to reach a consensus among the six as to who would be the proper candidate for the contested offices. However, what he failed to realize was that only three members of the new Committee were hardcore opponents of Muhammad Kura, while the rest saw no reason why they should defeat him, especially if they could fulfill their goals through him.

First, there was no disagreement regarding the office of party secretary; the feeling was that Shaykh Hammal had a clear advantage over everyone else since he enjoyed the confidence and respect of both Muhammad Kura and Ahmad Amir. Instead, the contest revolved around the office of assistant secretary and the four delegates to the Markaz Committee. The Kuras had slated 'Abd Ata, one of their faithful supporters, for the position of assistant secretary, but he was opposed by Ahmad Amir, who viewed Ata as a Kura client lacking independence. He wanted Mahmud al Sayid to become assistant secretary, hoping that he could swing the committee in his favor. He counted on the two reform cooperative members, who strongly opposed the Kuras, and Abdo Suhdi, who was promised support by Amir in his bid as a delegate to the Markaz Committee. He also was depending on Fikri Haris and Hadi Hammal. This arrangement was opposed by the Kuras, who were strong opponents of Mahmud al Sayid. In the face of a deadlock, a compromise solution was reached through the initiative of the Kuras, and they withdrew their candidate in favor of Abdo Suhdi, an independent. This plan won the grudging support of Amir, and Abdo Suhdi was elected despite his preference for a position on the Markaz Committee.

The only stubborn resistance to Abdo's election came from 'Ali al Shawi, who abstained from voting. Al Shawi's opposition to Muhammad Kura remained strong, partly because they had been rivals for leadership in the village and for national office in the 1964 elections and partly because 'Ali was one of the few local leaders acting with class consciousness, as illustrated by his use of the phrase "peasants against notables [al kubar]." His struggle extended beyond the limits of Shubra to the markaz and provincial levels. As a member of the cooperative board that included several hamlets in addition to Shubra proper, he had contacts and influence in ASU committees elsewhere besides his influence among leaders of the reform peasants in the province. He was hoping to win a working majority for peasants in the executive committee of the province, and this plan called for the defeat of Muhammad Kura. The Kuras became irate with 'Ali's extensive campaigning against them and described him as an arrogant man who did not know his proper station. Later, they sought unsuccessfully to oust him from membership in the village Committee of Ten.

While independents were elected to head the Committee of Ten in Shubra, the Kuras received the lion's share of the delegation to the Markaz Committee. Muhammad Kura headed the delegation with two of his allies, Bashir al Shubrawi and Shatir, and he succeeded in eventually reaching the ASU Central Committee. The only delegate elected in opposition to the Kuras was Fikri Haris, who, as mentioned elsewhere, broke with the Kuras immediately after the elections. This had no damaging effect on Muhammad Kura, but it served as an indication in Beheira Province that he had no absolute control over the Committee of Ten and, *ipso facto*, no power monopoly in Shubra.

The Committee of Ten politics was affected by individual sympathies and antipathies of the members toward one another. Despite their prominence, neither Muhammad Kura nor Ahmad Amir could overcome these personal factors. For instance, Shubrawi's hostile attitude toward Fikri considerably complicated the Kuras' relations with the latter, while Hammal's opposition to 'Ali al Shawi seriously constrained Amir in his efforts to outmaneuver the Kuras.

An interesting phenomenon throughout this election period, from the day the Committee of Ten was elected to the period during which the committee's officers were chosen, was that no outside force could or did affect the outcomes despite the fact that many forces on the markaz and provincial levels were interested in the results of Shubra's elections. The opponents of Muhammad Kura, especially Hasan Faris, the former ASU district secretary, and 'Abd al Mun'im Makram, a member of the National Assembly, were particularly interested in seeing anti-Kura forces, especially Ahmad Suhdi, come out on top. There was no obstacle to their interference, that is, to their actually campaigning in the village and influencing the voters on behalf of their candidates, other than the villagers' indisposition to allow outsiders openly to manipulate their elections. Such an invasion of village autonomy would not have been accepted passively.

Participation in the Elections

Only members of the ASU were allowed to vote, but this meant practically all eligible voters except for women. Women were legally eligible to vote, but the practice in Shubra was for them not to join the ASU, since in rural areas the ASU was considered a man's world. Thus the elections in Shubra were limited to adult males eighteen years and over. The issue of who was entitled to vote among them was complicated by two criteria: card carrying and dues paying. The membership record had never really been very well kept, and only those who had made a point of asking to have their name on the ASU roster and who paid the initial membership fee were on the party lists. When it came to paying dues, the picture looked dismal. Only eighty members in Shubra had paid their dues, and no special effort was ever made by the ASU local leadership to collect dues. Membership in the ASU had never been clearly defined or strictly observed, and it was generally assumed that all voters were party members. Thus two weeks before the elections, membership cards were made available by the ASU Secretariat for distribution to all voters regardless of whether they had paid their dues or not. Membership cards equal to the number of voters were sent to the Markaz Committee secretary, who then gave them to the secretary and his assistant of the defunct Leadership Group to distribute. It may be useful to note here that the ASU officers at the markaz and provincial levels continued to function as party officials until the election day, whereas the Leadership Groups at the village level considered their functions to have ended on March 30, when Nasser announced his plan to reorganize the ASU and hold elections. As they had been instructed to do, Ahmad Suhdi and Fikri Haris announced that voters could pick up their cards at the ASU village office from 8:00 a.m. to 2:00 p.m. and from 5:00 p.m. to 6:00 p.m., Tuesday through Friday. The number of people who picked up their cards during that period was not very large, and the deadline was extended to the following Monday. In the meantime, Fikri and Suhdi decided to expedite the distribution by sending cards to voters through friends and neighbors. This apparently went against the rules, which stipulated that cards should be handed to the voters in person. At the end of the period, 920 cards had been distributed, and 400 unclaimed cards were returned to the Markaz Committee secretary. As it turned out, Fikri and Suhdi were later criticized by friend and foe, by the former for returning cards that could have been for friendly voters and by the latter for the alleged banning of voters from receiving their cards.

On election day, 700 of the 920 eligible voters cast their ballots; 30 of their votes were declared invalid, leaving a total of 670 votes. Muhammad Kura and his ally Bashir Shubrawi received the highest number of votes, 72 percent and 60 percent, respectively. In view of the Kuras' popularity and Muhammad's skills, local observers were expecting that he would be able to carry to victory more than three other candidates on his list. Impressive as his showing was after his period of political withdrawal, the results were considered a qualified success.

The intensity of competition may be assessed from the number of candidates running in the elections. Twenty-four candidates contested 10 seats, a ratio of 2.4 to 1. In terms of degree of participation, 59 percent of the eligible voters actually took part in the elections, but only 53 percent cast valid votes.[3] These figures correspond fairly well with survey results, where 62 percent of the respondents manifested a participatory attitude (see chapter 12). It therefore may be concluded that in this rural community about two-thirds of the population participate in local politics, which is neither outstanding nor insignificant when viewed in the light of comparative voting behavior. At any rate, it is not as high a participation rate as is usually claimed by the regime.

As has been seen in the opinion survey results regarding kinship, family ties did not play an important role in the elections. For instance, kinship groups of patrilineal descent did not do well in the elections. The Rayyan family, one of the largest, had two of its members running in the elections, both of whom lost; and the next largest family failed to put up a candidate for elections, despite the fact that many of its members were active in

3. As in the survey, these figures were based on the total number of adult males 18 years and over. The total number of voting cards sent to Shubra by the ASU was 1320, while the total universe in the survey came to 1350.

village affairs. In response to my query on this matter, one of them said, "It is not a matter of family ties," meaning the elections. Rivalry among kinsmen was made conspicuous by the bitter opposition of the Suhdi brothers to one another. Although some candidates were assisted in their campaigns by close relatives, there was no evidence of clan solidarity.

The difference between the elections in a mobilization system such as Egypt's and those in single party systems of Communist countries is in the number of competitors for the same office and the absence of a clear definition of party membership. In Shubra, party membership is synonymous with voters. The fact that valid party cards were distributed to voters before the elections shows clearly that below the leadership level no clear party lines separated the voters from one another. Similarly, the fact that more than two candidates competed for each office shows that the ASU is not a single party in the classical sense but a group of citizens willing to participate in the political and social life of their community. The implication of this broad-based arrangement is clear: the regime intended to give legitimacy to political competition, if not struggle, on the popular level by including different economic and opinion groups in an all-embracing political organization.

The only individuals officially excluded from participating in the ASU elections were Mustafa Samad and a villager who had been dealing in drugs. Legally, the case against Mustafa Samad was based on the fact that he was convicted of irregular conduct in handling the finances of the cooperative society in 1959. The real motives, though, were political, since the Samads were associated with the rural oligarchy of the old regime. Indeed, as I was told in the village, Mustafa Samad was the only person who had been politically disenfranchised (*ma'zul siasiyan*), that is, prohibited from taking part in any political activity.

Tolerance of political competition and struggle in the ASU would not have been possible had the regime not clearly drawn the line between popular participation and its own power position. In no way did the regime allow its legitimacy and power to be questioned by the election of the ASU officers. As shown in this examination of the Shubra elections, free competition started to suffer from the limitations imposed by the regime once the elections reached the national level. However, it should also be remembered that the very act of permitting the electoral process to continue at the national level under a limited degree of freedom suggests that the gap between the ASU officers and the regime was not too wide. Had there been an indication of a serious schism, the regime would not have allowed the process to take place; or, it could have resorted to appointing all national party officers.

The range of groups that participated in the competition for offices in Shubra is indeed impressive. The elections included candidates from the lowest income and social groups in the community such as vendors and laborers, as well as small cultivators, shopkeepers, village officials, and rich farmers. In historical perspective, it is the participation of the lower socioeconomic groups that makes the difference in the political life of the community. These groups had never been able to participate freely in the political process or run for office themselves before 1954. Although the most humble among them did not become a member of the ASU Committee of Ten in 1968, it is worth noting that the vendor ranked eleventh in the number of votes received, and, should there have been a vacancy in the Committee, he automatically would have occupied that position.

The official party changed in character and leadership several times within fifteen years as a result of the shifting policies of its sponsor, the national regime. Ideological changes and shifts in attitudes toward various groups and individuals subjected the official movement to changes in organization and leadership in the community of Shubra as well as nationally. However, there has not been a complete reversal between 1953 and 1968, only changes in emphasis that brought some to the fore and pushed others to the background in the party leadership of Shubra.

Finally, it can be concluded that, since 1952, processes of change have resulted in a political pluralism in the community that has so far withstood the test of change. Since a high degree of lateral mobility and political movement now exists, future changes in national politics may result most likely in the villagers' reorganization of social groups and readjustment to new social conditions, not in their withdrawal from politics.

Conclusion

By organizing political competition locally, the national government neutralized some of the economic advantages of the privileged in Shubra and allowed for candidates to compete on a relatively equal basis. First, by undermining the economic basis of the Samads' power, it contributed to their political decline and eventual exclusion by official measures. Not all the economically privileged, however, were subject to official opposition. Many, such as the Kuras, were actually encouraged by the national government to assume leadership in order to contain and defeat the older and more threatening oligarchy that had been associated with the old regime. At the same time, villagers from the lower social stratum such as agrarian reform peasants were encouraged to participate in village politics through the official party.

The national government has contributed to the circulation of elites in Shubra in two basic ways. First to be noted is the category of government actions, such as electoral rules, taken with the intention of affecting local leadership composition and second are developments in national politics that had unexpected effects on local leadership mobility. National events such as the regime's turn toward socialism, starting in 1956 and culminating in 1963, supported the rise to political leadership of lower-stratum villagers such as the agrarian reform peasants. The continuation of the regime's move toward the left and activization of the ASU in 1965 contained well-to-do farmers such as the Kuras and gave rise to new leadership, including local officials and ordinary villagers. Then again, the turnabout by the regime after the 1967 war and the liberalization of recruitment to the ASU resulted in new changes in local leadership. As observed in this chapter, the Kuras returned to a position of political prominence in the village, though not one of hegemony as in 1961.

Local officials, who are often described as all-powerful in developing countries, were clearly not so in Shubra, since not many of them took an interest in village politics. The leaders who had emerged among officials in Shubra were subject to routine transfer, leaving their political base for other political competitors to fight over. The very fact that local officials had a short tenure of service in a community proved to be a serious limitation to their power. As mentioned above, the mayor of Shubra, Ahmad Amir, was transferred to another position at the most critical moment in the struggle of his local political group. His transfer, ordered by higher government officials irrespective of the local political situation, had a deleterious impact on the political fortunes of local leaders who had risen in the ASU Leadership Group under his sponsorship.

Change in the national government's orientation was another reason why political leadership by officials in the local community was seriously limited. Nasser's 1967 suspension of political activities in the Youth Organization and the abandonment of the 'Ali Sabri organization in favor of free ASU elections undermined the party cadres who had emerged in the Leadership Group in Shubra and in the Youth Organization chapter, both of which were led by local officials. Thus the physician and the agronomist, who had played central roles in the Youth Organization chapter in Shubra, found themselves in 1967 without a political base, and they, like Amir, were soon transferred to other places in a routine administrative shuffle.

In short, the effects of the national government on local politics have been to make local leadership roles insecure, as the high turnover rate in Shubra suggests. One effect of the high turnover rate has been the prevention of the hegemony of one dominant political group in place of the old Samad oligarchy. In 1961, the Kuras had almost reached the point of stabilizing their leadership and dominating the community's politics when intense political competition supported by national developments prevented them from enduring beyond 1965. Again, what seemed like the possibility of domination by the Leadership Group under the mayor was cut short by national events.

The election results of 1968 clearly reflect the intensity of the leadership struggle and turnover rate. All three political blocs that were active during the period of 1963 to 1967 emerged weakened in the Committee of Ten in 1968. The Kuras made a comeback, but without the strength they had enjoyed in the ASU committee of 1963, just as the agrarian reform peasant group lost some of its former strength. The Leadership Group, which had the upper hand between 1966 and 1968, suffered the greatest loss. However, in this political flux, a degree of continuity was maintained, since all three groups continued to be represented in the new basic committee of the ASU. Political pluralism in Shubra survived the difficult test of sudden political changes. Moreover, despite the momentous changes in leadership, partisanship has not hardened, as leaders of different groups still recognize the need to cooperate with leaders of other groups. Cooperation has been manifested clearly in the compromises reached in the Committee of Ten's election of local officers and district delegates. As leaders have not become more antagonistic toward their political opponents, one may expect that village politics will not become factionalized but that the citizens of Shubra will continue to manifest lateral mobility by maintaining political ties with more than one group at the same time.

Again, no class struggle was witnessed in the elections of 1968. More than ever before, individuals from a humble background ran in the elections, but hardly any of them raised class-oriented slogans or was discriminated against because of his background. The Kura group, which included the only candidate with high income, received support from a majority of low-income villagers. However, the members of the Kura group also included the largest number of educated villagers. Two exceptions to the observation about the lack of class struggle during the elections may be cited. 'Ali al Shawi, in campaigning against the Kuras, set himself up as a representative of "peasants against the notables," though this theme was advanced in muted tones on a person-to-person level. The second exception was an agricultural laborer who had been a member of the Youth Organization. He also made use of class appeal, calling on peasants to stop voting to please their social friends and consider the interests of their class. I could not, however, detect any signs that class appeals were making any strong impression on villagers. Indeed, both candidates who made use of them did not do very well in the elections. 'Ali and one of his supporters barely got elected, and the other candidate lost.

chapter 14

Crisis in the modern sector

It has been shown in this study of Shubra el Gedida that village organizations—the party branch, the municipal council, and the cooperative societies—have been the arenas where political competition occurs and where issues arise and are resolved. The cooperatives are economic organizations, but, since they affect the major economic resources of villagers and their officers exercise considerable influence in the community, they have also been politicized. Moreover, the regime itself has encouraged the political involvement of these organizations, as may be recalled from earlier chapters of this book.

The main question here concerns the impact of politics on the cooperative societies and their leaders. The fact that boards of the two cooperative societies in Shubra were dissolved by executive action of the governor of Beheira Province in 1967 and 1968 makes cooperative-society politics a pressing issue. Although the decision to dissolve the cooperative boards came from outside the community, the crisis originated in the internal politics of Shubra itself. By discussing the sequence of events that led to this situation, it is hoped to depict concretely the realities of the political process in the community and underline once again the thesis that politics is an essential part of socioeconomic reform. This discussion also shows how fragile local organizations may be in a society where national bureaucracy assumes a preponderant position.

Dissolution of the Cooperative Boards

The boards of the two cooperative societies in Shubra were dissolved by orders of Wagih Abaza, the governor of Beheira Province, one in July 1967 and the other in February 1968. These peremptory decisions were probably related to the strains that Egypt was experiencing as a nation just defeated in war. The national government then became preoccupied with the consequences of military defeat and turned its attention away from local concerns. Instead of calling elections when the terms of the cooperative board members expired in 1967, the government simply extended the terms of office without even specifying a date for new elections.[1]

The extension was resented by all aspiring village leaders as well as by cooperative members not satisfied with the boards. Particularly displeased were other local organizations such as the ASU branch that had hoped to influence the outcome of new elections. Thwarted by the national government, these interested parties resorted to nonelectoral means to attain their goals. This step is all the more understandable when it is recalled that the cooperative boards in Shubra were cohesive bodies that could not easily be affected by local opposition except during board elections. The first instance to be discussed involved a struggle between the ASU and the regular cooperative board, and it points to the vulnerability of a local organization whose political support in the community has been undermined.

The Case of the Regular Cooperative

The board of the regular cooperative was elected in the fall of 1961[2] after a fierce struggle between the old Samad guard and the Kuras. Cultivators of irreproachable personal integrity and knowledge of agriculture ran on the slate opposing the Samad candidates and won the election.

The board members were respected and capable individuals, strongly supported by ordinary cultivators but lacking a strong political commitment and the tenacity to withstand the pressures and slights to which public servants are usually subjected in a community suspicious of holders of public office. They were service-oriented individuals, ideologically committed to the reform efforts of the regime in the countryside. In addition, the office held the prospect of personal prestige and perhaps economic advancement. The main compensation for holding such an office, however, was limited to a share in the dividends and minor favors which they could discharge to themselves and their friends. As material benefits were negligible, board members became especially sensitive to criticism and felt that their free public service was not duly appreciated, although criticism and suspicion of their record came from only a militant few.

1. In the future, election dates may become a routine matter, but, in 1967, they still had to be called by the national government.
2. They assumed their responsibilities in January 1962.

More important than criticism, perhaps, in disheartening the board members and making them partially lose interest in their offices by 1966 was their involvement in the struggle between the ASU and the Kuras. As allies and supporters of the Kuras, their political position was weakened when the Kuras lost leadership of the ASU, and their commitment to the cooperative waned. As the board members gave less attention to the cooperative's business, the two clerks in charge of accounts and the storehouse became practically free from supervision. Some villagers started to make allegations of fraud and profiteering against the clerks, sometimes charging the board with complicity rather than negligence.

At this point, the Leadership Group of the ASU stepped in to supervise the activities of the cooperative through a committee of three knowledgeable members. Many villagers who had been critical of the cooperative admitted that irregularities stopped after the ASU intervened. The dissolution of the cooperative board, therefore, was not connected with alleged malpractice by the cooperative clerks.

Despite being an economic organization concerned with agricultural management, the cooperative could not remain isolated from village politics and continued to draw political leaders into its affairs. In this particular instance, the board members were second-order leaders leaning on the prominent Kuras. When the latter were still in a politically leading position, the board was very active, and the cooperative engaged the interest and respect of most villagers. As the Kuras' position weakened in 1965 and as the ASU became critical of the board members, the board members reacted diffidently and became indifferent to their cooperative duties.

It may be suggested here that, in a mobilization regime, political participation by members of a functional organization contributes to that organization's viability and effectiveness in performing public business. Obversely, when political support of such an organization becomes lax, the organization may become unable to withstand pressures and threats. The following therefore describes in more detail the manner in which political support of the cooperative board was undermined and how it was subjected to interference by administrative power.

When Amir was appointed mayor of Shubra in 1965, he found himself head of a community most of whose leaders were allies of the Kuras. The village council, the ASU Committee of Twenty, and the board of the regular cooperative were formed of sympathetic elements or allies. No other organization was free from Kura influence except the reform cooperative. Naturally, Amir felt a need for change in the leadership of local organizations to carry out his duties effectively in the community.

Developments in the ASU in 1966 allowed Amir to have party leaders with whom he could cooperate; however, the cooperative boards proved to be a hard target for the new mayor, since they did not fall under the direct authority of the ASU or the village council. He was nevertheless determined to change the boards even before the end of their legal term by soliciting the aid of provincial officials, but his efforts were unsuccessful. As for the village council, which he headed, only two influential councillors were in partial agreement with his policy on the cooperatives. It was thus obvious that Amir had no powers to dislodge the cooperative boards despite his great influence in the ASU and the village council.

The mayor's opportunity to settle accounts with the regular cooperative came in 1967 in the aftermath of the June war. In the desperation of military defeat, the Egyptian government was afraid of suffering another blow by having a poor cotton crop. The main danger to a good cotton yield is the boll weevil, and the government pressured local officials to fight the pest vigorously. The governor of Beheira Province issued orders to all cooperative boards in the province to lead the fight against the pest. Amir and the Leadership Group cadres claimed that the majority of the regular cooperative board members did not take part in the campaign against the cotton worm. Wasting no time, Amir reported the members to the governor and recommended dissolution of the board. He received prompt response from the governor, who took steps to ban the board, an act that curiously enough went unopposed by anyone in the village or elsewhere.

The dissolution of the cooperative board was not the result of any incriminating evidence against board members of deeds punishable by court or in violation of cooperative laws. There was no charge of embezzlement, fraud, theft, infraction of the rules, or mismanagement. Fighting the pest was actually the responsibility of cooperative officials, not board members. It is, therefore, surprising that the governor was able to carry out his decision so easily and with no objection from any source.

The fact that even the board members did not try to fight the dissolution is astonishing. Not very ambitious politically, members of the board had no incentive to stay in an office which was personally demanding and publicly unrewarding. "People are not appreciative," commented one board member, "they are quite suspicious of a person in office. If a board member repairs the ceiling of his house, buys a water buffalo, or improves his land, they think that he is using public funds of the cooperative for personal advantage." Actually, the board members were oversensitive; in fact, no widespread or serious criticism was in evidence against them. Neither through my informal contacts nor through the survey did I detect a strong feeling of discontent, except among a very small minority. Therefore, it may be that the board members' lack of interest in preserving their position was the result of political adversity and lack of material reward for service.

There were two other interested parties who could have challenged the governor's decision but did not: the Kuras and the General Cooperative Society (*al Jam'iyah al Mushtarakah*) of the district, a confederation of district cooperatives in the district of Damanhur. The Kuras did not stir because their influence with the governor and their political fortunes in the province were at the lowest ebb, and they could not afford to jeopardize their interests by provoking the governor. While he politically had turned against them, the governor treated their interests kindly and was generous to them on many occasions. Furthermore, it was not wise politics for those notables who were kindling hopes of a return to political eminence to confront the regime's representative in the province.

The inactivity of the General Cooperative Society is more surprising and may be indicative of the organizational weakness of the whole cooperative enterprise in Egypt. Action in the case of the Shubra cooperative should have been initiated by the General Cooperative Society, whose officers assembled in their headquarters in Damanhur more in the manner of club members than as leaders of an economic movement. I discussed the case of the Shubra cooperative with them and was surprised to find that they had taken no position on the matter nor had they shown any concern. It was obvious that they did not feel any solidarity as a cooperative movement of national importance and therefore did not defend or take interest in the case.

The cooperative movement in Egypt does not have an autonomous national organization but rather acts as a semi-official welfare agency to meet the agricultural needs of cultivators. In practice, each cooperative society in a community stands by itself, unrelated to others. It is like a local branch of the Agricultural Credit Bank, with local representatives on its boards yet with very little influence beyond the local society. In theory, the cooperatives have provincial and national organizations, which unfortunately are inactive, especially the national organization. After the board was dismissed, Shubra's cooperative was run as an extension unit of the Agricultural Credit Bank, and, to make matters worse, a new, inexperienced agronomist was appointed. Without a cooperative board to assist and advise him, the new agronomist found it difficult to carry out his daily responsibilities and felt bitter that no advice was available to him locally.

It is obvious from this case that an economic organization with a semi-public character and in the service of the community cannot remain immune from politics and, *ipso facto*, from political struggle and competition. Officers of an organization of this kind have to be prepared to be politically involved in order to protect its interests. In Shubra, officers of the cooperative board were political but not sufficiently motivated or interested to withstand the pressures that political leaders usually face. As a consequence, the cooperative society under their leadership became extremely vulnerable and succumbed to external pressures most readily. This was a blow to a cooperative society that had one of the best records of performance and achievements in the province.

Had the board members wanted to resist external intervention, they would have had to resort to the courts, not, unfortunately, to a higher cooperative body, since agricultural cooperation in Egypt was not a movement and lacked political leverage on the national level. The value of political commitment and leadership in protecting cooperative interests is demonstrated in the case of the reform cooperative, which was subjected to similar attacks.

The Case of the Reform Cooperative

The initiative in opposing the board of the reform cooperative originally came from the membership, independent of external influence. Twelve cultivators stood together in opposition to the board and rallied about eighteen others to their cause. Thus, whereas the conflict in the regular cooperative was generated by politically expansive efforts of the local party organization, in the reform cooperative it arose out of internal competition for leadership and allocation of cooperative resources.

The opposition leaders in the reform cooperative were ordinary members who had aspired to replace the incumbents by regular electoral methods but were frustrated when the government extended the term of the existing board. With their normal access route blocked, they resorted to other measures to unseat their opponents. One of the three leaders of the movement was Ibrahim Tukhi, the brother of the former board secretary who had been defeated by 'Ali al Shawi, the incumbent board secretary.

Unlike the incumbents, the Tukhi group did not seem to have any aspiration for leadership in the village community beyond the cooperative itself. The purpose of their action was to gain advantages available to leaders in the cooperative. These included the authority to appoint mechanics, drivers, guards, and farmhands for the cooperative. (Some of the advanced mechanics and of course the clerical and professional staff of the cooperative were appointed by the agrarian reform authorities in Damanhur, from whom they also received their wages.) Tukhi himself was a tractor driver in need of a job, having been laid off from the Kura farm for economic reasons. He had tried unsuccessfully to secure employment in the reform cooperative before he took up the banner of opposition. Although his collaborators themselves were not looking for employment, they were appreciative of the possibilities that a position on the board would give them in helping friends and relatives. For example, Shawi had given the job of labor contractor to one of his brothers and appointed another brother a switchboard operator for the cooperative's telephone. In addition to patronage possibilities and enhancement of his political fortunes in the community, a board member enjoyed certain pecuniary benefits such as receipt of ten percent of the dividends, not an impressive source of income but a prize nevertheless.

The Tukhi group started in the summer of 1967 to speak out against the board and rally supporters. Then, in January 1968, they organized themselves and presented formal charges against the board members by submitting petitions to the Agrarian Reform Commissioner in Damanhur; the governor of Beheira Province; Anwar al Sadat, then Speaker of the House in the National Assembly; and 'Ali Sabri, the Secretary General of the ASU. This massive assault resulted in three investigation committees' being sent to Shubra from the ASU Secretariat in Cairo, the agrarian reform authorities, and the governor of Beheira Province.

The Tukhi group charged the board members with corruption in collusion with the agronomist. In particular, they charged 'Ali al Shawi of having illegally prospered by diverting cooperative resources for his own personal use. Specifically, they claimed that he had sprayed his clover by using cooperative spraying machines free of charge and that he offered to spray his neighbors' fields at a low rate. They also charged 'Ali's brother with having cut down trees belonging to the cooperative and with using the cooperative's tractor to transport them to the family compound, where they were used in constructing a roof. They accused another board member, Yasin, with complicity from the board, of selling a waterwheel that belonged to the cooperative. Then 'Ali, the rest of the board members, and the agronomist were charged with having sold some of the provisions such as seeds and fertilizers and of having pocketed the money. They were also accused of having bought poor-quality cotton at low rates and crediting it to the cooperative at the regular price of high-quality cotton.

The conflict within the cooperative society had political implications beyond the cooperative proper, for 'Ali and his colleagues were village leaders, some holding positions in the ASU. Obviously, 'Ali's political opponents, especially the Kuras, viewed this development favorably and gave the Tukhi group advice and moral encouragement.

Of the three investigation committees, only the governor's found incriminating evidence which it thought would justify action against the board. The governor's committee found the board guilty in the following instances: an irregularity of conduct was committed by Yasin, who confessed to having sold one of the cooperative's waterwheels; 'Ali's brother was found guilty of cutting trees which belonged to the cooperative society; and board members in general were charged with favoring their own fields in the use of cooperative machinery. There were other irregularities charged, although guilt was not established to the satisfaction of the committee.

It is necessary to note here that, in the author's opinion, the governor's report was clearly biased, doubtless for political reasons. In discussing the issue with the Department of Legal Matters, which prepared the case for the governor, I was struck by the vehemence with which the officers of that department advocated the case against 'Ali in particular and their willingness to believe other charges against the board for which they had not themselves been able to find evidence. Neutral observers in Shubra were very wary of accepting some of the charges that the Department of Legal Matters had accepted.

The Tukhi group was not satisfied with the outcome of the committees' investigations; they wanted action. Rather than wait to hear again from the committees, they pleaded their case with the ASU provincial secretary, Ibrahim Adam, who pressed for action on the basis of the governor's committee findings. Adam's support was fruitful, and the governor dissolved the board with an injunction that the agronomist and the storehouse clerk be transferred. The order, which was made public and published in the newspapers, did not have the signature of the agrarian reform commissioner of Beheira Province, as he had not concurred with the governor's decision. The board members and the agronomist refused to comply with the governor's orders and continued working as usual. Only the storehouse clerk was transferred by the commissioner. Surprised by this defiance to the governor's orders, the Tukhi group requested an explanation from the commissioner, who told them flatly that the governor's orders lacked legal force (*qarar mayi'*). (The law requires that any action by the provincial government regarding agrarian reform business be signed jointly with the agrarian reform authorities.)

The conflict between the agrarian reform peasants of Shubra had clearly developed into a jurisdictional matter between two provincial government agencies. Since its inception, the Agrarian Reform Administration (ARA) was an autonomous government agency, shielded from the regular civil service. This autonomy was a legacy from the 1952 period, when the Free Officers discovered that implementation of the land reform law was hampered by rigid administrative rules and an unsympathetic bureaucracy. They consequently side-stepped the regular bureaucracy and created an autonomous agency for land reform that was responsible directly to the head of state. Thus, when provincial governors were given power over departments of various ministries in their provinces in 1960, they discovered that the ARA was a special case over which their authority was limited.

Since the governor's measure was ineffective, the Department of Legal Matters in the province, acting on advice from the governor's office, asked the agrarian reform commissioner to consider the governor's orders as "recommendations" until he gathered his own evidence against the board. But this did not satisfy the commissioner, who considered the request meaningless, since it came after the governor's orders had been made public. The request was ignored, and for four months the governor's orders went unheeded.

In the meantime, the governor of Beheira was transferred to Gharbiyah Province, and a new governor was appointed in his place. Although unrelated to the cooperative case, the change in governors served to reduce personal tension and gave the new governor an opportunity to smooth things over with the commissioner. Consequently, the agrarian reform commissioner conducted a *pro forma* investigation of his own in August 1968 and, in a conciliatory move toward the provincial government, charged Shawi, Yasin, and the agronomist of deviation (*inhiraf*) and the rest of the board with complicity. He then ordered the board dissolved and the agronomist transferred, but only the judgment against the latter came to pass. Refusing to submit to administrative order, 'Ali took the case to court as a last resort. The court ruling was in 'Ali's favor, and the cooperative board continued to function despite opposition from the provincial government and the commissioner of the ARA.

The board of the reform cooperative obviously showed more determination than the regular cooperative board and was able to resist interference from the provincial government for two important reasons. First, its leadership was politically involved and its political position hinged on maintaining its cooperative base. Second, the higher departments of the agrarian reform cooperatives were strong and maintained close connections with the local organizations. This connection proved useful when the governor used his superior powers against a local cooperative. Although the local political position of the reform cooperative board was on the decline, it was still very much a part of the local contest. It fought for its survival and, in the course of its struggle, preserved the autonomy of the organization.

Crisis in the modern sector

The board of the reform cooperative in Shubra enjoyed a position of local autonomy.[3] The very fact that its opponents had to resort to the highest provincial government authorities for the dissolution order is indicative of the board's independence from other local organizations. The Leadership Group and the mayor, who had hoped to dominate the cooperative boards without the assistance of outside agencies, failed in their attempts. Not until the mayor resorted to the provincial governor, in the case of the regular cooperative, did he obtain results.

Throughout Egypt, relations between a cooperative board and higher authorities vary according to the leadership of the local cooperative. In the case of Shubra's reform cooperative, strong leadership gave the society autonomy not only from other village organizations but also from the ARA as well. This independence was particularly in evidence when 'Ali went so far as to resist the ARA dissolution decision. He had also shown a measure of autonomy vis-à-vis the ARA earlier when he refused to employ non-native individuals recommended by ARA officials.

Another instance that illustrates the board's autonomy and how it withstood pressures from both village organizations and higher provincial authorities may be related here. Before the village council acquired its own television set, Ahmad Amir asked the reform cooperative board to lend the council its set so that the ASU could operate it for the village public. The cooperative board adamantly refused Amir's request, whereupon he raised the issue with the agrarian reform commissioner and asked him to intercede. The board still refused to comply, arguing with the commissioner that the cooperative board was ultimately responsible for the set in case of damage.

Administrative interference in the cooperative societies of Egypt continues to be a strong threat to their development. As in Shubra's cooperative societies, high-handed administrative interference was based more on arbitrary considerations than on incriminating evidence against the two societies. Minor infractions were given severe penalties that would not have been upheld if brought to a court of law. There were some leaders, particularly in the ASU, who argued and worked toward giving cooperatives greater autonomy, not only from administrative interference but also from the Agricultural Credit Bank and the Ministry of Agriculture. The peasants' representative to the ASU Secretariat for the years 1968–71 was a peasant from Beheira Province who strongly advocated this course.

3. The reform co-ops in hamlets, which are entirely under the Agrarian Reform Administration, are a different case altogether and are practically run by agrarian reform officials. Examples of this kind of co-op can be found in the Khazzan area of Beheira Province.

However, unless agricultural cooperatives themselves develop a regional or national movement that will give them power in the political life of the country, their autonomy will remain fragile.

Conflict between the Reform Cooperative and the Agricultural Workers

A conflict that developed between agricultural laborers and the board of the reform cooperative is related here to illustrate how two organizations created by the same regime to improve life in the countryside became incompatible. Of particular interest in this case is that the two organizations at odds were members of the lowest income groups in society. The role played by the ASU in this case gives an idea of the attempts and failures of that mass movement to solve the problem of surplus farmhands in Egypt.

Agricultural workers in Egypt, especially migrants, were traditionally recruited by labor contractors who assigned them to employers. The practice was for a labor contractor to hire farmhands below the market rate and sell their services to others at a profit. The whole institution of contract labor came under strong attack in the 1960s, the role of the middleman being considered exploitative. The socialist government of Egypt thus became opposed to the institution and planned to abolish it. However, finding no alternative means of maintaining a labor supply without contractors, the regime took no drastic action; rather, slow and half-way measures were taken to replace contractors by more palatable means. The manner in which this policy affected Shubra and its local political process is discussed here.

Agricultural workers constitute more than twenty percent of adult males in Shubra el Gedida. Some are employed in the village, while others are sent by labor contractors elsewhere, primarily to Liberation Province, the land-reclamation site west of Beheira on the Cairo-Alexandria desert line. Workers in Liberation Province are in the employ of the government but are supplied by labor contractors. In 1965, the national government tried to induce village councils, by giving the mayor and the village council special remuneration, to assume responsibility for supplying surplus labor in their villages to Liberation Province. Ahmad Amir, the mayor of Shubra, responded by appointing an employee of the village council to carry out the operation under the mayor's supervision. Except for some minor practical problems, the operation worked well but, by 1968, had not entirely succeeded in replacing labor contractors.

The labor problem that stirred up political matters in Shubra pertained to local workers supplied to the reform cooperative. The need of the reform cooperative for agricultural workers varied from approximately two hundred workers during peak seasons to fifty or fewer in off seasons. They were generally wanted for clearance of drainage and irrigation canals, work in the palm tree groves that the co-op managed, as well as for the regular services provided by the cooperative to cultivators. Until this practice was changed in 1966, the board employed a contractor. In 1959, 'Ali al Shawi gave the job to his brother, who managed the labor supply without difficulty until 1964, when political rivalry between 'Ali and the Kuras reached its peak. The Kuras then organized a labor "trade union" in the hope of taking over the contract from 'Ali's brother, an attempt that failed because they had the cooperation of neither the ARA nor the cooperative board. Moreover, no effort was made by the Kuras to involve the workers in the selection of the trade union officers or in other matters. Instead, Muhammad and Sayid handpicked six men: three agricultural laborers and three landed peasants. To the workers, the trade union was "a Kura business" and, as one of the six "officers" told me, "They registered our names and told us that we were selected representatives." The Kuras' effort in starting a trade union for agricultural workers failed for other reasons such as the problem of surplus farmhands and the lack of a trade union orientation among workers in Shubra.

This issue, however, did not die. In its nationwide drive to mobilize the population in 1966, the ASU took up the matter of labor contractors, revived the idea of trade unionism, and arranged for the acceptance of unionization by the Ministry of Agriculture. In Shubra, they found an already registered union but one that was not operative. The ASU was more successful than the Kuras, but the party's efforts fell short of organizing the workers at the mass level and instead focused on creating a trade union leadership. The district secretary of the ASU, Hasan Faris, invited the three labor members of Shubra's trade union (the landed three were dropped by the district secretary) to meet with other worker representatives in the district of Damanhur for lectures on socialist exploitation by labor contractors and on the organization of trade unions. They were informed that official and semi-official government agencies exploited them no less than did landlords and that the only means of self-improvement was for them to organize themselves and manage their own affairs without the services of a labor contractor. At the completion of the training course, the ASU district secretary told the worker representatives that they were henceforth in charge of labor recruitment and sent them back to take charge of organizing workers in their communities. Apparently, he considered these worker representatives to have received adequate political education to qualify them for such a leadership role.

'Ali's brother, the labor contractor for the cooperative, was consequently removed from the employ of the cooperative, and a "trade union" of three members was assigned his responsibilities. In effect, the only functions this so-called trade union of agricultural workers performed was to recruit laborers for the reform cooperative and to collect the laborers' wages from the Agrarian Reform Administration.

Although the cooperative board and the agronomist complied with these measures, they resented the action and were less than cooperative with the trade union leaders. Politically, the trade union deprived them of a lucrative patronage job and also constituted a personal affront, since the ASU secretary informed the laborers' representatives that cooperative societies were exploiting them.

The major problems of the trade union in Shubra, however, were of a practical and organizational nature rather than purely political. The "trade union" was a name without an object. It had no formal membership, dues, election of officers, or even common understanding of trade unionism. Only two of its three officers were active: Hasan Rayyan dealt with the reform cooperative proper, and Husni Salman was in charge of recruitment for the newly organized, second reform cooperative, the Mihtab co-op, which had been established in 1963 from the Mihtab *waqf* land. Workers conceived of the trade union officer as someone who performed the functions formerly carried out by the contractor—delivering them to the work site and paying their daily wages.

The most immediate problem facing the trade union officers was to secure the wages of the workers they had recruited. The difficulty stemmed from the fact that the ARA paid its employees once every two weeks, but, because of red tape, it was often longer between payments. Workers subsisted on their daily wages and could not afford to wait. In the past, the labor contractor had paid them on a daily basis, using his own funds, and then reclaimed his debt when the ARA paid. Under the trade union arrangement, the board in the Mihtab reform cooperative helped Salman, the trade union officer, by advancing him credit, but, in the main reform cooperative of the village, this practice was not possible because hundreds of workers were involved and especially because the board was not sympathetic to the trade union idea. Hasan Rayyan was paid for his services one piaster per worker per week, which gave him an income practically equal to that of a fully employed agricultural worker but provided no resources with which to pay his recruits in advance. Therefore, he was caught up in a problem situation that he could not solve without the assistance or cooperation of both workers and the cooperative society. He claimed that the board and agronomist of the cooperative society, instead of helping him, were obstructing his work by unnecessary delays in signing his workers' papers and were casting doubts on his integrity. Consequently, the trade union problem became an issue between Rayyan and the cooperative society.

The conflict between Hasan Rayyan and the cooperative reached its peak in the summer of 1968 and further complicated 'Ali's precarious position both in the cooperative and as a village leader. Rayyan had become convinced that 'Ali, in agreement with the agronomist, was trying to get rid of him in order to re-install his brother as a labor contractor. The day after Rayyan heard a rumor that he had been accused by the board of exacting more than the fee to which he was entitled, he entered the office of the agronomist in the presence of many members of the cooperative and challenged 'Ali and the agronomist to prove their charges. They denied that they had made such charges, and Rayyan left satisfied. Later in the day, he showed me his account book, and I talked to workers who appeared to be satisfied that Rayyan was not overcharging them.

By forcing a confrontation with the cooperative leaders, Rayyan was able to put them on the defensive and abort any effort to remove him. Indeed, it was a defiant move that put him in a strong position vis-à-vis the cooperative society and demonstrated that he could challenge these powerful individuals and make them publicly deny their allegation against him. By making a big issue of his conflict with 'Ali and the agronomist, Rayyan drew public attention to the real issue in case they tried to remove him under the pretext of failing to recruit workers for the society.

Rayyan's efforts to make known in the village and in Damanhur his differences with 'Ali al Shawi and the latter's alleged obstructions added to 'Ali's difficulties and made accusations of improper conduct against him more credible. 'Ali was known even among his closest colleagues as a stubborn person, and he certainly did not do anything to disprove the charge in the way he handled his differences with Rayyan. From his own point of view, 'Ali believed that the most important characteristic of a board secretary was to have the courage to say no when necessary. Thus his failure to follow the common practice of obliging others (*mujamalah*) cost him friends and supporters. His difficulties in the cooperative, in turn, contributed to the weakening of his political leadership in the village, as the ASU elections of 1968 have demonstrated. Furthermore, the conflict with the ASU-sponsored trade union turned the district and provincial party secretaries against him, and they helped in bringing about the governor's decree that dissolved the reform cooperative board.

It is of interest to note that, despite their similar humble backgrounds, agricultural workers and agrarian reform peasants found themselves in conflict. However, if one should look at this conflict without preconceived ideas of social class and assess the matter as a contest situation in the context of incompatible interests, the conflict seems quite normal. As it stood then, the two groups occupied contending positions: land reform peasants were the employers, while agricultural workers were their employees. This relationship was subject to all the familiar aspects of an employer-employee relationship such as cooperation, bargaining, and conflict.

The problem of organizing agricultural workers to manage their own affairs had not been solved when I left Shubra in August 1968. There were many impediments to a satisfactory resolution of this problem. For example, Egypt had a surplus of agricultural laborers, and therefore the supply of labor was not balanced by demand. During peak seasons almost all agricultural laborers would be employed, but during off seasons employment and wages dropped sharply. The labor market and the low productivity of workers' services determined actual wages despite regulation by the government, which, in the 1960s, set the daily wage of an agricultural laborer at a minimum of eighteen piasters and maximum of twenty-five. However, not even government agencies could honor the fixed rates, and the Ministry of Agriculture paid a minimum of eleven piasters daily and a maximum of twenty. Furthermore, farmers were not willing to pay agricultural workers more than what they considered to be reasonable compensation for the value of their services. They obviously thought that government-fixed wages did not permit them to operate profitably. This feeling was also shared by small cultivators, whose need for labor was limited.

These hard facts are well known to agricultural laborers and make trade unions superfluous to them. They see no avenue of improvement for their own occupation but merely hope to find regular employment and to be paid their daily wages on time. They live from day to day within their means, and, as one of them remarked to the interviewer, "I do not have financial problems. I receive a daily wage and keep my accounts on that basis."

The absence of support for unionization cannot be attributed in this case to ignorance or lack of exposure to the outside world but to the limited benefits of unionization. As pointed out elsewhere in this book, agricultural workers in Shubra were slightly younger and more literate than the average villager, and also more politically aware.

In short, problems of agricultural workers have, by and large, defied the solution offered by the regime, while the status of the cooperative movement is still uncertain. In 1968, a moderate national interest appeared for resolving such weaknesses in the cooperative movement, but again critical political issues affecting the regime prevented the matter from being concluded.

Conclusion

Politics in Shubra after June 1967 continued to thrive unabated though strained by the national crisis. Struggles within the ASU and the cooperative societies suggest that the political process unleashed since 1952 has been deep-rooted, and no reversal to earlier periods is envisaged. Political trends that seem consistent with this study's earlier findings can be observed.

As the crisis in the two cooperatives unfolds, a variety of groups are drawn into the arena, a development that suggests that public issues revolving around one group or organization tend to involve other groups and organizations both within the community and beyond it. Another pattern that appears in village political processes is that political hegemony by one group or organization tends to be unstable and short-lived. Changes in the political orientation of the national government and the continuing expansion of political participation in the community are primarily responsible for the constant turnover in leadership and the inability of any group to consolidate its powers firmly for a long time. Moreover, individual villagers avoid attaching themselves strongly to one political leader or faction and, as observed earlier, membership in various groups tends to overlap, with villagers moving in and out freely.

Each of the three political groups in Shubra—the Kuras, the Leadership Group under Amir, and the reform board under 'Ali al Shawi—has enjoyed a measure of hegemony over part or most of the village at alternate periods of time, but each has also suffered serious political losses. None of them, for instance, emerged unscathed from the elections of 1968 or the conflict in the cooperative societies. The Kuras, who won a precarious majority in the ASU Committee of Ten in 1968, lost on the issue of dissolution of the regular cooperative board and had to accept a compromise arrangement in the selection of the Committee's officers. Previously, Sayid Kura had withdrawn permanently from politics and left the village as a result of political frustrations. Ahmad Amir in turn failed to win a majority in the ASU Committee of Ten but gained his goal of dissolving the cooperative board. As for Shawi, his base of power was weakened by the struggle in the cooperative and with the laborers' "trade union," but he was able to win a seat for himself and one for another board member in the ASU Committee of Ten.

Political instability in Shubra has prevented a single group from achieving domination over the others. Pluralism implies not only the juxtaposition of different political groups but also a certain degree of autonomy for each. Political groups as well as functional organizations in Shubra have been related to national bodies via regional links, and all of them have been sensitive to regional and national considerations. Their autonomy, therefore, may be understood in terms of the jurisdiction, which was extensive, over their local affairs. Furthermore, solidarity among board members of the two cooperatives has been very strong and has reduced somewhat the possibility of interference from other local organizations.

Politics may be considered an important factor in developing local economic organizations. For instance, because the agrarian reform peasants were politically independent, their cooperative board was able to assert itself over the official staff, including the agronomist, whereas in the regular cooperative the balance of influence was in favor of the official staff. But again, in the regular cooperative, when board members enjoyed strong political leadership under Muhammad Kura, the official staff was subordinate to the board. In the second place, the board of the reform cooperative was able to defend itself and resist outside encroachments better than the politically weakened regular cooperative could. Third, survey results have demonstrated that politically involved officials in the cooperative societies were more effective and helpful to cultivators than were their colleagues who had shunned political involvement. Fourth, in the absence of appreciable material incentives for holding office on the cooperative board, the political resources that such a position offers may be the only reward left to encourage villagers to assume responsibility for cooperative affairs. The sooner the national government understands this point, the better are the chances for a normal growth of agricultural cooperatives. Finally, the existence of vigilant political groups such as the ASU has affected the management of cooperatives and put their officers on guard against committing glaring irregularities or taking an irresponsive attitude toward members. This local mechanism to oversee the cooperative proved more useful than external intervention by the civil bureaucracy.

In short, politics has contributed to the viability of the cooperative enterprise, which in Egypt is still entirely local in character without the benefit of a national movement to sustain and support it. Cooperatives are connected with the national government by bureaucratic rather than representational ties. Unless agricultural cooperatives in Egypt gain more autonomy and develop an effective national movement, strong leadership and political involvement at the local level may be the only measures available to sustain cooperatives in their present form. Political involvement in the community, however, provides them with limited power

Crisis in the modern sector

against higher authorities of the civil bureaucracy. No doubt, politics also involves waste, which may result from friction or factionalism, but its rewards may far exceed the ills of political disengagement among villagers.

Politics always involves the price of patronage and special favors for leaders, and the sooner the Egyptians decide to pay a reasonable price for politics in the cooperative, the stronger this organization will become. Reluctance to do so has weakened the position of representative board leaders and has increased the powers of officials, a tendency that made Shubra's regular cooperative less responsive to members. It also has subjected cooperatives to peremptory and arbitrary interference from the provincial government. Moreover, refusing to pay the price of politics locally will jeopardize the democratic development of cooperatives in favor of bureaucratization, which may prove to be more expensive to maintain.

chapter 15

Conclusion: reflections on political change

With cash in his pocket and a transistor radio in his hand, he talks about socialism and socialist countries as he watches a clerk of the local cooperative weigh his quota of fertilizers. He is a peasant from Shubra whose improved economic standards have led radicals of the ASU Youth Organization to charge that he has become a member of the burgeoning "bourgeoisie" in the village. For he is now, by village standards, a conspicuous consumer in an expansive market whose transactions are no longer limited to maize and clothes but extend to ideas and votes. Growth in per capita income is relatively easy to gauge, but to assess the development of new capacities and attributes among ordinary citizens is an arduous and subjective task.

Organizational innovation and increasing functional specialization have no doubt been major aspects of modernization in Shubra. With the introduction of a municipal council, cooperative societies, and a political party branch, the community has witnessed the rationalization of its economic and political management. Previously unavailable services such as electricity, schools, medical treatment, a veterinary unit, credit and marketing cooperatives, a new marketplace, and a crafts center have been introduced, making the village the focus of attention for its inhabitants. However, not unless attitudes and behavior become integrated into the new organizational structure can real change and development be said to have occurred.

Survey findings have shown that the ideas and attitudes of Shubra inhabitants have changed in a manner consistent with changes in the community's social structure. The villager, moreover, has become part of a nationwide communications network, and ideas have become part of the currency with which he deals. As a voter, he has the opportunity to make decisions that affect other members of the community.

Conclusion: reflections on political change

It also should be clearly noted that these new experiences, attitudes, and skills have become attributes of the *average* villagers, not of the distinguished village elite only. The ordinary villager, who lacks the visibility of the star performers in the history of the community, is not a stranger to the momentous developments that have occurred in his community. A study limited to the major decisions and history of the community would have brought to light only the elite and their record in the village, not the ordinary villager whose progress is essential in the development process.

Major aspects of the development process such as rationalization of administration, education, higher incomes, mass media exposure, and political participation have been manifested clearly in the recent transformation of Shubra under the Revolution. Growth and specialization of economic functions had started to a certain extent before the Revolution, as witnessed by the founding of a credit cooperative and the introduction of police services. These developments, however, failed to generate other modernizing activities or affect the conditions of ordinary villagers, particularly because they were bound to an oligarchic power structure irresponsive to the community. Not until vast, radical reform measures had been introduced by the Revolution did the ordinary villagers become part of the modernization process.

Proliferation of political leadership and groups, in addition to specialized organizations, developed under the Revolution. Thus, village pluralism has been marked by several characteristics. Each new organization, be it the cooperative society, the municipal council, or the party branch, has had its own formal rules, regulations, officers, and staff. Each has been run by more than one and less than twenty individuals who are prohibited from holding office in more than one organization at a time. Only officers of the political party may hold one other position in addition to the party post. Second, most of these organizations have had a built-in bias in favor of small cultivators, not only in terms of services but also with respect to leadership. As it may be recalled, boards of the cooperative societies were open only to cultivators who owned five feddans or fewer, allowing only one position for a wealthier farmer. Similarly, in 1963, new rules gave peasants and workers at least half the seats in the official party committees at all levels.

Finally, rationalization and pluralization of the village economic and political structures have generated a greater volume of work, responsibilities, and resources in the community. Commenting on the position of a village headman of the previous two generations, Gabriel Baer wrote that "the village shaykh's position [headman] waxed when centralized government waned."[1] In contemporary Shubra, an entirely different principle governed local leaders' relations with the national government. Increasing responsibilities of the national government have resulted in a concomitant growth in the powers and responsibilities of local leaders, a phenomenon that can occur only when there is growth and development.

The questions raised in chapter 2 of this book regarding the place of villagers in the larger society and regarding political elites and their relations with backward groups such as rural people have been answered to the extent possible on the basis of the available data. In effect, the findings call for reconsideration of generalizations derived mostly from studies of the national system regarding the political attitudes and behavior of rural people in Egypt. Rather than repeat the same conclusions drawn in each chapter of the book, I shall turn to the theoretical implications of this study, with particular reference to political change.

Identifying the characteristics of modernization is far easier than explaining change, the reason perhaps why development literature is burdened with descriptions of societies in terms of different development phases. Because of the complexity of the change phenomenon, the theory of political change is still in its initial stages. Empirical research, however, is continuously enriching our knowledge of change processes, and a summary of some theoretical formulations, as they relate to the findings in Shubra, is undertaken here.

The Environmental Impact

In dealing with the phenomenon of change within the framework of system analysis, social scientists tend to disaggregate a system from its environment, then detect and describe interrelationships between the two.[2] In the political system of Shubra, for instance, economic factors are considered environmental in relation to the political system. External factors that emanate from another society such as an urban center or an invading foreign nation also are classified as environmental. "The seeds of change," writes F. G. Bailey, "lie in the environment of a political structure." He adds that "the term 'environment' is defined very widely: it may mean a new law, a new ideology, an increase or decrease in

---

1. Baer, "The Village Shaykh . . . ," p. 152.
2. See for instance, David Easton, *The Political System: An Inquiry into the State of Political Science* (New York: Knopf, 1963), and *A Framework for Political Analysis* (Englewood Cliffs, N.J.: Prentice-Hall, 1965); Talcott Parsons, *The Social System* (Glencoe, Ill.: The Free Press, 1951).

population, a plague, a new technique of cultivation, a tender-hearted or rigid administrator, or many other things singly or in combination with one another."[3] Change occurs when the external force is stronger than the structure resisting its encroachment, or when other parts of the interdependent system have changed. The environmental explanation of change is particularly pronounced in structural-functional and communications analyses.[4]

In Shubra, the major forces that had set in motion the processes of change came from outside the community, namely, the national government. As observed in chapter 2 of this book, the national political system is the main reference point for the political and economic behavior of villagers. Practically every single major innovation in Shubra has been introduced by the national government: cooperatives, land distribution, political party, municipal council, medical and educational services, and so on. Many of the locally initiated changes such as the crafts center, the marketplace, the self-help projects, and others have been the products of the state-introduced organizations. It would be very difficult to see major changes in a community in Egypt now develop without taking the national or provincial government into account. For instance, the efforts to establish a trade union for agricultural workers did not materialize until backed by the national government through the official party. Innovative and wealthy farmers such as the Kuras failed to develop an enterprise that had the economic basis for success because of their inability to interpret the central government's intentions toward private property and business expansion. Innovations such as improving the yield of maize or the planting of fruit trees and vegetables also have been considerably affected by the central government, which encourages farmers to experiment with new crops. For farmers to take advantage of this policy, the government first had to waive certain requirements of land consolidation and the crop rotation system.

In short, the community of Shubra has become increasingly integrated

3. F. G. Bailey, *Stratagems and Spoils: A Social Anthropology of Politics* (New York: Schoken Books, 1969), pp. 190, 191. Parsons also stresses the diversity of external factors and adds the factor of internal conflict as a source of change, though using the psychological concept of strain; see *The Social System*, p. 493.
4. See David E. Apter, *Ghana in Transition* (New York: Atheneum, 1963), *The Political Kingdom of Uganda* (Princeton: Princeton University Press, 1961), and *The Politics of Modernization* (Chicago: University of Chicago Press, 1965); Marion Levy, *Modernization and the Structure of Society* (Princeton: Princeton University Press, 1966); Fred Riggs, *Administration in Developing Countries: The Theory of Prismatic Society* (Boston: Houghton Mifflin, 1964); Robert T. Holt and John E. Turner, *The Political Basis of Economic Development* (Princeton: Van Nostrand, 1966); and Lucian W. Pye, *Politics, Personality, and Nation Building*.

into the national system of government by means of intermediate steps; the individual becomes integrated first into political and economic organizations in his own home community, then through these organizations he is linked to provincial agencies, which in turn respond directly to the national government. Peasants therefore have primarily learned organizational skills—how to manage and behave in a new and rational environment. Local organizations have become the source of community activities and the center around which political and economic powers coalesce. The national government introduced these organizations, but villagers had to run them and make them useful, with limited assistance from the center. In other words, an external force may or may not generate a change in the ways of living and attitudes of inhabitants. To elicit a positive response, innovations should be relevant to the economic life of the people, and local political forces should be able to develop a vested interest in them. Entrenched political forces may thoroughly control innovative structures or may abort their intended consequences. Formal measures alone are not enough. To abolish the office of headman and institute instead a municipal council, for instance, does not necessarily put an end to the actual powers of the headman, for he could use his local political resources to infiltrate the government's formal organizations and maintain his control. Extensive economic changes and the national government's interest in local political organizations made slim the headman's chances to ride the wave. As fully described in this book, the effects of these changes have been mutually enforcing and have undermined the power of the headman.

Local conditions have proved to be a basic factor in determining local response in yet another instance, that of political indoctrination. As noted earlier, ideological messages emanating from the capital were localized to a marked extent as villagers understood them in a selective manner relevant to their own conditions, not necessarily as they were propagated by the literati. In effect, the outcome of change has been a product of the interaction between external forces and community culture and structures. This brief statement summarizes a large body of literature concerned with political change in developing countries, though it is too broad to be a very helpful generalization in explaining political change. Interactions of various forces ought to be defined more specifically if they are to be useful.

Structural Change

A major theoretical tradition in the social sciences views the social system in terms of functional requisites and roles that perform activities designed to fulfill these requisites. In every society, it is maintained, there are basic

Conclusion: reflections on political change

needs whose fulfillment is necessary for the survival of the system, such as procurement of life's essentials, defense, social control, communication among members, common cultural norms, coordination of various parts of the social order, and shared goals.[5] A family, for instance, is supposed to contribute to the functional requisite of procreation. The role of a headman may be to maintain security and order in a village and relate it to the larger political environment of the central government. When two or more interrelated roles such as those of the mayor and municipal councillors perform specialized and coordinated activities for the fulfillment of a functional requisite, they are referred to as a structure, in this case the structure of local government.

Functional requisites of a social system are considered constant, whereas structures are subject to change.[6] Thus societies differ from one another according to their organization and along lines of Parsonian pattern variables of particularism-universalism, diffuseness-specificity, ascription-achievement and affectivity-affective neutrality. It has already been shown how in Shubra the rationalization of economic and political structures has occurred and how this has affected individual villagers. When security functions were taken away from the headman, they were entrusted to a police department which was more complex in organization and more specialized. Similarly, when municipal functions were entrusted to a mayor and a council, formal rules were introduced and roles became specialized. In both instances, it was not the functional requisites of social control and adaptation that had changed but the structures fulfilling societal needs.

F. G. Bailey views change in terms of the impact of environmental factors on the normative rules of behavior. Since a role is a set of normative rules, that is, "guides to actions and expectations," [7] Bailey feels that one

---

5. The most elaborate statement on this subject is to be found in D. F. Aberle, A. K. Cohen, A. K. Davis, M. J. Levy, J., and F. X. Sutton, "The Functional Prerequisites of a Society," *Ethics* 60 (January 1950). See also Parsons, pp. 167–70, 483–84; and Talcott Parsons and Neil J. ɔmelser, *Economy and Society: A Study in the Integration of Economic and Social Theory* (New York: The Free Press, 1956), pp. 16–20. For formulations by political scientists, see the introduction in Gabriel A. Almond and James S. Coleman (eds.), *The Politics of Developing Areas* (Princeton: Princeton University Press, 1960); Gabriel Almond "Political Systems and Political Change," *American Behavioral Scientist* VI (June 1963), and "A Developmental Approach to Political Systems," *World Politics* XVII (January 1946); and Robert T. Holt, "Proposed Structural-Functionalism in the Social Sciences," in Don Martindale (ed.), *Functionalism in the Social Sciences* (Philadelphia: American Academy of Political and Social Science, 1965).

6. Almond and Coleman, *The Politics of Developing Areas*, especially pp. 11–19; Almond, "Political Systems . . . ," p. 8; Parsons, *The Social System*, pp. 480, 483; and Bailey, in *Rural Politics*, pp. 28–33, 34.

7. Bailey, in *Rural Politics*, p. 34.

way of looking at change is to detect the manner in which environmental factors encroach on normative rules, modify them, or perhaps lead to their destruction. Trends in behavior that pertain to environmental regularities are called pragmatic rules.[8] To illustrate, Bailey takes the example of Untouchables and clean castes in Bisipara, India. A tendency among Untouchables to become rich is a pragmatic regularity. In contrast, the rule that only clean caste members should have a voice in running village government is a normative regularity, because it specifies what is right and wrong behavior. It may be preferable to call Bailey's "pragmatic rules" empirical regularities, since this category refers to developments or activities that are not performed as an obligation. The tendency of Shubra villagers to become participants and to obtain information directly from the mass media are examples of empirical regularities. Rules in general may be consistent or inconsistent with one another. In case of inconsistency, conflict and change follow. For instance, an empirical regularity may be inconsistent with normative regularities, and this inconsistency may lead to a modification of normative rules. The more skilled and rich Untouchables become, the "more often will village leaders of the dominant caste be compelled to find pragmatic loop-holes in the normative rule that only clean caste members have a say in the running of the village."[9] In other words, those who have a vested interest in the normative rules feel that it is no longer feasible to resist the new force applied by the Untouchables to gain decision-making position in the community. In this case, inconsistency between empirical and normative rules has led to accommodation of new actors under a novel arrangement.[10]

Accommodation, however, is not necessarily an inevitable outcome of such conflicting demands; resistance and violence also may occur, depending on the extent of differences in demands, the magnitude of the threat, and the opposing forces' perception of their own strength. In my study of political change in nineteenth-century Lebanon, the tendency for commoners and clergymen to become more wealthy and influential resulted in an ambivalent reaction among the aristocracy who controlled access to political leadership roles. Those who felt that the new trend was a very serious threat to their leadership and control of political and economic resources fought back, and a protracted civil war that lasted nearly half a century ensued. Others found in the newly emerging forces allies from whom they could derive political strength regardless of

8. Bailey, *Stratagems and Spoils*, pp. 1–9. A variation of these categories introduced by Bailey is referred to as "definitional roles" and "optimal roles" in *Rural Politics*, pp. 28–31.
9. Bailey, *Stratagems and Spoils*, p. 15.
10. Bailey's phrase, see *Rural Politics*, p. 33.

Conclusion: reflections on political change

normative rules prohibiting them from acknowledging commoners as political leaders. The inconclusive outcome of warfare in this case resulted in the imposition of a compromise formula that fell short of the total demands of either side.[11]

The case of Shubra permits one to view political change in another perspective. Unlike nineteenth-century Lebanon and Bailey's Bisipara, the independent variable in the equation of political change has been the normative rules that were imposed on an extensive scale by a superior force from the outside. For this reason, the main inquiry in this book has been to assess the extent to which the imposition of new normative rules has changed the behavioral and attitudinal patterns of villagers. The assumption in undertaking such an inquiry, of course, is that the introduction of a normative rule may not necessarily lead to behavioral conformity.

It has been shown in the case of Shubra that new rules have affected behavioral and attitudinal patterns of villagers, though not necessarily to the extent of complete fulfillment. The rule that a private business enterprise cannot exceed a certain fixed size has led to a decline in the economic activities and wealth of large landlords and trading businessmen. Yet this rule has not stopped members of the business community from evading the land reform laws[12] nor from maintaining a larger enterprise than the law permits by means of collusion with the civil bureaucracy. Similarly, the rule that peasants and workers should occupy half the number of seats in all the organs of the official party has not prevented members of other influential classes from maintaining control in some party units by coopting partisans among peasants and workers to fill party posts. In other words, structural change affects but does not sum up attitudinal and behavioral developments.

The idea that environmental factors make changes in a certain structure necessary in order to fulfill functional requisites of the system is not only teleological but also posits performance as the basis of survival or decay. Under such a perspective, the paramount question is, "What functions must be performed to ensure the survival of that unit and all others of the same type?" [13] Or, as Bailey puts it, when roles "prove inefficient in these capacities [functions], they are likely to be changed." [14] There is no doubt that human behavior on the individual and the collective levels is to a large extent purposive. Yet social behavior cannot be viewed exclusively in

11. Harik, *Politics and Change.*
12. See Harik, "Mobilization Policy . . . ," in *Rural Politics.*
13. Apter, *The Politics of Modernization*, p. 17.
14. Bailey, in *Rural Politics*, p. 34.

terms of excellence of performance toward the collective good. Human history has not provided a mechanism for control of social behavior on the basis of excellence in performance. Moreover, the survival concept is not often the main criterion of social change, and it is too general to serve as a meaningful explanation of sociopolitical change. Indeed, history provides us with many instances where political structures survived at a mediocre level of performance, of which the last two hundred years of Ottoman history provide an adequate illustration.

Should we apply to Shubra the principle of structural change in relation to performance, that is, the principle that a structure changes in relation to the level of performance required by the social system, we would not be able to make any headway. For instance, to maintain that the headman's office disappeared in Shubra because it failed to perform its customary functions or meet the new requirements of Shubra's community would simply not be true. Similarly, the view that landlords in Shubra were not efficiently performing the requisite of procurement and adaptation would be hard to support. On the other hand, should we state that landlords had failed to contribute to the principle of social justice, we would be treading on very shaky normative grounds. For in whose system of values are we to determine what is social justice? In contrast to the functional view, if one considered the decline in the fortunes of the landlord-merchant class as the outcome of conflicting concepts of social justice, one would remain on an empirical level of inquiry that is possible to substantiate or disregard on the basis of empirical evidence. Undue emphasis on functional relevance in explaining behavior may lead to dismissal of important political phenomena as dysfunctional, above all conflict- and power-oriented activities.

Bailey notes that survival of a social structure is not always the issue in political change. He therefore introduces the concept of novel arrangement in normative rules[15] as the basic phenomenon of political change, but this overlooks the fact that modification of political rules is most often a manifestation of antecedent change in the power position of the contestants. When clean caste members allowed Untouchables to take part in political decision making, they did so because the actual power balance in the community had changed and material and ideological priorities had been redefined. Change in power positions cannot be considered fortuitous or transient in this case because it reflects an enduring trend toward more political participation and legitimization of leadership roles for commoners who had previously been excluded. In a similar example from Shubra, when the headman or, later on, the Kuras submitted to the political

15. Bailey, in *Rural Politics*, p. 33.

Conclusion: reflections on political change

ascendancy of ordinary peasants, they conceded that the balance of power had changed in favor of the opposing forces. As stated by Parsons, change is alteration by the overcoming of resistance.[16] Obviously, developments of this kind reflect important political processes that are not limited to cultural change in the perception of roles or the legitimate rules of conduct. The following are the major aspects of change seen in a political science perspective.

First, political conflict precedes and is at the root of political change, regardless of the source which activates it. Conflict generates activities whose purpose is to modify the status quo; and the outcome, if decisive, may lead either to change or to the maintenance of existing conditions. When a change occurs, a balance of forces develops in the interest of the challenger. In this book, the newly achieved balance is not conceived of as an equilibrium, for indeed this concept, which seems so suggestive, is also vague. Here, balance simply means tolerance of the resultant distribution of interests and forces in the system. For example, clean caste members in Bisipara and the Kuras in Shubra made concessions in the interest of the challenging parties. If equilibrium means tolerance of the distribution level of forces and interests, then an equilibrium emerged in both Bisipara and Shubra. However, equilibrium is not static but, as in the case of Shubra, is subject to disturbing influences or new efforts to renegotiate the distribution of shares among contestants.

Another aspect of political change in the cases under scrutiny is the new social definition of actors in the community. When political office is no longer limited to the Brahmins of Bisipara or the aristocracy of nineteenth-century Lebanon, the criterion for leadership recruitment is no longer the same. Commoners and members of various occupations, in the cases of Bisipara, Lebanon, and Shubra, acquired the right and strength to contest political leadership positions and determine the allocation of resources. Changes in the normative rules regarding political conduct were in these cases practically a formality signifying antecedent developments in favor of new groups. Therefore, changes in the composition of the elite are not to be viewed in these instances as a simple replacement of one particular actor by another, but as a change in the behavioral and normative rules regulating elite recruitment.

The sequence of change in Shubra el Gedida differed from the other two cases in that normative rules were introduced before the new balance of power took effect. Authoritative reorganization no doubt enhanced progress toward a new balance of interests and power in the community.

16. Parsons, *The Social System*, pp. 491, 492.

When considering change in Shubra, however, one should not lose sight of the fact that the community was part of a larger system where relevant contests had been won and whose outcome had a serious effect on the community. Thus, changes in the normative rules in Shubra, too, were reflections of antecedent changes in the power balance, but ones which occurred at the national level. With the encouragement of extracommunity forces, local actors sought to consolidate the powers guaranteed them by the new rules.

When viewing the problem of consolidation of interests and powers, the emphasis is on the links developed between the new local elite and their social base in the community. For, indeed, the changing characteristics of the elites as such do not necessarily guarantee a change in the interests and powers of a new group. Unless such a change is concomitant with actual change in the social base of power, it would most likely be of a limited impact on the political community. Elites from peasant backgrounds who are not strongly linked or not subject to pressures from their constituency may not necessarily behave differently from an elite made up of other occupational groups. By the same token, a landlord whose political position depends on a constituency made up of free peasants is more likely to respond to peasant needs than a peasant leader who is not strongly connected with his constituency. The community development projects introduced by the Kuras in Shubra clearly illustrate this point.[17] In brief, the changing definition of political actors points to important political trends: elite mobility and the broadening base of recruitment patterns.

A third political trend, related to the second, is the expansion of political participation among ordinary citizens, some of whom were previously excluded. We have observed how, in Shubra, this participating trend has been linked to the proliferation of political leaders and the formation of interest and political groups. The extension of political suffrage to the masses has been one of the major trends of change during the last 150 years in the world at large. Bisipara and Shubra el Gedida are more recent instances of strides already made elsewhere. By itself, change in the normative rules governing political participation is not a sufficient indicator of change in political behavior. For instance, the law permits women in Shubra to vote, yet they have not shown a tendency to do so. Similarly, some adult males who enjoyed voting rights in Shubra did not participate; only about two-thirds of adult males took advantage of universal suffrage. Thus, in gauging political change, a political scientist

17. This point has appeared also as a major feature of the elite's relations with their constituencies in contemporary Lebanon; see Harik, *Mann Yahkum Lubnan*.

focuses on the actual participatory behavior, that is, on changes in the empirical regularity under observation.

The theoretical point raised here is not a matter of refinement or semantics but has a definite implication for understanding social reality. A social anthropologist or political scientist may indeed point out that a citizen who starts to take advantage of free suffrage has changed his role, that is, has changed the norms which guided his behavior in the past. This is indeed so, but to conceive the change in this particular citizen's participatory behavior in terms of a change in roles from nonvoter to voter is of limited interest. Moreover, if such a view is strictly adhered to, it may lead to substituting a formal category for behavioral patterns. Almond has already suggested that this is indeed how politics should be viewed when he writes: "Social systems are not made of individuals but of roles; i.e. a family consists of the roles of mother and father, husband and wife, sibling and sibling, and the like. . . . In the same sense, the political system consists of the roles of nationals, subjects, voters, interacting—as the case may be—with legislators, bureaucrats, judges, and the like." [18] Each of the categories of voters, legislators, mayors, fathers, and wives in one community or a culture area may then be considered to have the same definition. To what extent, one wonders, can we rightly reduce a political actor to the formal scheme of roles and functions? Almond, who has contributed a great deal to freeing the study of comparative politics from the formalism of the legalistic approach, has substituted in its place a cultural formalism.

The criticism advanced here does not mean that a choice should be made between two irreconcilable approaches, one focusing on roles and another on the individual. Identification of social structure, whether in legal or cultural terms, is an important stage in our efforts to understand social reality; it is not, however, the end of the tunnel. Bailey looked at empirical trends to see how they affect the normative rules of behavior. Once the normative rules become stabilized, then the behavior of a social group is summed up in terms of roles. In the study of Shubra, I assumed no set of functions but turned rather to monitoring actual activities of citizens, councillors, mayors, and party leaders. Emphasis was on empirical regularities in the political field of actions, regardless of whether they led to change in normative regularities or not. Change in empirical regularities is not less important than cultural change. Again, rather than assess the influence of a person from the legal or cultural definitions of his role, I examined a leader's position in the context of a power network. A voter

18. Almond, "A Developmental Approach . . . ," p. 188.

may participate in a particular election or may not: we monitor that fact and elicit information relevant to his behavior. There is a great deal more to a voter who abstains from voting than a change in role from voter to nonvoter! It is those behavioral regularities that explain why a voter abstains or participates that constitute the focus of political inquiry. An individual, however, is not an end by himself; he is, rather, an instance (in the sense of the laws of enumeration and concomitant variation of the scientific method). Comparison and contrast of all individuals in the community[19] permit us to make generalizations about social, not only individual, behavior.

Emphasis on role analysis of political change stems from the particular concerns of some anthropologists with cultural matters, which, though relevant, do not necessarily constitute the main focus of political science, nor do they reflect the full meaning of empirical developments we have observed in a changing world.

Political Change and the Principle of Interdependence

Political change is sometimes explained in terms of the principle of interdependence, which is based on the assumption of complexity of the social system, that is, the specialization of activity, the division of labor, and the existence of coordinating mechanisms. The interdependence of political and economic powers in Shubra under the old regime was highlighted when the Revolutionary government passed new rules regarding the distribution of land. The powerful few became weaker politically as their economic source of power declined. Villagers who were no longer economically dependent on landlords became free to commit themselves politically as they wished.

Despite its central importance, the principle of interdependence remains vague and is usually treated in the course of other contexts. As it may be constructed from various writings, the proposition can be stated in the following way: A social system consists of constituent parts interrelated in such a way that (1) if A changes its properties, then other parts B,C,D, etc., will also change their properties; and (2) when A affects B, then the interaction will have a reciprocal effect, that is, a feedback. Expressed differently, the second part of the principle means that the causal relationship between variables is reversible.

These propositions are still too broad and leave many questions

19. Statistical techniques make this operationally possible.

Conclusion: reflections on political change 273

unanswered. For instance, will any change in one variable affect all the rest or only some of them? Why should a causal relationship always be reversible? Should the change in one variable be of major proportions to have an effect on the rest, or would any change produce systemic effects? Easton states that "any change will influence the rest";[20] while for Almond, it has to be a "significant" change,[21] though the term "significant" is left undefined. Broad responses such as these have led the sociologist Alvin Gouldner to charge that each constituent part of the system is given equal weight.[22] Obviously, the very general level at which this principle has been stated leads to criticism that the specific variables should be identified and values assigned to each.

In applying the interdependence proposition to the study of political change in nineteenth-century Lebanon, I identified on the basis of empirical evidence[23] three specific variables which were shown to have reciprocal causal relations. These were political legitimacy, the actors, and the normative rules governing political relations. While this conceptualization had the advantage of being specific, it was not necessarily inclusive of all the significant variables operative in the political transformation of the nineteenth-century Lebanese political system. Though some economic aspects such as transfers in landholdings were taken into account, the study came under criticism for not paying more attention to economic relations in the process of change.[24] Obviously, the growing economic independence of those acquiring land undermined their political relations with the actors and eventually led to conflict over who had the right to assume political leadership. This was shown in discussing the emergence of the Maronite Church as a political power, but it was not fully integrated into the conceptual framework dealing with change that was presented in the concluding discussion of the study. More could have been done to determine the weight of the land transfer variable and changes in market conditions on the course of events.

Another variable that was only implicitly taken into account was the structure of power and its relationship to change. The political behavior of the feudal elite was directly related to the structure of power in the system and was reflected in their constant striving to affect the power balance.

20. Easton, *The Political System*, p. 291.
21. Almond, in *The Politics of Developing Areas*, p. 8, and in "A Developmental Approach . . . ," *World Politics*, p. 185.
22. Alvin G. Gouldner, "Reciprocity and Autonomy in Functional Theory," in Llewellyn Gross (ed.), *Symposium in Sociological Theory*, pp. 263–266.
23. See Harik, *Politics and Change*.
24. See the review by Charles Issawi in *The American Historical Review* (December 1968), pp. 679–680.

Since the power structure was decentralized, the response of the feudal system to challenges from the peasantry and the clergy failed to be conclusive, as divisions in the actors' attitudes toward the new development prevented the necessary concerting of effort. Some actors broke the normative rules that defined access to authority positions and agreed to share leadership with commoners in an effort to augment their particular share of power vis-à-vis other feudal actors, who despised their unworthy conduct. Making room for commoners to join the elite circle was a major breakthrough in the revolution against feudalism. The inconclusive outcome of the ensuing armed conflict was certainly related to the decentralized structure of feudal authority and its limitations in facing novel conditions.

In explaining political change in Shubra, economic relations and power structure have been taken into account. As in nineteenth-century Lebanon, transfer of land to peasant groups has had great political implications. Another factor of no less importance in the developments that occurred in Shubra has been the organization of cultivation under a cooperative system which enforced the peasants' claim on the land and precluded the possibilities of mortgages and foreclosures. The fact that the central government has succeeded in imposing new regulations, both political and economic, on the small community of Shubra is indicative of the subordinate relation of Shubra to the national system. However, the explanation of Shubra's developments in terms of the superior power of the central government is not enough by itself, for Shubra el Gedida was only one of four thousand Egyptian villages that went through these changes and accepted new political and economic regulations. Had the new rules not met the interest of villagers or stimulated local leaders to uphold them, the course of political change in rural Egypt would have definitely been different.[25] Indeed, as some rural groups who did not have a vested interest in the regime's reform policies proved, local opposition to national reform is quite feasible, even in a dominant regime such as Nasser's.

Change of normative rules, as has been mentioned, is not the only major aspect of political or cultural change. Reform policies were buttressed in Shubra by political organization, extensive use of the mass media, and ideological indoctrination. If one accepted the new formal rules and ideology as the main aspects of change in Shubra, it would not have been necessary to set foot on the soil of the community, as information could have been obtained from national sources. In question was not only the issue of enforcing the new rules but, more important, the actual impact

25. Rural resistance to change in Tunisia illustrates this point.

they had on villagers. Above all, it was important to find out who would support the new measures locally to prevent hostile power structures in some communities from subverting the implementation of nationally conceived reforms.

It is obvious that the Revolution, which imposed new political and economic measures on Shubra, did not act inconsistently with the material and ideological interests of most villagers. The new principle of legitimacy was based on populist and egalitarian ideology, and, consistent with this principle, new normative rules opened the way for villagers to participate in local government and the economic management of cooperatives. Community leaders shared these political principles, since most of them came from the lower strata who had vested interest in the reforms.

If the receptivity of villagers to external sources of reform is a central issue, then it follows that community leaders play a pivotal role in the process of change. However, political leaders do not behave only in the context of ideology and normative rules, for these constitute general guidelines under which widely different courses of action are possible. The Kuras in Shubra, for instance, shared the regime's ideology and accepted its normative rules; yet their political behavior differed considerably from that of the ASU Youth Organization and the agrarian reform cooperative leaders. Political power considerations affect the actor's behavior to a considerable extent and therefore should be elaborated here.

Political Change and Political Power

Authority and power under the old regime were concentrated in the 'umdah's hands and associated with wealth, birthplace, and official connections. Economic resources were also concentrated, but less so than political power, which is often manifested in more skewed patterns of asymmetry. This relative discordance occurs because political power is always more scarce than economic resources and, second, because wealth is not always available for commitment to politics, whereas politics is more often used to affect economic conditions.

Most of the absentee landlords in Shubra under the old regime failed to commit their resources to political ends in the community, and they preferred the comfort of urban life, consumption of urban goods, and social prestige. Their life styles were separate from those of the community in which their wealth was generated. In other words, the relationship of the absentee landlords to Shubra was extractive: they drew an income but did not share with the community in any other aspect of its life.

Because much of the wealth generated in Shubra was not committed to political goals in the local arena, political power resources in the community were very scarce. Thus the headman, who controlled only a part of the wealth in Shubra, was able to dominate fully the political life of the community. For if only a portion of the resources that are convertible to political power are committed for that purpose, then that portion assumes a value equal to the full power capacity of the system. The headman enjoyed that full power capacity in Shubra because ordinary peasants were economically dependent and enjoyed no surplus in excess of their immediate consumption needs to commit for political purposes and, second, because estate holders did not take an interest in the community's politics. Since their property and personal safety were protected by the national government, absentee landlords did not play the role of a competing elite and thus deprived peasants of the opportunity to check the freedom of the headman.

The end of the monarchy did not, however, lift the authoritative presence of the central government; it increased it. The difference was that the monarchical regime sought to preserve the status quo, whereas, under the Revolution, the central government was committed to social change. The new regime questioned the justice of unlimited private property and imposed restrictions on ownership. Under these politically initiated economic changes, and with the moral support of the regime, new leaders in Shubra emerged with popular bases of support. The rise of new leaders in Shubra was clearly related to the changing principles of legitimacy and the new normative rules regulating economic and political behavior. New ideas of social justice brought about new normative rules which undermined the power of the economic and political elite. The new elite, in contrast, were resident villagers who formed competing groups and came mostly from medium- and lower-income strata. Their background characteristics were consistent with the principle of legitimacy and normative rules introduced by the Revolution, but attitudes and behavior of an elite are predicates primarily of the power structure in the system and secondarily of the elite's background and personal characteristics.

Models of Political Power

It may be useful at this point to draw up models of political power in terms of which developments in Shubra's politics can be interpreted. Relevant to this discussion are the zero-sum and the variable-sum models. Under zero-sum conditions, the quantity of power in the system is fixed, that is, it is not subject to any important variation. The gains of one leader are most often made at the expense of another, a condition that accentuates political rivalry and leads to chronic hostility or autocracy.

Conclusion: reflections on political change

Under the Samads, the situation can be characterized as zero-sum where autocratic rule prevailed. Social control was tight, and the generation of new political resources beyond the control of the autocratic headman was precluded. Had there been two clans competing for the power resources, as in some other villages, strife and factionalism would have been prevalent. Strife is the most likely outcome of zero-sum conditions, although this does not preclude the possibility of unstable peace, a kind of "cease fire" condition in which parties tolerate the existing balance of power and may even collaborate. Unstable peace usually occurs after further fighting, with no gains in sight, exhausts the resources of both parties.

Under a variable-sum condition, the quantity of power in the system grows larger and makes power sharing possible at minimal or, in some cases, no cost to the other power holders in the system. The emergence of new leaders does not necessarily lead to hostility and strife; because of the expanded room for action and achievement, socioeconomic reforms in Shubra increased the number of participants, the resources to be controlled, and the responsibilities to be discharged. Before interpreting the political history of Shubra in these terms, it may be helpful to explain what a power system, or, more specifically, "arena," means in this context.

An arena defines participants in a contest, the prize to be won, and the rules and conditions for winning.[26] For example, the election for the reform cooperative board in Shubra is a contest; its eligible participants are all the members of the cooperative, and the prize to be won is a seat on the board; the rules are those laid down in its statutes pertaining to how, where, and when to vote; and the condition for winning is a plurality of votes. Looking at Shubra, once the cooperative board is elected, it will constitute another arena in its own right. The members are those elected to the board, the prize or prizes are policy decisions, and, in order to win, one must be able to obtain the support of a majority of board members. When the cooperative at large is viewed as an arena, the number of voters is over one thousand, whereas in the cooperative board arena, the total is eleven.

A contender's power in the arena is relative to the total active force in

26. The concept of arena is fairly common in the language of political science and political anthropology. Its commonsense connotation as a contest setting is central in practically all the different usages it has had. Lasswell and Kaplan define it as "a pattern of encounters," in *Power and Society: A Framework for Political Inquiry* (New Haven: Yale University Press, 1963), p. 80. F. G. Bailey and Ralph W. Nicholas, wrote that "if the arena is viewed as the environment in which political contention occurs, then the term would refer to the rules and regularities of competitive interaction between contending groups," in Marc J. Swartz (ed.), *Local-Level Politics* (Chicago: Aldine, 1968), p. 271. Its theoretical relevance to the definition of power, however, has not been developed in any of these writings.

the system. It is measurable in terms of the number of voters an actor can draw to his support, that is, the resources he can effectively mobilize in the contest. In the cooperative arena, a winner will theoretically need more than five hundred votes to win. In the board arena, the value of each member's power is again relative to the aggregate of the votes, that is, eleven. In brief, the power of a political actor varies relative to the arena in which he is either a member or a contender, or both.

An individual or a group can be part of several arenas. As members of the cooperative board contest prizes in other arenas of the community, the value of each contender's power changes relative to the power capacity of the new arena. Thus 'Ali al Shawi of the cooperative board finds his power varying from one arena to another as he contests elections to the board, the village party branch, or a seat in the National Assembly. (The purpose of explaining the concept of arena in this context is made more explicit after Shubra's politics is interpreted in terms of the variable-sum model.)

The variable-sum model suggests a cooperative attitude on the part of political actors and reduced levels of strife, but not the absence of intense competition. In Shubra, under the mobilization regime, political struggle was often very intense. The question, then, is why did intense competition continue despite the expansion of political resources and increase in the number of leadership positions? Indeed, during this same period, some actors aimed primarily at taking away the resources of other actors in the village arena, an attitude which obtains under zero-sum conditions.

The first symptoms of political conflict that aimed at dispossessing incumbents were manifested at the beginning of the expansion period in 1953, when the Kuras launched their political campaign against the headman. The headman's first natural reaction was to expand his control to include the new political resources and contain their adverse effects on his position. Therefore, he tried to assume leadership of the newly created official movement in the village; but when the Kuras succeeded in capturing it, the headman conceded. In contrast, when the Kuras tried to undermine his traditional power domain, he reacted violently, and the ensuing strife led to physical clashes and litigation. In other words, the headman reluctantly acquiesced to the Kuras' playing a political role made possible by new opportunities, but he resisted efforts to take away his traditionally held powers.

Why were the Kuras not satisfied to acquire new positions and leave the headman in his established realms? First, the headman's powers over the villagers were extensive and any effort by others to claim leadership over some of them would amount to a challenge to the 'umdah. Moreover, national forces were on the side of the Kuras and it was an effective

Conclusion: reflections on political change

strategy for them to attack. Third, the growing interdependence in various aspects of village life made both sides sensitive to one another's achievements. Since municipal councillors in particular were to be recruited among party leaders, control of the municipal council was contingent on a commanding position in the new party branch. This made both the Kuras and the Samads obliged to contend for leadership of the National Union. Moreover, the policy of the Kuras to deprive the headman of his authority in local government and in the cooperative society was related to their political aspirations in arenas on higher levels. (This point is discussed below, since external factors affected other emerging leaders in the community as well.) In addition to the incompatibility of their political goals, the Samads and the Kuras differed ideologically and in their material interests, a fact that precluded the convergence of their political resources.

Strife with the headman and intense competition among the emerging groups of leaders may also be explained in terms of other factors derived from the variable-sum model. First, the growth in the volume of power was slow and limited in amount relative to the aspirations of the contenders. Consequently, some actors sought to augment their power at the expense of other leaders. Second, since some emerging leaders aspired to political positions beyond the local community arena, they needed as much of the power resources of Shubra as they could obtain, for the reason that the amount of power necessary to achieve an objective in one arena may not be sufficient in another. A local leader satisfied with a partial amount of power in his basic constituency will no longer be satisfied when he seeks to extend his power to a larger arena of which his basic constituency is a part. Expanding political objectives such as aspirations to higher political office leads political actors to maximize their control over their home base and to cultivate new resources in the larger constituency. Thus, regardless of his social or personal characteristics, a leader acting under such conditions seeks to expand his control in his basic arena at the expense of other leaders with little concern about the autocratic tendencies of such endeavors. (This is what 'Ali al Shawi feared the Kuras were doing.) It should make little difference whether the aspirant comes from a poor or a wealthy family, whether his personality is authoritarian or not, whether he inherited his position or personally acquired it by his own efforts. The political opportunities and constraints under which he operates guide him to seek more power units even at the expense of other leaders, should their cooperation not be voluntary.

The principle on which the preceding observation is based is that a leader or party will seek additional power until enough is acquired to attain the objectives in sight. No extra resources are invested in acquiring more available power units. When the same party seeks to achieve objectives at a higher level in a more inclusive arena, it will then need all the resources available in its basic constituency. Power resources previously spared will be sought after under the new situation.

We have witnessed how Muhammad Kura, who aspired for provincial and national leadership positions, tried to extend his control over the whole community of Shubra, despite the fact that he subscribed to the ideals of the Revolution and had fought against the autocracy of the Samads. 'Ali al Shawi, who was of humble origin, also sought to maximize his power in the cooperative as well as in the village-wide ASU arena in order to attain goals similar to those of Muhammad Kura. Both leaders were constantly striving to control more political units in the village arenas, despite their different backgrounds and personalities. Other local leaders whose political objectives were limited to Shubra showed more political tolerance and flexibility.

In seeking political hegemony in the village, Ahmad Amir, too, was acting under similar constraints. The overlapping of political arenas within Shubra induced him to generate political influence of his own in practically each one of them. In terms of influence beyond the community, the ASU political drive over which he presided in Shubra was related to the external arenas of the district, the province, and even the national scene. In other words, the constituency of Shubra was a political base of support in a more inclusive arena, where every unit of its resources counted.

The preceding explanation has stressed aspects of political behavior similar to those that occur under zero-sum conditions. Yet, as we look back at the course of events in Shubra, the intensity of competition among ambitious new leaders did not reach the point of strife or severance of relations. The sociograms have clearly demonstrated that lines of communications among the various political blocs remained in effect. Moreover, the extent to which one group sought to dispossess the other never reached the stage of "looting"; it was rather orderly and restrained. Again, this phenomenon may be explained in terms of the variability of the power aggregate in the system, which brings us to the third point regarding political behavior under variable-sum conditions.

Political strife did not become endemic in Shubra because the power position in the larger arenas could not be attained by dependence on Shubra's resources alone. A contender who bids for a leadership position in a larger arena will invariably need to cultivate new resources outside his original constituency. In generating additional political support, a serious political contender finds it more productive at a certain point to invest in other parts of the larger constituency than in his own basic arena

Conclusion: reflections on political change

exclusively. Should his basic arena, for instance, be strongly contested by others, as Shubra was, a concentration of investment capital will be subject to very costly and diminishing returns. Consequently, aspirants for higher political office look for political support elsewhere as well and do not act in terms of a zero-sum syndrome. This tendency limits the degree of political strife in a community.

The fourth point that explains the political behavior of Shubra's leaders in terms of the variability of the power aggregate is the distribution pattern of political resources and the intensity of the participants' political commitments. In Shubra, political support could shift from one group to another but only up to a point, beyond which it became too costly to obtain. The villagers' limited political commitment to a political group or leader made it possible for contenders to seek support in the opponents' camps. When the point of low returns was reached, contenders voluntarily maintained a "cease fire" line, since any further fighting for political support would have consumed resources of all concerned rather than generating new ones. Moreover, under conditions of continued strife, the contenders' dependency on their followers increased and they could even become vulnerable to an emerging third force.

In brief, the arena perspective directs attention to the importance of studying power as a network concept, in this instance to the relations of an actor to his political base of support, to other leaders, and to the distribution of forces in overlapping arenas.

The politics of growth in Shubra has manifested cohesive as well as competitive features. Cooperation and conflict are two primary characteristics of politics:[27] the first is predicated by the scarcity of power resources and the latter, by the necessity of achieving effectiveness. Both trends have been illustrated in the text, where courses of action taken by various leaders in Shubra are described, and in the sociograms.

Like capital, political power is a scarce resource that has to be generated, invested, accumulated, used up, or dispersed. It is a force that people use and to which they react, and, as such, it is no more an interpersonal relationship than a bank account is a personal attribute of the owner. It would not be realistic to consider relations of leaders who are in a bargaining or a competing situation as personal, because their interaction is based on the value of the power resources they command, just like a commercial transaction. To illustrate the point further, the head of the agricultural laborers' union in Shubra was an able person who demon-

27. This view has been stressed by Bailey, in *Stratagems and Spoils*, and in his essay in *Rural Politics*.

strated political skills in dealing with the cooperative board, but his political resources were still very limited. His friends in the village, including the mayor and a number of other prominent leaders, could not deal with him on the basis of their own favorable relations but on the basis of his stock of power. This is not to say, however, that personal qualities cannot be power resources. The headman under the old regime, for instance, enjoyed personal characteristics such as lineage and personal skills which improved his power position; but these were only part of his power resources.

The definition of political power, moreover, cannot be limited to the question of one actor's resistance to another, because power is a force subject to generation by positive factors such as convergence of interests and ideals, inducement, services, and sharing. Illustrations of this point can be found in the political tactics of the Kuras, who stressed their common cause with ordinary villagers and extended services to them. 'Ali al Shawi and Ahmad Amir followed the same methods but with more emphasis on convergence in their ideals and those of their constituents.

Since it is just as important to study the generation of power as it is to discuss its distribution and effects, actors cannot be viewed in isolation but must be viewed as part of a network of relations. The network concept can be illustrated in the context of Shubra's politics.

Political power in Shubra was manifested in a complex organizational setting and revolved around the party, the cooperatives, and the municipal council. Leadership in each one of these organizations was cohesive and centralized to the extent that if each one of these organizations were viewed in isolation from the rest of the field of action, it could be concluded that the community was ruled autocratically. But when examined from the viewpoint of power network, the relations of these organizations and the constraints they imposed on each other were highlighted. In other words, if the power of an organization is relative to others in an arena, then the autonomy of the organization or its dependency on the political environment become questions of central importance to the understanding of the political behavior of its officers. When power is viewed as the freedom of a collectivity to make decisions, it follows that a leader's power is not only a function of his standing in his organization but also of the autonomy-dependency standing of his organization in the field of action. The agrarian reform cooperative is a clear illustration of this point.

The pluralistic structure of the political field and the overlapping and limited commitments of villagers increased the dependency of Shubra's organizations. A villager is often a member of more than one organization and maintains links with more than one political group. As already observed in chapter 12, a villager moves easily between different political groups and this makes it necessary for leaders to try harder and remain responsive to their base of support. Thus the commitment of the individual to more than one political group makes the leaders' dependence on their organizational base greater. Under such conditions, power tends to become diffuse in a vast network of relations rather than highly dichotomized between leaders and followers. A second effect of organizational dependency is that leaders try to accommodate each other in order to reduce the extent of dependency on their constituencies. Third, the fact that the spheres of activities of various organizations overlap contributes to a state of vigilance on the part of leaders, that is, they take a keen interest in each other's activities. Thus different political blocs seek to contain each other and prevent the emergence of a hegemony by one leader or group. When vigilance proves ineffective and the power resources of one group become great in relation to the total active force in the field, then such a group is said to be dominant. During brief, alternate periods, the Kuras and Ahmad Amir achieved relatively dominant positions in the community, but they could not hold on to their hegemony because of changing conditions and intense competition.

Efforts have been made in this concluding chapter to underline observations relevant to the theory of political change. However, there is a practical aspect to the political history of Shubra in the last two decades that reflects on the Egyptian system of government. It has been observed that the Nasser regime intervened in the local community and introduced institutions through which villagers manage their own economic and political affairs. But, in so doing, the regime has succeeded in creating a local system that bears sharp contrasts with the national system: in Shubra, citizen participation is freer and more relevant to the ordinary villager, and the structure of power is pluralistic. Was this the intention of the regime? The evidence collected in Shubra does not definitively settle this question, but it strongly suggests that the national regime did seek to create such a pluralistic and participatory local system. This leaves open the question whether ordinary citizens will demand the extension of their local freedoms to the national level. No serious signs of such a course was in evidence at the time this study was concluded in the summer of 1968, and a suggestion of some of the reasons may be useful, even if speculatively.

One of the effective ways by which the regime has guarded itself from local political pressures has been to invest provincial government with sufficient powers to handle most subnational issues. In the second place, the advantages gained by cultivators from government-sponsored local reforms did not make them eager to press claims of a political nature on the national regime. This attitude on the part of rural people has considerably limited the desire and ability of provincial leaders to demand decision-making roles in the national government. Third, the nature of the reform introduced by the government was to provide organizational mechanisms for each community to solve its own problems. As a result, local organizations became the proper agencies for solving problems, acting in conjunction with district and provincial agencies.

Since the direct leverage of local communities at the national level is weak, is it possible that the government may feel free to reverse reform policies? The answer is obviously yes, but quite unlikely. For one thing, reform has reduced the sources of rural problems and put the national government in a better position to carry out agricultural policy. A reversal of the reform policies of the last two decades could not fail to generate massive unrest in the countryside, where more than half of all Egyptians still live. A more likely threat to the gains made by the country people may occur in the realm of political freedoms. Considering the chronic international crisis of Egypt, an insecure national regime might resort to replacing elected boards of cooperatives by appointed officials, immobilizing the party branch, or making the party an oppressive instrument of an unpopular government and policies.

Finally, should the course of political activity in Shubra continue unabated and without obstruction from external forces, we may look forward to seeing local organizations grow stronger and their representation in provincial government become more effective. There can be no doubt that success of local institutions will, at this stage and for a long time to come, require the continuing understanding of the national government. Failure to call for local elections, impatience with local conflicts, and increasing resort to administrative interference in popularly elected bodies would do irreparable damage to modern rural institutions. Freedom to elect their own officers and freedom to manage their local organizations have been great gains made by the country people under Nasser. The implications for the development of a political system based on the principle of self-determination are obvious. In the last twenty years, diversity has become a conspicuous feature of political and economic conditions in the countryside, and, as witnessed in Shubra, political and interest groups of different concerns and predispositions have emerged. It is less likely now that the countryside will be an undifferentiated source of support for conservative politics, nor is it likely that it will be politically monopolized by one party or group of politicians. The variety of political leaders and groups may indeed encourage the emergence of political diversity on the national level and contribute to the transformation of the single party regime in Egypt.

Appendix A
Questionnaire

Part One

1. Have you ever heard of the savings project?
   Yes_____ No_____
   a. From whom?
      Name_____
   b. Do you personally have a savings?
      Yes_____ No_____
      (If "yes" ask:)
   c. Where?_____

2. Do you read the newspapers?
   Yes_____ No_____
   (If "no" ask:)
   a. Does anyone else read them to you?
      Yes_____ No_____
      Who?_____
      (If "yes" ask:)
   b. How often?
      Daily_____ twice a week_____
      Once a week_____ once a month_____
      Less than once a month_____

3. Do you listen to the radio?
   Yes_____ No_____
   a. Where?_____
   b. What do you like best?
      _____

4. Do you watch television?
   a. How often?
      Daily_____ twice a week_____
      Once a week_____ once a month_____
   b. What do you like to watch best?_____

5. Have you traveled anywhere outside Shubra el Gedida?
   Yes_____ No_____
   a. When was the last time you traveled?_____
   b. Where do you usually go?
      _____
   c. How often?_____
   d. For what purpose?
      _____

6. Have you been through any training program in the village or elsewhere?
   Yes_____ No_____
   (If "yes" ask:)
   a. What program?_____
   b. What did you learn from it?
      _____

7. Do you ever go to the co-op?
   Yes_____ No_____
   a. How often?
      Twice a day_____
      Once a day_____
      Twice a week_____
      Once a week_____
      Once a month_____
      Less frequently_____
   b. Whom do you go to see in the co-op?_____
      Who else?_____
   c. For what purpose do you go to the co-op?_____
      What else?_____

8. Now I would like you to tell me, what does the Leadership Group in the village do?
   _____
   a. Has any one of them gotten in touch with you?
      Yes_____ No_____
   b. Who?_____
   c. Where did he contact you?
      _____
   d. For what purpose?
      _____

9. Who in the village, would you say, is liked by most people here?
   Name_____ Why?_____
   a. _____ _____
   b. _____ _____
   c. _____ _____
   d. _____ _____
   e. _____ _____

10. Do you ever go to the village council?
    Yes_____ No_____
    (If "yes" ask:)

a. How often?
   Once a day____
   Twice a day____
   Once a week____
   Once a month____
b. For what purpose?
   _____
c. Who do you go to see there?
   _____
   Who else?_____

11 Name four members of Shubra el Gedida's village council:
   a. _____
   b. _____
   c. _____
   d. _____

12 Would you also name four elected council members of your co-op?
   a. _____
   b. _____
   c. _____
   d. _____

13 Suppose a project was started in the village by people here, such as opening a new school or draining a pool, and you were asked to participate as a member of this community, what would you do?
   a. Ask someone for his advice first?
      Yes____ No____
   b. Wait to find out who the people are who will participate before you make up your mind?
      _____
      Why?_____
   c. Decide on your own?____
      (If "a" ask:)
      Usually whom?
      Name_____

14 Who would you say are the most influential persons here in the village?
        Name   Why?
   a. _____ _____
   b. _____ _____
   c. _____ _____
   d. _____ _____
   e. _____ _____
   f. _____ _____
   (Encourage him to continue until he says "that is all.")

15 You know, of course, that every village has its own problems. Now, what do you think is the biggest problem your village faces?
   _____
   _____

16 Do you think you can do something to help out in this respect?
   Yes____
   What, for instance?
   _____
   No____
   Why?_____

17 Who else do you think can do something about it?
   Name_____
   _____

18 Suppose you had a problem—to whom would you go for help?
   a. Family problem
      _____
   b. Financial
      _____
      (If "financial" is not understood, substitute "if you were in need of money.")
   c. A dispute over property, livestock, farming, irrigation, etc.

19 You know well that everywhere you can find some people who know more about things than others do. Who in the co-op do you think is best informed about the co-op's business?
   a. _____
   b. _____
   c. _____
   d. _____

20 Who in the co-op do you think is most helpful to the members?
   a. _____
   b. _____
   c. _____
   d. _____

21 Have you ever heard of the family planning project?
   (If he does not understand, use "prevention of births.")
   Yes____ No____

Appendix A

a. From whom?
   Name_____
   _____
b. What do *you* think of this project?
   _____
c. Why?_____
   (If applicable to respondent, ask:)
d. Are you planning your family?
   Yes_____ No_____
   (If "no" ask:)
e. Why not?
   _____
   (If the answer reveals that there is a particular obstacle such as lack of nurses and pills, ask:)
f. What do you plan to do, then?
   _____

22 Have you heard about socialism?
   Yes_____ No_____
   a. From whom?
      Name_____
      _____
   b. Would you tell me, now, what is socialism?
      _____
   c. Can you name some socialist countries?
      _____
      _____
      _____
      _____
   d. Do you think it would be a good thing for other countries to adopt socialism?
      Yes_____ No_____
      (If "yes" ask:)
   e. Which countries, for example?
      _____
      _____
      _____

23 Have you ever heard of the five-year plan?
   Yes_____ No_____
   (If "yes" ask:)
   a. From whom?
      Name_____
   b. Which plan is now in effect?
      First_____
      Second_____
      Does not know_____

24 Can you tell me what is the purpose of the cooperative society?
   _____
   How does it accomplish its purpose?
   _____

25 Do you approve of the way your co-op is run?
   Yes_____ No_____
   a. Why?_____
   b. Do you have any suggestions to make?
      _____
   c. What do you think you can do about it?
      _____

26 Would you tell me now what is the purpose of cooperative marketing? (i.e., selling the crops through the co-op.)
   _____

27 Name two members of the Executive Bureau of the Arab Socialist Union in Markaz Damanhur.
   a. _____
   b. _____

28 Which would you say are the Arab countries still dominated by reactionary regimes?
   a. _____
   b. _____
   c. _____
   d. _____

29 Name the governor of Beheira Province.
   _____

30 Do you know the name of the governor in any other province?
   Knows_____
   Does not know_____
   (If "yes" ask the name of the governor and his province)
   _____

31 Can you tell me the name of the present prime minister?
   _____

32 You are aware, of course, that the village here has:
   1. A Cooperative Society.
   2. A Committee of Twenty.

3. A Village Council.
4. A Cultural Club.
5. A Youth Organization.
6. A Leadership Group.

In your opinion, which of these are most useful to the village? (List in order of importance)

1. _____
2. _____
3. _____
4. _____
5. _____
6. _____

Part Two
Agree—Disagree

1 One can no longer depend on his relatives as in the olden days.
2 Nowadays, young people do not seek their parents' advice as they used to in the past.
3 A leader in the village should come from a large and respectable family.
4 In times of great need, a person has no one but his relatives to turn to.
5 Young people nowadays are better informed than their elders.
6 Leadership in the village should be in the hands of the young, not the old.

Part Three

Respondent's Personal and Background Characteristics

1 Age____
2 Marital status:
Single____ Married____
Widower____ Divorced____
3 Education:
Illiterate____
Can read and write____
Completed the literacy course in adult education classes____
Elementary education____
Preparatory education____
Secondary school____
Degrees____
4 Main occupation_____
_____
Secondary occupation_____
_____
5 Economic Status:

                        Feddan Qirat
a. Land ownership _____ ____
b. Land rented   _____ ____
c. Other sources of income:____
_____

6 Family status:
a. Number of wives____
b. Number of sons and daughters ____
c. Number of relatives residing in the same house with the respondent____
7 Do you have any educated children, or ones who now go to school?
Yes____ How many?____
Does any one of them hold a degree?____
8 Membership in village organizations.

Name of Society

a. _____
b. _____
c. _____
d. _____

              Position
(President, secretary, member, etc.)
_____
_____
_____
_____

Interviewer's comments:

Appendix B
The Sample and the Actual Population

The sample used in the survey consisted of one-tenth of all adult males, 18 to 60 years of age, a total of 135 respondents. This number corresponds very closely to official figures for this age group, as can be seen from the voters' records. ASU voters in rural Egypt are adult males 18 years of age and over; only the handicapped and the very elderly are usually left out. Those left out for political reasons do not make a statistically significant number; only two such persons were excluded in Shubra. In the summer of 1968, the ASU officials in Beheira Province issued 1320 party membership cards to Shubra's voters. Since party membership is practically synonymous with eligible voters, the membership cards should be equal to the actual adult male population, which is almost the same figure for the universe from which we derived the sample. The figure for the sample was derived from the local census conducted jointly by the Arab Socialist Union and the village council in March 1967.

The 1967 local census showed that Shubra had then a population of 6210 inhabitants: 3065 males and 3145 females. Age was not listed in this census, and it was determined with the help of informants. Every name on the census list was screened in the presence of four knowledgeable villagers who determined whether the person was in the right age category as well as his whereabouts. Those absent from the village for a prolonged period of time were left out. The result was a list of 1350 names of adult males from which the sample was drawn.

Based on the figures from the local census of 1967, the working force of Shubra comes to 2256 men, women, and children (see table I). In view of the fact that this includes working women and children, it is more than one and a half times larger than the universe from which we derived the sample. Most of this increase comes from the category labeled agricultural labor-

Table I
Occupational Distribution of the Population, 1967

Agricultural Laborers	Craftsmen and Tradesmen	Salaried Native Employees	Cultivators	Total
1081	162	122	891	2256

ers. Practically all employed women and children over the age of nine are farmhands who are paid in cash on a daily basis. They are employed mostly to pick infested cotton leaves, weed, help in harvesting, and to do other odd jobs. The inclusion of women and children in the labor force explains the wide discrepancy in the number of agricultural laborers in the sample and those listed in the census (see table II). According to the sample, 28 respondents mentioned that they were agricultural laborers, which should represent a universe of 280 adult male laborers, or less than one-third of the figure given by the census. There is no precise way to determine the number

Table II
Occupational Distribution According to Sample

Agricultural Laborers	Craftsmen and Tradesmen	Salaried Native Employees	Cultivators	Other	Total
280	200	170	670	30	1350

of women and children in this group, but to judge from consultation with informants and labor contractors, the figure in the sample for adult male laborers is representative.

A small discrepancy can also be observed in the figures for peasants as listed in the two tables. The term peasants refers to owner as well as tenant cultivators, who include some women and men over sixty years of age. The discrepancy should be due mostly to the exclusion of these last two categories from the sample.

As was mentioned earlier, the local census did not include an age listing, but it is possible to present an age-distribution indicator from the 1960 census. The official census, however, included some neighboring hamlets in the Shubra population figures, and its age-listing breakdowns differed from those in the sample. Regardless of these differences, a comparison is useful for giving a general idea of the situation. According to the 1960 official census, the male population of Shubra between 15 and 39 years of age was 1274 and for those in the age bracket of 40 to 69 years, 621. In the sample universe, there are 890 between 18 and 39 years, while there are 440 between 40 and 60 years (see table III). The ratio of those 40 years old and over to those under 40 in both the census and the sample is almost exactly 2 to 1, which indicates that the age distribution in the sample cannot be far wrong.

Table III
Age Distribution in the Sample

Age	Frequency	Percentage
18–19	6	4.4
20–29	37	27.1
30–39	47	34.2
40–49	17	12.5
50–59	23	16.1
60	5	3.5
Total	135	99.8

Appendix C
Leadership Code for Sociograms

40 ʿAhmad Suhdi
41 ʿAbd Raqqush
42 Sayid Kura
43 Sayid Haris
44 Haj Hammal
45 Mustafa Rayyan
46 ʿAbd Kura
47 Ahmad Kattab
48 Ahmad Qidi
49 Sayid Shawi
50 Hadi Hammal
51 ʿAli Akhras
52 Sad Hamada
53 ʿAbd al Muttalib
54 Bashir Shubrawi
55 Ibrahim Muzayin
56 Mukhtar Shad
57 Fikri Haris
58 ʿAli al Shawi
59 ʿAbd al Majid Rayyan
60 Mahmud al Sayid Samad
61 Ahmad Shayban
62 Mahmud Dawud
63 ʿAbd Samad
64 ʿAbd Latif
65 Ahmad Tay
66 Hamid ʿIqda
67 Raziq Rawd
68 Muhamad Sharq
69 Ahmad ʿAbdulla Rayyan
70 Yasin Kamil
71 ʿAbd Atta
72 ʿAbdo Zarqa
73 Maqsud ʿUmar
74 Mahmud Qidi
75 Nasri Rayyan
76 Mahmud Yunis
77 Abd Tukhi
78 Anwar Rayyan
79 Sadiq ʿAbd
80 ʿAbd Muzayyin
81 Shihata Tukhi
82 Ahmad Ziyada
83 ʿAbd Hamido

Selective bibliography

Books and Articles

Abdel Malek, Anouer. *Égypte, Société Militaire.* Paris: Éditions du Seuil, 1962.
'Abd al Malik, Anwar. *Dirasat fi al Thaqafah al Wataniyah.* Beirut: Dar al Tali'ah, 1967.
Abu-al Khayr, Muhammad Kamal. *Qanun al Islah al Zira'i.* Cairo: Dar al Ma'arif bi Misr, 1964.
Abu-Lughod, Ibrahim. *Arab Rediscovery of Europe: A Study of Cultural Encounters.* Princeton: Princeton University Press, 1963.
———. "The Mass Media and Egyptian Village Life." *Social Forces* 42 (October 1963).
———. "The Transformation of the Egyptian Elite: Prelude to the 'Urabi Revolt." *The Middle East Journal* 21, no. 3 (Summer 1967).
Abu-Lughod, Janet. *Cairo: 1001 Years of the City Victorious.* Princeton: Princeton University Press, 1971.
———. "Migrant Adjustment of City Life: The Egyptian Case." *American Journal of Sociology* 67 (July 1961).
———. "Urban-Rural Differences as a Function of the Demographic Transition: Egyptian Data and an Analytical Model." *The American Journal of Sociology* 69, no. 5 (1964).
Adams, John Boman. "Culture and Conflict in an Egyptian Village," *American Anthropologist* 59, no. 2 (April 1957).
Agling, S.A. *Twelve Portraits of Power.* London: Harrap, 1959.
Ahmad, 'Izz al Din Hammam. *Dirasat fi al Iqtisad al Zira'i.* Cairo: Matabi' Madkur, 1961.
Ahmed, J. M. *The Intellectual Origins of Egyptian Nationalism.* London: Oxford University Press, 1960.
Alderfer, Harold F.; el Khatib, M. Fathalla; and Fahmy, Moustafa Ahmed. *Local Government in the United Arab Republic, 1963.* Cairo: Institute of Public Administration, n.d.
'Amir, Ibrahim. *al Ard wa al Fallah: al Mas'alah al Zira'iyah fi Misr.* Cairo: Matba'at al Dar al Misriyah, 1958.
———. *Thawrat Misr al Qawmiyah.* Cairo: Dar al Nadim, 1957.
Ammar, Hamed. *Growing Up in an Egyptian Village: Silwa, Province of Aswan.* New York: Octagon Books, 1966.
Antoun, Richard, and Harik, Iliya (eds.). *Rural Politics and Social Change in the Middle East.* Bloomington: Indiana University Press, 1972.
Ashford, Douglas E. *The Elusiveness of Power: The African Single Party State.* Ithaca: Cornell University, Center for International Studies, 1965.
———. *National Development and Local Reform: Morocco, Tunisia, Pakistan.* Princeton: Princeton University Press, 1967.

Ayrout, Henry Habib. *The Egyptian Peasant*. Boston: Beacon Press, 1963.
'Awad, Lewis. *al Jami'ah Wa al Mujtama'*. Cairo: al Dar al Qawmiyyah, n.d.
Baha' al Din, Ahmad. *Afkar Mu'asirah*. Beirut: Jaridat al Muharrir, n.d.
Baily, F. G. *Politics and Social Change: Orissa in 1959*. Berkeley: University of California Press, 1963.
———. *Stratagems and Spoils: A Social Anthropology of Politics*. New York: Schocken Books, 1969.
———. "Decisions by Consensus in Councils and Committees." *Political Systems and the Distribution of Power*. Ed. Max Gluckman and Fred Eggan. New York: Praeger, 1965.
Baer, Gabriel. *A History of Landownership in Egypt, 1800–1950*. New York: Oxford University Press, 1962.
———. *Studies in the Social History of Modern Egypt*. Chicago: Chicago University Press, 1969.
———. "The Beginnings of Municipal Government in Egypt." *Middle Eastern Studies* 4, no. 2 (January 1968).
———. "The Dissolution of the Egyptian Village Community." *Die Welt des Islams*, 1959, pp. 56–70.
———. "Fellah and Townsman in Ottoman Egypt." *Asian and African Studies* 8, no. 3 (1972).
———. "The Village Shaykh in Modern Egypt (1800–1950)." *Studies in Islamic History*. Ed. Uriel Heyd. Jerusalem: Magnes Press, 1961.
Banfield, Edward. *The Moral Basis of a Backward Society*. New York: Free Press, 1967.
Befu, Harumi. "The Political Relation of the Village to the State." *World Politics* 19, no. 4 (July 1967).
Berger, Morroe. *Bureaucracy and Society in Modern Egypt*. Princeton: Princeton University Press, 1957.
———. *The Arab World Today*. Garden City, N.Y.: Doubleday, 1962.
———. *Islam in Egypt Today: Social and Political Aspects of Popular Religion*. New York: Cambridge University Press, 1970.
———. "The Mosque: Aspects of Governmental Policy toward Religion in Egypt." *Middle Eastern Studies* 6 (January, 1970).
———. "Socialization to National Identification among Turkish Peasants." *The Journal of Politics* 30, no. 4 (November, 1968).
———. "Surveying Peasant Attitudes in Turkey." *Public Opinion Quarterly* 27 (Fall, 1963).
Berque, Jacques. *Egypt: Imperialism and Revolution*. London: Faber and Faber, 1972.
———. *Histoire Sociale d'un Village Égyptien au XXème Siècle*. La Haye and Paris: Mouton, 1957.
Binder, Leonard, ed. *Crises and Sequences in Political Development*. Princeton: Princeton University Press, 1971.
———. *The Ideological Revolution in the Middle East*. New York: Wiley, 1964.
———. "Egypt: The Integrative Revolution." *Political Culture and Political*

Selective bibliography 295

Development. Ed. Lucian Pye and Sydney Verba. Princeton: Princeton University Press, 1965.
———. "Political Recruitment and Participation in Egypt." *Political Parties and Political Development*. Ed. Joseph LaPalombara and Myron Weiner. Princeton: Princeton University Press, 1966.
Blackman, Winifred S. *The Fellahim of Upper Egypt*. London: Cass, 1968.
Clark, Terry N. *Community Structure and Decision Making: A Comparative Analysis*. San Francisco: Chandler, 1968.
Cooper, Charles A., and Alexander, Sidney S., eds. *Economic Development and Population Growth in the Middle East*. New York: American Elsevier, 1972.
Coult, Lyman H., Jr. *An Annotated Bibliography of the Egyptian Fellah*. Coral Gables, Fla.: University of Miami Press, 1958.
Dekmejian, R. Hrair. *Egypt under Nasir: A Study in Political Dynamics*. Albany: State University of New York Press, 1971.
———. "The UAR National Assembly: A Pioneering Experiment." *Middle Eastern Studies* 4 (July 1968).
Deutsch, Karl W. "Social Mobilization and Political Development." *The American Political Science Review* 55, no. 3 (September 1961).
el Saaty, Hassan, and Hirabayashi, Gordon K. *Industrialization in Alexandria: Some Ecological and Social Aspects*. Cairo: American University of Cairo, 1959.
Fakhouri, Hani. *Kafr el-Elow: An Egyptian Village in Transition*. New York: Holt, Rinehart and Winston, 1972.
Fallers, Lloyd. "Equality, Modernity, and Democracy in the New States." *Old Societies and New States*. Ed. Clifford Geertz. London: The Free Press of Glencoe, 1963.
Frey, Frederick. *The Turkish Political Elite*. Cambridge, Mass.: M.I.T. Press, 1965.
Gadalla, Saad M. *Land Reform in Relation to Social Development, Egypt*. Columbia: University of Missouri Press, 1962.
Geertz, Clifford. "Ideology as a Cultural System." *Ideology and Discontent*. Ed. David Apter. London: The Free Press of Glencoe, 1964.
———. "Peasants." *Biennial Review of Anthropology*. Ed. Bernard Siegel. 1961.
———. "Primordial Sentiments and Civil Politics in the New States." *Old Societies and New States*. Ed. Clifford Geertz. New York: The Free Press of Glencoe, 1963.
Ghayth, Muhammad 'Atif. *al Qariyah al Mutaghiyirah*. Cairo: Dar al Ma'arif, 1964.
Ghonemy, Mohammad Riad el-. *Land Policy in the Near East*. Rome: FAO, 1967.
Greever, Leslie. *The High Dam over Nubia*. London: Cassell, 1962.
Hagras, Saad. *Agrarian Reform in the United Arab Republic*. Cairo: Agrarian Reform Organization, 1969.
Hakim, Tawfiq al. *Yawmiyat Na'ib fi al Ariyaf*. Cairo: Lajnat al Ta'lif, 1937.
Halpern, Manfred. *The Politics of Social Change in the Middle East and North Africa*. Princeton: Princeton University Press, 1963.
Hammond, Paul Y., and Alexander, Sidney S., eds. *Political Dynamics in the Middle East*. New York: American Elsevier, 1972.

Hanna, Sami A., and Gardner, George H. *Arab Socialism.* Salt Lake City: University of Utah Press, 1969.
Hansen, Bent, and Marzouk, Girgis A. *Development and Economic Policy in the U.A.R. (Egypt).* Amsterdam: North-Holland, 1965.
Haqqi, Yahya. *Dima' Wa Tin.* Cairo: Dar al Ma'arif, 1955.
Harik, Iliya F. *Mann Yahkum Lubnan.* Beirut: Dar al Nakar, 1972.
―――. *Political Change in a Traditional Society: Lebanon, 1711–1845.* Princeton: Princeton University Press, 1968.
―――. "The Single Party as a Subordinate Movement: The Case of Egypt." *World Politics* 26, no. 1 (October 1973).
Harris, Christina Phelps. *Nationalism and Revolution in Egypt: The Role of the Muslim Brotherhood.* The Hague: Mouton, 1964.
Haykal, Muhammad Husayn. *Zaynab Akhlaq wa Manazir Rifiyah.* Cairo: Dar al Hilal, 1930.
Haykal, Muhammad Hasanayn. *Azmat al Muthaqafin.* Cairo: al Sharikah al 'Arabiyah, 1961.
Heikal, Mohamed. *Nasser: The Cairo Documents.* Garden City, N.Y.: Doubleday, 1972.
Heaphey, James. "The Organization of Egypt: Inadequacies of a Non-political Model for Nation-Building." *World Politics* 18, no. 2 (January 1966).
Heyworth-Dunne, Gamal Eddine. *Egypt: The Cooperative Movement.* Cairo: The Rennaissance Bookshop, 1952.
Hilali, Abd al Razzaq al. *Qissat al Ard wa al Fallah wa al Islah al Zira'i fi al Watan al 'Arabi.* Beirut: Dar al Kashshaf, 1967.
Hirabayashi, Gordon K., and Khatib, M. Fathalla el. "Communication and Political Awareness in the Villages of Egypt." *Public Opinion Quarterly* 22 (1958).
Holt, P. M., ed. *Political and Social Change in Modern Egypt.* London: Oxford University Press, 1968.
Hopkins, Harry. *Egypt the Crucible: The Unfinished Revolution in the Arab World.* Boston: Houghton Mifflin, 1969.
Horton, Alan W. "The Officer Who Chose Progress." *American Universities Field Staff: Reports Service* 13, no. 1 (1967).
―――. "The Omda's Boy." *American Universities Field Staff: Reports Service* 11, no. 6 (1964).
Hourani, Albert. *Arabic Thought in the Liberal Age, 1798–1939.* London: Oxford University Press, 1962.
―――. *Minorities in the Arab World.* London: Oxford University Press, 1947.
Hurewitz, J. C. *Middle East Politics: The Military Dimension.* New York: Praeger, 1969.
Husayn, Taha. *al Ayyam.* 2 vols. Cairo: Dar al Ma'arif, n.d.
Idris, Yusif. *al Haram.* Cairo: Dar al Hilal, n.d.
Issawi, Charles. *Egypt in Revolution: An Economic Analysis.* New York: Oxford University Press, 1967.
―――, ed. *The Economic History of the Middle East 1800–1914.* Chicago: University of Chicago Press, 1966.
Kerr, Malcolm. *Egypt Under Nasser.* New York: Foreign Policy Association, 1963.

———. *Islamic Reform*. Berkeley: University of California Press, 1966.
———. *The United Arab Republic: The Domestic and Economic Background of Foreign Policy*. Santa Monica, Calif.: RAND Corporation, 1969.
———. "Arab Radical Notions of Democracy." *St. Antony's Papers, no. 16: Middle Eastern Affairs*, no. 3. London, 1963.
———. "The Emergence of a Socialist Ideology in Egypt." *Middle East Journal* 16, no. 2 (Spring 1962).
Kholi, Lutfi al. *Dirasat fi al Waqi' al Misri al Mu'asir*. Beirut: Dar al Tali'ah, 1964.
Lacouture, Jean, and Lacouture, Simonne. *Egypt in Transition*. New York: Criterion Books, 1958.
Lambton, Ann K. S. *Landlord and Peasant in Persia: A Study of Land Tenure and Land Revenue Administration*. New York: Oxford University Press, 1953.
Landau, Jacob. *Parliaments and Parties in Egypt*. Tel Aviv: Israel Publishing House, 1953.
Landes, David. *Bankers and Pashas: International Finances and Economic Imperialism in Egypt*. London: Heinman, 1958.
Lasswell, Harold. *Politics: Who Gets What, When, How*. New York: McGraw-Hill, 1937.
———. *Power and Personality*. New York, W. W. Norton, 1948.
Lazarsfeld, Paul F.; Berelson, Bernard; and Gaudet, Hazel. *The People's Choice*. 2d ed. New York: Columbia University press, 1948.
Lerner, Daniel. *The Passing of Traditional Society: Modernizing the Middle East*. New York: The Free Press of Glencoe, 1963.
Little, Tom. *Modern Egypt*. New York: Praeger, 1967.
Malikah, Lewis Kamil. *al Jama'at Wa al Qiyadat fi Qaryatin 'Arabiyah*. Sirs-al-Layyan, Egypt: Markaz Tanmiyat al Mujtama', 1963.
Mansfield, Peter. *Nasser's Egypt*. London: Penguin African Library, 1965.
Mar'i, Muhammad 'Abd al Majid. *Qanun al Islah al Zira'i*. 2 vols. Cairo: Dar al Fikr al 'Arabi, 1968.
Mar'i, Sayid. *al Islah al Zira'i Wa Muskilat al Sukkan fi al Qitr al Misri*. Cairo: al Dar al Qawmiyyah, 1963.
Mayfield, James B. *Rural Politics in Nasser's Egypt: A Quest for Legitimacy*. Austin: University of Texas Press, 1971.
Mitchell, Richard P. *The Society of the Muslim Brothers*. London: Oxford University Press, 1961.
Moore, Barrington, Jr. *Social Origins of Dictatorship and Democracy: Lord and Peasant in the Making of the Modern World*. Boston: Beacon Press, 1966.
Nasser, Gamal Abdel. *Egypt's Liberation: The Philosophy of the Revolution*. Washington: Public Affairs Press, 1955.
Nieuwenhiujze, C. A. O. van. *Social Stratification in the Middle East: An Interpretation*. Leiden: Brill, 1965.
———. *Sociology of the Middle East*. Leiden: Brill, 1971.
———. "The Near Eastern Village, A Profile." *Middle East Journal* 16, no. 3 (Summer 1962).
Nutting, Antony. *Nasser*. New York: Dutton, 1972.

O'Brien, Patrick. *The Revolution in Egypt's Economic System*. London: Oxford University Press, 1969.
Patai, Raphael. *Golden River to Golden Road: Society, Culture and Change in the Middle East*. Philadelphia: University of Pennsylvania Press, 1962.
Petersen, Karen Kay. "Villagers in Cairo: Hypotheses versus Data." *The American Journal of Sociology* 77, no. 3 (1971).
Pitt-Rivers, Julian, ed. *Mediterranean Countrymen: Essays in the Social Anthropology of the Mediterranean*. The Hague: Mouton, 1963.
Quint, Malcolm. "The Idea of Progress in an Iraqi Village." *Middle East Journal* 12, no. 4 (1958).
Quraishi, Zaheer. *Liberal Nationalism in Egypt*. Allahabad: Kitab Mahal, 1967.
Qutb, Sayid. *Tifl min al Qariyah*. Beirut: n.p., 1967.
Rafi'i, 'Abd al Rahman al. *Muqadimat Thawrat 23 Yulyuh Sanat 1952*. 2d ed. Cairo: Maktabat al Nahdah al Misriyah, 1965.
———. *Thawrat 23 Yulyuh 1952*. Cairo: Maktabat al Nahdah al Misriyah, 1959.
———. *Thawrat Sanat 1919*. Cairo: Matba'at al Nahdah, 1946.
———. *al Thawrah al 'Urabiyah was al Ihtilal al Inglizi*. 3d ed. Cairo: n.p., 1966.
———. *Fi A'qab al Thawrah*. 3 vols. Cairo: Maktabat al Nahdah al Misriyah, 1951.
Redfield, Robert. *Peasant Society and Culture: An Anthropological Approach to Civilization*. Chicago: University of Chicago Press, 1956.
Riad, Hasan. *L'Égypte Nassérienne*. Paris: Éditions de Minuit, 1964.
Rivlin, Helen Anne B. *The Agricultural Policy of Muhammad 'Ali in Egypt*. Cambridge, Mass.: Harvard University Press, 1961.
Rogers, Everett M. *Modernization among Peasants: The Impact of Communication*. New York: Holt, Rinehart and Winston, 1969.
Roos, Leslie L., and Roos, Noralou P. *Managers of Modernization: Organizations and Elites in Turkey (1950–1969)*. Cambridge, Mass.: Harvard University Press, 1971.
Rudebeck, Lars. *Party and People: A Study of Political Change in Tunisia*. Stockholm: Almquist and Wiksell, 1967.
Saab, Gabriel S. *The Egyptian Agrarian Reform 1952–1962*. New York: Oxford University Press, 1967.
Sabri, 'Ali. *Sanawat al Tahawwul al Ishtiraki*. Cairo: Dar al Ma'arif, n.d.
———. *Al Tatbiq al Ishtiraki fi Misr*. Cairo: al Dar al Qawmiyyah, n.d.
Sadat, Anwar el-. *Revolt on the Nile*. London: Allan Wingate, 1957.
———. *Ma'na al Ittihad al Qawmy*. Cairo: n.p., n.d.
Safran, Nadav. *Egypt in Search of Political Community*. Cambridge, Mass.: Harvard University Press, 1961.
Sayigh, Yusif A. *Entrepreneurs of Lebanon: The Role of the Business Leader in a Developing Economy*. Cambridge, Mass.: Harvard University Press, 1962.
Shabanah, Zaki Mahmud. *Al-Iqtisad al Ta'awumi al Zira'i*. Cairo: Dar al Ma'arif, 1965.
Sharqawi, 'Abd al Rahman al. *al Ard*. Cairo: Nadi al Qissah, 1954.
St. John, Robert. *The Boss*. New York: McGraw Hill, 1960.
Sweet, Louise E., ed. *Peoples and Cultures of the Middle East*. 2 vols. Garden City, N.Y.: The Natural History Press, 1970.

Tignor, Robert L. *Modernization and British Colonial Rule in Egypt, 1882–1914*. Princeton: Princeton University Press, 1966.
Vatikiotis, P. J., ed. *Egypt Since the Revolution*. New York: Praeger, 1968.
———. *The Egyptian Army in Politics: Pattern for New Nations?* Bloomington: Indiana University Press, 1961.
———. *The Modern History of Egypt*. New York: Praeger, 1969.
———. "Egypt: Politics of Conspiracy." *Survey* 83, no. 2 (Spring 1972).
Vaucher, Georges. *Gamal Abdel Nasser et Son Equipe*. Paris: Juillard, 1959.
Vidich, Arthur J., and Bensman, Joseph. *Small Town in Mass Society: Class, Power and Religion in a Rural Community*. New York: Doubleday (Anchor), 1960.
Warriner, Doreen. *Land Reform and Development in the Middle East*. New York: Oxford University Press, 1962.
Waterbury, John. *The Cairo Workshop on Land Reclamation and Resettlement in the Arab World*. American Universities Field Staff, Northeast Africa Series 17, no. 1 (1972).
———. *Manpower and Population Planning in the Arab Republic of Egypt*. American Universities Field Staff, Northeast Africa Series 17, nos. 2–5 (1972).
Wheelock, Keith. *Nasser's New Egypt*. New York: Praeger, 1960.
Wolf, Eric R. *Peasants*. Englewood Cliffs, N.J.: Prentice-Hall, 1966.
———. *Peasant Wars of the Twentieth Century*. New York: Harper and Row, 1969.

Documentary Sources

Al Gumhuriyah. January–May 1967. Articles by 'Ali Sabri on the Arab Socialist Union.
Arab Socialist Union. *al Ishtiraki*.
———. *al Shabab al 'Arabi*.
———. *al Kitab al Sanawy (1964)*. Cairo: Dar Matabi' al Sha'b, 1964.
———. *al Kitab al Sanawy al Thalith*. Cairo: Dar Matabi' al Sha'b, 1966.
———. *Intisarat al Fallahin*. Cairo: Dar al Ta'awun, 1966.
Dar al Ahram. *al Tali'ah*. 1965–1970.
U.A.R. al Jihaz al Markazi. *al Kitab al Sanawy lil-Ihsa'at al 'Ammah lil-Jumhuriyah al 'Arabiyah al Muttahidah, 1952–1965*. Cairo: 1966.
———. *al Mu'ashirat al Ihsa'iyah lil-Jumhuriyah al 'Arabiyah al Muttahidah, 1952–1966*. Cairo: 1967.
———. *Ziadat al Sukkan fi al Jumhuriyah al 'Arabiyah al Muttahidah Wa Tahaddiyatuhah lil-Tanmiyat*. Cairo: 1966.
———. *al Mithaq*. Cairo: al Dar al Qawmiyah lil-Tiba'ah Wa al Nashr, n.d. [1962].
———. Community Development Institutions, *Majalat Tanmiyat al Mujtama'*.
———. Idarat al Ta'bi'ah al 'Ammah, *al Kitab al Sanawy lil-Ihsa'at al 'Ammah lil-Jumhuriyah al 'Arabiyah al Muttahidah, 1952–1962*. Cairo: 1963.
———. Institute of National Planning. *Research Report on Employment Problems in Rural Areas, U.A.R*. Cairo: 1966.
———. Maslahat al Ihsa' wa al Ta'dad. *al Ta'dad al 'Am lil-Sukkan, 1960*. Cairo: n.d.

―――. Ministry of Agriculture. *al Islah al Zira'i wa Istislah al Aradi, 1952–1966.* Cairo: n.d.

―――. *Qanun Nizam al Idarah al Mahaliyah.* Cairo: 1965.

U.S. Department of Agriculture. *Agricultural Development and Expansion in the Nile Basin.* Foreign Agricultural Economic Report, no. 48, n.d.

Index

Abaza, Wagih, 11, 58, 84
Abduh, Muhammad, 4, 183
Absentee landlords, 33, 38, 55–56, 276
Adam, Ibrahim, 84, 249
Administrative interference, 284
Administrative ties, 10–12, 62
Agrarian reform, 8, 35–37, 49, 57. *See also* Cooperative system; Land distribution
Agrarian Reform Administration, 7, 8, 36; autonomy of, 11, 249–50; and local co-op boards, 251; and labor contracting, 254
Agrarian Reform Commissioner, 248
Agrarian reform laws, 35, 267
Agricultural Credit Bank, 40, 41, 44, 246, 251
Agricultural economy, 32, 34. *See also* Market economy; Rural capitalism
Agricultural inspection, 74, 94–95
Agricultural laborers: percentage of Shubra population, 10; economic status of, 32, 47; and land distribution policy, 36; media exposure of, 162; absence of class solidarity among, 171; social status of, 215, 218; as contract labor, 252; attempts to organize, 253, 256; and reform co-op, 255–56
Agricultural production, 38, 39, 46, 263
Agronomists, 45–47
Afghani, Jamal al Din al, 4
Alexandria, 3, 5, 6, 41, 131, 133; University of, 73
Algeria, 177
Arab-Israeli War, 12, 222, 245
Arab League, 178
Arab nationalism, 166–67, 177–78, 185
Arab socialism: local relevance of, 157; as Egyptian doctrine, 167; pragmatic approach to, 175, 184, 188
Arab Socialist Union (ASU): birth of, 66; command structure, 67; leftward shift in, 81; organizational structure, 81, 82; at subnational level, 83–84, 90–98; information transmission within, 92; watchdog activities, 92; information dissemination role of, 108, 156; working forces, defined by, 167–69, 224; political competition within, 168; and Sufi orders in Shubra, 182; 1963 structure restored, 223; peasant representation to, 251–52
ASU Central Committee, 82, 225
ASU Committee of Ten, 233–34, 238, 240
ASU Committee of Twenty, 71, 77, 86, 90
ASU district executive bureau, 83, 84
ASU district first secretary, 84, 88, 92
ASU Higher Executive Committee, 66, 67, 225
ASU Markaz Committee, 224, 234
ASU mobilization drive: three steps of, 81; in Shubra, 81, 84–86, 98–100; slowed down, 222–23
ASU Provincial Committee, 71
ASU Secretariat, 66, 67, 74, 81, 83, 251–52
ASU Secretariat of Peasant Affairs, 92
Arena, 277–78
Aristotle, 5
Artisans, 47
Ashford, Douglas, 63, 64
'Ashur, Na'man, 134, 135
Associated Cooperative Society, 77
Aswan Dam, 199
Ayrout, Henry Habib, 165, 177
Azhar University, al, 180

Baer, Gabriel, 262
Baily, F. G., 122, 123, 147, 262, 265, 266, 267, 268
Balance of power, 269
Barnugi, al, 6; Socialist Institute of, 6, 88
Beheira Province, 3–8 *passim*, 47, 51, 134, 242, 245, 248, 249, 251
Beni Suef Province, 7, 178
Berger, Morroe, 23
Bilad Barrah (Foreign Lands), 134. *See also* 'Ashur, Na'man
Binder, Leonard, 63, 64
Bisipara, India, 266–70 *passim*
Bourgeoisie: "older," 16, 17; narrowing of gap within, 19, 20; perceived emergence

301

of, in Shubra, 216, 260. *See also* Middle class
Bureaucrats, 16, 19–20

Cairo, 4, 130, 131, 180
Capitalism, 167
Censorship, 131
Christians, in Shubra, 10
Change: national government as source of, 21; and single party regimes, 79, 87; functional explanation of, criticized, 267–68; a political explanation of, 269; conditions of, 264
Change, cultural: mass media and, 140, 141; as feature of modernization, 164; religious support of, 182; among peasants, 192–97; attitudes toward, 205
Change, political: in Shubra, 62, 164, 200–04, 240; religion as agent of, 184; environmental explanation of, 262–63; national government and, 263–64
Class awareness: in Shubra, 138, 171, 172, 216, 234; agricultural laborers and, 218; during 1968 elections, 240–41
Class conflict, 167–68, 170–71, 185, 217–18, 240
Class solidarity, 171, 194
Coalition groups, 233
Coleman, James S., 64
Combined-services center, 5, 9, 59–60
Committee of Jurisdiction (*Lajnat al Shiyakhat*), 53
Committee of Ten. *See* ASU Committee of Ten; National Union
Committee of Twenty. *See* ASU Committee of Twenty
Communal property, 172
Communications revolution, 129, 169
Communist parties, 168
Communist Party of Iraq, 14
Communists, 169
Community, local understanding of, 173
Community ties, 15
Conflict: as cause of change, 266–67. *See also* Class conflict; Political conflict
Consensus. *See* Decision making
Constitution of 1956, 66
Conventionalists, 208–13, 214, 217
Cooperative boards: functions and powers of, 45–46; elections to, 57–58, 76–77, 243, 278, 284; membership regulations, 58; cohesiveness of, 123; local political struggle and, 244; autonomy of, 258; absence of material benefits to, 238, 243; dissolution of, 242–43
Cooperative marketing, 46, 190, 191
Cooperative production, 190
Cooperative societies: administration of, 44–46; free, Samad monopoly over, 57; administrative links, 62; representation in Leadership Group, 90; local attitudes toward, 189–92; and politics, 242, 246–47, 258–59; autonomy of, 251, 252. *See also* Reform cooperative; Regular cooperative
Cooperative system: 22, 28; initial emergence of, 35; new system instituted, 57–58; as described in the *Charter*, 189; organizational weaknesses of, 246–47; national interest in, as movement, 256
Cooptation of leaders, 62, 67
Courts, the, 54, 108
Crafts center, 59, 60
Credit, financial, 44, 45, 46
Crops, 10, 39, 94, 188
Cultivation area, 38
Cultivators: percentage of Shubra population, 10; under agrarian reform, 19; upward mobility of, 38; income, 47; media exposure of, 162; social status of, 215–16
Cultural formalism, 271

Damanhur, 3, 4, 72, 93, 133, 134, 248
Dar al Kutub, 180, 181
Dawwar, 52, 201
Decision making, 101, 110, 122–25
Delta Railway, 4, 72, 133
Delta region, 4, 8
Democracy, 126
Deutsch, Karl, 21, 212
Developing countries, 13, 64, 65, 79, 153
District. *See Markaz*
District executive bureau. *See* ASU district executive bureau
District first secretary. *See* ASU district first secretary
Domestic market, 18, 32

Education, 115, 139
Effendis, 15
Egypt: cultivation area of, 34; mass commu-

nications system in, 129; relations with other regimes, 177
Egyptian Communist Party, 81
Elders, 194, 196–97, 214, 221
Election campaigns, 121, 226–28
Election candidates, 228–32
Election regulations, 223–24, 232
Elections: 1968 local ASU, 121, 216, 222–23; lack of outside interference in, 235; exclusions from, 237
Electrical service, 60–61
Elite-mass gap, 16, 187, 205
Elite-mass gap theory, 22–26
Elites, 16–20 *passim*; use of ideology of, 24; background analysis of, 26, 159; behavior and attitudes, 27, 126, 212–18, 220–21; in Shubra, 125; communications with rural people, 146; local mobility of, 239; changes in composition of, 269, 270; new rural, 202–3, 276; attitudes of, explained in terms of power, 276
Empirical regularities, 266, 271
Entrepreneurs, 17, 19, 21
Extension centers, 8

Fallers, Lloyd, 15, 16, 21
Family disputes, 108
Family planning, 193, 197–200
Family planning policy: source of information on, in Shubra, 108, 156; described, 149; *imams'* support of, 181; ideological explanation of, 189; obstacles to, 200
Faruq, King, 6
Festivals, 182, 183
Feudalism, 6
Feudalists (*al iqta'iyun*), 33, 167, 171
Fi'at (miscellaneous groups), 71, 224. *See also* Election regulations
Field of action concept, 28. *See also* Arena
Financial problems, 108–9
Five Year Plan. *See* Savings policy
Foreign trade, 32
Free Officers, 35, 65, 129, 249
French forces, 4
Fruit cultivation, 10, 39
Functional requisites, 264–65

Geertz, Clifford, 24
General Cooperative Society (*al Jam'ujah al Mushtarakah*), 246

Generational differences, 195–96
Gharbiyah Province, 250
Government officials, 10, 47, 66; as "members of the community," 80; influence of, in Shubra, 104–6; social status of, 115, 216; as representatives of external influences, 115–16; viewed as second to native leaders, 125; as opinion leaders, 156–57; political participation of, 239
Gouldner, Alvin, 273
Guinea, 64

Hakim, Tawfiq al, 128, 187
Halpern, Manfred, 15, 16, 22, 23, 24
Headman. *See 'Umdah*
Health centers, 28
Higher Executive Committee. *See* ASU Higher Executive Committee
Housing-renewal project, 61
Hulul dhatiyah. See Self-help projects

Ibrahim, Prince Muhammad 'Ali, 38, 39, 40, 42, 55, 56
Ibrahimiyah, al, 183
Ideology: and elite-mass relations, 24–25; dissemination of, 30, 134–35, 141; and single party system, 63; local response to, 170; diffusion limits to formal, 185; as selective ideas, 184; humanizing role of, 187–89, 205; varying effects on individuals, 205; in mobilization regime, 207
Illiteracy: and social change, 23; and mass communication, 28; and assimilation of formal ideology, 65; failure to combat, in Shubra, 97–98; and newspaper exposure, 136; and mass media messages, 147; and news reception, 152; political awareness and, 161
Imams, 75, 179–82
India. *See* Bisipara, India
Individualism, 141, 207
Individualists, 209, 210–15
Influentials, 102, 103, 104, 112–16 *passim*
Information flow, 149–52, 156, 157. *See also* Two-step flow of information hypothesis
Inheritance rights, 199
Intellectuals, 23, 25, 133, 166, 169
Interest rates, 40, 41
Iran, 17, 19, 20

Iraq, 17, 177
Irrigation, 38
Irrigation Committee, 53
Islam, 48, 181, 182, 197

Jordan, 177
Journalists, 131–32

Katz, Elihu, 153
King, the, 50, 53
Kinship strife, 8
Kinship ties: peasant bound to, 15; Shubra leaders and, 110; as qualification for leadership, 194; decline in function of, 196–97; and political attitudes, 213–15, 221; and election regulations, 223–24; effect of, on elections, 236–37
Koran, 168

Labor contracting, 252–54
Land consolidation, 38
Land distribution, 35–36, 42–43
Land grants, 32
Landlord-merchant class, 268
Landlords, 17–19, 38–39; status before 1952, 32; as farm operators, 34–35, 41; downward mobility of, 38; mutual jurisdictional respect among, 55; factions among, 71; villagers' attitudes toward, 171, 172, 189. *See also* Absentee landlords
Landowners (*al mullak*): as term, defined, 33; large, effect of reform on, 36
Landownership, 8; inequality of, 33–34; ceilings on, 35, 36, 37, 62, 172; turnover in, 36–37; among Shubra villagers, 38
Landowning family, defined, 39
Land reclamation, 36, 38, 199
Land reform. *See* Agrarian reform
Land requisition, 35
Land sales, 35
Land taxes, 59
Lateral mobility, 218–21, 238
Lazarsfeld, Paul F., 147, 152
Leadership: broadening of local base of, 90; attributed, in Shubra, 101–104; diversity of, in Shubra, 110; change in traditional view of, 193; causes of turnover in, 257
Leadership blocs, 113, 125–26
Leadership Groups (*Jama'ah qiyadiyah*), 83–86 *passim;* recruitment of membership, 87–90; activities of, in Shubra, 92, 93, 97; backgrounds of members, 115; abolished, 121; coalition groups in, 233; and 1968 elections, 229–33 *passim,* 240
Leadership mobility, 79, 239–40
Leadership proliferation, 71, 90, 99, 125, 261
Leadership structure, 116
Leadership qualities, 124, 194, 195, 216–17
Leadership recruitment, 126, 239, 269
Leadership struggle, 77, 85–87, 240
Lebanon: elites in, 17–21 *passim;* social integration in, 18; radio ownership in, 136; modernizing effect of religion in, 184; political change in, 266–67; interdependence principle applied in study of, 273
Leisure time, 141
Lerner, Daniel, 164, 210
Liberation Province, 252
Liberation Rally, 57, 66, 68–89
Liberia, 64
Lipset, Seymour Martin, 126
Literacy, 159, 221. *See also* Illiteracy
Livestock: examined by vet in Shubra, 96–97
Local autonomy, 28, 79, 100, 235, 250, 258
Local community: as subordinate system, 274
Local government law of 1960, 11
Local leaders, 65; five types of, 66, 71–78; use of party as arena, 67, 78; relations among, 75, 112–16, 118–22, 125; officially recognized, 80; "general" and "specialized," 108; individual differences, 116; background characteristics, 26, 125, 159, 212–18, 220–21; ranking of, 103–4, 125, 109–10; restraints on, 110; media preferences of, 143–45; average age of, 194; rise of new, 276
Local party cadres, 81, 84, 94–95, 98

McLeod, Jack M., 163
Ma'dhun, 54
Mahmudiyya canal, 3, 4
Makram, 'Abd al Mun'im, 71, 88
Manifesto of 81, 168
Markaz, 3n2, 10
Market economy, 32, 34
Marketplace, 59, 60, 123, 153
Markets Department, 60
Maronite Church, 273
Marxism, 180, 181

Index

Mass media, 25, 28, 65; at national level, 129–33; marginal utility of, 139, 142; functional specialization of, 142; as linkage, 148; as policy information source, 149; effectiveness of, 159, 161; and political awareness, 163–64; ideological use of, 188. *See also* Press; Radio; Television

Mass media exposure: by media types, 134–38; comparative studies on, 136–37, 140; by mode of reception, 143; effect on communications flow, 150–52; and political awareness, 158–63; and political attitudes, 210, 211

Mass media exposure index, 158

Mass media preferences: variables in, 139; by mode of reception, 146

Mass media programs, 129–30

Mayor of Shubra, 5–6; appointment of, 58, 62, 70; duties of, 61; as government official, 84–87; opposition to, 86–87; and problem solving, 106; attributed leadership of, 117; as head of council, 123–24; as head of political bloc, 229; undermined, 240; vs. regular co-op, 244–45

Meat prices, 93–94

Medical examinations, 92, 96

Merchant middlemen: in Shubra, 38, 40–41, 46; role in tenancy abolished, 43; villagers' views of, 170, 171, 189

Merchants, 18, 19, 32

Middle class, 14–16, 19–20; "new," 16, 22, 23

Mihtab *waqf* cooperative, 254. *See also Waqf* land

Military elite, 20

Ministry of Agrarian Reform, 7, 8, 11. *See also* Agrarian Reform Administration

Ministry of Agriculture, 11, 59, 97

Ministry of Awqaf and Religious Affairs, 74, 115, 181

Ministry of Education, 69

Ministry of Information, 129–30

Ministry of Local Government, 11, 85; provincial services council, 59; Department of Legal Matters, 249, 250

Ministry of National Guidance, 129

Ministry of Public Health, 5, 59

Ministry of Social Affairs, 59

Ministry of the Interior, 11, 53

Mintaqah, 11

Minufiya Province, 7

Mobility. *See* Lateral mobility; Upward mobility

Mobilization, 21, 64, 212, 22. *See also* ASU mobilization drive

Mobilization regimes, 25; use of ideology in, 187, 207; Egypt as, 206; and local policy, 207–8; effectiveness of organizations in, 244

Modernization: effect on rural communities, 21–22, 80, 212; cultural change and, 164; and religion, 182, 184; as manifest in Shubra, 260–62; in the literature, 262

Monarchy, the, 32, 48, 50, 53, 276

Money rents, 34, 39–40, 42

Mortmain land. *See Waqf* land

Movie industry, 131

Multiparty system, 20

Municipal administration, 28

Municipal commune, 10, 11

Municipal council, 10; in Shubra, 58–61; link to provincial government, 62; ranked by villagers, 106; and information dissemination, 108; as elite council, 123–24

Municipal councillors, 58–59, 62

Muntazah Palace, 6

Murad, Dr. Hilmi, 180

Napoleon, 4

Nasser, Gamal 'Abd al: in Damanhur, 4; use of ideological symbols by, 25; coup staged by, 53; as head of party, 66; political concessions of, 67; speeches of, 141; and national ideology, 165, 169; postpones 1968 elections, 225

National Assembly, 67, 69–70, 71, 88, 203–4

National Charter, The: as national ideology, 66, 149, 165–69; on Arab nationalism, 77; eclecticism of, 185; on women, 188; on agricultural cooperation, 189

National Congress of Popular Forces, 66, 70, 149, 224, 225

National consensus, 185

National government: pre-1952 role of, in Shubra, 41; in contrast with local system, 65, 225, 283; as problem-solving agent, 110; change in traditional views toward, 190; as agent of change, 263; and local political pressures, 283–84

National integration, 18, 212

Nationalism, 19, 167. *See also* Arab nationalism
Nationalization: of trade and industry, 172, 189, 203
National party organization, 66–68. *See also* Arab Socialist Union; Single party system
National policies, 143
National Union: in Shubra, 58, 69–70; peasant participation in, 63, 76; designated as new party, 66; Committee of Ten, 121
Native capitalists, 169
Nawwar family, 6
News mediators: as information source, 150; dependence on, 153; public newspaper readers as, 155; *imams* as, 182. *See also* Opinion leaders
Newspaper readers: number of, in Egypt, 130–31; number of, in Shubra, 136; public, 155
Newspapers: and communications flow, 154; as source of policy news, 151
Normative constraints, 48, 55, 219–20
Normative rules of behavior, 265–66, 271, 275, 276
Nuclear family residents, 214, 215

Occupation, and political attitude, 221
Occupational groups: in Shubra, 10; among *effendis*, 15; within agricultural economy, 32; incomes of, 47; national representation of, 224; participation in 1968 elections, 238
Officials. *See* Government officials
Open meetings, 99
Opinion leaders, 147, 148, 151–61 *passim*
Opinion survey, 30, 101
Organization leaders, 66, 75–77, 115
Organizations: villagers' ranking of, 105–6, 108; and elites, in Shubra, 126; as news mediators, 156; resort to, among villagers, 197; membership overlap, 218; as political arenas, 242, 257; and political participation, 244; effect of politics on, 258; functional specialization of, 260; as political and economic center, 264
Orphans Property Committee, 53
Overpopulation, 38, 199

Parliament, 34, 50, 53
Parsonian pattern variables, 265
Participant observation, 29–30
Participatory attitude, 212, 220
Partisanship, 117
Passing of Traditional Society, The, 164, 210
Patrilocal residence, 213–15, 221
Patronage, 259
Patron-client relationship, 55, 66, 71
Peasant: in the literature, 13–15, 18, 205; and modernization, 21–22, 212; under rural capitalism, 33, 34; income of, in Shubra, 47; inactivism of, 48; leaders, emergence of, 75–77, 115; and landownership, 172; paternalism of government toward, 190; expectations of, 200; national representation of, 224; and political participation, 238; as consumer, 260; organizational skills learned by, 264
People's Choice, The, 147, 153
Philosophy of the Revolution, The, 165
Plays, 134
Police, 108, 197
Political activism, 168–69
Political alliances, 229, 230, 232, 244
Political awareness, 148, 149, 158–63
Political awareness index, 158
Political behavior, 221, 278–81
Political blocs, 126, 228–32, 240, 257
Political competition, 237, 238, 240
Political conflict, 278, 281
Political cooperation, 281
Political dependence. *See* Conventionalism
Political diversity, 284
Political hegemony, 224, 238, 240, 257, 280
Political indoctrination, 91, 99, 170, 264
Political instability, 257
Political interaction, 12
Political participation, 28; and dispersion of economic resources, 49; and the single party system, 63; and assimilation of formal ideology, 65; at national and subnational levels, 99; of officials, 105–6, 258; encouraged by national regime, 206–7, 225, 242, 283; attitudes toward, 207–8; and autonomy, 258–59; meaning of, with respect to change, 270–71
Political pluralism: encouraged by national regime, 58, 283; in Shubra, 87, 126, 240; as result of change process, 238; and autonomy, 258; characteristics of, 261
Political power: theories of, 25–26; distribu-

tion of, in field of action, 101; as source of change in normative rules, 268; political and economic compared, 275; models of, 276–84; quantification principle of, 281; personal theory of, criticized, 281–82; convergence principle of, 282; autonomy-dependency principle of, 282
Political strife, 277, 278–80
Political structure, 261
Political supervision, 92
Popular, the (leaders), 102, 103–4
Population size: of Egyptian villages, 7; of Shubra, 10
Populism, 64, 206
Power bases, 126, 270
Power considerations, 275
Power distribution, 78
Power network: as gradation network, 26, 27; leaders examined in context of, 271–72; concept of, 281, 282
Power structure, in Shubra, 27, 110
Power struggle, in Shubra, 68–71, 124, 244, 257
Pragmatic rules of behavior, 266
Preparatory Committee, 225
Press, the, 130–32
Primary groups, 213, 214
Prince, the. *See* Ibrahim, Prince Muhammad 'Ali
Private property: emergence of, 19, 32; rights, state support of, 34; rights, denial of, 35; under new regime, 46, 49, 169, 263, 276
Problem solving, 106–110
Professional farming, 34, 41, 73
Progress, 198, 200, 203
Province Committee (*Lajnat al Muhafazah*), 224
Provincial executive bureau, 83, 84
Provincial government: powers of, 283
Provincial governors, 11
Provincial party secretaries, 83, 84
Provincial services council, 59

Qaraqis, 4

Radio: broadcast time per program type, 129–30; exposure to, 135
Radio Cairo, 157
Radio ownership: in Egypt, 130; in Shubra, 136; obtaining information and, 150–51; and political awareness, 159, 161
Rafi'i, 'Abd al Rahman al, 51
Rahmaniya, al, 4
"Reactionary regimes," 177
Recreational services, 46
Reform cooperative: area under, in Shubra, 11; as political base, 75–76; board elections of, 76–77; conflict within, 247–48; resistance to efforts to dissolve, 248–49; autonomy of, 250–51; vs. agricultural workers, 252–57
Regular cooperative, 44, 75; dissolution of board of, 240, 243–47
Religion, 10, 178–84, 197–98
Religious fraternities, 71, 110. *See also* Sufi orders
Religious leaders. *See* Imams
Rental rates, 38
Representative bodies, 206
Representative leaders, 71–75, 84–85, 114–15
Reputational method, 110, 112; defined, 101–2; criticism of, 116–18; uses of, 122
Resberg, Carl G., Jr., 64
Residence, mode of: and political attitudes, 213–15
Resource allocation, 28, 218, 224
Revolution, the, 21, 32, 35, 201
Revolutionary-centralized model, 64–65
Revolutionary Command Council, 225
Road construction, locally, 93
Rogers, Everett, 162
Role analysis, 271, 272
Rose el Yusuf, 6
Royal family, 6, 36, 38
Rudebeck, Lars, 64
Rural capitalism, 32–35, 38–42
Rural notables, 41
Rural socialism, 172, 173

Sabri, 'Ali, 66, 239; leads mobilization drive, 81; launches self-help projects, 92; election of, to Supreme Executive Committee, 225
Sadat, Anwar al, 225, 248
Sa'dist party, 53
Saudi Arabia, 177
Savings policy: awareness of, 143; described,

149, 188–89; opinion leaders on, 156; religious justification of, 181
Second-order leaders, 116, 117, 125
Select, the: defined, 102; sociogramic analysis of, 112–16; media exposure of, 137–38; media preferences of, 143–45; define Arab socialism, 175; attitude of, toward youth, 196
Self-help projects, 92–95, 98, 181–82
Secretary General, 67
Shabab al 'Arabi, al, 91
Shaltut, Mahmud, 181
Sharecroppers, 18, 32
Sharecropping, 33, 34
Shopkeepers, 10, 155, 216
Shubrakhit, 4
Single party regimes, 19, 20
Single party system: views on, 63–65; at national and local levels, 65, 78–80; collaboration model, 65, 98; elections in, 237
Social cleavages, 15, 17–18. *See also* Elite-mass gap; Urban-rural gap
Social conflict, 7–8
Social contiguity, 218–19
Social differences: sense of, in Shubra, 171; and political attitudes, 212–13, 215–17
Socialism: information dissemination on, 108; as national policy, 149; opinion leaders on, 156; local understanding of, 170–75, 185; villagers' attitudes toward, 176–77; rural elites' view of, 202–3. *See also* Arab socialism
Socialist institutes, 88, 93; curricula of, 6, 85; in Shubra, 170, 181
Socialist justice, 168
Socialist regimes, 19
Social stratification, 37. *See also* Class awareness; Social differences
Social workers, 47, 97
Sociogramic analysis, 111–22
Street-repairs project, 95, 124–25
Suez Crisis, 66
Sufi orders, 110, 182–83
Sukarno, 169
Supreme Committee of Agrarian Reform, 199
Syria, 17, 177; secession from UAR, 66, 70, 165, 178
Systems analysis, 28, 262
System survival concept, 268

Tawfiq, Khedive, 151
Teachers, 47, 105
Telephone: as authority symbol, 50, 128
Television: broadcast time per program type, 129; ownership, 131, 136; frequency of watching, 135
Tenants, 18, 32, 35, 36, 43
Theater, 131
Third world, 147
Trade union, 97, 253–55, 263
Travel, 133–34, 159, 210
Tunisia, 64, 177
Turkey, 17–20 *passim*
Two-step flow of communications hypothesis, 147–48, 152–53, 210

'Ulema, 197
'Umdah: social status of, 40, 201; hereditary authority of, 50–52, 54–55; decline and disappearance of, 56–58, 262, 268; and political conflict, 278; prohibited to seek ASU office, 224
Upward mobility, 218, 221
University of Cairo, 180
'Urabi revolution, 4

Van Nieuwenhuijze, C. A. O., 15, 16, 23, 24
Variable-sum model, 277, 278–81
Vendors, 47, 215
Veterinarian, 96–97
Vidich, Arthur, 122
Village council. *See* Municipal council
Voting eligibility, 235–36
Voting participation, 210
Voting rights, 270

Wafd party, 53
Wage-laborers project, 59, 60
Wahdah al mugamma 'ah, al. *See* Combined-services center
Waqf land, 38, 40, 44, 254
Waqf Land Committee, 53
"Wise" leaders, 66, 77–78
Wolf, Eric, 13
Women, 30; illiteracy rate of, 136; regime's attitude toward, 179; seclusion of, 188; views on family planning, 200; voting of, 235, 270
Working forces. *See* Arab Socialist Union
World War II, 13, 19, 32

Yawmiyyat Na'ib fi al Ariyaf, 128, 187
Yemen, the, 167, 177
Youth: status of, in Shubra, 194–96, 212
Youth Organization: creation of, 83; political education program of, 85, 91, 99; lower meat prices, 93–94; villagers' ranking of, 106; campaigning of, 227, 228; 1968 electoral slate, 231–32; suspension of, 239

Zakat, 182
Zero-sum model, 276
Zimam. See Cultivation area